Planning Commission Reports on Labour & Employment

Planning Commission Reports on

Labour and Employment

Report of the Task Force on Employment Opportunities

Chairman: Montek S. Ahluwalia

Report of the Steering Committee on Labour and Employment for the 10th Five Year Plan (2002-07)

Chairman: S.P. Gupta

Report of the Special Group on Targeting Ten Million Employment Opportunities per Year over the 10th Plan Period

Chairman: S.P. Gupta

WITH AN INTRODUCTION BY

RAJ KAPILA & UMA KAPILA

ECONOMICAindia

INFO-SERVICES

ECONOMICA INDIA INFO-SERVICES IS A DIVISION OF ACADEMIC FOUNDATION

Published in 2002 by
ACADEMIC FOUNDATION
4772-73 / 23 Bharat Ram Road,
(23 Ansari Road), Darya Ganj,
New Delhi - 110 002.

Phones : 3245001, 02, 03, 04.
Fax : 011-3245005
e-mail : academic@vsnl.com
www : academicfoundation.com

Planning Commission Reports on Labour & Employment
with an Introduction by Raj Kapila & Uma Kapila
ISBN 81-7188-267-6

Laser-Typeset at AF's DTP Division.
Printed at Print Perfect, Mayapuri, Phase - II, Delhi.

Contents

Report of the Task Force on Employment Opportunities

(...Contents continued...)

Report of the Steering Committee on Labour and Employment for the Tenth Five Year Plan (2002-2007)

(..Contents continued...)

Report of the Special Group on Targeting Ten Million Employment Opportunities per Year over the 10th Plan Period

Editors' Introduction

WE have long recognised that productive employment is not merely a means to the ultimate ends of economic well-being and poverty reduction, but is an important end in itself. It is a basic source of human dignity and self-respect. In recent years, two trends have become apparent, which dictate a reappraisal of our approach to development and employment generation. First, demographic trends indicate that the rate of growth of population in the working age group is accelerating due to the high birth rates experienced in the late 1970s and early 1980s, and is likely to attain its peak during the current decade. Second, the pace of creation of work opportunities has not kept pace with the growing requirement during the 1990s, despite an acceleration in the growth rate of the economy. Taken together, these trends imply that if nothing is done, the country will face the spectre of rising unemployment with all its attendant economic, social and political consequences.

There is a wide-spread concern that the acceleration in GDP growth in the post reforms period has not been accompanied by a commensurate expansion in employment. Public sector employment is expected to fall because the public sector is withdrawing from many areas. There are fears that the process of internal liberalization and globalisation are creating an environment which is not conducive to expanding employment in the organized private sector. Existing industrial units are shedding excess labour in order to remain competitive and new technology, which is essential to ensure competitiveness, is typically more automated and therefore not job-creating. The net result of these forces, it is feared, could be a very slow expansion in employment opportunities in the organized sector, resulting in growing frustration among the youth.

It is in recognition of these facts that the Prime Minister announced to the nation that the government is committed to "create ten crore employment opportunities over a period of ten years". The Planning Commission was entrusted with the responsibility of giving shape to this vision. To this end, the Planning Commission set up the following Committees/Groups :

(1) A Task Force on Employment Opportunities under the chairmanship of Montek S. Ahluwalia (Member, Planning Commission) was set up in January 1999 which submitted its Report in July 2001;

(2) The Steering Committee on Labour and Employment for the Tenth Five Year Plan was set up under the chairmanship of S.P. Gupta, Member, Planning Commission. This Committee submitted its Report in December 2001; and

(3) The Special Group on "Targeting Ten Million Employment Opportunities per year over the Tenth Plan Period" constituted by drawing experts from the Steering Committee on Labour and Employment for the Tenth Plan and co-opting experts and specialists from within the Government, and from academics and practitioners in this area. The special group submitted its report on May 21, 2002.

The Task Force was to examine the existing employment and unemployment situation in the country and to suggest strategies of employment generation for achieving the target of providing employment opportunities to ten crore people over the next ten years i.e., providing employment opportunities to one crore people per year on an average.

The report consists of eight chapters discussing, among other things, The Employment and Unemployment Situation, The Role of Economic Growth in Employment Generation, Sectoral Policies for Employment Promotion, Role of Special Employment Programmes, Labour Force Skills and Training, and Reforms of Labour Laws.

According to the Report of the Task Force the rate of unemployment, as measured by NSS Surveys, appears to have increased in the 1990s with unemployment, on the basis of Current Daily Status, increasing from 6.03 per cent in 1993-94 to 7.32 per cent in 1999-2000.

Further, the growth of employment has dropped sharply from about 2 per cent per annum in the period 1983 to 1993 to less than 1 per cent during 1993-94 to 1999-2000.

A basic point which emerges from the Report is that the employment objective cannot be defined solely in terms of whether enough job opportunities are created for the projected increase in the labour force. This purely quantitative approach ignores the very important issue of the low "quality", low-income employment which is the source of much of the current unhappiness with the employment situation. This is evident from the fact that while unemployment, according to the CDS measure, was only 7 per cent in 1999-00, the percentage of the population in poverty was 26 per cent. In other words, large numbers of those currently employed, according to the NSS definition, earn income levels which are insufficient to take them above the poverty line. In this situation, an employment strategy which focuses on a mere creation of low income job opportunities will not address the real nature of the problem.

The Report, therefore, emphasises that Employment policy in future must focus not just on creating new employment opportunities in quantitative terms, but also on improving the quality of employment. There is a strong preference for employment oppor tunities in the organized sector rather than the unorganized sector and especially for employment in the government sector. Organised employment grew at only 1.2 per cent per year in the period 1983-1994 which is much lower than the growth rate of total employment in the same period. If the expectations of the labour force regarding creation of employment in the organised sector are to be met, it will be necessary to generate much faster growth in this sector. Similarly, there is a preference for regular wage employment rather than casual wage employment and for self employment which is economically viable in the sense of providing an adequate and reliable income level, rather than low income self employment of a residual category subject to high variability and uncertainty.

It is stated in the Report that some of these expectations definitely cannot be met in future. Expansion in government employment for example is unlikely to be an important source of future employment growth. There is evidence of excessive employment in the government sector as a consequence of fiscal indiscipline in the past when a large number of people have been added in the rolls, much beyond what is functionally necessary. In any case, fiscal constraints make it impossible to continue in this way. If government employment cannot be expanded the demand for organized sector jobs can only be met by a faster growth in employment in the private organised sector. This may require supportive action in other areas to encourage growth of the organized sector component. One of the steps needed for this purpose is a modification in labour laws.

India's labour laws have evolved in a manner which has greatly reduced the flexibility available to employers to adjust the labour force in the light of changing economic circumstances. In a globalised world, persisting with labour laws that are much more rigid than those prevailing in other countries only makes us uncompetitive not only in export markets but also in domestic markets. Some changes in the laws are therefore necessary if we want to see rapid growth.

The Report has identified five broad areas of policy which together would constitute an appropriate strategy for employment generation. These are :

i) Accelerating the rate of growth of GDP, with a particular emphasis on sectors likely to ensure the spread of income to the low income segment of the labour force.

ii) Pursuing appropriate sectoral policies in individual sectors which are particularly important for employment generation. These sector level policies must be broadly consistent with the overall objective of accelerating GDP growth.

iii) Implementing focused special programmes for creating additional employment and enhancing income generation from existing activities aimed at helping vulnerable groups that may not be sufficiently benefited by the more general growth promoting policies.

iv) Pursuing suitable policies for education and skill development, which would upgrade the quality of the labour force and make it capable of supporting a growth process which generates high quality, high income jobs.

v) Ensuring that the policy and legal environment governing the labour market encourages labour absorption, especially in the organized sector.

The basic message which emerges from the Task Force report is that it is only a rapidly growing economy, with a structural change in which labour intensive sectors see major modernisation and technological upgradation, that can provide the expansion in productive and high quality employment opportunities that we will need in the next ten years. *The ultimate solution to the problem of unemployment lies more in increasing the rate of growth than the special programmes for creating jobs.*

The second report of the Planning Commission i.e., the Report of the *Steering Committee* on Labour and Employment submitted in December 2001 has discussed in its nine chapters among other things, Employment Projections, Employment, Planning and Policies, Skill Development and Training, Occupational Safety and Health, Social Security for Workers, Labour Laws and Other Labour Regulations, Vulnerable Groups in Labour Force — (a) Child Labour, (b) Bonded Labour, (c) Migrant Labour, (d) Building and Other Construction Workers and (e) Landless Agricultural Workers.

A significant point made in the report is that more than 90 per cent of employment is in unorganized sector. The level of productivity and income in case of such workers is very low. One of the reasons for predominance of unorganized sector in total employment has been the inability of the organised sector to absorb the increase in the labour force.

The Report states that due to fiscal constraints facing the Governments at all levels, the growth of jobs in public sector declined sharply during the nineties. This led to an overall decline in the rate of growth of employment in the organized sector despite a much improved performance in organized private sector employment growth.

The process of restructuring of the economy in general and also within the public sector itself precludes any possibility for growth of employment in the public sector. It is, therefore, imperative to promote the growth of organized private sector to give further boost to momentum that it has picked up in the nineties so that over time the overall share of organised sector in total employment increases. But presently the private organized sector caters less than 2.55 per cent of employment. Therefore, to meet the demand of the growing labour force, dependence has to be on the growth of the informal sector and its improvement in productivity.

In the order appointing the Special Group, the Deputy Chairman of the Planning Commission, Shri K.C. Pant pointed out that the earlier Task Force (Chairman, Montek Ahluwalia) had not paid adequate attention to the issue of the large backlog of under-employment and therefore, has estimated the unemployment gap to be lower than the Planning commission's stated goal of 10 million a year.

While the two groups proceed on the same set of data, barring some difference in approach, they differ in the relative emphasis given to growth. The Task Force Report emphasises the importance of growth as a factor for reducing unemployment and is not convinced about the role of special programmes for creating employment. In this context, it points out the considerable leakage in resources, especially in the IRDP type of programmes.

The Task Force infact questions the wisdom of spending more money on job creation *per se* through such special employment programmes. The Report of the Special Group (Chairman S.P. Gupta), however, does not agree with the Task Force and argues that there is a specific role for special employment programmes, notwithstanding the complaints of leakage in efficiency.

The Task Force is also strong in its emphasis on labour reforms, which are necessary for higher FDI. In the same spirit, the Task Force has recommended considerable liberalisation in the use of agricultural land and for the food processing industry. The Task Force's emphasis is on higher investment in the economy, as a whole, while the Special Group stresses the unfeasibility of such higher investment.

In respect of agriculture, the Task Force recommends its opening up to corporate investments, which in the view of many economists, is an essential reform for agriculture to enter the modern age. However, the Special Group prefers the status quo.

The Task Force is in favour of de-reservation of small-scale industries as a step to modernisation and to encourage competitiveness in exports and recommends that reservation should be removed within a period of four years. The Special Group, however, recommends de-reservation only on a case-to-case basis. Both the Groups are, however, united in recommending a freer flow of credit to the small sector. They note that the flow of credit from the banking system is disproportionate to the contribution of the small-scale industries sector to overall GDP and to exports.

After a detailed analysis of the various special employment programmes, the Special Group has laid stress on improving the content and the potential for job creation.

In his forword to the Report of the Special Group, Shri K.C. Pant remarks, "the Report clearly indicates that it is possible to increase labour intensities in the economy and to reduce underemployment through well-designed policy and programme interventions which take into account sectoral and regional specificities". He further adds, "the findings of this report, along with the growth-augmenting macroeconomic policy recommendations of the Task Force, should pave the way for us to devise a more employment-sensitive development strategy and public policy".

Report of the Task Force on Employment Opportunities

Contents

Contd...

...Contd...

...Contd..

...Contd...

1

Introduction and Overview

The need to ensure adequate growth in employment opportunities to provide productive employment for the continuing increase in the labour force is widely regarded as one of the most important problems facing the country. There is widespread concern that the acceleration in GDP growth in the post reforms period has not been accompanied by a commensurate expansion in employment. Public sector employment is expected to fall as the public sector withdraws from many areas. There are fears that the process of internal liberalization and globalisation, inevitable though they may be, are creating an environment which is not conducive to expanding employment in the organized private sector. Existing industrial units are shedding excess labour in order to remain competitive and new technology, which is essential to ensure competitiveness, is typically more automated and therefore not job creating. The net result of these forces, it is feared, could be a very slow expansion in employment opportunities in the organized sector, with a rise in unemployment rates and growing frustration among the youth. The problem is perceived to be especially severe for educated youth, who have high expectations about the quality of employment opportunities that should come their way.

1.2 Recognising this problem, the Planning Commission established a Task Force on Employment Opportunities under the Chairmanship of Shri Montek S. Ahluwalia, Member, Planning Commission to examine the existing employment and unemployment situation in the country and to suggest strategies for employment generation for achieving the target of providing employment opportunities to 10 crore people over the next ten years, i.e. one crore on average per year. The detailed terms of reference of the Task Force and its composition are given in Appendix I.

1.3 In this chapter we provide an overview of our report and its basic message. The detailed recommendations for policy action proposed in individual chapters are not summarised here but are presented in Chapter 8.

1. Some Dimensions of the Problem

1.4 Our assessment of the employment and unemployment situation in the country along with an assessment of recent trends is presented in Chapter 2. The rate of unemployment, as measured by the NSS surveys appears to have increased in the 1990s with unemployment on the basis of current daily status increasing from 6.03% in 1993-94 to 7.32% in 1999-00. Other measures of unemployment also show an increase.

1.5 The NSS data show that the growth of employment has dropped sharply from about 2.0% per year in the period 1983 to 1993-94 to less than 1% in the period 1993-94 to 1999-00. The deceleration in employment growth has attracted a great deal of attention but it is not adequately recognized that the estimate of employment is derived by applying the unemployment percentage in the NSS Survey to the labour force estimate derived from the Survey. Since the NSS Survey shows a sharp deceleration in the growth of the labour force from 2.3% in the period 1983 to 1993-94 to a little over 1.0% in the period 1993-94 to 1999-00, the employment growth shows a comparable deceleration.

1.6 A basic point which emerges from our review is that the employment objective cannot be defined solely in terms of whether enough job opportunities are created for the projected increase in the labour force. This purely quantitative approach ignores the very important issue of the low "quality" of employment which is the source of much of the current unhappiness with the employment situation. This is evident from the fact that while unemployment according to the CDS measure was only 7 percent in 1999-00, the percentage of the population in poverty was 26%. In other words, large numbers of those currently employed according to the NSS definition earn income levels which are insufficient to take them above the poverty line. In this situation, an employment strategy which focuses on a mere creation of low quality job opportunities will not address the real nature of the problem.

1.7 Employment policy in future must therefore focus not just on creating new employment opportunities in quantitative terms, but also on improving the quality of employment. One aspect of quality is the income generated by the job opportunity but other aspects are also important. For example there is a strong preference for employment opportunities in the organized sector rather than the unorganized sector and especially for employment in the government sector. Our review of recent trends in Chapter 2 show that organised employment grew at only 1.2% per year in the period 1983-1994 which is much slower than the growth rate of total employment in the same period. If the expectations of the labour force regarding creation of employment in the organised sector are to be met, it will be necessary to generate much faster growth in this sector. Similarly, there is a preference for regular wage employment rather than casual wage employment and for self employment which is economically viable, in the sense of providing an adequate and reliable income level, rather than low income self employment of a residual category subject to high variability and uncertainty.

1.8 Some of these expectations definitely cannot be met in future. Expansion in government employment for example is unlikely to be an important source of future employment growth. There is evidence of excessive employment in the government sector as a consequence of fiscal indiscipline in the past when large number of people have been added the rolls, much beyond what is functionally necessary. In any case, fiscal constraints make impossible to continue in this way. If government employment cannot be expanded the demand for organized sector jobs can only be met by a faster growth in employment in the private organized sector. This may require supportive action in other areas to encourage growth of the organized sector component. One of the steps needed for this purpose is a modification in labour laws.

1.9 The quality of employment is important not only for the new employment opportunities to be created to absorb the new entrants to the labour force, but also for existing employment opportunities, a large part of which are clearly of low quality. A successful employment strategy must bring about a substantial structural change in the pattern of employment over the next ten years, with certain types of traditional low quality, low income, employment opportunities gradually disappearing, and being replaced by higher income, better quality employment. It is therefore important to recognize that a concern with employment should not lead to a desire to protect all forms of existing employment. On the contrary structural change in employment with the disappearance of low quality existing employment should be an important objective of policy.

2. Towards a Strategy for Employment Generation

1.10 The employment strategy needed to achieve our objective of providing sufficient expansion in total employment opportunities to absorb the net addition to the labour force, while also upgrading the quality of existing employment has to extend much beyond any narrow conception of employment policy and employment programmes. To this extent, the employment generation strategy cannot be distinguished from the broader policy thrust for growth and structural change in the economy as a whole.

1.11 We have identified five broad areas of policy which together would constitute an appropriate strategy for employment generation. These are:

- Accelerating the rate of growth of GDP, with a particular emphasis on sectors likely to ensure the spread of income to the low income segments of the labour force.
- Pursuing appropriate sectoral policies in individual sectors which are particularly important for employment generation. These sector level policies must be broadly consistent with the overall objective of accelerating GDP growth.
- Implementing focused special programmes for creating additional employment and enhancing income generation from existing activities aimed at helping vulnerable groups that may not be sufficiently benefited by the more general growth promoting policies.

- Pursuing suitable policies for education and skill development, which would upgrade the quality of the labour force and make it capable of supporting a growth process which generates high quality jobs.
- Ensuring that the policy and legal environment governing the labour market encourages labour absorption, especially in the organized sector.

The main message emerging from our review of each of these areas is summarized below.

3. Role of Growth in Employment Generation

1.12 A central message of our report is that the aggregate employment problem in the country cannot be solved except through a process of accelerated growth which would create additional demand for labour and also provide the increase in labour productivity needed to achieve the much needed improvement in employment quality. The implications of alternative growth rates of GDP for employment generation are explored in Chapter 3. The various projections of employment generated by alternative growth paths are compared with projections of the labour force to come to a broad assessment of the employment situation over the next ten years.

1.13 A sophisticated projection of the labour force over the next ten years requires detailed demographic information from the 2001 census, which will become available only later in the year and this exercise is being attempted as part of the Tenth Plan. For the purpose of our report, we have made a rough projection using available data from the census and the 55th Round NSS survey for 1999-00. An important feature of the 55th Round results is the deceleration in the labour force growth in the period 1993-94 to 1999-00 to 1.03% per year. This low growth rate has emerged because of a sharp decline in the labour force participation rates in 1999-00 compared with 1993-94. However we find that the decline is primarily a reflection of the fact that the participation rates in the 1993-94 survey were unduly high which has exaggerated the extent of the reduction in labour force participation rates between 1993-94 and 1999-00. We cannot therefore assume that the participation rate will decline at the same rate in the next ten years. This means the growth of the labour force will be lower than the growth of the working age population, which is likely to be around 2% per year, but it will not be much lower. Accordingly we have worked with two alternative assumptions with labour force growing at 1.5% and 1.8% respectively.

1.14 These projected growth rates for the labour force growth imply that the expected scale of addition to the labour force, and therefore the need for new employment opportunities, will be significantly less than assumed in our terms of reference. Even if we adopt the higher growth rate assumption of 1.8%, the addition to the labour force in the next ten years will be 8.3 million per year on average and not 10 million as stated in our terms of reference.

However, although the number of additional job seekers is likely to be less than was earlier assumed, the employment prospects remain a matter of concern.

1.15 Our growth simulations suggest that continuation of 6.5% GDP growth is not likely to bring about a significant improvement in the employment situation. The employment elasticities we have used imply that 6.5% GDP growth will only generate additional employment of 5.9 million per year, leading to a continuing worsening in the rate of unemployment. GDP growth of 6.5% with labour force growth of 1.5 to 1.8% will of course bring about a steady improvement in the productivity per person, which can be expected to generate an improvement in the quality of much of the existing employment, but it may not lead to an improvement in open unemployment.

1.16 Acceleration to 9% growth brings about a significant improvement in the employment situation, with a marked tightening of the labour market. In fact, since the supply of labour in our projections is independent of demand, we find that 9% GDP growth actually generates a labour deficit or "negative unemployment". Of course, in practice, we do not expect to see labour deficits because the progressive tightening of the labour market will raise real wages and automatically moderate the demand for labour. However, our projections can be interpreted as implying that growth rates of GDP between 8% and 9% are needed over the next ten years if we want to see a significant improvement in the employment situation.

1.17 The relative importance of accelerated growth in generating employment compared to targeted programmes for employment creation can be seen by comparing the additional employment generated by higher growth with the employment created by specific employment oriented programmes. Our simulations show that a shift from 6.5% growth to 8% growth generates an additional employment of 14.5 million in the terminal year 2012. In contrast, the total volume of employment created by all special employment programmes put together is only about 4.4 million and this level has actually declined over time. Because of severe resource constraints, it is unlikely that the volume of employment provided by special employment programme can be increased significantly in future. Indeed substantial additional resources may be needed simply to maintain the present level of employment while improving the quality of employment created. The role of growth in generating additional employment is therefore overwhelming.

4. *Macro Level Policies For Rapid Growth*

1.18 If accelerated GDP growth must be the core of any viable strategy for employment creation, the policy framework for achieving rapid growth of GDP must be regarded as essential pre-condition for successful employment generation. We regard the following areas to be critical at the level of macro-economic policy.

i) Higher Rates of Investment

1.19 Accelerated growth requires a combination of higher rates of investment and an improvement in efficiency in resource use. As far as investment rates are concerned, we estimate that it will be necessary to increase the gross domestic investment rate by about 4.5 percentage points of GDP to around 29 or 30% to achieve a GDP growth rate of 8%. The resources to finance this expansion in investment have to come dominantly from an improvement in public savings and from an increase in foreign investment. The required improvement in public savings calls for a major improvement in the revenue deficit of both the Centre and the States.

ii) Improvements in Efficiency

1.20 Investment alone will not suffice unless accompanied by a substantial improvement in the efficiency of resource use. This calls for policies to promote domestic competition and to continue the process of opening the economy to international competition.

iii) Improvements in Infrastructure

1.21 Deficiencies in infrastructure are currently a major constraint on India's ability to achieve 8% growth. This is true for infrastructure in rural areas, especially irrigation and rural roads which are critical for agricultural development, and also social infrastructure especially health and education in rural areas which is very deficient. Infrastructure deficiencies are also a serious problem for the non-agricultural economy. Power, telecommunications, roads, railways and ports are all critical sectors for the competitiveness of the economy, and substantial investments will be needed in these sectors along with an improvement in quality to support 8% growth. This calls for a combination of increased public investment and the evolution of a policy framework in which public private partnership in infrastructure can evolve, with a substantial expansion in the role of the private sector which is essential if total infrastructure needs are to be met.

iv) The Financial System

1.22 An efficient banking system and well functioning capital markets are an essential support structure to achieve 8% growth in the economy. Unless the financial system functions efficiently, channeling resources to productive sector in a manner which supports efficient firms and provides sufficient financial resources to permit investment and expansion, it will not be possible for the real economy to respond to the reform signals aimed at accelerating growth. This emphasizes the need for continuing reforms in the banking sector and in the capital markets.

v) Credit for the Informal Sector

1.23 The formal financial system is not well suited to meeting the credit needs of the informal sector and yet this sector is expected to play a major role in expansion of the economy and the provision of employment over the next ten years. It is therefore essential to ensure that the credit needs of the informal sector are adequately addressed. The co-operative system is a potentially important mechanism for providing credit for the informal sector but the system has been greatly weakened in most states. Non-bank finance companies are another potentially important mechanism for reaching the informal sector with several advantages over the formal banking system. It is necessary to find ways of strengthening NBFCs to enable them to perform this intermediation role with suitable prudential safeguards. Micro-finance through self-help groups is another potentially useful channel.

5. Some Critical Sectoral Policies

1.24 In addition to macro-level policies for accelerating growth, it is necessary to focus on policies in specific sectors which are critical for employment generation and for the quality of employment. In Chapter 4 we present a number of policy suggestions for individual sectors which would help to realize the overall growth objective while also helping to create high quality employment.

i) Agriculture and Allied Activities

1.25 This sector now accounts for just under 60% of total employment but we do not expect significant growth in total employment opportunities in this sector because it suffers from considerable under-employment at present. However acceleration of agricultural growth is important to increase labour productivity in this sector and thereby increase the quality of employment for large numbers of the existing labour force. This requires action on several fronts.

- It is necessary to increase public investment in agriculture especially in irrigation. This depends critically upon improving the fiscal position of state governments. There is a case for restructuring the existing allocation of resources by reducing implicit subsidies and increasing public investment.

- Controls on agriculture act as an impediment to the development of a national market and should be removed urgently.
- Laws regarding leasing of land need to be liberalized to allow marginal landholders to lease out agricultural land.

Agricultural exports will support diversification of agriculture and also promote employment in rural areas. Our policies towards agricultural export have not been sufficiently supportive. In particular, control on agricultural exports should be abolished. Other steps also need to be taken to promote agri-exports.

ii) Food Processing

1.26 This sector is highly under-developed compared to its potential. Development of food processing could be an important support for agricultural diversification which is necessary, and it would provide significant non-farm employment in rural areas. Government policy towards this sector has not been adequately supportive and needs to be comprehensively reviewed. There is a case for rationalization of multiple laws affecting this sector and in particular, modernization of the Prevention of Food Adulteration Act. The structure of taxation should also be reviewed to remove disincentive for food processing.

iii) Small Scale Industry

1.27 The small scale sector is an important source of industrial dynamism and growth of employment. It needs to be encouraged through multiple initiatives. The following are particularly important.

- Some of the larger issues of reforms in infrastructure development (especially power) and reforms in labour laws, are particularly important for the SSI sector, much more so than they are for large industry. Progress in these areas will therefore help SSI development and the growth of employment in this sector.
- The benefits currently given to the SSI sector in industry should be extended to small scale enterprises in the non-industrial sector, including services.
- Government should provide resources for upgrading

infrastructure for industry clusters where there is a sufficient agglomcration of SSI units.

- State governments must undertake concerted efforts, in close consultation with SSI organizations, to reduce the burden of "inspector raj" which is especially heavy on SSI units.
- The policy of reservation has become an impediment to the development of a strong SSI sector capable of competing effectively in the new more open trading regime. We recognize this is a sensitive subject but after careful consideration of all factors, we recommend phased abolition of reservation over a period of 4 years. This will give existing units time to adjust and will create a healthier and more vibrant SSI sector.

iv) Services

1.28 The services sector will be the major source for employment generation in future providing about 70% of the new job opportunities in the economy. Adequate attention has not been given to the many sectoral policy constraints which hold back employment in services. We have made recommendations in the following areas which we believe are critical for achieving our employment objectives in the next ten years.

- Travel and Tourism
- Information Technology
- Housing and real estate development
- Construction
- Road Transport
- Distributive Trade
- Education and Health Services

Our recommendations in these sub-sectors are designed to remove constraints which prevent rapid growth and modernization of these sectors. Some of these recommendations will lead to an expansion in total employment. Others may not contribute to an increase in total employment but will accelerate the shift from unorganized modes of production to organized sector modes, which is extremely important if we want to improve the quality of employment. It is important to emphasise that the structural shift in some areas may appear to displace traditional types of employment, but it needs to be encouraged nevertheless.

6. The Role of Special Employment Programmes

1.29 Special employment programmes aimed at providing wage employment or self employment opportunities have been an important element of our employment strategy over the years. In Chapter 5 we have reviewed the experience with these programmes and made an assessment of their potential role in the future. Our review of past experience suggests at best a mixed picture. Many of the major programmes, especially IRDP, suffered from major weaknesses. There was little evidence of success in generating sustainable self-employment opportunities. The wage employment programmes also suffered from weaknesses in design and implementation. The focus on pure employment creation in these programmes led to the specification of excessively high wage components which had the effect that the assets created under the programmes were insufficiently productive.

1.30 Since financial resources with the central government are scarce, and there are competing demands from the social sector and infrastructure, it is difficult to count on any substantial increase in the volume of resources devoted to these programmes. The shift of emphasis from pure wage employment generation to creation of durable infrastructure assets will also reduce the amount of direct employment generated for a given volume of resources. It is therefore unlikely that the total volume of employment created by these programmes can expand significantly in future. However, while special employment programmes may not make a significant contribution to the expansion in total employment in future, they will continue to play an important role in providing supplementary employment, especially to groups of the population that are specially vulnerable and in areas subject to sudden economic stress e.g. on account of droughts, floods or other natural calamities.

1.31 There is a case for continued support for programmes like PMRY and the Margin Money Scheme of KVIC which help new entrants into small business and potential village industry entrepreneurs. These programmes are relatively less dependent on budgetary support and rely to a greater extent upon parallel resource flows from the commercial banks. However in implementing these programmes it is important to ensure that the commercial viability of these activities is effectively established.

7. Labour Skills and Training

1.32 While faster GDP growth is necessary to generate a demand for labour, it can only be achieved if the labour force is sufficiently skilled. This is especially so if the growth is to come from expansion of more labour using sectors, which would generate a large demand for skills in all sectors. Unfortunately, the skill endowment of India's labour force leaves a great deal to be desired. Almost 44% of the labour force in 1999-2000 was illiterate and only 33% had schooling of secondary education and above. The latter category includes all those who have some secondary school education even if they did not complete secondary school. The percentage of those who had at least completed secondary school would be significantly lower. The position in relation to vocational skills is even more alarming. Only 5% of labour force in the 20-24 age category have vocational skills compared with 28% in Mexico and as much as 96% for Korea.

1.33 Part of the problem is a strong preference among the young for general education over vocational training because general education has traditionally been seen as a route to acquiring government jobs which are highly valued. This has led to a low demand for vocational training courses. However, there is also a problem with the supply side of vocational training. The physical capacity of the existing training institutes is limited and the quality of the training provided is also not up to the mark. Training courses in government run institutes are often not sufficiently reflective of market demand. There is also a perception among employers that the skill levels acquired by graduates of these institutes are inadequate.

1.34 Correction of these deficiencies calls for action on several fronts. Given the continuing low levels of enrollment and high drop out rates in middle and secondary school, there can be no doubt that a major expansion in general education is necessary.

However, efforts should be made to increase the vocational content of education. More generally, the education system must evolve in a manner which lays greater emphasis on acquiring marketable skills. The ITIs in the public sector need to be strengthened by providing additional resources for upgrading their facilities. They also need to be restructured to provide much greater interaction with industry and joint management.

1.35 At the upper end of the educational spectrum, the capacity for producing trained engineers needs to be expanded. Given the heavy demand for graduates of IITs abroad and the likelihood that many future graduates will continue to migrate, we need to expand the capacity of the existing institutes to ensure that our demand for high skills is met. There is a case for substantially expanding the capacity of existing IITs and also the total number of IITs by creating an IIT in each major state.

1.36 The role of the private sector in providing education and training needs to be encouraged as much as possible. Private training institutes have done well in many sectors though there are problems of assuring quality. Existing policies regarding private sector investment in education and training need to be reviewed to remove impediments which hamper the flow of private resources into this sector. The role of the government must change from being a direct provider of services to being a facilitator and source of certification.

8. Regional Dimensions of Employment

1.37 An aspect of employment growth which we have not explicitly addressed in the Report is the regional variation in the employment situation in future. The experience of the 1990s shows that growth rates of State Domestic Product vary considerably across states with the fastest growing state, Gujarat, recording a growth rate of about 8%, while the slow growing states grew at only 3%. Given the importance of GDP growth as a determinant of employment growth in our simulation of employment in Chapter 3, one can assume that continued disparity in regional growth rates will imply corresponding divergence in the rate of improvement of the employment situation. This will be moderated to some extent by migration from the slow growing states to the faster growing states, a trend that is already evident, but large scale migration is not the answer to inadequate availability of employment opportunities, especially for lower skill levels. A regionally balanced employment strategy therefore calls for much faster growth rates of SDP in the poorer states. This in turn points to the importance of policies which can accelerate SDP growth in the poorer states, including, especially in the agricultural sector, as the critical factors for improving the employment situation in these states.

1.38 Many of our recommendations on policy reform at sector level require initiatives by the State Governments, and to the extent it is not uniformly pursued by all States, the impact of our recommendations will differ across States. At the same time, some of the sector level reforms we have recommended will give much better returns in terms of generating employment and improving the qualities of employment in States that have done less thus far.

9. Reform of Labour Laws

1.39 To achieve a significant increase in the proportion of organised sector employment to the total, we will need to address problems with our labour laws which are widely regarded as being too rigid and therefore have the effect of discouraging growth of employment in the organised sector. This issue is examined in Chapter 7. Our assessment is that the existing labour laws, and in particular the way they have been administered and implemented, have this unintended effect of discouraging employers from investing and expanding in labour intensive areas. This has made us uncompetitive in these areas in export markets denying us the possibility of large expansion in organised sector employment. It has also made our producers uncompetitive vis-a-vis imports in an environment where the economy is increasingly becoming more open, a trend which is unavoidable and should be continued.

1.40 A comprehensive review of the labour laws will no doubt be undertaken by the Second Labour Commission. However there are some changes that are urgent. It is particularly necessary to introduce flexibility by deleting the provision requiring prior permission of the government for retrenchment and closure. This provision was introduced in 1976 and it has introduced a degree of inflexibility that does not exist in any other country. In a globalised world if we subject our producers to a labour regime which reduces their ability to adjust in the face of changing economic circumstances, the result is not to protect employment but to make production uncompetitive both in export markets and in domestic markets. We have also made a number of other suggestions for amendment of the Trade Unions Act (1926) and the Contract Labour (Regulation and Abolition) Act (1970), which in our view are desirable to make Indian industry competitive.

1.41 Reform of labour laws is a particularly sensitive issue and there is understandable reluctance to proceed with reforms which may appear "anti-labour". For this reason it is necessary to bring about a better appreciation of the negative effects of existing labour laws on total employment in the economy and the potential benefits to labour of introducing greater flexibility. It is also important to implement labour law reform as part of a package which could be seen as putting suitable pressure on inefficient managements. Reform of bankruptcy laws is particularly important in this context. It is also necessary to make a start towards implementing some form of unemployment insurance as a safety net to mitigate the hardship associated with retrenchment. Such a system would have to be based on contributions from labour and employers and should not involve an open ended burden on the state.

1.42 In the chapters that follow, we spell out in detail the policy implications of the broad approach overviewed in this chapter. We wish to reiterate that one most important message is that the employment strategy for the next ten years cannot be dissociated from the process of accelerating economic growth and bringing about structural change in the economy. This acceleration in growth has to be achieved in an environment in which competition, including international competition is inescapable. Our policies must therefore be tailored to ensure that the economy can achieve more rapid growth of output and employment in an enviro in which the process of integrating with the global economy is unavoidable. At a macro level, we need to push the policies which can help to achieve a more rapid rate of growth with an emphasis on the growth of labour using sectors, including especially agriculture and agro-based industries. This will create an environment conducive to growth of total employment and an improvement in the quality of employment. This macro level strategy needs to be supported by policies at the sectoral level which attempt to remove the sector specific constraints which hold back growth.

1.43 Many of the policies that emerge from the strategy proposed in this report may not seem to be directly relevant for employment generation, but they are in fact crucial if we want to achieve rapid growth in total employment with an improvement in the quality of employment of which is equally important. A viable employment strategy for the future must go beyond the limited concern with employment programmes which has dominated the policy debate in the past. It is only a rapidly growing economy, with a structural change in which labour intensive sectors see major modernisation and technological upgradation, that can provide the expansion in productive and high quality employment opportunities that we will need in the next ten years.

2

The Employment Unemployment Situation: An Assessment

Our terms of reference specifically require us to "examine the existing employment and unemployment situation in the country" and this chapter responds to this requirement. It presents unemployment situation and recent trends based on available data. We also draw some implications for policy which have to be kept in mind in evolving an employment strategy for the next ten years.

1. Measurement and Recent Trends

2.2 The terms employment and unemployment are frequently used in public debate and discussion but they are not easy to define and measure in our situation where there are considerable seasonal variations in the intensity of employment and the presence of underemployment in many forms is widely prevalent. For example, the census, which classifies people as employed or unemployed based on a single question, with no reference to the period involved over which employment is measured or the intensity of employment in the period, cannot capture these complexities. Recognising these problems, the National Sample Survey Organisation (NSSO) collects detailed information on the employment status of the population through large-scale, nation-wide sample surveys in which individuals are categorised as employed or available for work but not employed, using different criteria. These surveys are the most reliable source of data on the employment-unemployment situation in the country and they are the basis of our assessment of employment and unemployment.[1]

i) Measurement of Unemployment : Alternative Measures

2.3 The NSSO provides four different measures of employment and unemployment which capture different facets of the employment-unemployment situation following the recommendations of the Expert (Dantwala) Committee on Unemployment.

- *Usual Principal Status (UPS):* A person is counted as being in the labour force on principal usual activity basis if s/he was either engaged in economic activity (work) or reported seeking/being available for work for the major part of the preceding 365 days. Those classified as being in the labour force on this basis are further classified as being employed or unemployed depending on whether the majority of the days in labour force was spent in economic activity or in seeking/being available for work. The Usual Principal Status unemployment rate is the proportion of those classified as unemployed on this basis expressed as a percentage of those classified as being in the labour force. On this criterion, persons can be counted as being employed even if they were unemployed (or were outside the labour force) for a significant part of the year. Equally, a person can be counted as unemployed even though s/he may have been employed for part of the year.

- *Usual Principal and Subsidiary Status (UPSS):* This provides a more inclusive measure covering, in addition, the participation in economic activity on a more or less regular basis of those classified as unemployed on the Usual Principal Status as also of those classified as being outside the labour force on the same criterion. This would

---

1 We have used the employment-unemployment data drawn from the quinquennial, large sample, Employment-Unemployment Surveys of the NSSO conducted in 1977-78, 1983, 1987-88, 1993-94 and 1999-2000. Employment and unemployment rates (as percentage of the total labour force) drawn from these Surveys are combined with independent population data to obtain estimates of the absolute number of people employed or unemployed.

result in a larger proportion of the population as being in the labour force with a higher proportion of workers and lower unemployment rates relative to the UPS criterion.

- *Current Weekly Status (CWS):* The reference period here is the week i.e. the 7 days preceding the interview. A person is counted as employed if s/he was engaged in economic activity for at least one hour on any day during the reference week. A person not being engaged in economic activity even for one hour on any day but reporting seeking/being available for work during the reference week is classified as unemployed. To the extent that employment varies seasonally over the year, the labour force participation ratcs on the Current Weekly Status would tend to be lower. However, reflecting the unemployment during the current week of those classified as being employed on the UPS (and the UPSS) criterion, the Current Weekly Status unemployment rates would tend to be higher. The difference between the unemployment rates on the Current Weekly and that on the Usual Status would provide one measure of seasonal unemployment.

- *Current Daily Status (CDS):* Based on the reported time-disposition of the person on each day of the reference week (in units of half day where needed by the presence of multiple activities within a day), person-days in employment (unemployment) are aggregated to generate estimates of person-days in employment/unemployment. The person-day unemployment rate is derived as the ratio of person-days in unemployment to the person-days in the labour force (i.e. person-days in employment plus person-days in unemployment). This measure captures the 'within-week' unemployment of those classifies as employed on the Weekly Status. The CDS-measure of unemployment is widely agreed to be the one that most fully captures open unemployment in the country.

2.4 The four different unemployment rates emerging from successive NSSO surveys corresponding to each of the four measures described above are summarized in Table 2.1. The extent of unemployment varies considerably depending on the measure chosen. For example, the unemployment rate for the year 1999-

2000 is a low 2.23% based on the UPSS definition (which relates to percentage of individuals in the labour force classified as unemployed) but it rises to 7.32% based on the CDS definition (which refers to percentage of unemployment in terms of person days).

2.5 In evaluating the state of unemployment it is important to recognise that some degree of unemployment is normal in any labour market since even in a full employment situation there will always be some people looking for work. Full employment is therefore conventionally defined not as zero unemployment but as that level of employment where unemployment has fallen to the irreducible minimum. However this level has not been defined in the Indian context.

2.6 In order to assess the degree of unemployment in India it is relevant to compare the incidence of unemployment with unemployment in other countries. Differences in definitions make such comparisons tentative at best but subject to this caveat a comparison is presented in Table 2.2 based on the available data on unemployment rates in other countries in the World Employment Report. Since the data for other countries is based on the current weekly status, the CWS measure has been used for India. India's CWS unemployment rate is higher than the rate reported in Bangladesh and China, but it is comparable to Indonesia and significantly lower than in several other countries.

ii) Trends in Employment and Unemployment

2.7 A better assessment of the employment-unemployment situation can be made by looking at recent trends. Table 2.1 reveals a disturbing feature of an apparent rise in unemployment rates in 1999-2000 compared with 1993-94.[2] The UPSS measure shows a modest increase in the rate of unemployment in the 1990s from 1.9% to 2.23%, but the CDS measure shows a sharper increase

2. It is important to note that before 1987-88 the direction of change in the rate of unemployment over time depends upon the measure used. For example, between 1983 and 1987-88 the unemployment rate increased according to the UPS, UPSS and CWS measures, but fell significantly according to the CDS measure. After 1987-88 however, the direction of change has been the same whichever measure is chosen. The rate of unemployment declined between 1987-88 and 1993-94 using all four measures and increased again between 1993-94 and 1999-00.

from 6.03% to 7.32%. More importantly all four measures show an increase in unemployment rate reversing the decline witnessed in the previous period.

Table – 2.1

Unemployment Rates : Alternative Measures

(Percentage of Labour Force)

	Usual Principal Status (UPS)	Usual Principal and Subsidiary Status (UPSS)	Current Weekly Status (CWS)	Current Daily Status (CDS)
RURAL				
1977-78	3.26	1.54	3.74	7.70
1983	1.91	1.13	3.88	7.94
1987-88	3.07	1.98	4.19	5.25
1993-94	1.80	1.20	3.00	5.63
1999-00	1.96	1.43	3.91	7.21
URBAN				
1977-78	8.77	7.01	7.86	10.34
1983	6.04	5.02	6.81	9.52
1987-88	6.56	5.32	7.12	9.36
1993-94	5.21	4.52	5.83	7.43
1999-00	5.23	4.63	5.89	7.65
ALL INDIA				
1977-78	4.23	2.47	4.48	8.18
1983	2.77	1.90	4.51	8.28
1987-88	3.77	2.62	4.80	6.09
1993-94	2.56	1.90	3.63	6.03
1999-00	2.81	2.23	4.41	7.32

Note : These Estimates of Employment are based on NSS data combined with census data. The NSS gives Labour Force Participation Rate (LFPR) and Work Force Participation Rate (WFPR) for four categories : rural male (RM), rural female (RF), urban male (UM) and urban female (UF) separately. We obtain estimates of the total labour force and total work force in each year by applying LFPR and WFPR to the total population of each category (RM, RF, UM and UF) obtained from the interpolation for inter-census years. However, for the year 2001, the four component (RM, FR, UM & UF) are not available in the key results of Census released in April 2001. Hence, estimates of populations for these four categories made by the Technical Group (which was chaired by Registrar General) in 1996 have been used to combine the component-wise LFPR's and WFPR's to the level of Rural, Urban and All India.

Table – 2.2

Unemployment Rates @ : India and Selected Countries

Country	1996
India$	**4.4**
Australia	8.6
Bangladesh	2.5
China	3.0
Indonesia	4.0
Korea, Republic of	2.0
Malaysia	2.6
Pakistan *	5.4
Philippines	7.4
Sri Lanka	11.3

@ Current Weekly Status Basis
* Figures relate to 1995
$ Pertains to the year 1999-2000 (55th Round)
Source : World Employment Report

2.8 The growth rates of employment and the labour force derived from the NSS data are shown in Table 2.3. The rate of growth of employment declined sharply from 2.04% per year in the period 1983 to 1993-94 to only 0.98 per cent per year in the period 1993-94 to 1999-2000. This sharp deceleration in the growth of employment has naturally been the focus of much attention and comment, raising fears that economic growth in the 1990s has been of a "jobless" variety. However it is important to recognise that the absolute level of employment in 1999-2000 is estimated by applying the percentage of employed workers to the total number of workers in the labour force observed in the survey to an estimate of the labour force in that year. The estimate of labour force in turn is obtained by applying the Labour Force Participation Rates (LFPR) in the survey to the total population derived from Census data. An important feature of the 1999-2000 survey is that labour force participation rates have declined sharply compared with position in 1993-94 and this is reflected in sharp deceleration in the growth of labour force from 2.29% in the period 1987-88 to 1993-94 to only 1.03% in the period 1993-94 to 1999-2000. The observed deceleration in employment therefore can not be dissociated from the sharp decline in the growth of the labour force and indeed is derived from it.

Table – 2.3

Rate of Growth of Population, Labour Force and Employment

Period	Rate of Growth of Population (% per annum)	Rate of Growth of Labour Force (UPSS) (% per annum)	Rate of Growth of Employment (UPSS) (% per annum)
1972-73 to 1977-78	2.27	2.94	2.73
1977-78 to 1983	2.19	2.04	2.17
1983 to 1987-88	2.14	1.74	1.54
1987-88 to 1993-94	2.10	2.29	2.43
(1983 to 1993-94)	(2.12)	(2.05)	(2.04)
1993-94 to 1999-2000	1.93	1.03	0.98

2.9 This is not to deny that the employment growth has been inadequate. The data clearly show that the growth rate of employment is less than the growth rate of the labour force indicating an increase in the unemployment rate and this is a matter of concern. However, the sharp deceleration in the growth rate of employment should not be compared as is sometimes done, with the continuing growth rate of population. It must be viewed in the context of the growth rate of the labour force which is shown to have decelerated in the Survey.

2.10 It is relevant to ask whether the observed deceleration in the labour force growth in some sense reflects a structural change in economy which is likely to continue in future. Some deceleration in labour force growth was expected because of the decline in population growth from 2.10% per year in 1987-88 to 1993-94 to 1.93% in the period 1993-94 to 1999-2000 and this would normally be associated with a slower growth in the working age population, which in turn would also lead to slower growth in labour force. However, the observed deceleration in labour force growth from 2.29% to 1.03% is much sharper than the deceleration in population growth. This is because participation rates in all age groups have declined sharply. This decline needs to be carefully evaluated.

2.11 Table 2.4 summarises the participation rates thrown up by various NSS surveys from 1983 to 1999-00. The following features are worth noting.

a. The decline in the Labour Force Participation Rate (LFPR) in the younger age group in the period 1993-94 to 1999-00 is a part of longer term trend reflecting the expected shift in the activity status of this group towards education. This trend is likely to continue in future.

b. In prime age groups, especially among males in both rural and urban areas, the declines in LFPR are within the margins of sampling error.

c. In the age group 60 and above the decline in the LFPR can be explained by increase in the share of more aged in the age 60 and above population, where the LFPRs are expected to be low.

d. Finally, the decline in LFPRs in certain age groups between 1993-94 and 1999-2000 appears to be large primarily because the LFPR in 1993-94 showed a significant increase, contrary to the longer term trend. This is most evident in age groups 50-54 and 55-59 and 60 & above of the rural male. This raises the question whether the 1993-94 data were out of line with past trends. This would exaggerate the growth of labour force in the period 1983 to 1993-94 and also exaggerates the apparent deceleration in 1999-2000.

2.12 The slower growth of labour force has implications for the number of new employment opportunities that need to be created. The Working Group for the Ninth Plan had projected labour force growth at 2.5% in the period 1997-2002. The actual labour force growth implied by the NSS 55th Round in the period 1993-94 to 1999-2000 is much lower at 1.03 percent per year. This implies a considerable scaling down of the number of new jobs to be created. With a base year labour force of 406 million in 1999-2000, a 2.5% growth in the labour force means an annual addition of about 10 million to the labour force for which new jobs would have to be found. This is the figure referred to in our terms of reference. With the observed growth rate of 1.03 % the annual increase in job seekers would be only about 4 million. We return to this issue in Chapter 3 when we make projections about the future.

Table – 2.4

Labour Force Participation Rates by Sex and Age, 1983 to 1999-00

Age Group	Rural Male				Rural Female			
	1983	1987-88	1993-94	1999-00	1983	1987-88	1993-94	1999-00
5-9	25	23	11	7	23	24	14	7
10-14	239	193	139	93	225	183	142	96
15-19	658	630	598	532	442	415	371	314
20-24	915	918	902	889	494	484	470	425
25-29	976	981	980	975	543	539	528	498
30-34	986	990	988	987	577	588	587	557
35-39	988	991	992	986	607	608	610	579
40-44	981	984	989	984	611	620	607	586
45-49	978	982	984	980	589	590	594	566
50-54	957	962	970	953	526	530	543	515
55-59	920	929	941	930	476	463	468	450
60+	660	670	699	640	227	220	241	218
All Ages	548	549	561	540	332	331	331	302
	Urban Male				**Urban Female**			
	1983	1987-88	1993-94	1999-00	1983	1987-88	1993-94	1999-00
5-9	7	5	4	3	7	3	4	2
10-14	114	92	71	52	65	66	47	37
15-19	472	429	404	366	164	169	142	121
20-24	816	792	772	755	218	225	230	191
25-29	965	967	958	951	242	244	248	214
30-34	985	985	983	980	267	282	283	245
35-39	987	989	990	986	292	313	304	289
40-44	982	986	984	980	305	311	320	285
45-49	977	977	976	974	284	307	317	269
50-54	943	944	945	939	270	269	287	264
55-59	843	849	856	811	230	235	225	208
60+	509	482	443	402	124	123	114	94
All Ages	**536**	**534**	**542**	**542**	**155**	**162**	**164**	**147**

Note: Classification is based on those classified in the labour force on Usual Status Basis

Source: National Sample Survey 38th, 43rd, 50th & 55th Rounds

2.13 In addition to trends in total employment it is useful to consider the pattern of employment growth in different sectors from 1983 to 1999-2000. These trends are presented in Table 2.5

which shows that the deceleration in the total employment growth in the period 1993-94 to 1999-2000 compared with the previous period 1983 to 1993-94 was almost entirely due to slower growth in agricultural employment. In fact the absolute number of persons employed in agriculture shows a decline for the first time. As a result, the proportion of workers employed in agriculture, which declined from 68.5% in 1983 to 64.8% ten years later, declined more sharply to 59.8% in the next six years. Employment in sectors like Trade, Construction, Financial Services and Transport, Storage & Communication has grown faster than the average and the share of these sectors in total employment therefore increased. The share of manufacturing in total employment has also increased but only marginally.

Table – 2.5

Growth of Employment by Sectors (UPSS)

Industry	Employed workers 2/ (million)			Annual Growth Rate (percentage)	
	1983	1993-94	1999-00	1983-94	1994-00
Agriculture	207.23	242.46	237.56	1.51	-0.34
Mining & Quarrying	1.76	2.70	2.27	4.16	-2.85
Manufacturing	34.03	42.50	48.01	2.14	2.05
Electricity, Gas & WS	0.85	1.35	1.28	4.50	-0.88
Construction	6.78	11.68	17.62	5.32	7.09
Trade	19.22	27.78	37.32	3.57	5.04
Transport, Storage & Commn.	7.39	10.33	14.69	3.24	6.04
Financial Services	1.70	3.52	5.05	7.18	6.20
Community Social & Pers. Services	23.80	32.13	33.20	2.90	0.55
Total Employment	302.76	374.45	397.00	2.04	0.98

1. Notes to Table 2.1 refers.

2/ The NSS gives the percentage distribution across industries of each of the four categories of workers. We apply this distribution to the absolute numbers of workers of each category for each year and add up the four categories in each industry to derive estimates of total workers in each industry.

iii) The Quality of Employment

2.14 An important aspect of the employment problem, which

is missed if we focus only on employment and unemployment, relates to what may be called the quality of employment. Many people are "employed" in the technical sense that they are engaged during the reference period in an income earning activity, but the employment they have may not meet their expectations and this naturally creates dissatisfaction about their employment status. In our view, a great deal of the unhappiness on the employment front arises not from open unemployment but from the fact that much of the employment available does not come up to expectations which are rising rapidly.

2.15 There are several dimensions in which the employment opportunities available may fall short of expectations. The most obvious relates to the level of income which they provide. A large part of the employment generated in the economy at present provides very low levels of income either because productivity in self-employment is very low or because real wages in the relevant labour market are too low. This is evident from the fact that whereas unemployment in 1999-2000 on the basis of UPSS measure, which is a body-count measure, was only 2.23% and even according to the CDS measure it was only 7.3%, the percentage of the population in poverty in the same survey was as high as 26.1%. The fact of being employed is obviously no guarantee of escaping poverty, which in our situation refers to a very basic level of subsistence.

2.16 Income is not however the only aspect of employment that is relevant for quality. Several other features are also relevant and a mismatch between expectations and availability of jobs in any of these dimensions is part of the perceived employment problem.

- People may have a preference for desk jobs rather than jobs which involve manual work. This is particularly true of educated job seekers since our educational system reinforces the prejudice in favour of desk jobs or "white collar" jobs. Educated entrants into the labour force are typically unwilling to take on technical work i.e. "blue collar" jobs or self-employment as carpenters, electricians, plumbers, repairmen etc.
- There is a strong preference for secure wage employment in the organized sector (especially in government) over

other forms of employment which are less secure including wage employment in the unorganized sector or self-employment. Some of these alternatives, especially self-employment, may yield a satisfactory income but since these employment opportunities are perceived as involving some measure of risk, they are sometimes valued much less. The preference for security is itself a consequence of the lack of any insurance mechanism that would protect workers at least for a period from the loss of employment. As the economy undergoes a structural change because of competition and globalisation, the process is likely to increase the degree of perceived insecurity, at least in short run, and this is an important aspect of quality of employment.

- There is also a preference for employment in urban areas rather than rural areas because urban areas provide in many ways greater access to other facilities, which are usually heavily subsidized. However, it may not be possible or even desirable to encourage growth of employment in urban areas. Excessive migration is already placing unsustainable stress on urban areas. It may be more appropriate to focus on improving employment opportunities in rural areas so as to discourage urban migration. One consequence of this is that it may be necessary to tolerate a higher rate of unemployment in urban areas compared with rural areas since efforts to create urban jobs will only increase migration.

2.17 These considerations suggest that a meaningful solution to the perceived employment problem calls for more than the mere creation of a sufficient number of new employment opportunities. It is necessary to create employment opportunities of the right quality that can match the rising expectations of the labour force, especially of the new entrants who are generally better educated and therefore have high expectations. Some of these expectations e.g. of obtaining secure white collar jobs in government may not be feasible in view of the limited scope for expanding government employment in future. This only underscores the need to encourage sufficient growth in other high quality opportunities either in the self-employment category or in regular employment in the organized private sector.

2.18 It must be emphasised that the need for high quality job creation is not limited solely to the needs of the new entrants to the labour force. In fact a high proportion of persons who are currently employed are engaged in employment opportunities of low quality which are not only below their expectations but do not even allow them to cross the poverty line. It is therefore necessary to ensure that many of the existing work opportunities either experience very large increase in productivity, or are effectively phased out and replaced by new work opportunities which generate higher levels of incomes. Since many existing low quality employment opportunities do not have prospects for significant productivity increase, large reductions in the incidence of poverty in a relatively short period can only take place if these low productivity activities are phased out and replaced by new types of activity. A viable employment strategy must allow for the phasing out of low quality employment and its replacement by employment opportunities of higher quality.

2. Unemployment Among Particular Categories

2.19 The unemployment rate for the population as a whole masks important variations in the rate of unemployment for different categories of the labour force. These variations are relevant for policy since they indicate areas where the employment problem is most acute.

i) Urban and Rural Differences

2.20 Unemployment rates are traditionally higher in urban areas than in rural areas, partly because the greater dominance of the organized sector in urban areas forces people to be either employed or unemployed, with fewer opportunities to engage in low productivity subsidiary employment which can disguise an effective state of unemployment. This pattern is evident from Table 2.6 upto 1993-94. It is interesting to note however that the difference in unemployment rates between rural and urban areas narrowed considerably in 1999-2000, because of a sharp increase in rural unemployment rates for both rural males and rural females.

2.21 The reasons for the observed increase in unemployment rates in rural areas are not yet fully understood. One factor could be the shift from self employment to casual labour shown in Table 2.15. Since the extent of underemployment is effectively disguised in self employment, the shift in composition of employment away from self employment towards casual labour may lead to an increase in measured unemployment especially on the basis of the current daily status measure used in Table 2.6

Table – 2.6

Unemployment among Males and Females*

(per cent of labour force)

Survey Period	Rural Areas			Urban Areas		
	Male	Female	Persons	Male	Female	Persons
1977-78	7.1	9.2	7.7	9.4	14.5	10.3
1983	7.5	9.0	7.9	9.2	11.0	9.5
1987-88	4.6	6.7	5.3	8.8	12.0	9.4
1993-94	5.6	5.6	5.6	6.7	10.5	7.4
1999-2000	7.2	7.3	7.2	7.2	9.8	7.7

* Unemployment rate on current daily status basis

Source : NSSO Surveys

ii) Male-Female Differences

2.22 There are important differences between Male and Female unemployment rates which can be seen from Table 2.6. Female unemployment rates are significantly higher than male unemployment rates though the difference has narrowed down over time and was almost completely eliminated in rural areas in 1999-2000.

2.23 Female unemployment in urban areas was 9.8% compared with 7.2% for male unemployment. As the number of women entering the labour force is likely to increase, especially in urban areas, this suggests that employment policy in future will have to pay special attention to the need to create employment opportunities for women in urban areas.

ii) Age Differences

2.24 Unemployment rates are significantly higher in the younger age groups. Table 2.7 shows unemployment on the Current

Daily Status (CDS) definition for different age groups. The unemployment rate for the 15-29 age group was as high as 12.1% in 1999-2000 against 7.3% for the population as a whole.

2.25 Higher unemployment rates in the younger age group reflect the phenomenon that new entrants into the labour force, except those from the lowest income groups, may be more likely to wait until they find a job which matches their aspirations. The extent of mismatch between jobs available and the expectations of the labour force are therefore best captured by the extent of unemployment rate in this age group.

Table – 2.7

Unemployment across Age Groups : 1999-2000*

(per cent of labour force)

Age (years)	Unemployment Rate		
	Rural	Urban	Combined
15-19	13.3 (8.8)	19.0 (16.6)	14.4 (10.3)
20-24	11.8 (9.8)	18.7 (19.2)	13.5 (12.0)
25-29	8.7 (7.4)	10.9 (10.4)	9.2 (8.1)
Sub Group (15-29)	11.0 (8.6)	15.5 (15.0)	12.1 (10.1)
30-34	6.1	4.9	5.8
35-39	5.0	3.7	4.6
40-44	4.8	2.7	4.2
45-49	4.6	2.4	3.9
50-54	4.5	2.1	3.9
55-59	4.6	2.0	4.0
60 and above	3.5	3.8	3.5
All Age Groups	**7.2 (5.6)**	**7.7 (7.4)**	**7.3 (6.0)**

Unemployment rates on current daily status basis
Figures in parenthesis give the comparative estimates for 1993-94
Source : NSSO 50th (1993-94) and 55th (1999-2000) Round Surveys

iii) Educational Differences

2.26 A very important feature of the unemployment problem

is that the rate of unemployment is typically much higher among the educated than among those with lower levels of education. Table 2.8 presents unemployment rates on the UPSS definition for the labour force classified according to education level. The unemployment rates for the illiterate is as low as 0.2% rising to 1.2% for literates upto primary school and 3.3% for middle school. For the category of educated labour (i.e. education level of secondary education and above) the rate was 7.1%, which is more than 3 times the unemployment rate on the UPSS basis for the population as a whole. This difference clearly indicates the large mismatch between expectations and available employment opportunities for the more educated and highlights the need for employment strategies to focus on employment quality.

Table 2.8

Unemployment by level of education*

(per cent of labour force)

Education Level	Unemployment Rate		
	1987-88	1993-94	1999-00
Not Literate	1.1	0.2	0.2
Literate upto primary	1.9	0.9	1.2
Middle	5.3	3.4	3.3
Secondary	8.7	6.2	5.5
Higher Secondary	-	8.7	7.8
Secondary + Higher Secondary	-	7.1	-
Graduate & Above	9.9	9.3	8.8
Educated (Secondary & Above)	9.0	7.7	7.1
All	**2.7**	**1.9**	**2.2**

Unemployment rates on usual principal and subsidiary status basis.

Source : NSSO Surveys, 43rd Round (1987-88), 50th Round (1993-94) and 55th Round (1999-00)

2.27 The mismatch is most evident when the criterion of education is combined with age. As shown in Table 2.9, the unemployment rate for educated (secondary and above) persons in the age group 15-29 in 1993-94 was as high as 18.5%. If we focus on those in the age group 15-29 who have any form of technical education, the unemployment rate is even higher at 27.3% in 1993-94. It is interesting to note however that according to the NSS, the incidence of unemployment among educated youth, both for general and technical education, declined sharply between

1993-94 and 1999-2000. Unemployment rates for educated youth in 1999-00 are still high at 14.8% for secondary education and above and 23.7% for all types of technical education, but they are significantly lower than in earlier years.

Table – 2.9

Unemployment Rates (%) amongst Educated Youth*

Year	Secondary education & above			All types of Technical Education		
	Rural	Urban	Combined	Rural	Urban	Combined
1983	20.4 (2.5)	30.0 (10.7)	20.7 (4.2)	25.0	23.9	24.4
1987-88	15.9 (3.8)	16.6 (12.1)	16.2 (5.4)	24.0	20.7	22.1
1993-94	17.0 (2.9)	20.8 (10.8)	18.5 (4.6)	29.0	25.9	27.3
1999-2000	12.5 (3.7)	18.3 (11.2)	14.8 (5.4)	22.8	24.5	23.7

* On Usual Status Basis

Note: i) Technical Education comprises of Additional Diplomas or certificates in Agriculture, Engineering/Technology, medicine, crafts and other subjects.

ii) Youth means age group 15-29

iii) Figures in the parentheses show the unemployment rate among youth as a whole.

2.28 The high rate of unemployment among educated youth is in many ways the core of the problem because it creates a sense of despair across a wide section of the population including not only the educated youth but their parents and families. It needs to be emphasised that the aspirations of this group cannot be met just by creating any employment opportunities. Indeed, the reason why this group has high unemployment is precisely because their aspirations are high and they do not just want to take up any employment that may be available. The problem of unemployment in this category can only be solved if high quality employment is created.

iii) Variation in Unemployment across Per Capita Consumption Classes

2.29 The NSS data allow us to examine the incidence of unemployment in different groups of the labour force according to the per capita consumption class of the household to which they belong. Table 2.10a presents the incidence of unemployment in different consumption classes for 1999-2000 based on unemployment as defined in the UPSS definition while Table 2.10b uses the CDS definition. We find that the lower consumption groups show much lower unemployment rates using the UPSS definition but the pattern is reversed when using the CDS definition. This reflects two features of the labour force in the lower income groups. On the one hand, their poverty makes it impossible for them to wait for appropriate work for any length of time and they are therefore likely to take up work even if it is of sporadic nature. This accounts for lower rate of unemployment on the UPSS measure. However, the nature of employment that they get makes them more vulnerable to the uncertainties of labour demand in the market for casual labour. This is reflected in the higher rate of unemployment on the CDS measure which reflects intensity of employment.

Table 2.10 (a)

Expenditure Class (1999-00)

Monthly Per Capita (Rupees)		Expenditure Class Unemployment Rate (per cent of labour force)	
Rural	Urban	Rural	Urban
0-225	0-300	1.06	2.91
225-255	300-350	1.02	5.21
255-300	350-425	1.27	4.08
300-340	425-500	0.98	5.43
340-380	500-575	1.20	5.81
380-420	575-665	1.43	8.12
420-470	665-775	1.59	5.85
470-525	775-915	1.79	4.95
525-615	915-1120	1.78	5.08
615-775	1120-1500	2.21	4.21
775-950	1500-1925	2.44	3.49
950 & above	1925 & above	2.54	2.99
All	**All**	**1.43**	**4.63**

* Unemployment rates on Usual Principal and Subsidiary Status basis

Source : NSSO Survey 55th Round (1999-00)

Table 2.10 (b)

Unemployment Rates by Household Monthly Per Capita Expenditure Class (1999-2000)*

Monthly Per Capita (Rupees)		Expenditure Class Unemployment Rate (per cent of labour force)	
Rural	Urban	Rural	Urban
0-225	0-300	11.31	9.61
225-255	300-350	9.62	9.67
255-300	350-425	8.12	8.20
300-340	425-500	7.46	9.20
340-380	500-575	6.56	9.20
380-420	575-665	6.18	8.63
420-470	665-775	6.48	8.19
470-525	775-915	6.14	7.18
525-615	915-1120	5.60	6.65
615-775	1120-1500	6.06	5.68
775-950	1500-1925	5.57	4.67
950 & above	1925 & above	5.25	4.10
All	**All**	**7.21**	**7.65**

* Unemployment rates on Current Daily Status basis

Source : NSSO Survey 55th Round (1999-00)

vi) Regional Variations

2.30 The rate of unemployment also varies sharply across states. As shown in Table 2.11 the unemployment rate for 1999-2000 varies from levels of around 3% in Himachal Pradesh and Rajasthan to about 12% in Tamil Nadu, 15% in West Bengal and almost 21% in Kerala. It is interesting to note that these inter-state variations are consistent over time and the same states had high unemployment rates in 1993-94 and 1987-88.

2.31 The extent of variation across states is not easy to explain though some tentative hypotheses suggest themselves. States where wages are kept higher than the neighbouring regions either by strengthening the bargaining power of labour or by provision of social security (Kerala, West Bengal and Tamil Nadu) have a higher incidence of unemployment. However, the effect of economic and social conditions across States on employment situation, more particularly on quality of employment, requires to be explored further.

Table – 2.11

Unemployment Rates in Major States*

(per cent of labour force)

	States	Unemployment rate		
		1987-88	1993-94	1999-2000
1.	Andhra Pradesh	7.35	6.67	7.94
2.	Assam	5.09	7.96	8.00
3.	Bihar	4.04	6.25	7.35
4.	Gujarat	5.79	5.73	4.63
5.	Haryana	7.59	6.59	4.67
6.	Himachal Pradesh	3.12	1.82	2.93
7.	Karnataka	5.06	4.89	4.61
8.	Kerala	21.19	15.50	20.77
9.	Madhya Pradesh	2.86	3.42	4.60
10.	Maharashtra	4.67	4.97	7.09
11.	Orissa	6.44	7.28	7.38
12.	Punjab	5.07	3.08	4.15
13.	Rajasthan	5.74	1.33	3.06
14.	Tamil Nadu	10.36	11.44	12.05
15.	Uttar Pradesh	3.44	3.45	4.27
16.	West Bengal	8.13	9.87	14.95
17.	Delhi	4.77	1.91	4.58
	All India	**6.09**	**6.03**	**7.32**

* Current daily status basis

Source : NSSO

3. Some Structural Characteristics of Employment

2.32 In assessing the employment situation in the country it is important to recognize two other distinctions. The first is the distinction between organised sector employment and other employment and the second between wage employment and self employment.

i) Organised Vs. Unorganised Sector Employment

2.33 Much of the concern about the lack of employment opportunities reflects a strong preference for employment in the organised sector, which usually refers to employment in the government and in establishments employing more than 10 persons. These jobs typically provide much higher levels of wages than the unorganised or informal sector and also provide much greater job security and other benefits. In the case of government employment the wage rates for the lower skill categories are significantly higher than could be earned even in the private organised sector for similar levels of skills and the level of job security is virtually infinite.

2.34 While there is a large unsatisfied demand for these jobs, the size of the organised sector in our economy is relatively small and the scope for expansion of employment in this sector is therefore relatively limited. The main source of information on employment in the organised sector is the Employment Market Information (EMI) Programme of the Ministry of Labour which compiles data based on returns submitted by all establishments employing more than 10 persons. The available information is summarised in Table 2.12 and shows that organised sector employment in 1999 is only 28.11 million, or about 7% of the total employment of over 397 million in the economy. Furthermore, as much as 19.41 million, or over two-thirds of total organised sector employment, is in the public sector.

2.35 It is possible that the EMI data under-estimate the size of organized private sector employment because the EMI system is based on returns that are voluntary for establishments employing between 10 and 25 workers and mandatory only above that level. There is no census of establishments which would give a firmer fix. It is also very likely that private sector establishments understate employment. The likelihood that the EMI does not adequately capture organised sector employment is borne out if we compare the EMI based estimates of employment in the organised manufacturing sector with estimates from the Annual Survey of Industries (ASI). As per ASI data, (adjusted for non reporting units) the total factory sector employment in manufacturing, excluding repair services was 7.97 million in 1993-94. The corresponding estimate from EMI was only 6.40 million. The ASI figures are thus seen to be higher by 25%. It should be noted however that even if the EMI estimates of the share of employment in the organised sector are revised upwards to reflect this discrepancy, the size of organised sector in total employment will still be below 10%.

Table – 2.12

Total Employment and Organised Sector Employment

Sector	Employment (Million)				Growth rate (% per annum)	
	1983	1988	1994	1999-00	1983-94	1994-2000
Total Population	718.21	790.00	895.05	1004.10	2.12	1.93
Total Labour Force	308.64	3.49	381.94	406.05	2.05	1.03
Total Employment	302.75	324.29	374.45	397.00	2.04	0.98
Organised Sector Employment	24.01	25.71	27.37	28.11	1.20	0.53
– Public Sector	16.46	18.32	19.44	19.41	1.52	-0.03
– Private Sector	7.55	7.39	7.93	8.70	0.45	1.87

Note:

1. The total employment figures are on Usual Status (UPSS) basis
2. The Organised sector employment figures are as reported in the Employment Market Information System of Ministry of Labour and pertain to 31st March of 1983, 1988, 1994 and 1999
3. The rate of growth of total employment and organised sector employment are compound rates of growth

2.36 One reason why the share of the organised sector in total employment is relatively small is the predominance of agriculture which provides almost no organised sector employment. However this is not the only reason. As shown in Table 2.13, the share of the organised sector is also quite low in the other sectors. In the manufacturing sector, for example, it is as low as 14%, indicating that as much as 86% of the employment generated in manufacturing is in the unorganised sector i.e. handlooms and power looms, other village industries, the tiny sector and the smaller SSI units.

2.37 Trends in organized sector employment revealed by Table 2.12 show that organized sector employment is not growing rapidly and indeed is decelerating. Organised sector employment grew relatively slowly at 1.20% per annum during the 1983-94 but then slowed down further to only 0.53% between 1994 and 1999. This is certainly a matter of concern given the strong preference for organized sector jobs. However it is important to note that the deceleration was entirely due to the slowing down in employment in the public sector from a growth rate of 1.52% per year between 1983 and 1994 to a negative growth of –0.03% per year during 1994-99. The trend in the organised private sector was the reverse. It grew by only 0.45% per year between 1983 and 1994, but then accelerated to 1.87% per year between 1994 and 1999. The faster growth in private sector employment did not offset the effect of the slow down in public sector employment in the organised sector because the private sector share of the employment in the organised sector was only one third.

Table – 2.13

Organised sector jobs in employment by industry

Industry	Employment (million)				Share of Organised Sector (per cent)	
	1993-94		1999-2000			
	Total@	Organised Sector*	Total@	Organised Sector*	1993-94	1999-00
Agriculture	242.46	1.48	237.56	1.39	0.61	0.58
Mining & Quarrying	2.70	1.09	2.27	1.01	40.37	44.49
Manufacturing	42.50	6.40	48.01	6.75	15.05	14.06
Electricity	1.35	0.97	1.28	1.00	71.85	78.13
Construction	11.68	1.23	17.62	1.18	10.53	6.70
Wholesale & Retail Trade	27.78	0.45	37.32	0.49	1.62	1.31
Transport, Storage & Communication	10.33	3.11	14.69	3.15	30.11	21.44
Financial Services	3.52	1.53	5.05	1.65	43.46	32.67
Community, Social & Personal Services	32.13	10.93	33.20	11.49	34.02	34.61
All Sectors	**374.45**	**27.18**	**397.00**	**28.11**	**7.26**	**7.08**

* As on 31.3.1993 and 31.3.1999

@ As on 1.1.1994 and 1.1.2000

Source : 1. DGE&T for employment in organised sector

2. 55th Round Survey of NSSO for total employment

2.38 It is important to recognise that public sector employment is unlikely to accelerate in future. Both the Central and State governments are burdened with excess staff and both face severe financial constraints which will force measures to reduce the size of government. The central government has already declared that it plans to reduce the total size of government employment by about 2% per year over the next 5 years. Employment in the public sector enterprises is also unlikely to expand rapidly as most public sector undertakings are seriously over-manned. In fact their very survival in the more competitive environment they face today, which will only become more competitive in future, depends upon their being able to trim excess labour. Even if extent of actual retrenchment is limited, future expansion in employment is likely to be severely constrained until existing excess labour is absorbed through output expansion.

2.39 Rapid growth in organised sector employment in future therefore depends crucially upon employment growth in the private sector. The experience of the 1990s does show faster growth in organised sector employment in the private sector and this is reassuring. However this growth has to be accelerated very considerably if it is to offset the continued stagnation in public sector employment and generate faster growth in total organized sector. This clearly depends upon the rate of growth of the economy as a whole and the growth of the organised sector within the total. The latter depends critically upon reform of labour laws, which discourage expansion of employment growth in the organised sector. We will have more to say on this issue later in the report.

2.40 Since the potential growth of total organised sector employment in the next ten years will be limited, the employment strategy in the next decade must recognise that the bulk of the growth in employment will have to come from the unorganised sector as defined and identified under present conditions. How to ensure that this sector can provide a sufficient supply of high quality job opportunities is a major challenge.

ii) Self Employment vs Wage Employment

2.41 The distinction between self-employment and wage employment is also important for employment policies. Table 2.14 presents the share of self-employment in different sectors of the economy and in the rural and urban areas separately. It shows that as much as 53% of the total workforce in all sectors was engaged in self-employment in 1999-2000. The proportion was higher at 56% in rural areas, reflecting the classification of farmers as self-employed, but it is interesting to note that even in urban areas the proportion of self employed was as high as 42%.

Table – 2.14

Proportion of self-employed among the workers by industry: 1999-2000

(Per cent)

Industry	Rural	Urban	Combined
Agriculture	57.9	57.2	57.7
Manufacturing, mining, electricity, gas and water supply, construction	45.4	33.8	40.3
Trade, transport, financial, ownership of dwellings, Community, social and personal services	52.9	44.6	48.2
All industries	**55.9**	**42.1**	**52.9**

Source: NSSO Surveys

2.42 Self employment covers a large spectrum of economic activities with high income professional services such as doctors, lawyers, consultants, architects etc. at one end while at the other end of the spectrum there are self employment activities involving much lower levels of skills and incomes, e.g. certain types of khadi and handloom activity, village and tiny industries and traditional services such as barbers, artisans, craftsmen, small retail outlets etc.

2.43 Changes in the composition of employment between self-employment, regular salaried employment and casual employment are shown in Table 2.15. The share of self-employment has declined from 58.9% in 1977-78 to 52.9% in 1999-2000. This has occurred primarily in rural areas reflecting the decline in the proportion of farmers cultivating their own land owing to fragmentation of holdings. The proportion of self-employment to total employment in the urban areas has been more or less constant around 42%.

Table – 2.15

Distribution of Workers (Usual Status) by Category of Employment

(per cent)

Year	Category of Employment		
	Self Employment	Regular Salaried	Casual
1. Rural Areas			
1977-78	62.6	7.7	29.7
1983	61.0	7.5	31.5
1987-88	59.4	7.7	32.9
1993-94	58.0	6.4	35.6
1999-00	56.0	6.7	37.3
2. Urban Areas			
1977-78	42.4	41.8	15.8
1983	41.8	40.0	18.2
1987-88	42.8	40.3	16.9
1993-94	42.3	39.4	18.3
1999-00	42.1	40.1	17.8
3. Rural and Urban Combined			
1977-78	58.9	13.9	27.2
1983	57.4	13.9	28.7
1987-88	56.0	14.4	29.6
1993-94	54.8	13.2	32.0
1999-00	52.9	13.9	33.2

Figures for the share of self employed, regular salaried employed and casual workers for the year 1972-73 are 61.4% , 15.4 % and 23.2% respectively for the Rural and Urban combined.

Source: NSSO Surveys

2.44 The share of regular salaried employment has fluctuated marginally around 14% for the economy as a whole. As we would expect, it is much higher in urban areas at around 40% and lower in rural areas at around 7%. However, there is a sharp increase in the share of casual employment over time. This reflects the displacement of marginal cultivators and their conversion into agricultural labour. As a result casual labour increased from 29.7% of rural employment in 1977-78 to 37.3% in 1999-2000. The share of casual labour in urban employment has fluctuated over the past two decades. It increased from 16.9% in 1987-88 to 18.3% in 1993-94 but then declined again to 17.8% in 1999-2000.

2.45 The increase in the share of casual labour in total employment is sometimes regarded as an indication of deteriorating employment quality since this type of employment is not associated with job security or other employment benefits. However it is worth noting that the increase in casual labour in the 1990s has been associated with a significant acceleration in the growth of real wages. Table 2.16 presents estimates of the annual growth in wage rates of casual labour between 1987-88 and 1993-94 and between 1993-94 and 1999-2000. The rate of growth in the second period was much faster than in the first. This suggests that while dependence on casual labour may have increased, this was accompanied by a sufficient growth of productivity and tightening of the labour market to allow growth in real wages.

Table – 2.16

Growth of Average Daily Wage Earnings in 1993-94 Prices in Rural India

	Rural Males		Rural Females	
	1987-88 to 1993-94	1993-94 to 1999-00	1987-88 to 1993-94	1993-94 to 1999-00
Public Works	1.55	3.83	1.90	5.04
Casual Labour in Agriculture	1.36	2.80	2.34	2.94
Casual Labour in Non-Agriculture	1.33	3.70	1.32	5.07
Casual Labour in all Activities	0.77	3.59	1.95	3.19

Source : NSSO Surveys for 1987-88, 1993-94 and 1999-2000

2.46 Self-employment in the urban areas will remain a very important source for growth of employment in future and this is broadly in line with patterns observed in other developing countries. Self-employment is particularly important for women in urban areas as this type of employment is often particularly well suited to the needs of many women workers. As female participation in the work force increases in future, growth of self-employment opportunities will be an important factor matching employment possibilities with employment needs. However it is important to emphasise that self-employment requires access to capital and entrepreneurial skill and this means that many forms of self-employment may not be best suited to meet the employment needs of the lowest income groups which will continue to depend heavily upon the availability of wage employment.

2.47 The quality of a great deal of wage employment is very low and this is a major problem. It could be improved if there is a progressive shift from casual employment to regular wage employment but this depends upon the growth of the organised sector relative to unorganised sector and partly also on the pace of reform of the labour laws. More flexible labour laws would encourage greater dependence upon regular employment with an improvement in the quality of employment for labour as a whole.

4. Some Implications for Employment Policy

2.48 The assessment of the employment unemployment situation presented in this chapter suggests the following broad conclusions about the nature of the unemployment problem in India.

a. Although the extent of open unemployment in India, as conventionally measured is not high, the rate of unemployment has increased in the 1990s which is matter of concern.

b. There are two factors which underlie the perception that employment continues to be a serious problem. First, the quality of a large volume of employment generated in the system is very low, in the sense that it does not provide an adequate level of income even to keep a family out of poverty. Second, unemployment is very high among certain groups, especially among educated youth, indicating a serious mismatch between the expectations of new entrants to the labour force and the quality of employment opportunities available to them.

c. Given the high expectations of the increasingly better educated new entrants to the labour force the employment problem for this group cannot be addressed simply by creating more jobs of the same low quality as exist at present. What is needed is a strategy that will create more high quality jobs which generate higher levels of income.

d. In addition to creating sufficient number of new employment opportunities to meet the rising expectations of the new entrants into the labour force, it is necessary to replace existing low quality employment in which a large section of the existing labour force is engaged, with higher quality employment which will improve their income levels significantly. This would be desirable even if it implies the disappearance of existing low quality jobs and their replacement by higher quality jobs.

e. There is a very strong preference for organised sector jobs, especially government jobs which are associated with near total employment security and remuneration levels which are often higher than those prevailing in the market for comparable skill levels. This presents a major problem in meeting expectations since employment in the government sector has been decelerating in the 1990s, and this trend is certainly likely to continue over the next ten years. The demand for organized sector jobs can be met in future only if there is a rapid growth in organized sector employment in the private sector.

f. In order to encourage a faster rate of growth of regular salaried jobs in the organised sector than has been seen in the past it may be necessary to make conscious efforts to remove some of the disincentives which discourage rapid expansion of regular employment in the private sector. One of these is the inflexibility of labour laws. Changes in the labour laws to allow greater flexibility to employers are therefore necessary to give employers sufficient incentive to increase employment.

g. With the best efforts at promoting the growth of regular salaried employment in the organised sector, the contribution of this type of employment to total employment expansion is likely to remain modest in the next ten years. Much of the need for productive and remunerative employment in this period will have to be met through self-employment. This requires supportive policies in other areas, including especially banking and also the regulatory framework regarding self-employment, to ensure adequate growth of employment opportunities in self-employment.

h. Notwithstanding all possible efforts to promote regular wage employment and productive self employment, a sizeable proportion of work force would still be dependant on the market for casual labour. Improving the quality of this type of employment – in terms of both rising days of employment in a year and rising real wages – is crucially dependant on acceleration of growth with rising productivity accompanied by a sufficient demand for labour to ensure tightening of the labour market.

2.49 In the rest of this report we outline a multi-pronged strategy for employment generation which can respond to these problems.

3

The Role of Economic Growth in Employment Generation

Our assessment of the employment situation presented in Chapter 2 suggests that the employment strategy must have a two-fold objective. It must provide a sufficient expansion in total employment opportunities to absorb the net addition to the labour force and it must also aim at improving the quality of existing employment by replacing some of the low quality employment in which large numbers of the existing labour force are currently engaged by new employment opportunities. The creation of new employment opportunities which displace existing forms of employment, does not create a net addition in total employment, but it is an extremely important part of the structural change needed to improve the quality of employment in the country.

3.2 Employment objectives defined in these terms cannot be achieved through a narrow focus on what are traditionally called employment oriented policies and programmes. They require policies that will affect the behaviour of the economy as a whole and the structure of employment generated. The policy interventions needed are therefore wide-ranging often going beyond issues which are normally discussed in the context of employment generation. We have identified the following five broad areas of policy which are relevant in this context.

- Accelerating the rate of growth of GDP, with a particular emphasis on sectors likely to ensure the spread of income to the low income segments of the labour force

- Pursuing appropriate sectoral policies in individual sectors which are particularly important for employment generation. These sectoral policies must be broadly consistent with the overall objective of accelerating GDP growth.
- Implementing focused special programmes for creating additional employment or enhancing income generation from existing activities aimed at helping vulnerable groups that may not be sufficiently benefited by the more general growth promoting policies.
- Pursuing suitable policies for education and skill development which would upgrade the quality of the labour force and make it capable of supporting a growth process which generates high quality jobs.
- Ensuring that the policy and legal environment governing the labour market encourages labour absorption, especially in the organized sector.

In this chapter we focus on the first area i.e. the role of growth in employment creation and the critical macro-economic policies needed to achieve high growth. The other four issues are examined in Chapters 4, 5, 6 and 7 respectively.

1. Employment Generation Through Growth

3.3 The relationship between growth of GDP and growth of employment is usually characterized by a summary parameter such as the elasticity of employment with respect to GDP, which can be calculated either for employment in the economy as a whole or for employment in individual sectors. The elasticity of employment indicates the percentage growth in total employment (or sectoral employment) to be expected from a one percent growth in GDP (or GDP in individual sectors). In this section we present an assessment of possible employment growth over the next ten years based on alternative scenarios for GDP growth using employment elasticities which reflect recent experience.

i) Employment Elasticities in India

3.4 Since labour is an input into production, an increase in output is normally associated with an increase in labour use or employment, which implies that the elasticity of employment is generally expected to be positive. However, employment elasticities are typically expected to be less than unity because productivity per person employed is expected to increase over time, which implies that employment increases proportionally less than output. Since productivity per person employed is an important determinant of wage rate and therefore the quality of employment, it is important to recognize that high employment elasticities are not necessarily the best way of achieving employment objectives. Ideally, what is needed is a growth rate of GDP which is high enough to allow employment to expand, while also allowing for growth in productivity to ensure rising real wages and growth of income per person employed in self-employment.

3.5 Table 3.1 presents estimates of employment elasticities for the major sectors of the economy, and also for the economy as a whole, based on data on employment growth and GDP growth for three different periods spanning the past two decades. The estimated elasticities are less than unity in almost all cases though there are some exceptions (especially construction). Table 3.1 also shows that the elasticity of total employment has been declining consistently in each sub-period. This obviously reflects an acceleration in the growth of productivity per person employed, which is a desirable outcome, especially if it is taking place in sectors where productivity per person employed is very low. We note also that employment elasticities may be very low in sectors where there is a great deal of under-employment, which means there is considerable room for output to expand without an expansion in measured employment.

3.6 A remarkable feature of Table 3.1 is that although the employment elasticity declined in the earlier period, the decline was especially sharp in the 1990s. The employment elasticity for the economy as a whole was 0.53 in the period 1977-78 to 1983 and this declined to 0.41 in the period 1983 to 1993-94. It then declined very sharply to 0.15 in the period 1993-94 to 1999-2000 which is less than half the elasticity of 0.38 which was assumed when making employment projections for the Ninth Plan.

Table – 3.1

Elasticity of Employment to GDP

Sector	Estimated Elasticities			Projected Elasticities	
	1977-78 to 1983	1983 to 1993-94[2]	1993-94 to 1999-00	As used in the 9th Plan Projections	Projected for the future
1. Agriculture[1]	0.45	0.50	0.00	0.50	0.10
2. Mining & Quarrying	0.80	0.69	0.00	0.60	0.00
3. Manufacturing	0.67	0.33	0.26	0.25	0.22
4. Electricity	0.73	0.52	0.00	0.50	0.00
5. Construction	1.00	1.00	1.00	0.60	0.60
6. Wholesale & Retail Trade	0.78	0.63	0.55	0.55	0.50
7. Transport, Storage & Construction	1.00	0.49	0.69	0.55	0.40
8. Finance, Real Estate, Insurance & Business Services	1.00	0.92	0.73	0.53	0.50
9. Community, Social and Personal Services	0.83	0.50	0.07	0.50	0.30
All Sectors	**0.53**	**0.41**	**0.15**	**0.38**	**0.22**[3]

Note: Manufacturing includes workers engaged in repair services, except for the year 1977-78.

1 Estimated elasticities for agriculture have been calculated on the basis of 3 year moving average of GDP at 1980-81 prices for the period 1977-78 to 1983 and 1983 to 1993-94. For the period 1993-94 to 1999-00 we have used the GDP series with base 1993-94 but a three year average is not used since data are not available for 1992-93 or 2000-01.

2 This period combines two distinct periods for which data are separately available i.e. 1983 to 1987-88 and 1987-88 to 1993-94. However, 1987-88 was a drought year when employment was abnormally low and this distorts elasticities in both periods. The combined period 1983 to 1993-94 has been used to avoid this distortion.

3 Implicit elasticity based on 6.5% GDP growth.

3.7 The low employment elasticity in the 1990s reflects the fact that employment growth decelerated in this period while GDP growth accelerated. As shown in Table 3.2, total employment growth decelerated from 2.04% in the first period to 0.98% per year in the second period. Much of the slowdown in total employment growth was due to developments in two important sectors viz. agriculture (including forestry and fishing) and community, social and personal services. These sectors, accounting for almost 70% of total employment, experienced no growth in employment in the period 1993-94 to 1999-2000. Employment elasticity in Agriculture and Manufacturing sectors was therefore 0.00 and 0.07 respectively whereas the elasticity used in the Ninth Plan projections was 0.50. Employment growth in manufacturing also slowed down reflecting a continuing decline in the employment elasticity from 0.33 in the period 1983 to 1993-94 to 0.26 in the period 1993-94 to 1999-2000 but this was almost identical to the level of 0.25 assumed in the Ninth Plan (see Table 3.1). The low growth in total employment is therefore not due to slower than expected growth in employment in the manufacturing sector. In transport and communication the elasticity of employment actually increased, compared with the previous period, and was also higher than projected in the Ninth Plan.

Table – 3.2

Growth of Employment by Sectors

Industry	Employed workers[2] (million)			Annual Growth Rate (percentage)	
	1983	1993-94	1999-00	1983-94	1994-00
Agriculture	207.23	242.46	237.56	1.51	-0.34
Mining & Quarrying	1.76	2.70	2.27	4.16	-2.85
Manufacturing	34.03	42.50	48.01	2.14	2.05
Electricity, gas & water supply	0.85	1.35	1.28	4.50	-0.88
Construction	6.78	11.68	17.62	5.32	7.09
Trade	19.22	27.78	37.32	3.57	5.04
Transport, Storage & Commn.	7.39	10.33	14.69	3.24	6.04
Financial Services	1.70	3.52	5.05	7.18	6.20
Community, Social & Pers.Services	23.80	32.13	33.20	2.90	0.55
Total Employment	**302.76**	**374.45**	**397.00**	**2.04**	**0.98**

1. Notes to Table 2.1 refers.
2. The NSS gives the percentage distribution across industries of each of the four categories of workers. We apply this distribution to the absolute numbers of workers of each category for each year and add up the four categories in each industry to derive estimates of total workers in each industry.

3.8 In order to project employment growth in future consistent with alternative assumptions about GDP growth, it is necessary to make some assumptions about how employment elasticities will behave in future. This is inherently difficult because much depends upon changes in technology which are not easy to anticipate. In general however, one would expect that employment elasticities will continue to fall in sectors where productivity per man is currently low and also in sectors where technical change is likely to be labor-saving. Keeping in mind these factors and recent experience we have adopted a set of employment elasticities given in Col.6 of Table 3.1 for projecting future employment. The rationale for our choice is as follows:

a. Although employment elasticity in agriculture was zero in the period 1993-94 to 1999-2000, we have assumed a small positive elasticity of 0.1 for the future primarily because the higher growth rate being projected for agriculture implies a structural shift towards non-cereal agriculture, which is more labor-using. The very low elasticity for agriculture compared with some of the other sectors is however reasonable because productivity in this sector is relatively low with considerable under-employment, at least in large parts of the country. It is therefore reasonable to assume that the growth of value added in this sector should not be expected to generate a large increase in total employment but rather to reduce the degree of under-employment with an increase in both wage rates and self-employment income per person.

b. Employment elasticities have been assumed to be zero in Mining and Quarrying and in Electricity. These are sectors where there is considerable over-manning at present reflecting the dominance of public sector enterprises and rationalization of the labour force has been unavoidable. Keeping total employment constant in these sectors would enable the excess labor to be absorbed by expansion expected over the next ten years.

c. The elasticity of employment in manufacturing is assumed to be 0.22 which is slightly lower than the 0.26 observed in the period 1993-94 to 1999-2000. A further reduction in employment elasticity in this sector is reasonable since liberalization has accelerated the process of technological modernization and industrial restructuring, including labour rationalization, and this process is expected to continue in the next ten years. However, we expect the decline in the employment elasticity, in the manufacturing sector as a whole to be moderated compared with past trends because we would expect that manufacturing growth in future will involve a shift away from the highly capital intensive industries emphasized which absorbed a large part of total investment in the past, towards more labour using industries. Even though the employment elasticities in each individual industry may fall reflecting technology changes, the shift towards more labour using industries would moderate the decline in the total employment elasticity for the manufacturing sector as a whole. It is worth noting that the employment elasticity of 0.22 assumed in our projections implies that a 10% growth in value added in manufacturing will lead to only 2.2 per cent growth of employment in this sector.

d. Elasticities for other sectors are projected on the basis of a further decline compared with the observed elasticity in 1993-94 to 1999-2000 (see Table 3.1). The only exception is community, social and personal services which showed employment elasticity of only 0.07 in the period 1993-94 to 1999-2000. This category includes public administration and defence, where growth in employment may well be zero or even negative, but it also includes health and education services which will certainly need to expand and are likely to generate considerable additional employment. We have therefore assumed an employment elasticity of 0.30.

ii) Alternative Employment Projections

3.9 Using the employment elasticities reported in Table 3.1 we have made alternative projections for employment in the period 2002-03 to 2011-12, i.e. the period of the Tenth and Eleventh Plans using three different assumptions about economic growth. The three growth assumptions we have used are: a base line scenario in which GDP grows at 6.5%, a high growth scenario with GDP growth at 8 percent and a rapid growth scenario with GDP growth at 9%. The sectoral growth rates associated with these scenarios are presented in Table 3.3. Tables 3.4, 3.5 and 3.6 present the detailed employment outcomes for the economy as a whole and also for individual sectors associated with each scenario.

Table – 3.3

Alternative Growth Scenarios

Projections	GDP Growth		GDP Growth 2002-03 to 2011-12		
	1995-96 to 1999-00	2000-01 to 2001-02	Base Line	High Growth	Rapid Growth
1. Agriculture	3.9	2.7	3.9	4.2	4.8
2. Mining & Quarrying	2.5	4.2	4.0	4.7	5.5
3. Manufacturing	5.6	7.1	7.0	10.0	12.0
4. Electricity, gas and water supply	7.2	6.2	7.2	8.3	10.0
5. Construction	7.0	5.7	7.0	8.3	9.7
6. Trade	6.8	8.4	6.7	8.0	9.5
7. Transport, Storage & Comm.	7.7	8.0	7.3	10.3	11.0
8. Financial Services	9.1	7.7	9.0	10.0	11.5
9. Community, Social & Personal Services	9.9	7.7	6.8	7.6	7.8
10. GDP growth	6.5	6.2	6.5	8.0	9.0

3.10 The major features of the employment projections presented in Tables 3.4, 3.5 and 3.6 can be summarized as follows.

a. The level of total employment in the economy will be significantly affected by the overall growth rate of GDP. In the base line scenario, with GDP growing at 6.5% the total employment increases from around 397.0 million in 1999-2000 to 467.81 million in the terminal year 2011-2012. However, terminal year employment increases to 482.26 million in the high growth scenario with 8% GDP growth and further to 495.18 million in the rapid growth scenario with 9% GDP growth.

b. The quantitative significance of the impact of a higher rate of growth of GDP on employment creation can be seen by comparing the additional employment generated by higher growth with the employment generated by various special employment schemes. Acceleration in GDP growth from 6.5% to 8% generates an extra 14.45 million employment opportunities by the terminal year 2012 and a shift to 9% growth yields an additional 12.92 million in the terminal year. Against this, the total employment generated from special employment programmes was 6.0 million in 1993-94 and it has declined to 4.4 million in 1998-99 (see Chapter 5). This comparison actually underestimates the beneficial effect of high growth on employment because it focuses only on the additional employment generated by higher growth. However, faster GDP growth will also bring about an improvement in the quality of existing employment with a faster growth in real wages and an acceleration of the process of high quality jobs replacing low quality jobs.

c. Some indication of the extent of the structural shift in employment to be expected in future can be had from the structure of employment shown in Table 3.4 to Table 3.6. In the baseline scenario, the share of agriculture in total employment falls from just under 60% in 1999-2000 to 53.11% in 2011-12. The share of manufacturing increases only modestly from 12.09% to 12.38%. The share of the services sectors (construction, trade, transport storage etc., financial services and community and personal services together) increases from 27.17% to 33.75%. In the high growth scenario the share of agriculture in the terminal year is lower at 51.65% while manufacturing increases to almost 12.81%. The share of the services group increases to 34.8%. In the rapid growth scenario the agriculture share falls to 50.63% manufacturing increases to 13.02% while the services group increases to 35.63%.

d. An important feature of the projection is that the share of agriculture in total employment falls over time while the share of services increases. The fall in the share of agriculture reflects the fact that total employment growth in agriculture is much slower than the growth in total employment. Nor should this be a cause of alarm since the focus in this sector should be on increasing productivity of the persons employed, which is very low due to under employment. The dominant source of new employment possibilities will be the Services sector including construction, trade, transport, storage and financial services and communication and personal services. This sector will provide over 70% of the increase in employment. Employment in manufacturing also expands, but its contribution to the total increase in employment is only around 17%.

Table – 3.4

Employment Projection : Baseline (6.5% growth)

(million)

Industry	Employment in 1999-2000	Projected Employment 2007	2012
Agriculture and Allied activities	237.56	243.68	248.47
Mining and Quarrying	2.27	2.27	2.27
Manufacturing	48.01	53.65	57.91
Electricity, Gas and Water Supply	1.28	1.28	1.28
Construction	17.62	23.35	28.69
Trade	37.32	48.25	56.89
Transport, Storage & Comm.	14.69.	18.20	21.02
Financial Services	5.05	6.85	8.54
Community, Social & Personal Services	33.20	38.65	42.76
Total Employment	**397.00**	**436.18**	**467.81**
Labour Force A (1.5% growth)	406.05	452.33 (A)	487.29 (A)
Labour Force B (1.8% growth)	406.05	462.12 (B)	505.23 (B)
Unemployment Rate(%)			
With Labour Force A	2.23	3.57 (A)	4.00 (A)
With Labour Force B	2.23	5.61 (B)	7.41 (B)

Note: 1. Employment Estimates for the year 1999-2000 has been derived by applying the labour force participation rate from the NSS 55 th Round on the Provisional Totals of Census-2001.

2. Employment projections for 2007 & 2012 has been made using projected sectoral elasticities & projected growth in GDP, 6.5, 8.0 and 9.0 per annum during 2002-12.

Table – 3.5

Employment Projection : High Growth (8% growth)

(million)

Industry	Employment in 1999-2000	Projected Employment 2007	2012
Agriculture	237.56	243.99	249.10
Mining and Quarrying	2.27	2.27	2.27
Manufacturing	48.01	55.41	61.78
Electricity, Gas and W.S.	1.28	1.28	1.28
Construction	17.62	24.25	30.93
Trade	37.32	49.79	60.57
Transport, Storage & Comm.	14.69	19.29	23.60
Financial Services	5.05	7.02	8.96
Community, Social & Pers. Services	33.20	39.11	43.78
Total Employment	**397.00**	**442.40**	**482.26**
Labour Force A (1.5% growth)	406.05	452.33	487.29
Labour Force B (1.8% growth)	406.05	462.12	505.23
Unemployment Rate(%)			
With Labour Force A	2.23	2.20	1.03
With Labour Force B	2.23	4.27	4.55

Table – 3.6

Employment Projections: Rapid Growth (9.0% growth)

(million)

Industry	Employment in 1999-2000	Projected Employment 2007	2012
Agriculture	237.56	244.77	250.70
Mining & Quarrying	2.27	2.27	2.27
Manufacturing	48.01	56.62	64.49
Electricity, Gas & W.S.	1.28	1.28	1.28
Construction	17.62	25.22	33.45
Trade	37.32	51.61	65.08
Transport, Storage & Commn.	14.69	19.55	24.24
Financial Services	5.05	7.27	9.62
Community, Social & Pers. Services	33.20	39.22	44.03
Total Employment	**397.00**	**447.80**	**495.18**
Labour Force A (1.5% growth)	406.05	452.33	487.29
Labour Force B (1.8% growth)	406.05	462.12	505.23
Unemployment Rate(%)			
With Labour Force A	2.23	1.00	-1.62
With Labour Force B	2.23	3.10	1.99

iii) Projecting Labour Force Growth

3.11 To explore the implications of these projections for the unemployment situation we need to compare the employment projections with the projected growth of the labour force. A detailed projection of labour force growth over the next ten years requires a combination of demographic and behavioural modeling. Demographic modeling would yield projections of the growth of population and its age structure which determines the growth of the working age population and this needs to be combined with behavioural modeling to yield projections of labour force participation rates in different age groups. The rural-urban composition of the population is also relevant in this context since participation rates vary between rural and urban areas. A detailed labour force projection along these lines requires detailed data from the 2001 census which would only become available later in the year and this is being attempted by one of the Working Groups set up in the Planning Commission in connection with the Tenth Plan. However, for the purpose of this report, we have made some assumptions about the likely growth of the labour force over the next ten years taking into account such information as is available from the 55th Round of the NSS and the initial data from the 2001 census.

3.12 The results of the 2001 census confirm that population growth has decelerated in the period 1991-2001 (though the deceleration is less than was expected) and this deceleration is expected to continue over the next ten years yielding a growth rate of population of about 1.6% per year over the next decade. Given the age structure of the population, the working age population will definitely grow faster than the growth of total population and a growth rate of 2% can be assumed for the working age population. Moving from the working age population to the labor force requires projection of labor force participation rates and this presents numerous difficulties.

3.13 As pointed out in Chapter 2, the 55 th Round of the NSS for 1999-2000 showed a sharp decline in participation rates in certain age groups which led to a considerable slowing down in labour force growth to a little over 1% per year even though population growth was almost 2%. Although a further decline in participation rates in the younger age groups can be expected because of the expansion of schooling, the rate of decline in other age groups is not likely to be as sharp as suggested by the 55th Round data. This is because, as pointed out in chapter 2, the deceleration between 1993-94 and 1999-2000 was perhaps exaggerated by the unusually high participation rate observed in 1993-94. It is therefore reasonable to assume that while labour force growth will be much closer to the growth rate of the working age population of around 2%, it will not be as low as 1%. Accordingly, we have made two alternative projections of the labor force over the next ten years based on a growth rate of 1.5% per year and 1.8% per year, respectively.

3.14 These growth rates imply that the net addition to the labour force over the next ten years will be between 6.6 million and 8.1 million per year. It may be noted that even the higher labour force growth assumption implies a growth that is significantly less than the growth of 10 million per year indicated in our terms of reference. To that extent, the need for additional jobs is somewhat less than envisaged in our terms of reference though, as pointed out below, it will not be easy to absorb even this reduced flow.

iv) Implication for Unemployment

3.15 The unemployment picture which results if the employment projection from each of our alternative GDP growth scenarios is combined with each of the two alternative labour force assumptions, is reported in Table 3.4, 3.5 and 3.6 respectively. These projections of the rate of unemployment have important limitations which we point out below, but they are nevertheless instructive. The main conclusions can be summarized as follows :

a. The 6.5% GDP growth scenario yields total employment growth of only about 1.37% per year. This means that if the labour force grows at 1.5% per year, the unemployment rate will continue to rise over the next ten years, increasing from 2.23% in 1999-2000 to 4.00% by 2011-12. If the labour force grows faster at 1.8% per year, then this employment projection actually yields a sharply worsening unemployment situation, with the unemployment rate reaching 7.41% in 2011-12.

b. In the High Growth scenario, with GDP growing at 8.0%, total employment growth accelerates to around 1.68% per year. If labour force grows at 1.5%, the unemployment rate declines to 1.03% in the terminal year but if labour force grows at 1.8%, then unemployment will still increase sharply to 4.55% in the terminal year.

c. In the rapid growth scenario where GDP grows at 9%, the situation is much better with total employment increasing by 1.95%. In this case, unemployment falls on both labour force assumptions. Indeed with labour growth at 1.5%, the rate of unemployment actually becomes negative indicating a labor deficit. If labour force increases at 1.8% there will be a decrease in unemployment to 1.99%.

3.16 An obvious limitation of these projections is that the demand for labour (i.e. employment) is projected independent of supply with no room for the impact of adjustment mechanisms which operate in the labour market in response to the emergence of excess demand or excess supply situations. For example, in the real world, if growth of labour demand is inadequate relative to growth of labour, then instead of the sharp increase in open unemployment shown in our projections, we are more likely to see a more moderate increase in open unemployment together with a tendency for surplus labour to be absorbed to a greater extent in residual sectors (e.g. agriculture and certain types of services). Similarly, a scenario of rapid growth in labour demand will not lead to as sharp a reduction of unemployment, and certainly not to negative unemployment rates, as in our calculations if only because the very process of tightening of the labour market will lead to a faster growth in real wages, which will automatically encourage a shift to more labour saving technologies which will moderate the growth in demand for labour though improving the quality of existing employment. Faster growth in real wages could also lead to a supply side response, with an increase in labor force participation rate. Such equilibrating reactions of the labour market can only be quantified through explicit general equilibrium models in which technology choices, real wages and the supply of labor are endogenously determined. It is doubtful whether the information needed to construct such models is available and in any case the exercise is well beyond the scope of this report.

3.17 These limitations notwithstanding, the projections reported above provide some useful guide for assessing the rate of growth of GDP needed to make a significant difference to the employment situation in the next ten years. With labor force growth at 1.5% the addition to the labor force will be 6.6 million per year whereas the higher labour force growth rate of 1.8% yields an addition of 8.1 million per year. Continuing with GDP growth of 6.5% will certainly not bring about the desired improvement in the employment situation but will only lead to further increases in unemployment albeit with some improvements in the quality of existing employment resulting from the growth of productivity. Our projections suggest that growth rate of GDP between 8% and 9% is needed if we are to achieve our objective of generating enough additional employment to absorb the addition to the labour force and also ensure a sufficient tightening of labour markets to improve the quality of existing employment. An important feature of our projections is that much of the additional employment generated will be in the services sector and not in manufacturing.

2. Policies for Accelerating Growth

3.18 Since rapid growth is important for generating additional employment and for improving the quality of existing employment, any employment strategy must emphasize the policies needed to accelerate growth, especially in sectors which employ large numbers of people. These issues are being examined separately by the Planning Commission in the context of the formulation of the 10 th Plan and detailed proposals for accelerating growth are expected to emerge from the exercise. In the rest of this chapter we focus on some of the critical macro-level policies that are essential if growth is to be accelerated to 8% or more.

i) Investment Levels

3.19 The rate of investment expressed as a percentage of GDP and the efficiency of investment measured by the incremental capital output ratio (ICOR) are two critical determinants of growth and both are important for policy if we want to accelerate growth in future. The rate of investment (gross domestic capital formation as a percentage of GDP) has fluctuated in recent years averaging around 24.4% in the period 1992-93 to 1999-2000. When the average growth rate was around 6.5%. An investment rate of 24.4% yielding 6.5% growth, implies an ICOR of 3.75. Using this ICOR, an acceleration from 6.5% growth to 8% would require an increase in the investment rate by 5.6 percentage points of GDP, taking the total investment rate to 30%. On the same basis, an acceleration to 9% would require an investment rate of almost 34%.

3.20 These estimates are broadly in line with the experience in East Asia which achieved 8% growth over a long period. Most of these countries typically had investment rates around 35%, with China's investment rates being even higher. However, the contemporary consensus is that investment rates in these countries were perhaps unnecessarily high, with evidence of "wasteful" investment projects. Even if the investment is not actually wasteful, it can certainly be argued that these countries invested heavily in the creation of infrastructure assets in excess of their immediate requirements. There are other examples of fast growing countries such as Chile, which have achieved rapid growth with much lower average levels of investment.

3.21 Keeping in mind past experience and the experience of other countries, and also recognising the scope for reducing ICORs through policies which increase the efficiency of resource use, we feel that an acceleration of growth to 8% could be achieved with an aggregate investment rate of around 29% of GDP, i.e. an increase of 4.5 percentage points of GDP, provided this is accompanied by a significant reduction in ICOR reflecting the pursuit of efficiency enhancing policies. Even so, an increase of 4.5 percentage points in the investment rate would require a major effort and cannot be achieved instantly.

3.22 The proposed increase in the rate of investment has to be financed by some combination of an increase in domestic savings and an increase in the foreign resource inflow. In our view, the strategy for achieving the increase in investment could be as follows:

a. The increase in the rate of investment of 4.5 percentage points of GDP could be financed by a combination of an increase in domestic savings of around 3 percentage points and an increase in the net foreign investment inflow of 1.5 percentage points.

b. Additional FDI flows of 1.5 percent of GDP imply an increase in the FDI flow from about $6 billion inclusive of FII investments at present to around $12 billion. This is not an impossible target given the level of inflows attracted by many developing countries, but success in this area depends critically upon other policies being suitably supportive. We note that the proposed expansion in FDI flows would require the current account deficit to expand from a little over one percent of GDP at present to around 2.5 percent. This is well within prudent limits, especially if the increase is financed by foreign direct investment.

c. The proposed increase of around 3 percentage points of GDP in domestic savings would have to come from household savings, corporate sector savings or public sector savings. Table 3.7 shows recent trends in savings from these three sources. The household sector shows a steady increase in its savings over time as a percentage of GDP. The private corporate sector also shows an increase with some reduction in recent years. Public sector savings on the other hand show a steady deterioration from a positive contribution of 2.0% of GDP in 1991-92 to a negative savings of 1.2.% in 1999-2000. These estimates of public sector savings include gross savings of public sector units. If we focus only on government savings the deterioration would be more marked.

d. These trends suggest that the improvement of about 3 percentage points of GDP in domestic savings will have to come largely from a turnaround in government savings. If the entire turnaround of 3 percentage points of GDP, were achieved by the government sector it would enable the combined fiscal deficit of the Centre and States to be reduced from 10% of GDP at present to 7%, while keeping the rate of investment in the government sector unchanged. However, if public investment by the government also needs to be increased as a proportion of GDP, and we shall argue later that such an increase is indeed necessary to make up deficiencies in the infrastructure and social sectors, then government savings have to increase by a larger amount. For example, if the rate of public investment (both Centre and States) has to increase by 1 percentage point of GDP while keeping the combined fiscal deficit at 7%, then the government savings rate has to be increased by 4 percentage points of GDP. If the combined fiscal deficit of the Centre or the States has to be reduced to 5% of GDP, which is surely desirable, and public investment raised by 1 percentage point, then the improvement in government savings needed is around 6 percentage points of GDP.

e. The above target is broadly consistent with the degree of fiscal correction envisaged in the Fiscal Responsibility and Budget Management Bill recently submitted to Parliament. The Bill envisages a reduction in the Centre's revenue deficit from 3.6% in 2000-01 to zero by the year 2005-2006, i.e. an improvement of 3.6 percentage point of GDP by the Centre alone. If the State can reduce their revenue deficit by 2.4 percentage points the total improvement for the Centre and States combined would be 6 percentage points of GDP over a five-year period

f. Reducing the revenue deficit is only possible if strong fiscal measures can be taken to reduce subsidies and increase tax realisation. Some examples of what is needed are:

   – reducing subsidies by raising user charges in a number of areas where the subsidy is not justifiable because it is not targeted at the poor. In the case of the Central government this includes raising passenger fares in the railways, raising university fees in Central Universities and raising prices of kerosene and LPG both which are heavily subsidised and not effectively targeted at the poor. State governments have to act to raise power tariffs for agriculture and household consumers, which at present are heavily subsidised, water charges for irrigation which cover only a fraction of the maintenance cost, fares in state transport corporations, fees in state universities, and municipal charges for water which are heavily subsidised.

- Eliminating the burden of losses in public sector enterprises by closing down loss making public sector enterprises or handing them over to the private sector.
- Realise asset values in profit making public sector enterprises by privatising these units and using the resources thus obtained to develop much needed social and economic infrastructure.
- Simplifying the tax system and modernising tax administration to achieve greater revenue realisation through better compliance and coverage.
- Trimming the government bureaucracy which suffers from massive over staffing

g. While the fiscal measures outlined above will have a positive effect on public savings, they could have a negative effect on private savings because of the reduction in private disposable income consequent to higher tax realisation and lower subsidies. This reduction in disposable income is unlikely to be accompanied by an equivalent cut in private consumption so private savings are likely to be lower than they otherwise would be. Special efforts will therefore be needed to ensure that the private savings rate is maintained as a percentage of GDP which implies an increase in private savings as a percentage of disposable income. To some extent, the achievement of high growth will itself stimulate private savings, since there is evidence that private savings increase when growth accelerates. However, some additional efforts will be needed to ensure that private savings do not suffer.

h. The most effective means of promoting private savings is the development of long-term contractual savings schemes. The recent opening of the insurance sector to private entrants is an important development in this context, since it will bring an improvement in insurance services and innovation in insurance products not only from the new private sector entrants but also from the existing public sector incumbents which can be expected to improve in the face of competition. Speedy implementation of policies already announced must be undertaken so that new insurance and pension products become available as quickly as possible.

Table – 3.7

Domestic Savings Rates

(% of GDP at current market price)

	Public Sector	Private Corporate Sector	Household Sector	Total
1991-92	2.0	3.1	17.0	22.0
1992-93	1.6	2.7	17.5	21.8
1993-94	0.6	3.5	18.4	22.5
1994-95	1.7	3.5	19.7	24.8
1995-96	2.0	4.4	18.1	25.1
1996-97	1.7	4.5	17.0	23.2
1997-98	1.5	4.2	17.8	23.5
1998-99	-0.8	3.7	19.1	22.0
1999-00	-1.2	3.7	19.8	22.3

Source: Economic Survey 2000, Ministry of Finance

3.23 The broad approach outlined above, as well as the specific suggestions offered, are not new. They have long been advocated by many expert bodies and also within government. Our purpose in listing them here is simply to point out that they are essential for mobilising the resources needed to promote growth in the economy, which is an essential requirement for employment creation.

ii) Policies to Promote Efficiency

3.24 As pointed out earlier, a higher investment rate is only one of the elements of a strategy for higher growth. The other element must be an improvement in efficiency. Higher levels of efficiency in all sectors are absolutely essential if the economy is to be brought to a growth path of 8% or more within the constraints of total invertible resources described above. The most effective instrument to ensure efficiency is competition, which in today's world must be both domestic and international.

(a) Domestic Competition

3.25 Intensification of competition is sometimes perceived to be against the interest of employment since the survival of weaker firms may seem to be endangered by stronger competitors, leading to concern about the loss of employment in these firms. This approach ignores the fact that a high employment strategy for the economy as a whole is not the same as a strategy of protecting employment in particular firms. A competitive environment puts pressure on all firms to improve their efficiency. While it is possible in principle that every firm gains sufficiently in efficiency to survive in the new environment, this is not likely to happen in practice. Typically, competition will lead to a generalised improvement in efficiency in many firms which will become more competitive and will flourish, but all firms will not be able to show the same efficiency gains and many of the weaker firms, which are not be able to improve sufficiently, will therefore be pushed out. It is important to recognise that a wake out of domestic industries, in which weaker firms die out or are taken over by stronger firms, is an inevitable and indeed even desirable process in our situation where many units are operating below economic scale. Such restructuring is not necessarily harmful for total employment. The decline in employment in the weaker units may be offset by the expansion of employment in stronger units. The total employment generated by the restructured industry is likely to be more sustainable and more capable of showing growth in the longer term. Given the challenges posed by globalization a failure to accept restructuring will only jeopardize employment and growth in the medium term. However, it must also be recognised that the process can be dislocating in the short run. It is necessary to explore ways of minimizing the costs of dislocation, especially when these are concentrated in particular industries or regions.

3.26 The economic reforms implemented since 1991 have already created an environment when domestic competition is much freer. Policies such as industrial licensing, limits on size, restrictions on foreign investment etc. all of which limited the scope for competition in the domestic economy are things of the past. However, the process is still incomplete. Important industries such as sugar remain subject to controls in terms of restrictions on the ability to set up new sugar mill within a certain radius of another and also a continuing obligation to surrender a portion of the output at an administered price to the government for supply through the public distribution system. In the case of dairying, the Milk Marketing Products Order limits potential expansion by competing dairying units based on arbitrary assessments of milk shed capacity. Coal mining is a major sector which has not yet been opened up to domestic competition except for captive coal mines. The pharmaceutical industries remain subject to extensive price control. The policy of reservation for the small scale sector, which is discussed in greater detail in Chapter 4 is another example of a policy which restricts domestic competition.

3.27 In our view, the Central Government should initiate action to increase competition in all the areas where government policy continues to impose restrictions and controls. Continent controls in these areas when the rest of the industrial sector has been liberalized is an anachronism. There is also need for parallel action at the State government level to remove a large number of regulatory restrictions, which currently limit competition. Several such restrictions exist in the areas of agriculture, road transport and real estate which are discussed individually in Chapter 4.

(b) International Competition

3.28 International competition is the other spur to efficiency which is especially important in our situation because the economy has been insulated from international competition to a much greater extent than other developing countries. The past ten years of reforms have seen considerable improvement in this area with a gradual reduction in quantitative restrictions (QRs) and also a reduction in tariff levels. QRs on imports have been completely phased out with effect from April 1, 2001 bringing India's trade policies in line with current international practice in this respect. The principle impact of the QR removal is that consumer goods, which have long been insulated from international competition, now face competition from imports, subject only to tariff protection. Our tariff rates have also come down from the very high levels that existed earlier, but they are still among the highest in the world and it is in this area that policy must concentrate.

3.29 It has often been stated that it is the objective of government policy to bring our tariff level down to levels comparable with those prevailing in East Asia. The Finance Minister's Budget Speech for 2001-02 provides the most recent and clearest statement of this objective with monitorable milestone in this regard.

> "I have already promised that our customs tariff would be brought down to East Asian levels. I will like to move progressively within three years to reduce the number of rates to the minimum with a peak rate of 20%. The modalities for this will be worked out in time for the next budget."

We welcome the statement of a target for the peak rate and the intention to announce modalities for the three year transition before the Budget for 2002.

3.30 Some indication of the extent of tariff protection in India can be seen from Table 3.8 which shows weighted average tariff rates for various broad import groups. It may be noted that although the average tariff rate declined steadily from 1991 to 1996, thereafter it edged up again, due to the imposition of various surcharges. The weighted average tariff level (excluding CVD) on the basis of the 2001-02 Budget is about 34%. The corresponding import weighted tariff rates in East Asia are much lower amounting to 14.3% for Indonesia, 7% for Korea, 9.4% for Malaysia and 8.5% for the Philippines. The figure for China is 18.5% at present and is expected to be phased down to less than 10% in the coming years as part of China's agreement in connection with its WTO entry. If the target for India is taken as a weighed average (excluding agriculture) of 10% to be achieved at the end of three years, it requires a reduction of approximately 8 percentage points per year in the weighted average tariff.

3.31 It is important that the proposed phasing of tariff reduction for different items should be indicated as early as possible to allow domestic industry sufficient time to adjust. To encourage investment in an environment where tariff levels are expected to fall, it is necessary to ensure that the phasing of tariff reduction is such that tariffs on capital goods are reduced as early as possible to their final resting position. This in turn draws attention to the need to lower tariffs on critical inputs into capital goods, including especially components, steel and other metals. In order to facilitate dispassionate discussion of these issues, and to enable industry to take a composite view in full knowledge of what is intended for both outputs and inputs, we recommend that the proposed phasing should be published in the form of a discussion paper by September 2001.

3.32 The prospect of reducing protection levels for domestic industry is likely to create fears and uncertainties. However, it needs to be kept in mind that reduced protection is an essential part of the process of bringing our cost structures in line with those prevailing the rest of the world and enabling our producers to become competitive internationally. This is a process being undertaken by all emerging market countries and India cannot be the sole exception. Indian industry has managed the transition from the very highly protected environment of 1991 to the much more open environment today fairly well, and there is every reason to believe that continued progress along these lines brings us to East Asian levels need not be disruptive provided it is appropriately phased, with supportive policies aimed at strengthening the competitive capability of Indian producers. It must be kept in mind that a policy of reducing tariff levels across the board need not have a damaging effect on domestic industry if it is accompanied by a parallel depreciation of the exchange rate which will boost the competitiveness of domestic industry with the additional advantage that it will be much more beneficial for exporters.

iii) Infrastructure Development

3.33 The state of infrastructure development is another major constraint on achieving rapid growth in both rural and urban areas and corrective policies in this area are absolutely essential if we want to achieve rapid growth of GDP and employment. Our rural areas lack basic economic and social infrastructure for agricultural and other rural development. This includes a well functioning system for irrigation and water management, rural roads to provide basic connectivity, a reliable extension service to disseminate best agricultural practices, adequate and reliable supply of electric power and basic social infrastructure in health and education. Industry is also severely constrained by lack of reliable and reasonably priced electric power and good quality transportation services (both road and rail). Telecommunications services have improved in metropolitan areas, but are still far behind levels prevailing in our competitor countries. Operational efficiencies in Indian ports are much lower than in our competitors and this is an important factor limiting the potential global competitiveness of Indian producers. Urban infrastructure services such as drinking water supply, sewerage and municipal cleaning are also under severe strain, which not only affects the welfare of our expanding urban population but is also a constraint on efforts to make India an attractive destination for foreign investment and also for tourism, both of which are important for employment.

3.34 A comprehensive analysis of the policies needed to set infrastructure development on the right track is outside the scope of our report but it is appropriate to highlight some of the critical policy issues relevant for infrastructure development which must be resolved if we are to achieve GDP growth of 8% or more in the next ten years. The first issue is the relative role of public vs. private investment in infrastructure development. Infrastructure has traditionally been developed almost exclusively by the public sector, but today the public sector simply does not have the resources needed to make investments on the scale required to support high rates of growth. It is therefore necessary to attract private sector investment to promote infrastructure development wherever possible. The quality of infrastructure services has also become a major issue because of the compulsions of global competitiveness and improvements in quality are best assured by encouraging competition, which again suggests the need for private sector involvement.

3.35 While private investment is important, it cannot possibly replace public investment entirely in our situation. Policy towards infrastructure development must therefore be formulated on the assumption that a very large part of the responsibility will continue to remain in the public sector. This is certainly true of infrastructure development in rural areas e.g. irrigation, land development, rural roads, rural schools and primary health centre.

There is room for community participation in the design of programmes in these areas and in their maintenance, but the finances for investment will have to come from the government. It is also true of some other sectors where private sector investment is possible in principle, but the scale of investment in practice is likely to be limited e.g. development of national and state highways and also railways. If public investment is essential, it is important to ensure that adequate resources are available in the public sector for this purpose and this depends upon implementation of the various measures for fiscal correction listed above. The need to raise user charges in critical areas such as power, irrigation, urban municipal services etc. where user charges are feasible is particularly relevant in this context. However, in several areas of rural infrastructure (schools, health care centres and even certain type of land development) user charges are not feasible and these investments have to be funded from the budget. This in turn depends upon achieving an improvement in the general fiscal position of state government.

Table – 3.8

Weighted Average Import Duty Rates in India

	Agriculture	Mining	Consumer Goods	Intermediate Goods	Capital Goods	All Commodities
1991-92	47.0	56.9	97.8	69.5	94.8	72.5
1992-93	22.8	32.6	83.2	62.6	85.2	60.6
1993-94	19.8	33.4	68.7	47.6	58.4	46.8
1994-95	16.8	30.3	55.9	38.4	45.5	38.2
1995-96	16.7	29.9	36.1	22.9	29.1	25.9
1996-97	14.7	22.0	39.0	21.9	28.8	24.6
1997-98	14.0	21.9	33.8	46.1	25.1	25.4
1998-99	24.2	19.9	37.9	31.1	29.4	29.2
1999-00	24.4	21.4	37.4	33.1	31.0	31.4
2000-01	58.6	16.1	56.2	36.2	34.4	35.7
2001-02	57.7	15.8	67.1	34.8	31.8	35.1

Source: Planning Commission Estimates

3.36 There is considerable potential for private investment in sectors such as power, telecommunications, ports etc., but it is important to recognise that private investment will not flow simply because a sector is opened for private investment. Experience in the power sector exemplifies the situation. Private investment in power was initially invited into the generation segment, but since the new power plants were expected to sell power to State Electricity Boards (SEBs) investors perceived serious risks of non-payment because of the poor financial condition of the SEBs. Investors therefore sought various types of risk mitigation through government counter guarantees, escrow arrangements etc., not of which have worked well. The net result is that although a large number of MOUs were signed initially, implementation has been very poor. Nor can much progress be expected until the root cause of the financial unviability of SEBs is tackled. This involves reforms in two critical areas. First, it is necessary to move away from the present system of heavy cross-subsidization in which tariffs are very low for some users (mainly agriculture and domestic households) with very high tariffs for industry. Second, it is necessary to reduce and reducing operational inefficiencies, especially the large transmission and distribution losses, most of which represent theft of power. Privatisation of the distribution segment would help to improve efficiency in this area and is urgently needed. Reforms along these lines are long overdue and will help to improve the viability of the public sector system, increasing its ability to invest, while simultaneously also making it possible to attract private investment to supplement the public sector effort.

3.37 Similar problems have arisen in telecommunications, where many private players have entered the field, but there are persistent complaints about the lack of a level playing field. The government has taken a number of steps in recent years to sort out problems as they have arisen, but this is an area where technology is changing so rapidly that new regulatory challenges are bound to arise. Government policy will have to be flexible to anticipate technology changes and to create a regulatory environment which is seen to be fair to both producers and consumers.

iv) Finance and Banking

3.38 The health and efficiency of the financial system plays an extremely an important role in financing development and ensuring efficiency of resource allocation, and this is especially so in a situation where the relative role of private investment is expected to increase. The development of a strong financial sector, encompassing both commercial banking and the capital markets is therefore a critical pre-condition for achieving rapid growth. A number of initiatives have been taken in this area over the past several years and they have definitely improved the situation in many ways, but the process of reforms is far from over.

3.39 Reforms in the banking sector were initiated as early as 1992, when the government began to implement some of the recommendations of the Narasimham Committee. Since then, considerable progress has been made in upgrading prudential norms and standards bringing closer to international levels, and strengthening the supervisory system. Nevertheless, there is still considerable scope for improving the efficiency of the banking system and these improvements are essential if we are to achieve GDP growth rates of 8% and more.

3.40 The cost of credit from the banking system is still quite high with real interest rates varying between 6% and 10%. Much of this is not due to the inefficiency of intermediation but because of the high rates which banks have to pay for mobilizing deposits, which in turn reflect the pressure on domestic interest rates arising from the high fiscal deficit. This can only be remedied by reducing the fiscal deficit and the various measures mentioned earlier in this chapter, if implemented in practice, would go along way to meeting this objective. However, high deposit rates are not the only problem. Indian commercial banks also display inefficiencies in intermediation reflected in the interest spread of 2.7 percentage points in the banking system, which is much higher than the international norm of around 1 percent. These high spreads reflect the need to make provisions for the high volume of non-performing assets generated by the system and also to cover high operating costs arising from extensive overstaffing and the existence of an over-extended branch network, with far too many loss making branches.

3.41 Apart from cost related inefficiencies, the banking system also suffers from poor quality of service which limits the competitive strength of the economy. Delays in clearing cheques and effecting payments are common, though with the gradual induction of information technology in the public sector banks, the situation is expected to improve. A more serious problem is that credit decisions in public sector banks are often delayed and the decision itself is typically driven by a culture which accords primacy to following procedures with multiple layers of approval. This greatly reduces flexibility of decision making and the net result is that many worthwhile ventures are denied access to credit or do not receive credit in time.

3.42 One of the causes of inefficiency in the banking system is the persistence of directed lending in the shape of priority sector lending requirements. The desire to ensure that credit reaches critical sectors such as agriculture and the small-scale sector is entirely understandable. It is a means of extending much-needed institutional support to sectors that are potentially important for both growth and employment but not otherwise adequately linked to the financial system. However the obligation to lend to the priority sector has created a culture of mechanical lending in public sector banks in which there is little effort at credit appraisal in priority sector lending, leading to a higher proportion of non-performing assets for priority sector advances than for non-priority sector advances. The Narasimham Committee had suggested a drastic reduction in the share of priority sector lending limiting it to a more precisely defined target group but this recommendation was not accepted. If the priority sector obligation is to continue, it is essential to ensure that credit appraisal is not compromised so that priority sector lending does not lead to high non-performing loans. The current practice of limiting the interest rate on loans below Rs.2 lakhs to the prime lending rate could be reconsidered. Small loans are inherently more costly for banks and there is ample evidence that for the borrower, what matters is the timeliness of availability of credit rather than the rate of interest especially since the interest paid by priority sector borrowers to money lenders is very high.

3.43 Competition among all categories of banks, including public sector banks, Indian private sector banks and foreign banks should lead to an improvement in the quality of banking sector services and this competition needs to be encouraged by following suitably liberal bank licensing policies which will allow qualified private banks (Indian and foreign) to expand their presence. Needless to say, competition should be accompanied by strict regulation which will ensure that banks observe minimum prudential standards. Banks that fail to meet these standards should be suitably penalized, and in any case restrained from expanding commercial advances, thus encouraging the more efficient banks to expand and prosper.

3.44 An aspect of the banking systems that deserves particular attention is the difficulty in present circumstances of obtaining bank credit for service sector activities. Traditionally, banks have concentrated on financing working capital for a manufacturing enterprises and banks are familiar with the needs of such units. However, as pointed out earlier in this chapter, the services sector is critical for employment generation and is expected to provide 70% employment over the next ten years. Indian banks are not well geared to meeting the credit needs of service sector units and this lacuna needs to be corrected.

3.45 The capital market is an important element of the financial systems and an efficient capital market can help lubricate the growth process. A well functioning capital market provides a means for individual savers to participate in the benefit of equity ownership with a high degree of liquidity, it allows dynamic companies to raise resources for expansion in the form of both debt and equity and it also provides mechanisms for take-over of companies by those willing to offer shareholders a better deal. All these functions are important in a situation where the objective of policy is to achieve a transition to more rapid growth. Considerable progress has been made in establishing a regulatory framework for the capital market and in introducing modern methods of trading or settlement. Nevertheless, the functioning of the capital market in recent years suggests that there has been some loss of confidence on the part of investors and the market has not been as effective as expected in channelling funds to productive investment. A high level review of policies for the capital markets on the lines of the review conducted by the Narasimham Committee for banking is desirable

v) Credit For the Informal Sector

3.46 A major problem in all developing countries is that the formal banking system is ill-suited to meeting the credit needs of the informal sector and yet this sector accounts for the bulk of the total employment generated. We have noted earlier that it must be an objective of employment policy to increase the relative size of the organised sector in total employment, but there are limits to the pace at which this can take place and the informal sector is therefore likely to remain a major source of employment and also growth of employment in future. Special efforts must therefore be made to ensure that the financing needs of this sector are adequately met so that it can expand at a role commensurate with the growth of GDP being projected.

3.47 This calls for initiatives on several fronts. First, the banking system itself must be encouraged to reach out to enterprises in the informal sector through innovative means. This is effectively what is intended by the various targets specified for priority sector lending by commercial banks. However, priority sector lending has its own problems as noted earlier. The effectiveness of bank lending to the informal sector must be greatly increased. Banking practices and procedures need to be reviewed to enable banks to adopt a more pro-active approach to lending for economically viable activities in the informal sector. The cooperative credit structure can play a major role in extending credit to the informal sector but it has become very weak in most States. There is an urgent need to strengthen the cooperative system. This calls for legislative changes which would free cooperatives from what at present is pervasive government control.

3.48 A great deal of informal sector activity can be more effectively serviced by non-bank financing intermediaries which are perhaps better able to handle such intermediations, charging interest rates which cover the high cost of managing an informal sector loan which is inherently more risky. They are also able to enforce claims on collateral. It is necessary to review the regulatory constraints on commercial banks which may prevent them from lending to such non-bank financial intermediaries for on-lending to finance informal sector activity.

3.49 Another important mechanism through which banks can meet the credit needs of the informal sector is by announcing self help groups (SHGs) which provide micro-credit for informal sector activities. A pilot project linking SHGs to banks was launched in 1992. It was envisaged that NGOs could help build up capacity among the poor to organize themselves into SHGs and approach the banks for financing. In 1992-93, a total of 255 SHGs were linked with banks under this project. The number had expanded to 1,21,744 as on September 30, 2000. The programme has provided credit to 1.9 million poor families. More than 85 percent of the SHGs are exclusively women's groups.

3.50 The experience thus far has been very encouraging. Recovery rates of SHGs are very high (over 90 percent) reflecting the impact of peer pressure in ensuring loan recovery. Impact studies of micro credit extended by SHGs show very positive outcomes in terms of the effectiveness of the loans in reaching the poor and in improving their income levels[1]. An important aspect of the programme is that it envisages a process of graduation whereby families can begin to finance informal sector activity through macro-credit extended by SHGs but can, in due course, access larger amounts of loans directly from the banks in due course.

3.51 The Reserve Bank of India has taken a number of steps to encourage bank lending to SHGs as a part of mainstream banking activity. Credit extended by commercial banks to SHGs is treated as part of priority sector lending in order to encourage banks to engage in the type of activity. Banks have also been given considerable flexibility to determine procedures and design loan products for SHGs responding to local conditions. A Micro-Finance Development Fund has also been established in NABARD to give training to SHG members, partner NGOs, banks and government agencies, provide start up funds to micro-finance institutions and meet their initial operating deficits and meet the cost of formation and nurturing of SHGs. We would strongly recommend that the programme of providing credit to SHGs, which has made a very good start, is a potentially important mechanism for expanding credit to the informal sector and should be greatly expanded in the year ahead.

3.52 To summarize, it is necessary to act on a wide front to

---

1 See "Micro Finance for Rural People — An Impact Evaluation" by V. Puhazhendi and K.J.S. Satyasai, NABARD, Mumbai (2000)

bring about rapid growth of GDP, which in our view will be the most important factor in generating a high growth. The policy initiatives needed to achieve this objective are not usually emphasised in discussions on employment policy, but they are in fact critical to achieving any significant improvement in the employment situation in the next ten years.

3.53 An aspect of particular importance in the future is that employment generation in future, especially of high quality jobs, cannot be as dependent as it has been in the past, on the growth of public sector employment. Employment policy must recognise that the objective of government cannot be to create jobs directly, but to facilitate the growth of employment opportunities by promoting GDP growth. The bulk of the new employment opportunities will necessarily be created in the private sector. Inevitably, they will consist of a combination of self-employment and wage employment. Agriculture will constitute only a small amount to the generation of new employment. The bulk of the new employment opportunities will be in the services sector and a large part of these will be in the informal sector.

4

Sectoral Policies for Employment Promotion

The macro-economic policies for accelerating growth outlined in the previous chapter need to be supported by sector specific policies aimed at stimulating efficiency and economic restructuring in individual sectors which will help achieve the overall growth objective. Sector specific policies are particularly important in case of sectors that are inherently more labour using since growth in these sectors can be expected to generate new employment opportunities or improve the quality of a large volume of existing employment. In this chapter, we focus on some of the sectoral policy issues which are most important from this perspective.

1. Agriculture and Allied Activities

4.2 Agriculture accounts for just under 60% of total employment and what happens in this sector is therefore extremely important for the employment situation in the economy. However, it is important to recognise that this is not a sector where we should be planning for a large increase in total employment. On the contrary, agriculture has traditionally served as a residual employer, and is therefore characterised by considerable underemployment with seasonal variation in employment and relatively low real wages. Our longer term employment strategy should therefore aim at absorbing as much of the expansion in the labour force as possible in the non-agricultural sector, thus reducing the pressure of labour on land and thereby tightening the labour market, so that incomes per head in farming and real wages of agricultural labour rise significantly.

4.3 This is reflected in the growth scenarios in Chapter 3 which project GDP in agriculture to grow by 4.2% in the high growth scenario (8% GDP growth) and 4.8% in the rapid growth scenario (9% GDP growth), but since the elasticity of employment is only 0.1, the growth in agricultural employment is only 0.42 to 0.48% per year. The resulting productivity growth of 3.5 to 4% per year should help to improve the quality of employment in agriculture through faster growth in real wages of agricultural labour and in incomes per head of the self-employed. However, the desired level of growth in agricultural output and labour productivity will only take place if a number of policy issues in this sector are successfully addressed and market based incentives are created to facilitate greater capital, credit and technology flow. These are discussed below.

i) Public Investment in Agriculture

4.4 Agricultural GDP has been growing at around 3.3% per year in the 1990s and the projected acceleration to between 4.2 to 4.8 % per year will definitely require higher levels of investment in this sector. While much of the investment needed will be private on farm investment, the role of public investment in agriculture (including especially irrigation) is extremely important. Unfortunately, public investment in agriculture has been declining in real terms in the 1980s and most of the 1990s[1], though there has been some increase in the last three years. Private investment in agriculture has been rising but the trend is offset by decline in public investment so that total investment in agriculture has increased at only a modest rate. Accelerated growth in agriculture in future will require a substantial increase in public investment in agriculture related infrastructure such as irrigation and drainage, land development, water conservation, development of rural road connectivity etc. Such investments are especially needed in the poorer, low rainfall areas of the country, which must now play a

1 This assessment of trends in public investment in agriculture may need to be modified if we take account of the fact that investment in agriculture in national accounts include investment in the form of irrigation but does not include investment in rural roads or development of markets, which are extremely important for agricultural production. It is possible that if these investments are included the decline in total investment may be less than it appears otherwise

larger role in achieving rapid agricultural growth since productivity levels in green revolution areas appear to have plateaued.

4.5 Public investment in agriculture is the responsibility of state governments and is therefore severely constrained by the fiscal problems of state governments. Resolution of these problems along the lines indicated in Chapter 3 is therefore critical for accelerating agricultural growth. It is important to note that although some of the solutions lie in a general improvement in fiscal performance, there is also room for restructuring the existing allocation of resources to agriculture by reducing implicit subsidies in this area and utilizing the savings thus achieved to increase public investment. For example, undercharging farmers for power and for irrigation is ostensibly designed to benefit farmers, but in practice it only leads to the power and irrigation systems being starved of resources. The net result is poor maintenance of existing assets and an inability to invest to expand the system, both of which reduce agricultural productivity.

4.6 The price distortions introduced by some of the present subsidies also have damaging effects. Low irrigation charges and power tariffs lead to excessive use of water, with harmful effects on soil fertility. The excessive subsidization of nitrogen compared with potash and phosphates leads to excessive use of urea. It can also be argued that the subsidy on urea is improving irrigation and pursuing watershed development would be much more beneficial for agricultural production and would promote the employment objective.

4.7 The lack of resources to finance investment is not however the only constraint in this area. Equally serious is the problem of inefficiency in the use of available resources. The tendency to start new irrigation projects when existing projects are underfunded, leads to a thin spread of available resources, with consequent loss of efficiency. Better prioritization of expenditure to focus on completing ongoing projects is urgently needed.

4.8 Poor design of public investment in rural areas is also a serious problem. Many rural development programmes are of a "top down" variety, with little participation by the beneficiaries. The effectiveness of public investments in rural areas in improving productivity can be greatly increased if there is effective participation which requires genuine decentralisation and empowerment of panchayats and zila parishads. There has been some attempt at such decentralization in many States but the situation on the ground varies considerably and there are serious deficiencies in most States. It must be emphasised that these are the areas which fall in the purview of State Governments. Much depends upon the political commitment at the top to bring about these changes which are bound to be resisted by vested interests.

ii) Private Investment in Agriculture

4.9 Private investment in agricultural at present consists mainly of on farm investment by the farming community itself. The flow of corporate and institutional investment into this sector which is needed now for next stage of agricultural transformation is negligible. It is necessary to encourage the private corporate sector to invest in agriculture and related activities by facilitating the creation of organised and corporatised entities like Integrated Agricultural Complexes and Food Parks that would attract commercial investments. Innovative policies are needed to facilitate large scale investment into the area of agricultural infrastructure, including irrigation by way of public private partnership.

iii) Controls on Agriculture

4.10 One of the factors holding back agricultural growth at present is the failure to extend the benefits of decontrol to the agricultural sector. Liberalisation has had beneficial effects in industry but it has bypassed agriculture which continues to suffer from innumerable controls which hamper realization of potential efficiency. We would recommend the following initiatives to remove existing controls which throttle agricultural development.

a. The *Essential Commodities Act* is a Central Legislation which provides an umbrella under which States are enabled to impose all kinds of restrictions on storage, transport and processing of agricultural produce. These controls have been traditionally justified on the grounds that they are necessary to control hoarding and other types of speculative activity, but the fact is that they do not work in times of genuine scarcity and they are not needed in normal times. Besides, they are typically misused by the lower levels of the administration and become an instrument for harassment and corruption. At a time when European countries have integrated their national markets and regard the resulting large European market as a feature which strengthen their position globally, it is an anomaly that we have laws that actually prevent the development of an integrated national market for agricultural products. After full consideration of this issue, we are of the view that the Essential Commodities Act should be repealed.

b. Repeal of Central legislation may not suffice as States can introduce controls under State laws. In the interest of creating an integrated national market for agricultural produce, there should be a central legislation that would actually ban imposition of any restrictions on the movement, stocking or forward trading in agricultural commodities. The Ministry of Agriculture in the Central Government, in collaboration with the Planning Commission, should undertake a systematic review of State laws and control orders which impose harmful controls on agriculture and actively seek their repeal. Vested interests and inertia will resist such a move, but we feel that it is an essential step for extending the benefits of economic reforms to agriculture.

c. Forward trading in agricultural products should be allowed in a systematic manner with suitable regulation. The introduction of forward markets would help farmers obtain price information and would allow hedging of price risks.

d. The marketing of agricultural produce, especially fruits and vegetables is governed by laws that stifle the development of agriculture. The existing laws require that wholesalers must purchase agricultural produce only in regulated mandis controlled by the Agricultural Produce Marketing Committee (APMC). Since most farmers are small farmers, they cannot directly bring vegetables and fruits to the mandis. They typically sell their produce to village commission agents who collect produce on behalf of the market commission agent who sells to wholesalers in the mandi. Although sale in the mandi is supposed to be by open auction to ensure fair pricing, in practice the price is determined in highly non-transparent manner by negotiations between market commission agents and wholesalers. Lack of transparency is perpetuated by the fact that produce is not graded before it is sold. The prices arrived at in this fashion are declared as the mandi price and the farmer receives the residual price after the commission of the village commission agent and the market commission agent is deducted from the declared market price. Not only is the price determination non-transparent, the large number of middlemen, each of whom charges a commission, squeezes the realization of the farmer so that the gap between the farm-gate price and the retail price paid by the consumer is very large. Although originally designed to protect farmers' interests by creating regulated markets, the system has actually created a monopoly situation in which a small group of traders and agents are able to extract huge benefits. It is absolutely essential to liberalise the existing laws and allow competing markets to be set up. The Government of Karnataka has amended the Agricultural Produce Marketing Act by ordinance to allow National Dairy Development Board (NDDB) to set up a modern fruits and vegetable market in Bangalore. This is a welcome development. We would recommend full decontrol so that any group of persons should be allowed to set up modern marketing infrastructure to facilitate marketing of agricultural produce subject to paying the normal mandi tax. The establishment of competing market will help farmers.

e. In order to improve the transparency in the operation of APMCs, these Committees should publish on the internet in real time, the daily arrivals, maximum and minimum prices as well as balance of stocks available. This will be a first step towards building on integrated national market for agricultural products.

f. Another control instrument which operates against the farmer is the reservation of certain agricultural implements for production by small scale industry. Six of these items were dereserved in 1999 but several other items remain reserved such as cultivators, disc harrows, insecticide dusters (manual), forks, hoses, seed treaters, hand shovels, water lifters, sickles and other agricultural implements. Many of these items can be produced efficiently by SSI units serving local markets and will continue to be produced by them. However, it is surely in the interest of the farmer to allow larger scale units to try to produce superior types of agricultural implements and market them in rural areas. It is illogical to regard agriculture as a priority sector and assert primacy of the objective of improving the conditions of living of agricultural workers, but to deny this sector the best implements which could be produced in India.

g. The time has come to review the entire gamut of policies governing procurement and distribution of foodgrains, including the role of the FCI. As we move away from the earlier years of a scarcity economy, we need to take initiatives to encourage the development of private traders who can compete freely with existing public sector entities such as FCI. It is impossible to develop modern private sector trading companies as long as the present system with movement restrictions, restrictions on stocks and lack of forward market continues. Our proposal in (i) above deals with this problem. It is also necessary to so away with the present preferential treatment of FCI in the matter of provision of transport and credit.

iv) Liberalising Leasing of Land

4.11 The progressive fragmentation of land holdings, leading to proliferation of very small holdings, poses serious problems in transiting to a high productivity agriculture. There is no doubt that much of agricultural technology is scale neutral and small holdings therefore can be highly productive but this is not necessarily the case for very small or marginal holdings. According to the 1990-91 agricultural census almost 60% of the operational holdings were less than 1 hectare and these accounted for 15% of the total area operated. Both percentages are likely to have increased since then because of the continued effect of fragmentation. As fragmentation of land continues in rural areas while real incomes in the rest of the economy increase, more and more of the very small holdings will become unviable in the sense that they will not be able generate sufficient levels of income to encourage the owners to cultivate them as owner cultivators.

4.12 It is therefore necessary to liberalise the present laws regarding the leasing of land to allow marginal land owners to lease out land to others to create operationally viable holdings. The legal position regarding leasing varies across states, but at present many states e.g. Uttar Pradesh, Orissa, Bihar, Kerala, Telengana area of Andhra Pradesh, Himachal Pradesh, Karnataka restrict leasing. In other states, leasing leads to the acquisition of tenancy rights which effectively discourages leasing by small farmers. These restrictions are an impediment to the evolution of economically viable operational holdings. It is necessary to consider changes in the land laws which can free up the land market and facilitate the development of viable sized operational holdings.

4.13 We recognise that changing the leasing laws is a potentially sensitive issue because these laws are perceived as protecting the interest of small cultivators. However, with the growing commercialisation of Indian agriculture and other changes in the economy, some of the safeguards, which were thought necessary under very different conditions 50 years ago may no longer be relevant. There is now an urgent need to develop a well functioning land market if we are to move to the next level of productivity. Marginal farmers must be enabled to lease out very small holdings with no fear of alienation of land. This requires freeing up the restrictions on tenancy in a manner which would promote efficient agglomeration and development of commercial farming. Tenancy laws can also be relaxed in areas such as Western UP and coastal Andhra Pradesh. To protect the rights of farmer owners, recovery of land by the owner could be made legally unchallengeable. As a measure of abundant caution, these changes need not apply to specified areas, which may be classified as feudal or semi-feudal.

4.14 Another dimension along which the rural land market can be freed is with respect to degraded and wasteland, including desert land, saline land & ravines. There are 24 million hectares of land characterised as cultivable wasteland and permanent fallows. Commercial leasing of degraded and wasteland could help to exploit available resources better. Concern is sometimes expressed that such flexibility could be misused and that non-degraded forest land will be misclassified and then leased out. However, such problems could be addressed through careful delimitation. After detailed delimitation, genuine wasteland can be taken out of the purview of land ceiling and tenancy laws, and agro-companies allowed to buy, mortgage, develop, cultivate and sell this land. Commercial leasing can also create problems of environmental degradation as in the case of prawn farming in certain areas where land became highly saline. It would be necessary to protect the interests of lessors in such cases.

v) Development of Non-Cereal Crops

4.15 Faster growth in agriculture necessarily requires agricultural diversification away from cereals towards non-cereal crops such as vegetables and fruits and other allied activities such as floriculture, dairying, poultry etc. These activities are much more labour using than cereal agriculture and will therefore help to improve the employment situation. The critical constraint for development of such crops is the lack of marketing linkages and also the lack of development of food processing. As far as marketing is concerned, liberalization of restrictions under the Agricultural Produce Marketing Acts is essential. Private & co-operative organisations should be allowed by urban authorities to set up their own marketing yards in urban areas. This will help in breaking the monopolistic/oligopolistic supply structures for fruits and vegetables existing in some metros, introduce competition and benefit both consumers and farmers.

vi) Agricultural Exports

4.16 Export markets are a potentially important source of demand for Indian agriculture in future as Indian agriculture diversifies out of cereal production. The potential for agricultural exports has not been adequately exploited in the past and needs priority attention in future. This is especially so if the renewed WTO negotiations on agriculture succeed in opening markets for our products and controlling the very high trade distorting subsidies to agriculture in many industrialised countries.

Agricultural exports are particularly important for employment generation since they are typically very labour using and a more rapid growth of agriculture or agriculture based exports would increase the demand for labour in the agricultural sector.

4.17 A major constraint on the development of a dynamic agricultural export sector is the uncertainty generated by frequent resort to export restrictions at the first sign of rising domestic prices. This stop-go approach to agricultural export has created an environment in which no one has an incentive to invest in building export markets for agricultural products and those that attempt to develop such markets can easily lose credibility and be classified as unreliable suppliers. Export restrictions when they are imposed may appear to hurt only traders, but the ultimate burden is borne by farmers who are denied the benefit of steady access to world markets. We recommend that restrictions on export of wheat, rice, dal, cotton, oilseeds, etc. should be lifted and government should announce a policy that it will not resort to bans on exports of agricultural commodities even if there is a domestic shortage.

4.18 In times of shortage of exportable agricultural commodities, government policy should aim at enhancing domestic availability by allowing imports more freely rather than by banning exports. We recognise that pressure on domestic prices can also come from increase in world prices and in such a situation imports may not help in containing prices since import prices will be high. However, in such situations, agricultural exporters should not be denied the benefit of high world prices. If vulnerable groups of consumers are to be subsidised, we recommend that this should be done by providing subsidised supplies through the PDS and making provision for the subsidy in the budget. Furthermore, the quantities to be procured for such subsidized supply should not be obtained only by importing at a high price and subsidising the imported supplies for domestic consumers. They should be obtained competitively from the market, leaving it to suppliers to tender either from domestic sources or from imports.

2. Food Processing

4.19 India is the second largest producer of fruits and vegetables in the world, but the food processing industry remains highly under-developed. Less than 2% of fruit and vegetable production is processed compared with 30% in Thailand, 70% in Brazil, 78% in the Philippines and 80% in Malaysia! The very low processing percentage means that wastage and spoilage in India is very high. Tapping the unutilised potential of food processing including fisheries and marine products, is an ideal way of bringing industry to rural areas, providing assured markets for farmers enabling them to diversify into higher value horticultural crops and expanding non-agricultural employment by creating new work opportunities in rural areas.

4.20 There are many reasons why food processing has not developed in India as it should have. Part of the explanation lies in the lack of assured electric power in rural areas and also high cost of power to industry. Poor road connectivity to urban markets is another important infrastructural constraint. These are areas where generalized improvements in infrastructure would help the development of non-agricultural activity in rural area in general and food processing in particular.

4.21 Government policy has also not focussed adequately on the role of the organised sector in the development of food processing. At present the food processing industry is dominated by small-scale producers, including traditional village industries, with a very small segment of large units including MNCs. The small scale sector is undoubtedly an important segment of the economy and they deserve full support. However, this should not lead to neglect of the role of the corporate sector in developing a modern food processing industry. Food processing industry is not a simple matter of taking agricultural products currently grown by farmers and using them as raw material to produce a standard processed product. In fact it is necessary to restructure the food chain from production to consumption keeping in mind the special requirements of the processed food market.

4.22 Traditional varieties may not be suitable for processing because the particular requirements of the processed food market are different from food for direct home consumption., or because of the requirements of processing itself. For example, potatoes with high sugar content are not suitable for frying because they change colour. Tomatoes required for making tomato paste need a different solid content than tomatoes for direct consumption.

Corporations or modern co-operative organisations are needed to manage the entire chain from farming to food processing to marketing. They have to develop institutionalized relationships with farmers providing them with seeds and other inputs for the varieties needed for the processed food industry along with extension services to overcome technical difficulties which may arise in growing these varieties. They must develop modern storage facilities at the processing stage and also develop methods of handling produce which minimize damage. The identification of varieties that meet the requirements of different markets is obviously crucial since consumer tastes vary across markets, including especially export markets. Standards of quality are also extremely important especially in accessing export markets, though this aspect will become increasingly important even domestically, as consumers become conscious of quality and hygiene standards.

4.23 Some of the important policy initiatives that are needed to help promote food processing are the following.

a. Although government policy allows the entry of larger units including foreign investment into food processing, it is necessary to adopt a more pro-active attitude. Major national and international food processing companies should be approached to ascertain the nature of the problems which limit their activities and interest in India and consideration should be given to making changes in policy which would encourage expanded investment by these companies.

b. Government should focus on R&D, information dissemination, extension & training and development of rural industrial estates (food parks). It should also create a policy environment, which supports both private sector and co-operative sector development of post-harvest preservation, quality testing & control labs, silos & warehouses, cold storage facilities, air-conditioned transport and agro-processing.

c. A major impediment to the development of a modern food processing industry is the present legal framework which is characterized by a multiplicity of laws and regulations related to food processing which are administered by different ministries and which are often inconsistent with each other (see Box 1). These disparate laws should be integrated into a single Food Act, and a single Food Regulatory Authority should be set up to regulate all the health and safety aspects of food processing, handling etc.

d. The Prevention of Food Adulteration Act, which is administered by the Ministry of Health and Family Welfare exemplifies the problem with existing legislation. The Act dates back to 1954 and is extremely restrictive in the category of permitted additives which do not reflect technological options which are now available and widely used internationally. Although changes are possible, the procedure for making changes is extremely complicated and the authorities concerned have shown little flexibility in these matters. The Act is also rigidly administered in the sense that any deviation from what is prescribed, even in the matter of the descriptive content of labels, is treated as an offence equivalent to adulteration which can invite criminal prosecution. There have been instances when smudged labels have been treated as mislabeling and made a basis of criminal prosecution. In one case a label indicated the weight in "kg." whereas the prescribed form under the rule was "kg" and the mere addition of a dot at the end of "kg" was regarded as a material deviation from the prescribed rules! Such provisions clearly deter organized sector companies from expanding in this area while leaving the unorganized sector, which is not effectively policed at all, largely unaffected. We would recommend repeal of the Prevention of Food Adulteration Act and its replacement by a modern Act in line with prevailing international practice.

e. The Central level and State level implementation agencies lack adequate manpower and training with the result that implementation is not uniform across states. There needs to be uniformity.

f. The present taxation system constitutes a significant disincentive for food processing because the agricultural sector is not subjected to excise taxation and excise taxes are first applied at the food processing stage. Ideally, only the value added at each stage should be taxed. However, since agricultural products are not taxed, no credit can be given for excise paid on these inputs as would happen in a normal modvat chain. Sudden application of the tax rate at the stage of food processing clearly discourages moving up the value chain. The Budget for 2001-02 has exempted processed food based on fruits and vegetables from excise duties but this leaves other processed food e.g. cereal and dairy based foods unaffected. One way of achieving a more rational tax structure would be by granting a notional excise set off on agricultural inputs. If that is not possible, then a lower rate of tax on the output is desirable.

Box – 1

Multiplicity of Laws and Enforcement Agencies

The following is a list of some of the major Acts and orders that govern food processing and the Ministries responsible for administration under the Acts. The multiplicity of Acts or Ministries creates contradictory definitions which make it difficult to comply with all requirements:

— Ministry of Agriculture
  - Insecticide Act
  - Milk & Milk Products Control Order - (MMPO), 1992
  - Meat Food Products Order, 1973.

— Ministry of Rural Development
  - Agricultural Produce (Grading & Marketing) Act, 1937

— Ministry of Health & Family Welfare
  - Prevention of Food Adulteration Act, 1954

— Ministry of Food Processing Industries
  - Fruits & Vegetables Products (Control) Order - FPO, 1955

— Ministry of Commerce
  - Export (Quality Control & Inspections)Act, 1963

— Ministry of Civil Supplies, Consumer Affairs & Public Distribution
  - Standards of Weights & Measures Act & Standards of Weights & Measures (Enforcement) Act.

3. Small-Scale Industry

4.24 Small scale industry (SSI) is an important source of employment all over the world because small industries typically involve less use of capital per man than large industries. They also play an important incubator role by developing entrepreneurship. Issues related to the small scale sector have been examined in detail by a Study Group on Development of Small Enterprises which was set up by the Planning Commission. The Group submitted an interim report in July 2000 which was considered by a Group of Ministers and formed the basis for a Comprehensive Policy Package for the SSI sector announced in August 2000 by the Prime Minister. The final report of the Group has also been submitted in May 2001 and it makes a number of valuable suggestions, including especially the need to redefine small scale industries, improve fiscal incentives, provide easier access to credit, capital subsidy for technology upgradation and improved infrastructure.

4.25 We agree with the broad approach of the Study Group on the need to reformulate policy for the small scale sector to take account of new challenges and the changing economic environment. This calls for a radical shift in policy from protection to promotion. The relationship between SSIs and large industries must also be seen as a mutually supportive and not as inherently adversarial. In this report, we have limited ourselves to commenting on only few key issues.

i) Strengthening Promotional Measures

4.26 We strongly endorse the need for pro-active support for small-scale enterprises to counter the fact that they do not face a level playing field vis-à-vis large industries on account of innumerable market imperfections. It must be emphasised however that many of the problems affecting the small scale sector adversely are the direct result of major policy failures in critical areas which are not easily offset by actions outside those areas. For example, the crisis in the power sector has made power from the grid unduly overpriced for industry and also of uncertain quality. This is a general problem facing all industry but it hurts small-scale industry much more because, unlike larger industries, the SSI sector cannot set up captive generating plants. Even when some of the more modern SSI units are able to set up small captive generating sets, the cost of such captive power is generally much higher for SSI units than for large units because of economies of scale in power generation. Similarly, inflexibility in our labour laws (discussed in detail in Chapter 7) affects all units, but it has a more damaging effect upon small-scale units because they are generally more labour intensive and therefore the share of wage cost in total cost is higher. The high "transaction costs" involved in dealing with the bureaucracy and the banks, which is another major source of complaint, also involves economies of scale which give larger units an advantage.

4.27 Efforts to offset the impact of these disadvantages on the small scale sector by various sops and incentives are of limited use because these so called incentives are minor compared to the adverse impact of the disadvantages. The problems facing SSIs therefore have to be tackled at the root by implementing reforms in the power sector as discussed in Chapter 3, or addressing labour laws as discussed in Chapter 7. We wish to emphasise that the benefits of such reforms to the small sector will be proportionately much larger than for the large sector and progress of reforms in these areas may therefore be the most effective support that can be given to the small scale sector.

4.28 In addition to these measures, there are a number of SSI specific policy support measures which should be considered to effectively target three key concerns - credit, marketing and technological upgradation. The Study Group on Development of Small Scale Enterprises has dealt with many proposals in its interim and final report, and these deserve full consideration. In our view, the following measures are especially important:

a. Globalisation of the Indian economy as well as the emergence of sunrise and knowledge based industries such as information technology, biotechnology, etc. have created a new industrial climate in which the traditional focus on small scale enterprises needs to be expanded into a composite policy focussing on small and medium enterprises which would also facilitate seamless growth of small to medium and ultimately even to large scale. The Study Group has recommended that tiny, small and medium establishments could be redefined in terms of investment limits of Rs.25 lakhs, Rs.5 crores and Rs.10 crores respectively. To reflect the new focus, the administrative ministry should be renamed the Ministry of Small & Medium Establishments. This is in our view the right approach and should be implemented expeditiously.

b. At present, the focus of small-scale policy is on units engaged in industrial production to the exclusion of smaller units in the service sector. Small-scale enterprises in the non-industrial sector are eligible for support only upto an investment limit of Rs.10 lakhs in plant and machinery. This approach is not conducive to employment objective since the bulk of growth in employment opportunities in future are expected to come from the services sector. We therefore recommend that support measures, including especially support from the banking system and institutional finance designed for the small industrial sector should be extended to cover small and medium establishments (SMEs) irrespective of whether they are engaged in industry or services. The benefits currently given to SSI should be extended to SMEs in the service sector even though investment in these units exceeds Rs.10 lakhs.

c. International experience suggests that SSEs flourish in situations where they can be clustered together in an area where it is then easier to develop common infrastructure facilities of high quality and where technical assistance, market assistance and other market information, credit institutions and also skilled labour are all available as a package. Many such clusters have already emerged in the country but at present we do not have any policy for providing special assistance for the development and upgradation of such clusters. The Abid Hussain Committee had recommended that the State governments should identify existing SSE clusters and promote types of organisations which are joint ventures between the State government or local authority and business associations in these clusters. We would recommend that the Central Government should provide additional resources for such programme through a special Centrally Sponsored Scheme aimed at upgrading infrastructure in areas where well defined industry clusters have already emerged in individual States with a sufficient agglomeration of SSI units. The aim should be not so much to create facilities that would attract new industries, as has been the case with industrial estates in the past, but to upgrade facilities and services in areas where industrial clusters have already developed with a view to making them more competitive and capable of withstanding competition in the emerging globalised environment. This assistance should be provided for infrastructure development provided a policy framework and institutional structure is in place which ensures that the upgraded infrastructure will be properly maintained. The facilities provided in these clusters would have to be tailored to the sector specific character of each cluster.

d. A major problem affecting small scale units is the burden imposed by inspection by a large number of different agencies, mostly of State Governments responsible for the implementation of different laws and regulations. The power given to the inspectors and the lack of transparency in their operations gives them extensive opportunities for arbitrary decision making with attendant harassment and corruption. As pointed out above, this problem affects large industries also but there are "economies of scale" in this area, which means that larger units by contrast are able to handle these problems with much greater ease, often devoting specialized personnel to deal with regulatory inter-phase, something which small units obviously cannot do. State Governments must take concerted steps to reduce the burden of inspector raj on small-scale enterprises. Announcements to this effect are frequently made but the impression on the ground is that there has been little improvement. The system is deliberately used to harass business in order to extract illegal payment and this continues despite periodic administrative efforts at simplification. State Governments need to interact closely with SSI units and organizations to evolve working arrangements and procedures that will carry credibility.

ii) Reservation for Small Scale Industry

4.29 The policy of reserving certain items for production only in the small scale sector is a unique feature of India's policy. At present almost 800 items are so reserved which means that they can only be produced in units where the total investment in plant and equipment does not exceed Rs.1 crore. The limit was Rs.60 lakhs earlier and was raised to Rs.3 crores in 1997 but was lowered again to Rs.1 crore in 2000 on representations from the industry.

4.30 The rationale of the policy of SSI reservation was extensively studied by the Expert Committee on Small Enterprises (the Abid Hussain Committee) which submitted its report in 1997. The Committee listed the following arguments against reservation which are worth recalling.

a. The policy has not actually helped the growth of small scale industry because SSI units in the unreserved sectors have actually grown faster than SSI in the reserved sector. In other words, SSI units have shown more dynamism in areas where they compete with larger units.

b. Reservation in many areas seems to have been irrelevant since a number of the reserved products are not produced at all or are produced by only one unit.

c. Reservation is inconsistent with the evolving trade policy which allows a large number of the items reserved for SSI production to be freely imported under OGL or under special import licenses, though with payment of duty.

d. Reservation has hurt our ability to expand exports in many critical areas e.g. textiles and leather because we are unable to supply large volumes of the right quality and within the required delivery time. This problem will be compounded when the MFA is abolished and we lose quota-based access.

The Abid Hussain Committee considered point (iv) above to be particularly important and recommended that SSI reservation should be abolished.

4.31 The issue of reservation was considered again by the Study Group on Development of Small Scale Enterprises. The Group came to the conclusion that "in spite of the present scenario of economic liberalisation and WTO regime the policy of reservation should continue. However, the position could be reviewed periodically to take stock of the changing economic scenario." Our assessment is somewhat different. We feel that it would be counterproductive to delay action in this area. It is now generally recognised that the policy of imposing a limit on investment in areas which have export potential has prevented India from exploiting world markets in many areas. China's dramatic success in exporting relatively simple products such as standardised garments, shoes, toys, etc. achieving export levels that are 40 to 80 times higher than India is well known. One major reason for China's success is that they are able to engage in large-scale production and achieve levels of quality and technology which is not possible with constraints on investment. The consequence has been a tremendous growth in income and employment in China. India could have reaped similar benefits if Indian producers had been allowed to produce on a competitive scale and received the support to achieve export orientation.

4.32 The recent dereservation of the garments sector and the announcement in the Budget that another 14 items, including leather goods and toys will be dereserved are important steps in the right direction. However, we would emphasise that the case for de-reservation cannot be limited only to areas where we have strong export potential. It is also necessary to dereserve in other areas because the opening up to imports has made continuation of reservation an unsustainable option. With the lifting of quantitative restrictions (QRs) on imports on 1 st April 2001, a large number of consumer items which are currently reserved products have become freely importable, subject only to tariffs. While tariff rates for many of these items, especially consumer goods, are relatively high, it has also been announced that within 3 years we will move to a peak tariff level of 20%. This means that imports produced abroad in economic scale units will be able to compete with Indian SSI producers in the domestic market with relatively modest tariff protection, but Indian producers will not be allowed to increase investment beyond the specified SSI ceiling level in order to become more competitive. With preferential access allowed for some SAARC countries, (eg. Sri Lanka and Nepal) producers located in these countries will be able to access our markets with zero or low tariffs. Continuing with reservation in this environment is completely illogical. It will only tempt Indian entrepreneurs to set up production facilities in neighbouring countries and import products from these locations rather than produce and generate employment at home, a trend that is already in evidence.

4.33 The Study Group on Small Scale Enterprises has suggested raising the investment limit for SSE in export related and hi-tech areas to Rs.5 crores. We agree that this would provide a significant degree of flexibility to existing SSI units to upgrade their capacity and increase efficiency in designated areas. However, it is necessary to go further and phase out SSI reservation completely over a defined period. We therefore recommend as follows.

a. All items where there is an export potential should be identified and dereserved immediately, on the lines already announced for garments, leather goods etc. The list should include those items where actual exports at present may be low but which are potentially high export earners.

b. For all other items, the existing reserved items should be classified into two Groups. The investment limit in the first group should be raised immediately to Rs.3 crores and in the second group to Rs.5 crores. All items initially placed in Group 2 with the Rs. 5 crore limit should be fully dereserved at the end of two years. Those in Group 1 should be moved to group two with the higher investment ceiling at the end of 2 years and then dereserved in the next two years. If this phasing is accepted, SSI reservation can be ended by 2005. The proposed enhancement of the investment ceiling and phasing out of dereservation gives existing units an opportunity to expand their capacity and upgrade technology to reach economies of scale, while preventing large scale units from moving in immediately, as they could if dereservation is implemented at one go. The grouping of items into two groups may be done by the administrative ministry in consultation with the stakeholders.

c. The existing foreign investment limit of 24% in small scale industry should be reviewed. Higher limits should be permitted if the entrepreneur wishes, as a means of upgrading technological capacity and getting marketing linkages.

4.34 Small scale reservation is a sensitive area, and there may be hesitation in taking bold steps because of the fear that this would hurt a large number of existing units. We would emphasise that dismantling of reservation in a phased manner as proposed above will not lead to a wholesale destruction of SSI. On the contrary, it will strengthen the small industry sector by allowing many existing SSIs to expand investment to reach critical minimum size. It must be kept in mind that many existing units have proliferated horizontally by creating multiple units solely in order to avoid the investment ceiling restriction. These units will consolidate to increase their efficiency. There may also be mergers and joint ventures between existing SSI units and some of the larger domestic units interested in entering these areas to produce a more economically rational industrial sector. Such developments may not lead to a reduction in total employment. Foreign investment could help to expand many of these units to a credible scale, thus enabling domestic SSI producers to acquire technical and management tie-ups.

4.35 We recognise that as restructuring takes place, the number of small-scale units may indeed be reduced and some of the weaker units displaced by others which will expand as a result of enhanced competitiveness. This is a normal process of structural evolution and is consistent with strengthening the sector as a whole. Fears that it will lead to a reduction in output or employment from the sector as a whole may not be valid since restructuring may permit deeper penetration of world markets which would generate a larger volume of employment and higher quality of employment than is the case at present. As pointed out earlier, the remarkable success of China in developing exports of labour intensive manufacturers is a pointer to what is possible in this context. Of course, small scale reservation is not the only constraint holding back exports of labour intensive manufacturers. Infrastructure constraints and outdated labour laws are also important and these are addressed in chapters 3 and 7 respectively.

4. Employment in the Services Sectors

4.36 In developed countries, the services sector is growing faster than manufacturing and is the dominant source of high quality employment. Our situation is different because GDP in manufacturing can still be expected to grow faster than services for sometime. However, this does not mean a correspondingly faster growth in employment in the manufacturing sector. Many manufacturing units in India suffer from serious over-manning and the compulsions of competition will force them to trim the labour force to cut costs with the result that growth in employment in the manufacturing sector may be much slower than the growth in value added. As pointed out in Chapter 3, 70% of the growth in employment opportunities generated over the next ten years will be in the services sector.

4.37 Services in India cover a very wide spectrum. There are formal sector services at one end, such as banking, communications, insurance, certain categories of transport, print and electronic media, high income hotels and restaurants, education and health, all of which generate high quality work opportunities. There are also traditional consumer services such as retail shops, low income restaurants, hair cutting saloons, tailoring, photographers, taxis and small truckers, etc where most of the establishments are small in terms of a formal or recorded employment size; declared employment being no more than one or two including the proprietor. Many of these services can in principle be provided by more organised establishments and over time the role of the organized sector will and should increase. This will imply some shift away from self-employment in very small establishments towards regular employment in more formal sector establishments. It will also imply an increase in the quality of wage employment which at present is often very low.

4.38 Some of the sector policy issues which constrain growth of services in critical sectors where faster growth could lead to a faster growth in employment and an improvement in the quality of employment are discussed below.

i) Travel and Tourism

4.39 Travel and tourism is one of the fastest growing industries in the world and accounts for 10.6% of the world's employment.

India has enormous potential for both domestic and international tourism but this potential, especially for international tourism, is largely unexploited. According to the World Tourism Organisation India stands 43rd in the list of tourist destinations worldwide, with a total of only 2.2 million tourist arrivals. This is ridiculously low compared with 23 million tourists in China. While this comparison may be vitiated by the fact that it includes visitors from Hong Kong, even if these visitors are excluded, the Chinese figure is as high as 12 million, which is almost six times the Indian figure. Other developing countries ahead of India include Turkey (8.0 million), Thailand (7.2 million), Malaysia (7.1 million), Singapore (6.6 million), Indonesia (5.0 million), South Africa (4.9 million).

4.40 Larger volumes of international tourism could contribute a substantial expansion in productive employment opportunities in the years ahead. However, this calls for dramatic action on several fronts most of which are outside the tourism sector narrowly defined. A major factor limiting India's attractiveness as an international tourist destination is the poor quality of infrastructure. It is difficult to attract high spending foreign tourists if the quality of airports, airlines, railways, roads and tourist buses available for travel within the country are much below the standard of other competing tourist destinations, including even developing countries. The deficiencies in these areas reflect the general inadequacy of investment in infrastructure which needs to be corrected in any case to support rapid economic growth. As this process proceeds, it will also help to achieve faster growth of the tourism industry. However, the process of upgrading infrastructure should be accelerated, especially in critical areas which have a high tourism potential.

4.41 The following policy initiatives are especially important from the point of view of developing tourism.

a. Investment in tourism development often gets very thinly spread over a large number of activities. It is important to adopt a much more targeted approach. Development of each tourism circuit needs to be taken up as a specific investment proposal based on potential foreign exchange earnings. The emphasis should be on total development of that circuit as opposed piecemeal development in a number of circuits at the same time. Total development should encompass the entire gamut ranging from the look and feel of the airport, immigration procedures, transport facilities, approach road to tourism destination and the comfort of stay. Some of these are discussed in some detail in next few paras.

b. The scarcity of good quality hotels at reasonable prices is an important constraint in the expansion of international tourism in India. This scarcity is due to the enormous difficulties in acquiring land for hotel development. The delays involved in getting necessary permissions, and the uncertainty which is often involved in the process adds to costs and the result is that hotel rooms in Bangkok typically cost 50% of what they do in India for hotels of comparable class. With growing business travel, which is typically not price sensitive, the existing good quality hotels in the metropolitan cities in India are able to charge high prices for business travelers and this inevitably discourages tourism. Expansion in medium priced hotel capacity in the major metros and tourist centers is essential. This requires focused attention of the local authorities in making land available and in ensuring expeditious grant of other necessary permissions.

c. The limited availability of airline seats into India, especially from the major tourist destinations, is another major constraint in tourism. Much of the problem arises because our policy on bilateral air service agreements has been too restrictive in granting additional seats to foreign airlines, especially on routes that are otherwise crowded, mainly because of the desire to protect Air India, which would lose market share if foreign airlines are granted additional capacity. This is especially so because Air India is not able to upgrade its own service or expand capacity sufficiently. We note that a number of bilateral agreements have been signed recently, but many of these are with carriers which do not fly the critical routes where there is congestion. Air India's poor financial performance, deteriorating service quality and inability to expand its fleet have been the subject of much comment in many fora, and we do not propose to pronounce on this subject. Whatever the reasons for Air India's problems, the concern to protect Air India's market share should not lead to imposing limitations on the ability of other airlines to increase total seat capacity to India. This only inconveniences business travel (already a frequently heard complaint) and also limits our ability to exploit our tourism potential. If we want to expand international tourism into India and benefit from its enormous employment generating capacity, we must plan for creation of excess airline capacity on the major routes. It is sometimes argued that the potential for tourism can be achieved by freely allowing charter flights to tourist destinations and we note that policy in this dimension is indeed liberal for certain destinations, e.g. Goa. However, not all tourism takes place through charter flights and at present charters to Delhi or Mumbai, which would be the preferred point of entry for many tourists, are restricted. An expansion and improvement in regular air services to India is therefore absolutely essential. We recommend that the policy on bilateral air agreements should be urgently reviewed to ensure sufficient expansion in airline seat capacity over the next few years consistent with rapid exploitation of tourism potential.

d. Another constraint on developing tourism in India is the very high level of internal air fares. In the past, this was partly due to the artificially high prices of Aviation Turbine Fuel which were driven by the need to cross subsidise kerosene and LPG. With the decontrol of ATF this particular problem may be resolved but there are other factors which keep domestic airline fares on the major routes higher than they should be. Tourism is a highly competitive business world wide, and high domestic airline costs are bound to discourage traffic.

e. Tourism is also subject to fairly high rates of taxation in the form of the combined effect of Luxury Tax and Expenditure Tax on hotels, very high rates of duty on imported alcohol i.e. beverages (which actually only encourages massive smuggling and leakages through diplomatic supplies). In many States, the rate of vehicle tax on tourist buses is very high. Of these taxes, only the Expenditure Tax on hotels and the import duty on alcohol are within the Centre's control. Consideration needs to be given by both the Centre and the States to whether the taxes on tourism could be moderated in some way to promote tourism. State Governments need to be made aware that expanded tourism will generate additional incomes and employment and higher sales tax revenues which may more than offset the loss on tourism related taxes.

f. Finally, India's visa regime is not tourist friendly. Until the 1980s it was possible for tourists to obtain a tourist visa on arrival at the airport and this is the practice in many important tourist destinations. The policy was abandoned due to security considerations and all tourists have to obtain visas in advance. The scope for re-instating the facility should be considered at least for designated nationalities corresponding to important tourist origination centres to allow them to obtain tourist visas at major points of entry relying on computerized checking to screen out known undesirables. We understand that in any case Indian Consulates abroad undertake such a check relying upon a centralized computer data base before granting visas and there is no reason why a computerised checking facility cannot be introduced in the major airports.

ii) Information Technology

4.42 Information technology is a new area which holds out very promising prospects for large income generation, much of it in foreign exchange, with a substantial expansion in high quality employment. India's IT sector, which at present is concentrated on software, has done remarkably well over the past ten years and there is reason to believe that we have a good base on which we can now build.

4.43 The potential employment opportunities provided by IT cover highly skilled activities such as software development as well as a large number of IT enabled services such as call centres, customer relations management, back office accounting, medical transcription etc. which also produce high quality work opportunities in the organized sector. A study commissioned by NASSCOM and conducted by McKinsey has projected that by 2008 the IT sector could grow to a total turnover of $ 80 billion of which $ 50 billion would consist of exports. On this basis, total employment in IT and IT enabled services is projected to increase to 2 million by 2008. The quantitative significance of this projection can be appreciated when we consider (Table 2.12) that the growth in total organised sector employment in the private sector between 1994 and 1999 was less than 1 million.

4.44 The NASSCOM-McKinsey projections are subject to the usual caveats which apply for any long term projection and we note that there has been a distinct downturn in the IT sector worldwide since the projection was made. There is evidence of a slow down in growth in the IT sector in India consequent upon the world wide downturn but we would emphasise that short term developments should not weigh too heavily in evaluating medium term prospects. Even with the short-term slowdown, the growth prospects of the IT sector remain very good over the medium term provided our competitiveness in this sector can be maintained. Complacency must be avoided at all costs and government policy must give high priority to ensuring that the environment facing the IT sector remains conducive to rapid growth. In this context, Government must ensure continuous bench-marking of our performance against our emerging competitors internationally.

4.45 The most important pre-requisite for growth of IT is the availability of fault free, internal & external broadband telecom access at reasonable cost. A number of important steps have been taken in this area over the past year to expand telecom services and to open up the sector to new private sector suppliers. The corporatisation of the Department of Telecommunications Services into the new Bharat Sanchar Nigam Ltd, the opening up of domestic long distance telephone services to competition, the ending of the VSNL monopoly on international telephony by April 1, 2002, and the decision to induct a strategic partner into VSNL are all landmark decisions taken over the past 12 months which should help to create a supportive environment for the development of high quality telecommunication.

4.46 Despite these favourable developments, it is important to recognize that telecommunications is an area where the pace of change in technology is likely to make many policies obsolete even before they are fully implemented. Since it is impossible to anticipate with certainty the directions in which technology will develop and the pace of development, it is necessary to ensure that the telecom policy retains flexibility to cope with the technological changes so that the country is not denied the benefit of new technology. The policy must ensure that the enormous potential for private investment in telecommunications is effectively exploited.

4.47 Competition is the major factor which will push the various players in this sector to bring in new technologies quickly and both policy and the regulatory framework must ensure that competitive pressures work towards improving the quality of service and ensure that costs are not out of line with international costs. The regulatory framework must ensure transparency and a level playing field to ensure fair competition among all players which is necessary to attract private investment.

4.48 The supply of trained professionals will be an important constraint in achieving the full potential of IT in the years ahead. This issue is separately examined in Chapter 6 which deals with training and skill development.

iii) Housing and Real Estate Development

4.49 Real estate development, because of the construction activity it involves, is one of the most labour using sectors and can generate a large number of work opportunities. Unfortunately, the development and growth of this sector has been severely constrained by outdated laws and policies governing land development and rent control which have pushed the market underground and spawned a host of undesirable practices. The stock of housing available to meet the demand of honest, law-abiding citizens seeking rental accommodation falls far short of demand and the gap has been widening. The contrast with the situation after partition, when a large housing stock was created through private investment in many of our cities, is stark.

4.50 The Central Government has taken an important step in this area by repealing the Urban Land Ceiling Act which had the effect of freezing the market for urban land. However State Governments must follow the Central Government's action by repealing their own Acts where they exist so that the land market can be freed up. While a number of States have followed suit, several States have yet to do so. The Repeal Act, initially applicable to Haryana, Punjab and all the Union Territories, has subsequently been adopted by State Governments of Uttar Pradesh, Gujarat, Karnataka and Madhya Pradesh. Some important States such as Andhra Pradesh, Bihar, Maharashtra, Orissa, Rajasthan and West Bengal have not adopted the Repeal Act so far.

4.51 Another piece of legislation which impedes rapid growth in the real estate sector is the Rent Control Act in many States. The Rent Control Act was originally introduced as an emergency measure in World War II but, like so many other World War II regulatory instruments, it became a permanent feature which effectively allowed the tenant to alienate rented property. The result is that there is no incentive to construct property for rent and property owners in a position to rent properties often prefer to leave them empty rather than risk losing them forever. Low and middle income families typically live in rented accommodation all over the world and the need for such accommodation in our cities will only increase as the economy modernises, labour mobility increases and urbanization takes place. Continuing with the present laws in rent control will effectively prevent a sufficient growth of such accommodation and will deny the economy the benefits of construction boom.

4.52 In the absence of rent control, dilapidated urban housing would be periodically pulled down and replaced by modern apartment buildings and other complexes leading to more rational use of prime locations and also creating a continuous process of urban renewal. This has not happened in India because of rent control combined with security of tenure. This explains the run down appearance of many of our buildings in prime locations which gives Indian cities a much more shabby appearance than their counterparts in other developing countries Repeal of the Rent Control Act could unleash a construction boom as has happened in many major cities all over the world. This is not only necessary to meet the growing unmet demand for housing, it would also have a highly favourable effect upon employment generation.

4.53 In 1992, the Central Government proposed a model rent control legislation which was circulated to all States. The Model act proposed modification of some of the existing provisions regarding inheritance of tenancy and also defined a rent level beyond which rent control could not apply. A new Delhi Rent Control Act based on this model law was passed in 1997 but it has not been notified to date because of resistance from traders who are sitting tenants. A few States have introduced Rent Control Model Act but most States have yet to enact new legislation.

4.54 These basic legislative steps would have to be accompanied by other policy reforms, such as:

a. Ending the monopoly of the urban development authorities over city land: The record of these authorities e.g. the Delhi Development Authority (DDA) is very poor and justifies a comprehensive reexamination. Policies should allow private developers a greater role in this important area as this will give a boost to high quality construction.

b. Giving freedom for conversion of rural land into urban usage may help to stimulate housing development. At present, we have the absurd situation in which historical village land ("Lal Dora villages") situated within the city limits of Delhi cannot be converted into urban colonies. The current cumbersome procedures for the expansion of urban limits into surrounding village areas should be simplified.

c. Modernisation of municipal laws and planning practices: The law must make provisions for private investment in supply of all public utilities and services and these services must increasingly be privatised subject to appropriate control over prices. Municipal authorities must increasingly focus on data gathering, analysis, planning, organisation, regulatory functions and monitoring rather than direct provision of public services.

d. Framing of a law to facilitate private development of townships and estates. The law must specify both the rights and obligations of private developers with respect to urban services and utilities. These include inter connection with existing water mains, sewer etc, and the processing of wastes and disposal of pollutants.

e. Stamp duties on transfer of property also needs to be reduced. The very high rates prevailing at present in most States deter legal sales and encourage grey transactions such as for example transfer under power of attorney.

iv) Construction

4.55 The changes recommended in the real estate sector would contribute to the expansion of construction sector and of employment in this sector. This needs to be supplemented by action to remove the bias which exists at present against large construction firms in order to ensure an improvement in the quality work opportunities in this sector. Small construction companies use migrant labourers who move from construction site to construction site with their spouses and children. These migrant labourers obviously find their occupation more remunerative than the alternatives available in the villages from which they come, but their mode of daily existence around the workplace imposes a strain on the urban areas to which they migrate and the employment opportunities generated in this process are also not of a high quality. If work opportunities in the construction industry are to be improved in quality, it is necessary to encourage the development of large construction companies which can reap the advantages of scale economies that would allow them to pay more to their employees and provide superior work conditions.

4.56 One source of bias militating against the development of large construction companies arises from government contracting practices, which give overwhelming weight to the lowest price bid relative to quality and durability of construction and also often deliberately break up large construction contracts e.g. roads, into smaller units to encourage wider sharing of construction contract. The practice of competitive bidding for award of contracts is essential for transparency but it is necessary to give much more weight to quality consideration in defining specifications and also in determining eligibility. Government construction and contracting manuals must be upgraded to reflect modern construction practices and the need for speed in construction and durability of assets.

v) Road Transport

4.57 The road transport sector provides an example where there is considerable scope for expansion in future with a favourable effect on employment and especially the quality of employment. At present, passenger traffic by road is dominated by highly inefficient State Road Transport companies while freight traffic is organised largely on the basis of small truck owners. Individuals and agencies operating a handful of trucks and buses are the general norm rather than organised corporate sector trucking companies. According to one estimate 85% of the transport operators own only 1-5 trucks each and another 12% own less than 20 trucks. Only 1% of the operators own more than 100 trucks. Truck drivers employed by small companies are typically over-worked, enjoy very few facilities on the road and in general have a wage structure and related employment terms that are well below any acceptable norm in the organized sector. To some extent this reflects low levels of production efficiency. The operational efficiency of the commercial road transport vehicles in our country (about 8500 km/month) is about one sixth that of USA and Europe. This is mainly due to poor road infrastructure, high accident rates due to insufficient training of drivers, poor maintenance of vehicles and high turnaround time due to manual handling of loading and unloading operations.

4.58 The importance of transport as a part of the logistics chain, and the compulsions of modernization and increasing competitiveness, suggest that we need to develop a modern road transport industry over the next ten years. This is a sector with considerable economies of scale and the emergence of national transport companies would improve the quality of road transport services – an important objective for a growing economy – and also provide better on-the-road facilities to its workers, have better equipped truck-stops that will allow drivers a better form of rest after a long drive, and also have better vehicles to begin with. It will also generate associated services like hotels, repair shops and construction activity in and around these national hubs. Most importantly, it will deliver a more humane employment opportunity than is currently being offered to our long distance commercial drivers who spend most of their nights on the road sleeping in the vehicles.

4.59 Several initiatives are needed to make this possible.

a. The most important pre-condition for the development of a modern truck industry is the development of high quality roads since expensive modern trucks can realise operational efficiencies only if roads are upgraded to levels that will allow such vehicles to demonstrate their superior capabilities. This underscores the importance of the recently launched National Highway Development Programme with its initial focus on upgrading the routes on the Golden Quadrangle. Similar upgradation of roads is needed on other heavily trafficked stretches. In the longer run, there is a case for developing tolled expressways in segment where traffic demand exists for high speed transit.

b. The establishment of mechanised truck terminals for the operation of truck services on the lines of container terminals and bus terminals would help bring about a transition to a better organised trucking industry. The improvement in handling of containers has been possible due to initiative taken by Railways, since long haul of containers is on rail network and short haul is by road. To facilitate quicker and better handling of more volumes, the inter-face between rail and road facilities was improved by establishing Container Terminals. Similar improvements for normal goods handling by trucks should be made. State Governments should attempt to set up common facilities outside major cities ("transport nagars") for loading and unloading of large vehicles which would help to decongest cities and increase the efficiency of the road transport industry.

c. There is at present poor planning of the interface between "highways" and "local economic social activities". Central Government's scheme of "Wayside Amenities", if implemented properly, with the involvement of local authorities and private sector can bring in a lot of resources into highway support infrastructure - wash and rest rooms, food, repair services, banking, etc. All these have scope for providing good quality employment opportunities.

d. The system of granting licenses and permits by State governments and municipalities to a restricted number of small operators limited to specific routes is an impediment to expanding and modernising this sector. It would be desirable to shift to an open and transparent system that encourages competition. Any individual or company should be free to operate transport services on each and every route in the city or state, subject only to a safety certificate. The purpose of safety certification would be to exclude irresponsible and unsafe small operators who can disappear without facing the legal consequences of their irresponsibility. There could also be a nominal license fee to ensure fiscal neutrality.

e. The tax system to which road transport is subjected, including Road Tax, Sales Tax, Octroi and other levies, varies greatly across the States and is a major impediment to trade and therefore efficient transport. The administration of the system also encourages corruption with bribes extracted from truckers at several points. It has been reported to the Committee that these amount to 20% of the cost of transport on the Delhi-Mumbai route. It must be noted that the prevalence of such practices militates against the development of an organised trucking industry.

f. In the longer run, opening up road routes to neighbouring SAARC countries may provide opportunities to increase in road traffic business opportunities and also employment potential.

vi) Distributive Trade

4.60 Retail trade in India is characterized by relatively small family establishments generating self-employment and a limited amount of relatively low quality wage employment. Modern retailing involving large department stores has not yet emerged in any significant way although a beginning has been made in recent years to set up such stores in the major metropolises. However, it is important to recognize that rapid growth in future will be accompanied by structural change and in particular the growth of modern organized retailing sector.

4.61 Concern is sometimes expressed that the modernization of retail trade and the growth of larger scale department stores may displace self-employment in the more traditional retail segment since productivity per worker in modern retailing is typically much higher. This leads to the fear that there may be a net reduction in total employment potential. However, it is important to emphasise that expansion of modern retailing is extremely important for several reasons. It will certainly improve the quality of employment provided in this sector, and as emphasized earlier in the report, improvement of quality of employment must be an important objective over the next ten years. Modern supermarkets and department stores will also help to develop effective supply chains linking producers with potential customers, provide quick feedback on consumer tastes and a mechanism for locating alternative cheaper production sources. This encourages competition, reduces distributive margins and ultimately helps to expand the market to the benefit of both the producer and the consumer at large. The potential benefits of modern retailing in terms of lower prices is not evident in the early stages because modern retailing tends to concentrate at the upper segment of the market where price is not a dominant consideration and consumers are actually willing to pay higher prices for convenience and a superior shopping environment. They also help new producers and new products to gain access to potential consumers thus spreading the growth of employment more generally.

4.62 An important factor holding back the development of modern retailing is the distorted rental market because of which a large number of existing shops survive primarily because they occupy rented premises at very low rents while the growth of modern retailing outlets are held back because they cannot be established without paying exorbitant rents or purchasing land (with vacant possession) at inflated cost. Liberalising land and rental markets is an important precondition for developing an efficient and modern retail sector which is necessary to support the high growth scenarios projected in Chapter 3.

4.63 Another policy constraint on modern retailing is that foreign direct investment in this sector is not allowed. Experience of other fast growing developing countries shows that foreign direct investment is allowed in retailing and has had a generally favourable effect. There is a case for opening up this sector for FDI.

4.64 Non traditional retailing such as direct selling by salespersons approaching consumers at home is an emerging area that may provide additional quality employment and the same needs to be supported by way of rationalization of tax procedures and suitable changes in weights and measures Act with respect to declaration about various features of the commodity and the prices.

vii) Education and Health Services

4.65 These are clearly areas where existing facilities are highly inadequate, especially in rural areas and considerable expansion is needed to provide minimum levels of access to every citizen. Much of this expansion has to be financed by the public sector which may also need to be major provider of these services. However, there is also room to consider a combination of public and private sector suppliers to meet essential needs in this area. Expanded supply of these services to meet existing deficiencies clearly holds prospect for a substantial expansion in employment. The critical constraint is the availability of public resources, especially in State Governments, to support expansion needed in health and education.

4.66 The entry of the private sector can help reduce costs, improve efficiency, productivity and quality of output in both health and education. It is important to note that the highly lauded success of Kerala in literacy and school education has not been based only on public provision of schooling. Private schools have played an important role, a role supported by the Government by providing the right atmosphere. The structure of oppressive controls and dysfunctional regulation of private education in most States needs to be replaced by a modern regulatory system that minimises compliance cost for honest private educational establishments and focuses instead on creating transparency and detecting fraudulent practices.

viii) New Emerging Services

4.67 The specific services areas identified above are only the major areas in the services sector. Rising income levels, accelerated urbanisation, technological changes, globalisation and the communications revolution are all producing structural changes in the economy which are giving rise to a host of emerging services many of which necessarily belong to the organised sector which will provide new opportunities for employment. A list of such services provided by the Confederation of Indian Industries (CII) is given in the Appendix to this chapter. Policy and regulatory constraints affecting employment in this sector need to be constantly reviewed.

4.68 To summarise, the macro level policy initiatives aimed at supporting faster rates of growth, discussed in chapter 3, need to be supported by sector policy initiatives in areas which can generate growth of employment or improve the quality of employment. There is a wide range of such policies and bold steps to push these policies to maximum extent possible will yield positive dividends in terms of both growth and employment. Some of these policies are in the purview of the Central Government but many of which are in the purview of State Governments. The sectors reviewed in this chapter are not exhaustive. However, they illustrate the kind of policy changes needed in individual sectors to remove bottlenecks in order to accelerate growth of output and employment.

Appendix

Emerging Service Sector Activities

1. Business Services

A. Professional services

a) Legal services

b) Accounting, auditing and book keeping services

c) Taxation services

d) Architectural services

e) Engineering services

f) Integrated engineering services

g) Urban planning and landscape architectural services

h) Medical and dental services

i) Veterinary services

j) Services provided by midwives, nurses, physiotherapists and Paramedical personnel

k) Others

B. Computer and related services

a) Consultancy services related to the installation of computer hardware

b) Software Implementation services

c)

d) Data processing services

e) Database services

f) Others

C. Research and development services

a) R&D services on natural science

b) R&D services in social sciences and humanities

D. Real Estate Services

a) Involving own or leased property

b) On a free or contract basis

E. Rental/Leasing services without operators

a) Relating to ships

b) Relating to aircraft

c) Relating to other transport equipment

d) Relating to other machinery and equipment

e) Others

F. Other business services

a) Advertising services

b) Market research and public opinion polling services

c) Management consulting services

d) Services relating to management services

e) Technical testing and analysis services
f) Services incidental to agricultural hunting and forestry
g) Services incidental to fishing
h) Services incidental to mining
i) Services incidental to manufacturing
j) Services incidental to energy distribution
k) Placement and supply services of personnel
l) Investigation and security
m) Related scientific and technical consulting services
n) Maintenance and repair of equipment (not including Maritime vessels, Aircraft or other transport equipment)
o) Building-cleaning services
p) Photographic services
q) Packaging services
r) Printing, publishing
s) Convention services
t) Others

2. Communication Services

A. Postal services

B. Courier services

C. Telecommunication services

a) Voice telephone services
b) Packet-switched data transmission services
c) Circuit-switched data, transmission services
d) Telex services
e) Telegraph services
f) Facsimile services
g) Private leased circuit services
h) Electronic mail
i) Voice mail
j) On-line information and data base retrieval
k) Electronic data interchange (EDI)
l) Enhanced/value-added facsimile services including store and forward, Store and retrieve
m) Code and protocol conversion
n) On-line information and/or data processing (including transaction Processing)
o) Others

D. Audiovisual services

a) motion picture and video tape production and distribution services
b) motion picture projection service
c) radio and television services

d) Radio and television transmission services
e) Sound recording
f) Others

E. Services

3. Construction and Related Engineering Services

A. General construction work for building
B. General construction work for Civil Engineering
C. Installation and assembly work
D. Building completion and finishing work
E. Others

4. Distribution Services

A. Commission agent's services
B. Wholesale trade services
C. Retailing services
D. Franchising
E. Others

5. Educational Services

A. Primary education services
B. Secondary education services
C. Higher education services
D. Adult education
E. Other educational services

6. Environmental Services

A. Sewage services
B. Refuse disposal services
C. Sanitation and similar services
D. Others

7. Financial Services

A. All Insurance and Insurance-related services
   a) Life, accident and health insurance services
   b) Non-life insurance services
   c) Reinsurance and retrocession
   d) Service auxiliary to insurance (including broking and agency services).

B. Banking and other Financial Services (excluding insurance)
   a) Acceptance of deposits and other repayable funds from the public
   b) Landing of all types including consumer credit, mortgage credit, factoring and financial of commercial transaction
   c) Financial Leasing
   d) All payment and money transmission services
   e) Guarantees and commitments
   f) Trading for own account or for account of consumer, whether on

An exchange, in an over-the-counter market or otherwise, the following:

- money market instruments (cheques, bills, certificate of deposits, etc.)
- derivative products including, but not listed to, futures and options
- Exchange rate and interest rate instruments products such as swaps, Forward rate agreements, etc. transferable securities.
- Other negotiable instruments and financial assets.

g) Participation in issue of all kinds of securities, including under writing and placement as agent (whether publicity or privately) and provision of services related to such issue.

h) Money binding

i) Asset management, such as cash or portfolio management, all forms of Collective investment management, pension fund management, custodial Depository and trust services.

j) Settlement and clearing services for financial assets, including securities, Derivative products and other negotiable instruments.

k) Advisory and other auxiliary financial services on all the activities listed in article is of MTN, TNC/W/50, including credit reference and analysis, Investment and portfolio research and advise, on acquisitions and own corporate restructuring and strategy.

l) Provision and transfer of financial information and financial data processing and related software by providers of other financial services.

C. Others

8. Health-related and Social Services (other than those listed under 1.A h j)

A. Hospital services

B. Other human health services

C. Social services

D. Other

9. Tourism and Travel-related Services

A. Hotels and Restaurants (including catering)

B. Travel agencies and tour operators services

C. Tourist guides services

D. Others

10. Recreational, Cultural and Sporting Services (other than audiovisual services)

A. Entertainment service (including theatre, live bands and circus services)

B. New agency services

C. Libraries, archives, museums and other cultural services

D. Sporting and other recreational services

E. Others

11. Transport Services

A. Maritime transport services
   a) Passenger transportation
   b) Freight transportation
   c) Rental of vessels with crew
   d) Maintenance and repair of vessels
   e) Pushing and towing services
   f) Supporting services for maritime transport

B. Internal waterways transport
   a) Passenger transportation
   b) Freight transportation
   c) Rental of vessels with crew
   d) Maintenance and towing services
   e) Supporting services for internal waterways transportation

C. Air transport services
   a) Passenger transportation
   b) Freight transportation
   c) Rental of vessels with crew
   d) Maintenance and towing services
   e) Supporting services for internal waterways transportation

D. Space transport

E. Rail transport services
   a) Passenger transportation
   b) Freight transportation
   c) Pushing and towing services
   d) Maintenance and repair of rail transport equipment
   e) Supporting services for rail transport services

F. Road transport services
   a) Passenger transportation
   b) Freight transportation
   c) Rental of Commercial vehicles with operator
   d) Maintenance and repair of road transport equipment
   e) Supporting services for road transport services

G. Pipeline transport
   a) Transportation of fuels
   b) Transportation of other goods

H. Services auxiliary to all modes of transport
   a) Cargo-handling services
   b) Storage and warehouse services
   c) Freight transport agency services
   d) Others

I. Other services not included elsewhere

5

The Role of Special Employment Programmes

One of the elements of the employment strategy we have followed thus far has been the financing of various types of special programmes designed to create additional employment opportunities to supplement the employment generated by the economy in the normal course. Some of these programmes are targeted to provide wage employment or self-employment to specific target groups such as the poor in urban and rural areas, women, scheduled castes and scheduled tribes. In addition to targeted employment programmes, there are wage and self employment programmes which are not targeted.

5.2 The total expenditure on the major programmes for wage employment and self-employment in rural and urban areas in recent years is shown in Table 5.1. Expenditure on these programmes increased sharply from Rs.4121.33 crores in 1990-91 to Rs.8697.63 crores in 1999-2000. However, as a percentage of the total Central Budget support for the Central Plan the allocation for these programmes has decreased from 23.6 % in 1990-91 to 20 % in 1999-2000. This reduction reflects the pressure of other plan schemes on the limited resources available from the Budget to support the central plan. The individual programmes of wage employment and self employment have been modified from time to time on the basis of experience gained and a substantial restructuring involving merger of similar programmes has taken place recently. In this chapter we present an assessment of the effectiveness of these programmes based on past performance and their potential role in the employment strategy for the future.

Table – 5.1

Expenditure for major Employment Programmes

(Rs.crores)

	Wage Employment					Self-Employment		
	JRY/ JGSY	MWS[2]	IAY[2]	EAS	IRDP/ SGSY	PMRY	KVIC[3]	Total (1) to (7)
1990-91	2588.52	279.74	213.07	-	809.49	44.51[a]	186	4121.33
1991-92	2663.23	495.18	263.01	-	773.09	50.00[a]	193	4437.51
1992-93	2709.59	534.05	233.84	-	693.08	45.00[a]	193	4408.56
1993-94	3878.71	639.74	481.00	183.75	956.65	137.00	208	6484.85
1994-95	4268.33	776.18	500.38	1235.45	1008.32	872.00	216	8876.66
1995-96	4466.91	559.07	1368.34	1720.61	1077.16	1378.00	337	10907.09
1996-97	2156.93	499.10	1383.90	2138.35	1126.90	114.94	309	7729.12
1997-98	2439.38	462.83	1591.48	2904.97	1109.54	1217.43	444.78	10170.41
1998-99	2518.92	474.34	1802.67	2819.77	1160.89	975.79	346.23	10098.61
1999-00*	2205.60*	2132.30	2432.10	1260.70	465.00	201.93	8697.63	—

Sources: Ninth Plan Document Vol.II, (ii) Annual Plans, and (iii) Basic Rural Statistics.

* Figures for 1999-2000 are based on Budget outlay and not expenditure.

a The figures are for Self Employment Scheme for Educated Urban Youth (SEEUY).

Note: 1 The Million Wells Scheme (MWS) which was originally a part of Jawahar Rozgar Yojana (JRY) had separate allocations between 1996-97 and 1998-99. But from 1999-2000 it was merged with Swarn Jayanti Gram Swarozgar Yojana (SGSY).

2 With effect from 1992-93 names were attached to rural well construction and rural housing constructions under JRY. From 1992-93 rural well constructions were made under MWS and rural housing constructions under Indira Awas Yojana (IAY). IAY and MWS became separate schemes in 1992-93. MWS was merged to SGSY in 1.4.1999 but IAY continued to be a separate scheme.

3 Expenditures of Khadi & Village Industries Commission (KVIC) are obtained from Deptt. of Small Scale Industry and Agro & Rural Industry.

1. Employment Programmes for the Rural Poor

5.3 The major ongoing employment programmes for the rural poor are the Employment Assurance Scheme (EAS) which is a wage employment programme, the Swarnjayanti Gram Swarozgar Yojana (SGSY), which is a self employment programme involving merger of the erstwhile IRDP and its various component programmes, and the Jawahar Gram Samriddhi Yojana (JGSY), which is now conceived as a rural infrastructure development scheme, but which also provides employment to the rural poor.

i) Employment Assurance Scheme

5.4 The Employment Assurance Scheme (EAS) is the only major wage employment programme for rural areas. It was launched in 1993 and was initially limited to the 1778 economically most backward blocks. The scheme was designed to provide supplementary wage employment for the unskilled rural poor in these specially backward blocks where incomes were low and employment opportunities were lacking. The programme was administered by the district administration. In order to ensure that only persons from households below the poverty line obtain employment under this programme, all eligible persons had to register themselves with district authorities and only registered beneficiaries were supposed to get employment. In 1997, the programme was extended to all blocks converting it to a geographically universal programme. The programme has been restructured with effect from 1st April 1999. Along with providing wage employment opportunities to rural poor during the period of acute shortage of employment, the secondary objective of the restructured programme is creation of durable community, social and economic assets for sustained development.

5.5 A comprehensive evaluation of the EAS by the Programme Evaluation Organisation (PEO) of the Planning Commission has revealed a number of flaws. The wage : material norm of 60:40 has not been observed. Genuine muster rolls have also not been maintained. Prescribed norms relating to the type of assets to be created (40% for watershed development and 20% each for minor irrigation link roads and buildings for schools and anganwadis) have not been followed. There has been a tendency to prefer assets such as school buildings and buildings for anganwadis which are not the most labour intensive. However, because of the requirement that employment can only be provided to registered beneficiaries the average employment per beneficiary was found to be 31 days per year, which is much higher than for the JRY (see below).

ii) Jawahar Gram Samriddhi Yojana

5.6 The JGSY was introduced on 1.4.99 as the restructured version of the erstwhile Jawahar Rozgar Yojana (JRY), which was itself initiated on 1.4.89 by merging two pre-existing separate wage employment programmes, the National Rural Employment Programme and the Rural Labour Employment Guarantee Programme. The total allocation for the JGSY in 2001-02 is Rs 1650 crores (BE).

5.7 The JRY, like its predecessors the NREP and RLEGP was initially designed as a programme for direct employment generation through the construction of various types of durable assets in rural areas. Some of the infrastructure assets created e.g. irrigation or water conservation works were also expected to contribute to farm productivity in rural areas and thus generate indirect employment, as for example when irrigation increases cropping intensity and thereby the demand for labour increases. However, this type of indirect employment creation was not the main consideration in choosing the durable assets to be created in the short term. For example, construction of school buildings may improve the quality of education and thus increase productivity and possibly also employment in the longer term, but it has limited indirect employment effects in the short term. Similarly, construction of rural houses or panchayat buildings helps develop rural areas in a broad sense, but does not generate indirect employment in the short run.

5.8 Since the primary objective of the programme was the creation of direct employment, projects selected for implementation under JRY had to conform to the requirement that at least 60% of the expenditure had to be on the wage component. The insistence upon a high wage proportion often made it difficult to undertake work of a durable type that would add to the productive employment potential of rural areas. In other words, there was often a potential conflict between the objective of creating direct wage employment in the short run and the objective of promoting broader based rural development, with indirect employment creation which is permanent.

5.9 An important feature of JRY was that, unlike the EAS, it was implemented at the panchayat level, with funds being devolved to village panchayats, intermediate bodies at tehsil level and district panchayats in the ratio of 70:15:15. Devolution of resources has brought about involvement of elected representatives in selection and implementation of the rural works which will in the longer run ensure greater participation. However, a concurrent evaluation of JRY conducted in 1993-94 revealed several problems.

- Projects selected often bore little relationship to local needs and conditions reflecting inadequate planning and design capability at the decentralised level.
- Resources were spread thinly to ensure wide coverage of area and as a result the quality of individual works has suffered. The duration of employment created in any area has also been relatively limited
- At the village level there was a strong preference for construction of durable assets. Since these could not be fitted within the prescribed norms for labour:material cost, muster rolls were fudged to get around these norms. The volume of employment reported as being created under the programme is therefore exaggerated.
- Fudging of muster rolls is also used for misappropriation of funds and has become a major source of corruption. This also implies that officially reported figures of employment created are exaggerated. According to one study actual employment created may be only one-third of the reported amount.
- JRY was meant to be implemented by use of local labour but, in practice, works in many areas were carried out by contractors. As a result, employment was provided to labour from outside the area. The timing of work was often not consistent with seasonal periods of slack labour demand in agricultural activity. As a result, the employment generated may not have helped to supplement

incomes of the poor in the local area.

5.10 These problems were sought to be addressed by the restructuring of JRY into JGSY. It was recognised that there is a strong preference at the village level for creation of durable assets which often required acceptance of a lower wage component than 60%, it was also recognised that a programme for construction of community assets must involve the community and therefore be "demand driven" with direct employment creation being a secondary objective. In consequence, wage: material norms have been abolished. This is likely to reduce the volume of direct employment creation under JGSY though it could increase the potential indirect employment created by the programme if the assets created are production enhancing. However, this depends upon the rural works being well designed and implemented. There is evidence of improvement as a result of these initiatives especially in the selection of projects based on local needs and also ensuring that local workers get work.

5.11 Since both JSGY and EAS are major programmes, which provide rural employment, it is useful to consider their contribution to rural employment creation by taking the two schemes together. The estimated total number of mandays generated under the two schemes based on official records is shown in Table 5.2 along with the equivalent manyears (see footnote to the Table for the basis of conversion). The total employment generated by these two programmes in 1998-99 (the last year for which full year information is available) is equivalent to 4.4 million manyears. Compared to the size of the total rural labour force of over 300 million this is only 1.5% and if adjustments are made for the likely over-reporting in official figures, the percentage is even lower. However, comparing the employment created under these schemes to the total labour force in rural areas is not appropriate since these schemes are aimed specifically at the rural poor. If we assume that this segment is about 30% of the rural labour force, the contribution of the employment schemes increases to about 5% of the labour force. This is still small but considering the scale of unemployment in rural areas (around 7%) it can be said to make a significant difference. One can therefore conclude that the schemes do help to contain the level of unemployment at the margin.

5.12 An important feature revealed in Table 5.2 is that the total volume of employment generated by these schemes is not increasing over time. This is because rising material cost and wage rates, and also a shift in emphasis towards asset creation, has made it difficult to increase volume of employment provided by these schemes within budgetary resources available. Since budget constraints are likely to remain very severe, it is reasonable to assume that while special employment programmes play an important role in providing supplementary employment which will support income levels among the rural poor, they cannot be expected to generate significant additional employment to meet the needs of the growing labour force. We, therefore, recommend that these schemes should continue but their limitations in contributing to future growth in employment and therefore their role in the overall employment strategy should also be appreciated.

Table – 5.2

	Mandays of Employment (Lakhs)			Manyears of Employment (millions)[1]
	JRY/ JGSY	EAS	Total (1) + (2)	
	(1)	(2)	(3)	(4)
1990-91	8745.59		8745.59	4.9
1991-92	8092.01		8092.01	4.5
1992-93	7821.01		7821.01	4.3
1993-94	0258.40	494.74	10753.14	6.0
1994-95	9517.07	2739.56	12256.63	6.8
1995-96	8958.25	3465.27	12423.52	6.9
1996-97	7453.88	4030.02	11483.90	6.4
1997-98	3958.00	4717.74	8675.74	4.8
1998-99	3752.10	4165.31	7917.41	4.4
1999-00	1450.05 (P)	1515.16 (P)	2965.21	1.6 (P)

Source: (i) Ninth Plan Document Vol.II, (ii) Annual Plans, and (iii) Basic Rural Statistics-various issues, published by Ministry of Rural Development.

Note: 1 While converting man days into man years, 180 days' work has been assumed as work for the whole year.

(P) Data for 1999-00 are not for the full year. Data are as per report on physical progress prepared on 3.3.2000 by Ministry of Rural Development.

iii) Self-Employment for the Rural Poor : From IRDP to SGSY

5.13 Promotion of self-employment for the rural poor has long been an important element in the overall employment strategy and the Integrated Rural Development Programme (IRDP) started in 1980-81 has been a major instrument for this purpose. IRDP was designed to assist identified beneficiaries below the poverty line to take up some form of self employment as a means of generating additional income which might take the households above the poverty line. Eligible beneficiaries below the poverty line were identified by the District Rural Development Agency (DRDA) and assisted through a combination of capital subsidy provided by the government plus credit provided by the commercial banks. The banks were supposed to ensure that credit is extended only to projects which are commercially viable.

5.14 Over the years a number of subsidiary and allied programmes evolved under the umbrella of IRDP such as the Training of Rural Youth for Self-Employment (TRYSEM), the Development of Women and Children in Rural Areas (DWCRA) and the Million Wells Scheme (MWS) all of which were introduced in the 7th Plan, the Ganga Kalyan Yojana (GKY) introduced in 1.2.1997, and the Supply of Improved Toolkits to Rural Artisans (SITRA) introduced in 1992.

5.15 On 1.4.99 all rural self-employment programmes were merged into the Swaranjayanti Gram Swarozgar Yojana (SGSY) in order to ensure greater integration of the programmes at the implementing level. It is too early to evaluate the impact of the restructuring brought about by SGSY, but it is worth reviewing the limitations of the earlier IRDP, revealed by numerous independent evaluations. It should be noted that these assessments are based on studies of the working of IRDP prior to the recent restructuring of the programme, and some of these deficiencies may have been overcome.

- Beneficiaries were often not of the targeted group and subsidies and loans were appropriated by non-poor individuals through political connections. This vitiates the effectiveness of targeting though it does not by itself negate the employment generating effect.

- The average investment per family was often too low to generate additional income on the scale needed to take families out of poverty. This investment amounted to Rs.7889 at the beginning of the Eighth Plan. It had risen to Rs.16,753 at the beginning of the Ninth Plan, but because of inflation the increase in real terms was not very substantial. The inadequacy of the investment means that projects were unviable and therefore did not generate sustainable employment.
- The projects selected were often unviable because the beneficiaries were typically not in a position to choose viable projects and manage them. A variety of problems including access to raw materials or lack of markets for their production remain unresolved. The assessment of viability by commercial banks was generally perfunctory because banks typically regarded IRDP lending more as a social compulsion than as normal commercial banking activity.
- The target driven approach to IRDP lending meant that banks engaged in mechanical lending to meet targets. For some time, IRDP became a scheme for distributing milch animals without regard for whether feed or veterinary care would be available, or whether the milk offtake could be assured. The same animal was often sold over and over again to new IRDP loanees. Over time a variety of tertiary activities became eligible for financing but the quality of lending did not improve significantly. In UP, a bank branch gave 20 loans for setting up shops in a village of 143 households!
- There is evidence of massive leakage and corruption. Beneficiaries receiving loans often have to bribe officials of banks and the district administration and this situation is accepted by beneficiaries because there is in any case an impression that bank loans under IRDP do not have to be repaid. The recovery rate from IRDP loans was as low as 32% in 1999-2000 whereas other micro-credit programmes implemented through NGOs such as the Rashtriya Mahila Kosh have recovery rates of 90%.

- TRYSEM was designed as a training scheme linked to IRDP in the hope that the provision of training would help to ensure project viability. However, only 3% of IRDP beneficiaries actually received training under TRYSEM. What is more disturbing, only 23% of those trained under TRYSEM received assistance from IRDP. The training imparted was not related to the capacity or aptitude of the trainees nor to demand for the respective skills. Many TRYSEM beneficiaries viewed the programme simply as a means of receiving a stipend during the training period and not as a way of developing genuine skills which would help in self-employment.

- SITRA provides artisans with a kit of improved handtools. The financial limit for the value of tools is Rs.2000 of which the beneficiary pays 10% the rest being covered by a subsidy. This scheme is reportedly well received by beneficiaries.

- DWCRA is another sub-component of IRDP which aims at improving the living condition of women. It encourages collective work in the form of group activities which are known to work better. The nature of the programme varies from state to state but it has worked very well in some states such as Andhra Pradesh, Kerala, Tripura and Gujarat. In Andhra Pradesh, DWCRA is essentially a programme implemented through Self-Help groups. The group approach creates more opportunities for better employment. Watershed development, which generates more employment, is also being encouraged in Andhra Pradesh.

5.16 The number of families assisted through IRDP has declined steadily from around 3.7 million per year in the Seventh Plan to 2.2 million in the Eighth Plan and further to 1.8 million per year in the first two years of the Ninth Plan. A large part of the explanation lies in the fact that the total size of the investment required for viable projects has increased whereas the total resources available under the programme have not increased commensurately.

5.17 From 1980-81 when the programme began, to 1989-90,

the programme has assisted 53.5 million families which is almost equal to the total number of rural poor families in the country. If the programme were really able to achieve its objective of raising assisted families out of poverty it would have achieved near complete elimination of poverty in rural areas! It has clearly not done so for all the reasons documented above. As noted above, some elements of IRDP e.g. SITRA and DWCRA are working well, but the programme as a whole has suffered from serious deficiencies. The restructuring of IRDP into SGSY is definitely a step in the right direction and may lead to improve performance in future.

2. Employment Programmes for the Urban Poor

5.18 Parallel with the effort in rural areas, there have been special employment programmes for urban areas also, focussing on both wage employment as well as self-employment for the urban poor.

i) Wage Employment Programme in Urban Areas

5.19 The Urban Wage Employment Programme (UWEP) is a successor to an earlier wage employment programme called Scheme for Urban Wage Employment (SUWE), which was a part of the Nehru Rozgar Yojana for urban areas. UWEP seeks to provide wage employment to beneficiaries below the poverty line living within the jurisdiction of Urban Local Bodies with a population less than 5 lakhs. Community Development Societies are expected to identify missing basic minimum services which will be prioritised and these works will then be financed under UWEP. The material:labour ratio for works under this programme is 60:40 and the wage paid shall be the minimum wage as notified in the relevant area.

5.20 The total expenditure for this programme in 1999-2000 was Rs. 177.81 crores. It is estimated that the programme generated about 10.1 million mandays of work, which is about 56,000 equivalent manyears of full time employment assuming 180 days equals 1 man year. This is less than one-tenth of one percent of the urban labour force.

ii) Self-Employment for Urban Poor

5.21 A programme of Self-Employment Programme for Urban Poor (SEPUP) was launched in 1986 aimed at assisting beneficiaries from urban poor households living in cities with a population of 10,000 and above. Loans of Rs.5000 were provided by the banks with a capital subsidy of 25% of the total loan. From 1986 to 1991 about 1.5 million beneficiaries were sanctioned loan amount of Rs.566 crores i.e. an average loan of Rs.3773 per beneficiary, for starting various types of town services including services requiring no special skills such as tea shop, pan shop, rickshaw pulling etc and also services requiring special skills such as repairing of TV, radio, carpentry, electrical etc. Financing was also provided for micro manufacturing units such as plastic toys, washing powder, ball pen, and ready made garments etc.

5.22 From 1992-93, SEPUP was merged with a Scheme of Urban Micro Enterprises (SUME) which was part of the Nehru Rozgar Yojana launched in 1989. When the NRY was replaced by SJSRY on 1.4.99, SUME was merged into the Urban Self-Employment Programme (USEP) which is one component of SJSRY. The maximum loan was limited to Rs. 50,000 and the maximum allowable subsidy will be 15% of the project cost, subject to a limit of Rs. 7500. The beneficiary is required to contribute 5% of the project cost as margin money. For comparison, under IRDP maximum loan is limited to Rs. 25,000 and the maximum allowable subsidy is 30% of the project cost, subject to a limit of Rs. 7500.

3. Self-Employment for Educated Youth

5.23 In addition to the programmes discussed above, which are targeted to benefit the poor in rural and urban areas, the employment strategy has also sought to provide employment opportunities for growing numbers of educated youth who may not be from poor families but who face severe difficulties in finding gainful employment. As pointed out in Chapter 2, this category has the highest unemployment rate of any group in the labour force. Responding to this problem, a Self-Employment for Educated Urban Youth (SEEUY) Programme was launched during 1983-84.

5.24 SEEUY was targeted at educated youth in the 18 to 35 years age group satisfying the criterion of belonging to families with income not exceeding Rs.10,000 per annum, which was much higher than the poverty line at the time. Assistance was to be in the form of a loan from commercial banks upto a maximum of Rs.25000 with the central government providing capital subsidy of 25% of the loan. The scheme covered urban areas other than cities with a population of more than one million.

5.25 During the years 1983-84 to 1989-90, about 1.3 million beneficiaries were sanctioned loans amounting to Rs.2620 crore. SEEUY was later incorporated into the Prime Minister's Rozgar Yojana (PMRY) which was launched on 2 nd October 1993. In 1994-95, the PMRY programme was extended to cover rural areas also. The programme aimed at setting up seven lakh micro enterprises during the VIII Plan period (1992-97) providing employment to more than a million persons over the period. Educated youth in the age group of 18-35 years, belonging to families with annual income up to Rs.24,000, were eligible. The income criterion ensured that the individuals assisted, though not from poor families, would also not be from upper income groups. Eligible activities include a wide range such as horticulture, piggery, poultry, fishing and small tea gardens. All economically viable activities are covered excluding direct agricultural operation. Activities under industry, service and business are assisted. Assistance takes the form of a bank loan with a subsidy of 15%, subject to a maximum of Rs.7500 per beneficiary* without collateral guarantee.

5.26 The performance of PMRY in 1994-95 has been evaluated by the Institute of Applied Manpower Research and the evaluation showed a number of positive features. The scheme generated four times the targeted level of applications for assistance indicating substantial interest. The loans sanctioned by banks were 80% of target. The average value of investment per PMRY unit was just over Rs.63,000 and the investment cost of full time employment was Rs.26,479 per man year which is substantially larger than for the rural poverty programmes. An important aspect of PMRY is

---

* If two or more persons join together in a partnership, the limit of subsidy for a project increases correspondingly.

that 75% of the beneficiaries made additional investment from their own resources in addition to the amount provided by bank loans and the capital subsidy. Of these, 58% invested up to Rs.10,000 and the remaining 17% more than Rs.10,000.

5.27 The average annual profit generated per PMRY unit was about Rs.35,000 in the case of industrial units and Rs.39,000 in service units. This amount is net of wages paid to hired labour but it includes imputed cost of own labour. This suggests that the programme is succeeding in generating relatively good quality employment. The PMRY evaluation also showed that 65% of the beneficiaries are repaying loans, which suggests that the enterprises set up under the PMRY were economically viable. However, data available from the RBI show that the recovery rate is only 35%.

5.28 A conceptual problem in evaluating self-employment programmes is that it is not easy to determine whether the employment created by these programmes represents additional employment which would not otherwise be created, or whether the employment opportunity would have come up in any case though it may have been availed of by a different person. One can envisage a situation for example where the scope for taking up self-employment in the various activities eligible for PMRY assistance is determined primarily by the demand in the economy. In the absence of PMRY these opportunities for self-employment would be taken up by individuals who are able to do so without special assistance and what PMRY effectively does is that it helps certain categories of the population to gain access to these employment opportunities which may otherwise be closed to them because of lack of access to credit. In this case, PMRY does not actually create additional employment opportunities as much as help distribute existing opportunities better. It must be emphasised however that even if this is so, the scheme helps achieve a legitimate objective of broadening the range of opportunities available to educated youth.

4. Khadi and Village Industries

5.29 An important element in the Government's strategy to promote employment in rural areas is the support provided for khadi and for a number of traditional village industries including beekeeping, handmade paper, ghani oil, pickle masala, dalia, agarbathi, leather products, soap etc. There is no explicit linkage to poverty in the choice of beneficiaries and any entrepreneur willing to promote these industries in rural areas is eligible. The Khadi and Village Industries Commission (KVIC) estimates that in 1998-99, the khadi and village industries assisted sector provided full time employment for 2.6 million persons and part time employment for another 3.3 million.

5.30 The promotion of Khadi and Village Industries is the responsibility of the KVIC at the apex level, with statutory KVI Boards in each State which assist various implementing agencies, including societies of producers. KVIC has a total budgetary allocation of around Rs.400 crore in 1999-2000, which is used for the following activities.

- It provides grants and rebates to the implementing agencies to support Khadi and polyvastra. The grants are for interest subsidy, training, marketing.
- Marketing assistance for both khadi and village Industries is provided by sales outlets managed departmentally by KVIC as well as by non-department outlets.
- KVIC also has a small training programmes for artisans and entrepreneurs through which a total of 11797 persons were trained in 1998-99.
- KVIC operates a Margin Money Scheme for village industries whereby 25% of the project cost up to Rs.10 lakhs and 10% for additional cost above Rs.10 lakhs is provided as a grant, which has a lock in period of 2 years. The scheme is implemented through the nationalized commercial banks and regional rural banks.

The annual value of output from this sector is estimated at Rs.5000 crores and the net earnings from this activity is estimated at Rs.1500 crores.

5.31 The Rural Employment Generation Programme (REGP) of KVI was launched in Eighth Plan and was initially targeted to create 2 million jobs in the Eighth Plan period 1992-93 – 1996-97. The programme envisaged five types of employment generating activities: (i) Khadi, (ii) district level employment programmes;

(iii) 125 blocks employment programme introduced in the Gandhi Jayanti year; (iv) national projects for production of hand-made paper, bee-keeping and leather production in rural areas; and (v) the margin money scheme (MMS). Progress of REGP was not found very satisfactory and taking into account the slow pick up of the scheme, the target of 2 million jobs under REGP had to be scaled down to 1 million jobs by the end of Ninth Plan. The main emphasis under REGP also shifted mainly to the MMS component.

5.32 Under the Margin Money Scheme, 60 per cent of resources needed for a venture are provided by the commercial banks at a subsidised interest rate, about 25 per cent by Government through KVIC, and about 15 per cent by the beneficiary. Eligible agencies under the scheme are (i) individuals (rural artisans/entrepreneurs) for projects upto Rs.10 lakhs and (ii) institutions, cooperative societies, trusts registered with KVIC/KVIB for projects up to Rs.25 lakhs. 25% of the project cost up to Rs.10 lakhs will be provided by KVIC as Margin Money by way of backend subsidy. For projects above Rs.10 lakhs and upto Rs.25 lakhs rate of margin money will be 25 per cent of Rs.10 lakhs plus 10% of the remaining cost of the project.[1] The borrower is required to contribute 10% of the project cost (5% in case of weaker section). The margin money is deposited by KVIC with the banks initially in its name, and after the sanction of credit by banks, it is transferred as a term deposit of two years in the name of the borrower at the loan-sanctioning branch. This amount will be first available for adjustment by banks to the borrower's loan account after a period of two years from the date of disbursement of the loan.

5.33 One of the weaknesses of KVI activity revealed by data provided by KVIC is that the quality of employment opportunities generated from these activities is relatively modest. For example, KVIC data indicate an annual income of only Rs.4000 for full time workers (ie only Rs. 333 per month) and only about Rs.1500 (ie Rs. 125 per month) for part time workers. These figures are very low even for rural areas. The khadi programme in particular suffers from some basic infirmities. Costs are high and the product

---

1 For the weaker section beneficiaries, the margin money grant will be at the rate of 30% of the project cost upto Rs.10 lakh and plus 10% of the remaining cost of the project up to Rs.25 lakh.

at the lower end of the quality range is not able to compete with mill-produced fabric available in the market. This explains why the production of khadi is decreasing. It was 109 million sq.metres in 1990-91 and has declined to 98 million sq.metres in 1998-99. Employment in this sector has also fallen from 14.15 lakh persons in 1990-91 to 13.85 lakh persons in 1998-99.

5.34 The potential for generating employment opportunities in rural areas through establishment of rural enterprises definitely needs to be fully exploited. The scope for expansion of employment in the Khadi sector is very limited and it is likely that employment in this sector will continue to fall. However, employment in village industries could expand provided these units are provided appropriate support in term of credit or marketing assistance. The emphasis under the KVIC programme should, therefore, be given to setting up economically viable rural enterprises with financial assistance from banks, and close monitoring by the banks of the fulfillment of the terms of credit.

5. Other Programmes

5.35 Other Programmes of Centre and States which are primarily for generating self employment among special sections of labour force are National Minorities Finance and Development Corporation, National Backward Classes Finance and Development Corporation, National SC/ST Finance and Development Corporation, National Handicapped Finance and Development Corporation, Training cum Production Centres (NORAD), Support for Training and Employment Programme and National Credit Fund for Women (RMK). However, no evaluation of these corporations etc. has been made so far.

6. Overall Assessment and Recommendations

5.36 It is evident from our review of special employment programmes that although the resources devoted to these programmes have increased substantially, the total volume of employment created by these programmes is relatively small and has not been increasing. If allowance is made for the fact that the official figures of employment creation almost certainly exaggerate the numbers the real contribution of these programmes would be even smaller. This does not mean that these programmes are not important. In our view, wage employment programmes can play a very useful role in providing supplementary employment to vulnerable sections of the population especially in seasonal lean periods, which are common in agriculture. They are also a potentially useful form of social safety net to deal with situations of exceptional distress e.g. droughts. In the absence of extensive system of social security the use of employment programmes as a form of social security to deal with a targeted population has a great deal of merit.

5.37 We are of the view that wage employment programmes should be focused as much as possible on maximising the developmental impact on rural areas through the creation of durable assets in the area of economic and social infrastructure. The restructuring of JGSY to give primacy to the creation of durable assets is therefore a step in the right direction. There is an urgent need to invest in such infrastructure, as the existing deficiencies in infrastructure especially in rural areas are glaring, and given the scarcity of resources it is desirable to use available resources for such investments even if the direct employment created is slightly lower. We would also recommend that in view of the fact that EAS has been universalized to all districts, there is merit in merging the EAS and the JGSY into a single employment programme in which funds devolve to panchayats.

5.38 The experience with self-employment programmes aimed at the poor is mixed at best with some outstandingly successful examples based on self-help groups involving women, but the general experience with IRDP has not been very encouraging. Part of the problem is that it is not easy for individuals or families below the poverty line to transform themselves into entrepreneurs capable of producing marketable products and services, which have to survive in competitive markets. We recommend that the functioning of the self-employment component in the restructured SGSY programme needs to be re-oriented as much as possible towards programmes supporting self-help groups with the assistance of NGOs with a good track record. Until there is clear evidence that the traditional IRDP type assistance produces results, it may not be desirable to expand the resources devoted to these types of schemes.

5.39 The experience with PMRY, which relates to self-employment for educated youth, is more encouraging although even in this area there are significant weaknesses, reflected for example in the very low recovery rates. Looking to the likely expansion in educated new entrants in the labour force in future, and the fact that self-employment has to play a major role in providing employment opportunities for this group, we would recommend an expansion of PMRY scheme. We would emphasize however that the provision of subsidy in such schemes is much less important than is generally made out. What is essential is that credit should be available to finance viable projects and that there should be effective means of training and providing advice on technology and marketing.

5.40 The inevitable decline in employment opportunities in Khadi production needs to be met by strengthening the village industry component through which rural enterprises are established. We suggest that economic viability of the expanded rural enterprises programme be closely monitored. The Margin Money Scheme implemented by KVIC through the banks has the advantage of building in stronger checks on economic viability but very little feedback from the field is available at present in terms of the volume of sustainable employment opportunities created and the quality of jobs created.

5.41 In a situation where resources are severely constrained and there are several other demands on the system our ability to expand the total volume of resources devoted to special employment programmes in the years ahead will be limited. In these circumstances a large expansion of the size of these programmes in future is unlikely to take place and is also difficult to justify given the experience thus far. We would recommend that an independent assessment of the impact of these programmes as recently restructured should be commissioned by the Planning Commission before there is any increase in total resources allocated to these programmes. Pending such a review, the total allocation to these programmes should be held constant at current levels, though resources could be shifted from programmes perceived to be less effective to those perceived to be more effective on the basis of current monitoring and evaluations.

6

Labour Force Skills and Training

The macro-economic and sector specific policy issues aimed at generating rapid growth in output and employment can succeed only if the skill level of the labour force can support rapid growth. In this Chapter we examine the current state of skill development of our labour force and make recommendations which could help to close some of the critical gaps in this area.

1. Current State of Labour Force Skills

6.2 It is not easy to quantify the level of skills in the labour force because data on skill levels are not readily available. What is available is information on the educational attainments of the labour force and the relevant data for 1999-2000 are summarized in Table 6.1. It is evident that education levels in the labour force in India are very low. About 44.0 % of all workers in 1999-2000 were illiterate and another 22.7% had schooling only up to the primary level. If we define the minimum level of education necessary to function in a modern economy as schooling up to the middle level, then only about 33.2% of the labour force had schooling of that level and above. The percentage was higher at 57.4% for the urban labour force, but it was correspondingly worse in rural areas, with only 25.4% for the rural labour force meeting these standards.

6.3 A positive feature of the situation is that education levels will improve over time because the younger age groups are much better educated. Table 6.2 presents the educational attainment of youth (15-29) in labour force for the year 1999-2000 (and 1993-94). The percentage with middle school education or above in this age group for the country as a whole is 49.3 compared with

33.2% for the total labour force. This percentage itself is increasing over time. It was 42.5% in 1993-94 and has increased to 49.3% in 1999-2000. There are of course sharp variations across gender and place of residence; for urban males it is as high as 72.1 (66.7 in 1993-94), whereas for rural females, it is as low as 29.0 (21.7 in 1993-94).

Table – 6.1

Composition of workers of age 15 years and above by level of education 1999-2000

(percentage)

	Not literate	Literate & schooling upto primary level	With schooling upto middle & higher level	Total	Share in Work Force
Rural Areas					
Male	39.6	27.3	33.1	100	49.74
Female	74.0	15.5	10.5	100	25.77
Person	51.3	23.3	25.4	100	75.51
Urban Areas					
Male	16.0	21.9	62.0	100	19.72
Female	43.9	17.6	38.5	100	4.76
Person	21.5	21.1	57.4	100	24.49
All Areas					
Male	32.9	25.8	41.3	100	69.46
Female	69.3	15.8	14.9	100	30.54
Person	44.0	22.7	33.2	100	100.00

Source: National Sample Survey on Employment & Unemployment, 55th Round.

6.4 It should be noted however that the category "middle school and above" includes all those who have had some middle school education even though they may have dropped out before completing middle school. Provisional gross enrollment rates for the year 1998-99 in the primary and the middle school levels are 92% and 58%, respectively (Table 6.3). However, the provisional dropout rates at primary and middle levels are quite high at 42% and 57%, respectively, in the year 1998-99. According to a rough estimate from the 52nd round (1995-96) of National Sample Survey, around 44% of the population (age group 14–16 years) was enrolled in the Class IX and X levels. However, only about 20% of the population in this age group actually completes secondary school education. These figures indicates that significant deficiencies in the general education level of the labour force are likely to remain in the next ten years though one can say from the past trends of increase in enrolment ratio and decrease in dropout ratio that the new entrants to the labour force will be significantly better educated than at present.

Table – 6.2

Percentage of persons in labour force educated middle and above 1999-2000 [a]

Sex	Age Groups	Rural	Urban	All areas
Male	15-29	50.9 (44.2)	72.1 (66.7)	56.4 (49.8)
	15-19	55.1 (49.5)	71.9 (67.4)	58.7 (52.1)
	20-24	53.8 (47.4)	73.8 (69.7)	59.2 (53.1)
	25-29	45.2 (36.6)	70.7 (63.5)	52.3 (44.0)
Female	15-29	29.0 (21.7)	62.5 (54.5)	33.5 (26.5)
	15-19	40.6 (30.6)	69.7 (63.6)	44.3 (34.7)
	20-24	28.9 (21.1)	64.6 (56.0)	33.9 (26.2)
	25-29	21.3 (14.2)	55.9 (47.0)	25.9 (19.6)
Persons	15-29	43.4 (36.6)	70.3 (64.1)	49.3 (42.5)
	15-19	50.2 (43.1)	71.4 (66.5)	54.2 (47.2)
	20-24	45.3 (38.0)	72.1 (66.7)	51.5 (44.3)
	25-29	36.7 (29.4)	68.0 (60.2)	44.1 (36.9)

Source: NSSO

Note : NSS Reports on Employment/Unemployment Survey give (i) labour force participation by age groups and (ii) level of education of population by age group. However, the Reports do not give labour force participation rates by age groups cross-classified by level of education. Therefore, estimates presented in this table are based on the assumption that distribution of labour force, in an age group, by level of education, is the same as the distribution of population in that age group by level of education.

@ Figures in parenthesis are for the year 1993-94

6.5 The statistics discussed above relates to general education which is not the same thing as possession of "marketable skills". While some jobs in a modern economy, especially clerical office

Table – 6.3

Enrolment in different stages of education as percent of population in the appropriate age groups 1961, 1981, 1990 & 1999

(percentage)

Education stage/ Age group	Enrolment as proportion of appropriate age group			
	1961	1981	1990	1999
Primary classes (6-11 yrs.)	62.4	80.5	95.9	92.1
Middle classes (11-14 yrs.)	22.5	41.9	57.4	57.6
High/higher Secondary (14-17 yrs.)	10.6	17.3	24.0	N.A.

Source: Manpower profile of India, year book 2000 (IAMR); Table 2.1.2.0

Table – 6.4

Percentage distribution of persons by possession of marketable skill: 1993-94

Possessing	Rural		Urban	
	Male	Female	Male	Female
No Skill	89.9	93.7	80.4	88.8
Some Skill[2]	10.1	6.3	19.6	11.2
Total	**100.0**	**100.0**	**100.0**	**100.0**
Sample persons	(183464)	(172835)	(109067)	(99283)

Source: NSSO Report No.409 on Results of 50th round (1993-94) survey on Employment and Unemployment.

Notes: 1 Information for 1999-2000 not yet available, since the results released by NSSO for that year Employment Survey give the skill classification of Non Workers.

2 Marketable skills that are reported by respondents are specified in Annexure 6.1.

jobs, may not require anything more than specified levels of formal academic education, most other jobs require specific skills. The NSSO Survey on Employment and Unemployment (1993-94) sought information on the possession of 30 specific marketable skills by persons in the labour force and the results are summarized in Table 6.4. The skilled percentage of the work force is evidently very low. In the rural areas, only 10.1% of the male workers and 6.3% of female workers possessed specific marketable skills. The percentages were higher in urban areas, but they were still woefully low in absolute terms – only 19.6% for male workers and 11.2% for female workers.

6.6 The level of vocational skills in the labour force in India compare poorly with the position in other countries. Table 6.5 shows the percentage of younger members of the labour force (age group 20-24), which have vocational training. Only 5% of the Indian labour force in this age category has vocational skills whereas the percentage in industrial countries is much higher, varying between 60% and 80%, except for Italy, which is 44%. The percentage for Korea, which has recently been categorised as an industrialised country, is exceptionally high at 96%. The developing countries listed have percentages which are significantly lower than the developed countries, but they are still much higher than India e.g. Mexico at 28% and Peru at 17%. Differences in definition may make inter-country comparison somewhat unreliable, but the level in India is clearly far too low.[1]

6.7 These figures reveal that education and skill levels of our labour force are relatively low compared with other fast growing developing countries. The system is also excessively oriented towards general academic education with little or no vocational orientation. The preference for general education is driven primarily by the perception that an academic degree is necessary to obtain a government job, which is highly valued because job security is virtually complete and pay scales are typically much above market wages. The net result is that the education system has neglected the need to provide vocational skills and also to generate awareness and demand among students for acquiring, marketable skills.

---

1 One reason why the comparison may exaggerate the difference is because, as pointed out in the footnote to Table 6.4, it is based on those having received training in formal institution.

Table – 6.5

Proportion Vocationally Trained among the youth in Labour Force-International Comparison[2]

Country	Age Group	Vocationally Trained (per cent of those in Labour Force)
India	20-24	5.06@
Developing countries		
Botswana	20-24	22.42
Colombia (1998)	20-29	28.06
Mauritius (1995)	20-24	36.08
Mexico (1998)	20-24	27.58
Developed Countries		
Australia (1998)	20-24	64.11
Canada (1998)	20-24	78.11
France (1997)	20-24	68.57
Germany (1998)	20-24	75.33
Israel (1998)	18-24	81.23
Italy (1997)	20-24	43.88
Japan (1997)	15-24	80.39
Korea Republic (1998)	20-24	95.86
New Zealand (1997)	20-24	63.03
Russian Federation (1998)	20-24	86.89
Singapore (1998)	20-24	66.24
United Kingdom (1998)	20-24	68.46

Note:

1 Vocationally trained persons are defined here as those having education level 3 or 5 as per ISCED clarifications which classifies the population across & levels of education starting with level X i.e. no education and the highest level being level 7 which post graduate level specialisation in a field. Levels 4 & 8 are not used. Level 3 of education: General education continues to be an important constituent of the programmes, but separate subject presentation and more specialisation are found at this level. Also to be classified under Level 3 are programmes consisting of subject matter mainly with a specific vocational emphasis of apprenticeship programmes, with an entrance requirement of eight full years of education, or a combination of basic education and vocational experience that demonstrates the ability to handle the subject matter of that level. Level 5 of education: Programmes of this type are usually "practical" in orientation in that they are designed to prepare students for particular vocational fields in which they can qualify as high level technicians, teachers, nurses, production supervisors etc. It may be noted however that in developing countries, economically productive skills are acquired not only in training/education institution but also through the family. Only the formal institute/school vocationally trained are shown above.

2. Only those who have received formal vocational training are shown as trained in this table. To the extent that training and skills in India are acquired through informal methods, including training in the family, the Indian figures are understated

@ Estimates are based on (NSSO Report No.409 on Results of 50th round (1993-94) survey on Employment and Unemployment; Table 20) distribution of persons by technical education in India adjusted by labour force participation rate by sex. The corresponding percentages by sex and residence are rural female 1.7, rural male 2.3, urban male 9.4, and urban female 17.0.

2. *Present Training System*

6.8 There are several methods of acquiring skills, which are used by persons entering the labour force, and these are briefly described below.

i) Hereditary skills acquired in the family

6.9 This is the typical method of acquiring skills in traditional family based crafts e.g. weaving, pottery, carpet weaving, etc. This method is also relevant for a range of contemporary skills within small family businesses e.g. tailoring, haircutting, repair work etc.

ii) On the job training:

6.10 This is the process whereby workers join businesses to do unskilled or semi-skilled work and then pick up specific skills in the course of their employment with or without explicit guidance. Training of this type takes places in an informal manner in smaller industrial organizations and in a more organized manner in larger industrial units, some of which may have substantial in house training facilities to upgrade skills.

iii) Education related to work

6.11 The educational system directly produces trained persons in disciplines where professional qualifications are needed e.g., doctors, lawyers, engineers, MBAs etc. General academic degrees also satisfy basic educational requirements for a number of managerial and administrative positions, where subsequent training is provided on the job or through in-house training. However, there is a large mismatch between the number of generalist graduates being produced and the availability of such jobs. General education can generate marketable skills if vocational training is integrated into the school syllabus, as is the case in some countries (see Fig. 6.1). An effort at such integration has been made in India by introducing Vocational training courses at the 10+2 level in 6486 schools under a Centrally Sponsored Scheme. However progress under the scheme is much behind the target. At present only about 8% of the students are estimated to be in the vocational stream compared with a target of 10% by 1985, which was expected to increase to 25% by 2000.

Figure 6.1

School-to-work-transition: How different training systems operate

Figure 6.1.a "German dual system" Figure 6.1.b."French system": secondary vocational/technical schools

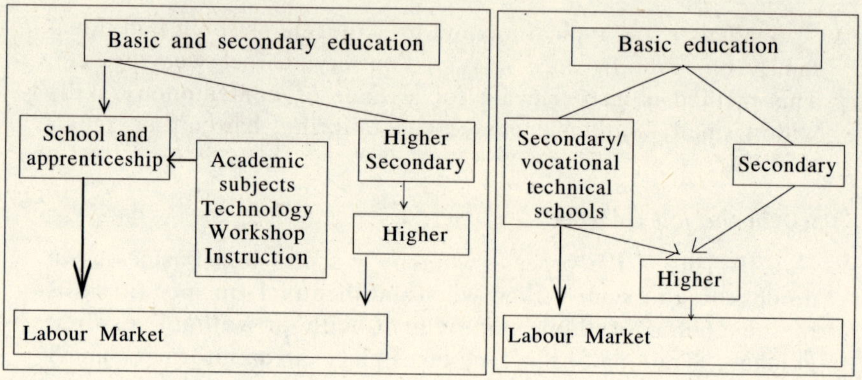

Figure 6.1.c

"American system": Diversified high school Figure 6.1.d "Latin American system": Vocational training institutes

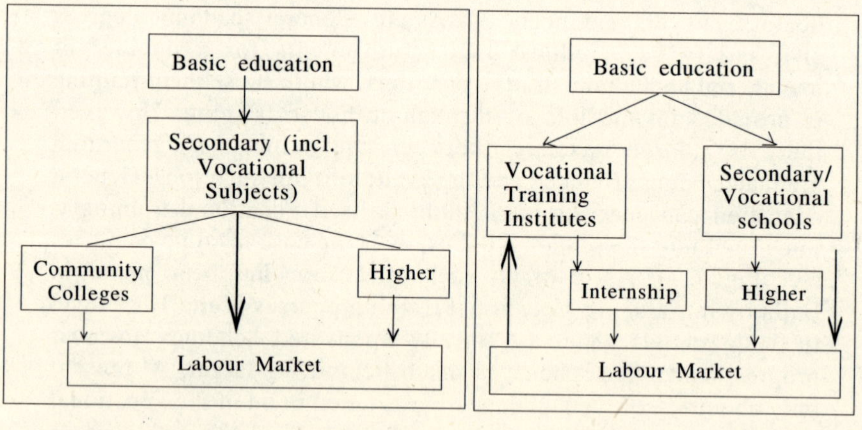

Source: World Employment Report 1998-99.

iv) Vocational training in specialised institutions

6.12 Vocational skills can also be acquired through formal vocational training in specialised institutions. There are about 4274 Industrial Training Institutes (ITIs) imparting training in 43 engineering and 24 non-engineering trades. Of these, 1654 are government run ITIs (State governments) while 2620 are private. The total seating capacity in these ITIs is 6.28 lakh. In addition to ITIs, there are 6 Advanced Training Institutes (ATI) run by the Central Government which provide training for instructors in ITIs and 2 ATIs for Electronics and Process Instrumentation offering long and short courses for training of skilled personnel at technician level in the fields of Industrial, Medical and Consumer Electronics and process instrumentation. Apart from ITIs, there are private proprietary institutes organized as businesses, which provide training of various types in areas such as computer application or hardware maintenance, readymade garments, textiles, refrigeration, air conditioning and electronics, catering etc. The training provided by these private institutions varies in quality but there are many examples of success industry especially in computer applications where private institutions have produced a considerable stream of recruits for this sector.

v) Formal Apprenticeship

6.13 Apprenticeship is an important means of training semi-skilled workers in industrialised countries. The most sophisticated system is the German "dual system" (see Fig.6.1) where vocational schooling is undertaken parallel with apprenticeship. In India, the system of formal apprenticeship was introduced through the Apprenticeships Act 1961, which requires employers in notified industries to engage apprentices in specified ratios in relation to the workforce. Apprentices obtain training for periods ranging from 6 months to 4 years and at the end of the period they are trade-tested by the National Council for Vocational Training and successful candidates are awarded National Apprenticeship Certificates. As on June 30, 2000 there were a total of 2.27 lakh seats for apprenticeship training in central or state/private sector enterprises combined. However, of these, only 1.65 lakh seats had been utilized.

vi) Vocational Training linked to Development Programmes

6.14 In addition to formal sector vocational training methods, there are some facilities specifically designed to provide vocational training for the informal sector e.g. the schemes for training of women by the Department of Women and Child Development.

vii) Overall assessment of present situation

6.15 The total supply of trained persons entering the labour force in a year can be roughly estimated from the data in Annexure 6.3, which pieces together the capacity of various institutions providing technical degrees or diplomas. The data relate to different years and are therefore subject to significant version of error, but the total capacity that emerges is only about 1.7 million.

6.16 The actual number of persons expected to enter the labour force on the 1.8% labour force growth assumption is about 12.3 million per year (see Table 6.6). Allowing for underutilization of seats in training institutions and some overlaps the percentage of those entering the labour force with some degree of formal training is probable around 1.5 million or about 12% of the gross new entrants into the labour force. While a significant number of the new entrants will be absorbed in various types of unskilled labour in agricultural and non-agricultural occupations, where skills are not needed, the level of skill endowment of new entrants to the labour force revealed by these numbers is clearly not consistent

Table – 6.6

Entrants to Labour Force in Rural and Urban Areas 2000-2012[a]

(Million persons 15+)

Entrants to the Labour Force	2000 to 2007 (7 years)	2007 to 2012 (5 years)
Rural Areas[1]	52.4	40.3
Urban Areas[2]	33.8	28.1
All India	**86.2**	**68.4**

Notes: [1] Excluding migrants from rural areas

[2] Including migrants to urban areas

[a] Corresponds to 1.8 percent per annum labour force growth scenario.

with triggering a process of rapid economic growth and high quality employment generation.

3. Quality of Training

The inadequacy of training capacity in quantitative terms is not the only problem. There are also serious problems relating to quality. While the quality of the output of IITs, engineering colleges or Medical colleges is very good; this is not the case with the vocational training institutions.

i) Problems with ITIs

6.17 Evaluation studies of the ITIs have shown that there is a great deal of variation in the quality of different ITIs reflecting partly differences across States, and partly also characteristics of individual ITIs. Many States have encouraged creation of new ITIs to cover areas not covered earlier but without adequate preparatory work, or resource input or effective follow-up action. The following deficiencies have been noted:

- Much of the training provided in the ITIs is for skills for which there is little current demand. The curriculum had not been revised for many years and was therefore not attuned to current market requirements. Some revision has taken place more recently, but more needs to be done. One reason for the lack of attention to market requirements is the lack of involvement by industry in the management of ITIs.
- The transference of skills in the ITIs also needs to be improved and the testing process at the end made more unreliable. All Govt ITIs and private ITIs affiliated with the NCVT, as well as the private training institutes running DOEACC accredited course, rely on formal trade testing or certification by an independent authority. However, there is a widespread perception among employers that students obtain certificates even though actual skills absorbed are very poor.
- The facilities and infrastructure in most ITIs are inadequate, with obsolete equipment in laboratories and workshops. Maintenance is also poor which means that

such equipment as is available is not well maintained. These deficiencies reflect the scarcity of resources with State Governments which is exacerbated by the tendency to create new institutions in places where they don't exist, even though existing institutions are under funded.

6.18 There is a shortage of suitably trained faculty in the institutions engaged in training. Six Advanced Training Institutes, (ATIs) established by DGET have been partly meeting the needs of trained instructors required by the ITIs, but the facilities available in ATIs are not being fully utilized by the State Directorates of Employment and Training due to their internal administrative problems. The State Governments have been requested to establish instructor-training institutes to train and retrain their instructors, but the States Governments have not been able to do so due to financial constraints.

ii) Problems with the Apprenticeship Scheme

6.19 Some of the problems characterising training institutes are less likely to arise in formal apprenticeship training schemes where apprentices are attached to functioning industries and obtain on the job training. However, the quality of apprenticeship programmes varies greatly depending upon the firm. The bulk of the apprenticeship seats are in the public sector organisations with private sector firms generally not complying with the requirement, though there are exceptions. One of the problems that has arisen is that apprentices view apprenticeships primarily as an avenue for subsequent employment, rather then as a mode of training. Although the law clearly does not entitle them to employment, the courts have interpreted the law to mean that apprentices must get preference, and this in turn discourages employers from fulfilling their obligation under the Act.

iii) Training for Informal Sector

6.20 There are almost no training facilities oriented towards the needs of the informal sector, which is otherwise expected to provide a large part of the expansion in employment. The principal economic activities here are retail trade, road transport, equipment repair, construction related jobs, household industries and a growing variety of community and personal services. Productivity improvements in the informal sector or absorption of new technology, which is essential for rapid growth, is possible only if the new entrants into this sector have adequate skills but there is virtually no effective system for ensuring some training for all those entering this sector.

4. Suggested Remedial Steps

6.21 It is evident from our review that the system of training and skill development currently in place needs substantial modification and strengthening if we want the economy to be launched onto a high growth employment-generating path. There is no single system of training, which is universally prevalent in the rest of the world, which can be used as a role model for reforming the system of training in India. Internationally, there is a considerable variety of models that have been adopted by different countries. See Annexures 6.4 and 6.5. We have to draw selectively from international experience in the light of our particular circumstances to evolve a suitable model Based on this approach; we have the following recommendations for the future.

i) Expansion of specialised Technical Education

6.22 While bulk of this Report deals with vocational training, the system of general and technical education also requires considerable improvement. Given the low level of attainment in general education and expansion in the education system is necessary but it has to be given a bias towards vocational education. This is discussed in para 6.22 below.

As far as engineering education is concerned, it has to be strengthened to avail of the labour intensive activity opening in the domestic and international labour market. The present IITs have demonstrated their capability for developing high quality skilled personnel who have played a leading role in the IT revolution abroad and have been at the forefront of the growth of the Indian IT sector. Given the demand for such trained personnel from the Indian software sector and the likelihood that many will continue to migrate abroad and it will be necessary to expand the output of engineers very substantially. The aspect of the existing IITs should be trebled, and ultimately each major State should have at least one IIT. The role of private sector in higher-level general education, and higher technical education must also be expanded. While many initiatives have been taken, further policy restructuring is called for, particularly in regard to the restrictions on charging of fees from students.

ii) Strengthening the existing ITIs

6.23 The existing National Vocational Training System (NVTS) based on government run ITIs needs to be radically overhauled. Since these are State Government institutions, relevant decisions have to be taken by State Governments but the Central Government could take the lead by suggesting an approach to reform of the ITIs and also offering to assist States willing to undertake such reform. The following initiatives deserve urgent consideration.

6.24 Industry must have much greater involvement in the management of ITIs including involvement in the matter of design of curriculum, selection of instructors, training of instructors in factories and other establishments in the area to familiarise them with the market demand for skills and also providing equipment for training. In 1998 a joint effort between CII and the Central Labour Ministry was launched. So far, only 7 states and a union territory (Punjab, Haryana, Himachal Pradesh, J&K, Chandigarh, Gujarat, Maharashtra, Tamilnadu and Karnataka) have put one government ITI under a Joint Industry Institute Management Committee. Experience with this experiment needs to be reviewed and the experiment expanded in scale.

6.25 At present, ITIs are essentially run as departmental organisations under the full departmental control of the State Government departments responsible for technical education. It may be desirable to convert selected ITIs chosen for joint management with industry into autonomous bodies receiving government funds with a management structure in which industry representatives can be formally inducted on the governing boards and the institutions are also given sufficient autonomy to become effectively board managed.

6.26 In the longer term we have to consider the direction in which the training system should evolve. Of the various types of systems listed in Table at annexure 6.3 we feel the cooperative system, in which there is cooperation between the State, employers organisations and trade unions may be the most suitable for India.

If the experiment with autonomous jointly managed ITIs mentioned above succeeds it should be replicated on a much broad scale.

6.27 *Strengthening* the government vocational training institutes will require substantial funds for upgrading infrastructure and facilities and also an assured flow of resources to maintain the assets the created. Capital financing can be obtained from the multilateral institutions along the lines of the modernization of 565 ITI's by the World Bank in 1990. a similar project should be devised to modernize all remaining ITIs over the next ten years. Provision must also be made to ensure an adequate flow of resources to the institutions for maintenance. At present, 90% of the budget of the ITIs goes to pay salaries leaving very little for maintenance. It is necessary to review the present policy whereby training in Government ITIs has traditionally been provided free. It may be desirable to allow ITIs to charge fees, at least for the more specialised courses from the trainees, or from their industry sponsors.

6.28 In the medium term, the resource requirements of training require some dedicated source of funding. A cess could be levied on the pay roll of all establishments, which should be credited to a special fund directed at creation of infrastructure for vocational training. A very small fraction, say in the range of 0.1 to 0.5 per cent of salary and wages paid to organised sector workers should be utilized to create an initial corpus. Some rebate in income tax should also be considered to the employees contributing to vocational training fund. Two third of the cess that is collected in a district should be deployed in the ITIs in the same district. It should be utilized under the guidance of an advisory committee chaired by representatives of the local industry or trade chamber/ association.

6.29 One of the reasons why demand for services of vocational training appears limited is the excessive demand for the degree level professional/technical education. This problem could be mitigated if graduates of ITIs and other vocational training institutions are eligible for entry into polytechnics and +2 level medical and engineering courses. Entry criteria and course curriculum would need to be redesigned for this purpose. This would also help to inculcate a culture of shifting between training and work in the formative stages of career of a professional. This practice is at present confined to post degree level in management education (MBA etc.) and specialisation in medicine (MD and super specialisation training).

iii) Entrepreneurship training for the informal sector

6.30 A large part of the employment generated by the economy will be self-employment in the informal sector. These self-employed entrepreneurs need training of the multi-skill variety, going beyond production skills to include marketing, finance and accounting and elementary management. Such skills cannot be developed through structured formal training but requires the guidance of "mentors" in actual business conditions.

6.31 The Bhartiya Yuva Shakti Trust (BYST), which is a CII initiative established in 1991, is a relevant model in this context. The Trust fosters entrepreneurial activity by providing seed capital loans and practical business advice through mentors. About 1700 people have been employed in 500 ventures between 1991-2000 spread over rural and urban areas. However, it is worth noting that the loan recovery rate is 94%, indicating strong economic viability. Such experiments need to be replicated on a much larger scale.

iv) Strengthening the Apprenticeship System

6.32 The number of apprentices taken by public sector enterprises has been declining down due to industrial sickness and other reasons. This form of training should be extended to cover many other enterprises where the opportunities for employment are growing or are expected to grow. This would require surveying and re-surveying industrial establishments more frequently. Furthermore, the Act should be amended to make it clear that apprenticeship does not imply any presumption of preferential employment.

6.33 The informal sector and the small scale sector can give the earliest returns to training, in terms of job placement, through training provided in 'apprenticeship' mode. We recommend that all enterprises should be brought under the purview of Apprentices Act. However, payment of stipend to apprentices taken in by small establishments should be voluntary, and not mandatory, under the Apprentices Act.

v) Improving Vocational Education at School Level

6.34 Integration of vocational education at the school level is the only practical way of imparting basic technical skills to large number of new entrants to the labour force. It is relevant to consider in this context whether vocational training should be added on to the general school system or whether it should be imparted through separate schools. Korea, which has recently graduated from developing country to industrialised country status, has relied upon vocational training provided in specialised schools. The curriculum is in the local languages and such as can be comprehended by a middle school level student. Most of these schools are owned and run by the private sector and there is active involvement of industry in supporting such schools. Equally important, there are possibilities for vertical movement from vocational schools to higher (degree) level of education. Opting for vocational education therefore does not deny students the option subsequently to switch back into the mainstream. A comparison between the Indian and Korean approach may be seen at Annexure 6.5.

6.35 It is not possible to expect the education administration dealing with the general school system to administer and promote vocational education, which requires a multi-disciplinary approach. The present Department of Technical Education focusses primarily on funding IITs and IIMs but this function is not really necessary as these institutions have matured sufficiently to look after themselves. The department should be restructured to focus on vocational education and vocational training. A parallel institution is needed in State Governments to focus on vocational education schools.

vi) Vocational training by firms or industry associations

6.36 Industry must also take the initiative to remove bottleneck of trained manpower by taking on the job of 'applied situation training' as distinct from lecture based training'[2]. These kinds of

---

2 Examples of direct interaction between Industry (through a particular firm, or through an association of firms) is the training of masons in Gujarat by a cement manufacturer, when it faced prospect of skill shortage affecting sales of its output in that region, and of Society of Automotive Manufacturers (SIAM) training the automobile drivers.

initiatives, which can help to train and retrain people, should be assigned a role in public policy on training by way of:

- recognition of courses for employment,
- making the premises and infrastructure of the local ITI available, and
- giving the expenditure on such effort the same treatment in tax policy as is given to expenditure on high tech education[3].

vii) The role of the public sector in skill development

6.37 The role of public sector in nurturing the market for skill development services has not evolved, as it should have. Government has tended to act as a training provider and not as a facilitator encouraging others to get into training. This is partly because of historical reasons. The bulk of the infrastructure services; both industrial and social infrastructure were owned by the government as railways, civil aviation, highways, communication, electricity, petroleum, coal, etc., on industrial infrastructure side, and health, education, housing and related support services like, sanitation, and drinking water and a host of others on the social infrastructure side. On the assumption that the producer is the best provider of training, the publicly owned establishments came to own and deliver the 'training services'.

6.38 As a result the role of the public sector as a facilitator of 'training institutions, was ignored' and this has had undesirable consequences. Private sector training has been discouraged because of highly subsidized training services provided by the public sector, an undesirable nexus between public owned training delivery institutions and placement for jobs in public sector, excessive regulation in extending recognition to the institutions.

6.39 In our view, the time has come to reduce the balance. The Central Government should withdraw completely from delivery of vocational training services, and foster autonomous professional bodies that give recognition to training institutes by declaring them as eligible training providers. The Government's

---

3 Such incentives were introduced for IIT's etc (*note not the ITI's!)* in Union Budget around the year 1995.

role should be one of monitoring the institutions that set up standards of training, and evaluating and assigning rating to the private training establishments. The Central Government should continue its role in the delivery of training services in specialized fields like instructor training, up gradation of skill level of industrial workers, supervisory training etc.

6.40 Government should set up a system of displaying wage levels associated with particular skills as essential public information like it does for commodity and foreign exchange price indices etc[4].

6.41 The state government will have a continuing role in promoting vocational training institutes such as the ITI's but these should be made into autonomous societies and be jointly managed with industry. A Centrally sponsored scheme or an aid institution like the UGC should be set up for the ITI's. Barring certain exceptions, the ITI's have a physical environment, which is much inferior to the engineering college, diploma awarding polytechnics and the medical colleges. For the latter, there are UGC type schemes for up-gradation of buildings and equipments and even to run special training courses. But for vocational training a forum for reaching the public resources to State-level institutions does not exist. And normally State Governments give a very low priority to vocational training.

iv) The role of the private sector

6.42 The private corporate sector should be encouraged to make equipment and some training infrastructure available. Government owned ITI's, which are able to attract resources from private corporate sector, should be rewarded by a matching inflow of resources from Government. Training activity should get the same preferential treatment in public policy for allocation of urban land and related civic infrastructure as is given to 'schools'. Resources put in by employers for training the workers themselves or through their sub-contractors should be encouraged through tax incentives.

6.43 *To summarise,* the rate of growth of economy cannot be accelerated, in particular in the labour intensive sectors, if there

---

4 For a fuller coverage of education and training statistics for employment, refer Annexure 6.8

is a general lack of skills among the work force. The example of software industry is sufficient to illustrate what can be done by the Indian youth if the right training facilities are afforded by the society. This requires strengthening of the existing training system. The role of public sector has to be restructured and conditions created for inflow of funds at a much larger scale than at present. Role of private sector has to be expanded sharply if the requisite resources are to be brought in to bridge the large capacity gaps that exist. The vocational training policy has to respond to this challenge.

6.44 The IITs require a much larger base, spread across all states, if the potential of Indian technical manpower is to be fully utilised for the benefit of the economy. A larger base of IITs, and facilities to vocational trained youth to enter into higher technical education stream will provide inspiration to those who take to vocational training right from the school stage.

Annexure – 6.1

Profile of Persons having some marketable skill by type of skill possessed - 1993-94

Skill	Code	Rural Male	Rural Female	Urban Male	Urban Female
Typist/Stenographer	01	3	2	14	10
Fishermen	02	5	-	2	-
Miner, Quarryman	03	2	-	1	-
Spinner including Charkha operator	04	1	3	2	3
Weaver	05	6	10	11	8
Tailor cutter	06	6	18	15	54
Shoemaker, cobbler	07	1	-	2	-
Carpenter	08	6	-	8	-
Mason, bricklayer	09	5	-	9	-
Moulder	10	-	-	1	-
Machine man	11	2	-	8	-
Fitter die maker	12	1	-	6	-
Welder	13	1	-	4	-
Blacksmith	14	2	-	2	-
Goldsmith	15	1	-	4	-
Silversmith	16	-	-	1	-
Electrician'	17	2	-	8	-
Repairer of electronic goods	18	1	-	5	-
Motor vehicle driver, tractor driver	19	11	-	27	1
Boatman	20	-	-	-	-
Potter	21	2	1	1	-
Nurse midwife	22	-	-	-	2
Basket maker, wicker product maker	23	3	4	1	1
Toy maker	24	-	-	-	-
Brick maker, tile maker	25	2	1	-	-
Bidi maker	26	3	7	-	7
Bookbinder	27	-	-	2	-
Barber	28	3	-	3	-
Mud house builder & thatcher	29	9	1	1	1
Others	30	24	15	57	21
Any skill possessed (Sub total)	01-30	101	63	196	112
No skill possessed		899	937	804	888
Total		**1000**	**1000**	**1000**	**1000**

Source: NSSO Report No.409 on Results of 50th round (1993-94) survey on Employment and Unemployment.

Annexure – 6.2

1999-2000

Currently Attending

Age Groups	Total	Not Attending	General education upto Higher Secondary level: middle level	General education upto Higher Secondary level: Higher Secondary & equ. level	Degree courses in agri., engg., medicine & other subject	Diploma or certificate courses in agr. engg/tech./ medicine & other subjects
				RURAL MALE		
15-19	1000(a)	586	94	291	21	9
20-24	1000(b)	888	5	35	46	16
				URBAN MALE		
15-19	1000(c)	407	69	395	74	30
20-24	1000(d)	763	3	46	128	53

Source: Table 42 of NSSO Report 458(55/10/2) on 55th Round (1999-2000) survey on Employment & Unemployment

Notes: (a) Sample size 26249

(b) " " 20997

(c) " " 17483

(d) " " 15569

Annexure – 6.3

Facilities for Education and Training in Applied Courses[1]

000 Nos.(Year)

1.	**Industrial Training**[2]	
	Apprentices from Industrial Establishments	227.0(2001)
	Seats in ITIs	628.0(2001)
2.	**Para-medical Courses**	
	Nurses out-turn	11.4(1996)
	Mid-wives	6.3(1996)
	Health Workers Female	6.5(1996)
	Health visitors	0.5(1996)
3.	**Engineering**	
	Admission at Degree level	138.4(1997)
	Admission at Diploma level	186.2(1997)
4.	**Medical**	
	Admission to Degree level in Allopathy & Dental	17.0(1992)
5.	**Agriculture & Forestry courses**	
	Enrolment	45.0(1987)
6.	**General Education Courses**	
	Enrolment	188.6(1999)
7.	**Veterinary Science Colleges**	
	Enrolment	22.2(1999)
8.	**Journalism, Library Science, Social Work Physical Education and others**	
	Enrolment at Graduate level	272.9(1987)
	Total	**1750**

Sources: 1. IAMR Manpower profile India (2000) unless otherwise stated.

2. Ministry of Labour (Director General of Employment & Training).

Annexure – 6.4

Training Systems[a]

System	Countries	Main features
"Cooperative"		
(effort of enterprises, Government and Trade Unions)	Australia, Germany, Switzerland, many countries in Latin America	Pressures to undertake training resulting from strong cooperation amongst employers' organisation, the state and trade unions
"Enterprise-based"		
* Low Labour Turnover *(long tenure of employee with an enterprise)*	Japan	Low labour mobility, life time employment for many staff. "Long-termism" arising from absence of stock market pressure. Wage system based on seniority and enterprise-based trade unions.
* Voluntarist *(Little initiative by Government or the Unions)*	United Kingdom, United States	Few institutional pressures on firms to provide training.
"State-driven"		
*Demand-led	Hong Kong, Republic of Korea, Singapore, Taiwan, China	State plays a leading role in coordinating the demand for and supply of skills. Operates in an open and competitive economic environment.
* Supply led	Economies in transition; many	Government takes on a prime responsibility for
developing countries, Asia pressure on employers to	formal sector in training institutes. Little or no	especially in and Africa train.

Source: Table 3.2 of World Employment Report 1998

Annexure 6.5

Comparison of technical-vocational education; India and the Republic of Korea, 1990

India	Republic of Korea
* Pre-vocational education is offered in limited numbers of schools and to limited number of students at primary and middle schools	* Education for introduction to the world of work, career awareness and career exploration are offered at primary and secondary school as part of a general education
* The annual intake in technical-vocational education schools is extremely low	* The share of students going to technical-vocational high schools in 1970s was about 50 per cent. In 1990 it was about 32 per cent.
* Practically all technical-vocational institutes are public	About 65 per cent of technical-vocational high schools and 84 per cent of junior colleges are private.
* There are few continuing education programmes (B-tech) for men.	* Most junior colleges offer short-term or regular evening classes for providing continuing educational opportunities to industrial workers who graduated from technical/vocational high schools. Also there are correspondence, university and open colleges for workers who graduated from junior colleges.
* Technical- vocational institutes for women are far fewer than for men.	* Girls can apply to any technical-vocational institute according to interest and competency; 46 per cent of students enrolled are female.
* Not much vernacular local literature in state of art practices in the trades. Union Ministry of Labour has set up a Society for instructional media. However for most of the modern techniques, the textbooks are imported and written in English	* All textbooks are compiled by the Ministry of Education and written in Korean.

* Technical-vocational teacher education is not systematized.	* Departments have been established at 4- year colleges or universities to produce qualified vocational teachers since the early 1960s.
* A substantial percentage of teaching posts are lying vacant.	* Technical-vocational teachers are actually oversupplied.
* Student drop-out rates from vocational training institutes are very high	* An average of 10 per cent of technical- vocational high school students drop out every year.
* Teaching-learning materials, especially raw materials for practice and audio-visual equipment, are very poor.	* The budget for laboratory practice and shopwork is adequately met by Government.
* Vocational education programmes with work experience are not operated	* Work experience for technical-vocational students is compulsory, ranging from one to six months.
* There are no close links between schools and industry barring a very limited number of exceptions.	* Schools and industries make a conscious attempt to develop closer relations. Industry provides scholarships and many have sister relationships with technical schools.

Source: World Employment Report 1998-99 for Korea. Situation in India is based on a typical South Asian Country reported in that Publication, modified in the light of initiatives taken by the Ministry of Labour, Government of India.

Annexure – 6.6

*Involvement of Central Government Ministries/Departments in Training for Specific Sectors***

** Report to Task Force Sub Group on Training, Annexure 2

Rural Agricultural Sector	Non-farm Rural Sector	Training For Women	Worker Education And Labour Development Related Training	Training For Industrial Sector	Training for Infrastructure Sector	Training for the Services Sector
* Ministry of agriculture	* Ministry of rural area & employment	* DWCD (other than Step & Norad-assisted programme)	* Central Board of worker education (Ministry of Labour)	* Ministry of Industry	* Ministry of Power	* Ministry of Civil Supplies
* Dept. of biotechnology	* Dept. of youth affairs & sports	* Women labourcell, Ministry of labour	* National Labour institute (Ministry of labour)	* Dept. of Electronics	* Ministry of Railways	* Ministry of Information & Broadcasting
* Dept. of non-conventional energy sources	* Dept. of biotechnology	* TREAD Programme of	* DGFASLI (Ministry of	* Ministry of Textiles	* Ministry of Surface Transport	* Dept. of Personnel & Training
				* Ministry of Environment		

(Contd...)

...Contd...

** Report to Task Force Sub Group on Training, Annexure 2

Rural Agricultural Sector	Non-farm Rural Sector	Training For Women	Worker Education And Labour Development Related Training	Training For industrial Sector	Training for infrastructure Sector	Training for the services Sector
		Ministry of industry	Labour)	& Forests	* Ministry of Civil Aviation	
* Ministry of rural area & employment	* Dept. of non-conventional energy sources					* Dept. of Culture
			* Institute of Labour Development (IFCI)	* Ministry of Petroleum		
	* Ministry of water resources			* Ministry of Coal	* Ministry of Urban Development	* Ministry of Home Affairs
	* Ministry of health		* NSTEDB (Ministry of Science & Technology)	* Ministry of Commerce		* Ministry of Parliamentary Affairs
				* Ministry of Supply		
				* Ministry of civil supplies		

Annexure 6.7

*Vocational Education and Training System in India at a Glance**

UNDER GOVERNMENT AUSPICES					OTHER THAN GOVERNMENT
Department of education, Govt. of India	DGET, Ministry of labour, Govt. of India	DWCD, Ministry of HRD, Govt. of India	Ministry of Rural Area & Employment	Ministry of Industry Govt. of India	Industrial Enterprises * IN-PLANT TRAINING
* Vocational Education Secondary school Lower school First degree level	* Craftsmen training scheme	* Step * Norad-assisted programme	* TRYSEM (now replace by other programmes)	* Training through DCSSI Institutes	Private training providers * PRIVATE PROPRIETARY TRAINING
* apprenticeship (For graduate engineers, diploma holders and vocational school passout(s))	* Apprenticeship (trade apprentices)	* Condensed courses of education & vocational training		* Training under NRF	Non-Govt. Organisations
* technical education	* Advanced vocational training scheme			* Training activities of KVIC	* INFORMAL SECTOR TRAINING
* community polytechnic project	* Vocational Training Programme for Women * CSTRI * CSMI * CTIS * FTIs				Employers Organisations
* shramik vidyapeeths					* SUPPORT TO INDUSTRY'S TRAINING ACTIVITIES
OTHER TRAINING ACTIVITIES ADMINISTERED BY CENTRAL AND STATE GOVT. DEPARTMENTS					

* Report of Task Force Sub Group on Training, Annexure 1

Annexure 6.8

Issues in education and training statistics for employment[1]

The data and information needs

Comprehensive statistics on education and training should over:

- demand for education and training: indicators of the current and future demand for education and training in particular sectors in relation to changes in workplace requirements, size and structure of the population, industrial structure of the economy, and occupational composition of the labour force;
- supply of education and training: financial, human and physical resources for various types and levels of education and training covering pre-employment, enterprise, private sector and individual training;
- participation and progression in education: data on enrolment rates at various levels of education and training, on student progression and on the expected duration of schooling; participation and a progression rates should relate to pre-employment education and training and continuous education and training;
- the learning environment: data on class size, student-teacher ratios, curricula and other aspects of the classroom experience of students, and qualifications, workload and earnings of teachers;
- outcome and performance data: data on how resources are utilized in the education and training sector on the performance of those resources.

Gaps in education and training statistics. In most countries, the deficiencies in statistics relate to:

- the lack of clarity and uniformity in statistical concepts, definitions and classifications;
- the difficulties of measuring the knowledge, skills and attitudes (KSAs) that work demands from workers;
- problems of measuring the KSAs obtained from education and training;

- the limited coverage and poor quality of information on how the demand for education and training is met; and
- problems of measuring the impact of education and training in performance of individuals, enterprises and economies.

The relationship between education and training and work. There should be better understanding of what work demands from education and training, and of how work affects education and training. To answer the first question, analysts need to measure the effect of education on job and organizational performance, for which better data are needed in two areas:

- identifying KSAs produced by education, especially among those excluded from academic and skills testing;
- measures of performance in the workplace and success of individuals and their employers.

The second question involves measuring the effect of work on lifelong learning. Better data are needed in two areas:

- detailed information on individuals' work experience, including the nature of tasks performed;
- data on learning experiences from in-plant training, training by private providers and training by individuals.

Data Collection methods

Longitudinal surveys provide retrospective data on employers and employees. They are useful for data on lifelong learning and on how structural change affects training decisions.

Enterprises surveys provide data on employers' formal training provisions and related expenditures, and on whether firms retain their own staff or recruit externally.

Employee surveys provide data on all forms of on-the-job training. They are best done in conjunction with enterprise (employer) surveys.

There are many other types of data collection methods, including household surveys, administrative data (public sector records), informal sector surveys, and employment and training observatories.

---

1. *Source*: World Employment Report 1998-99.

7

Reform of Labour Laws

One of the factors which is often said to restrain expansion of employment in the organised sector in India is the rigidity of our labour markets arising from the nature of our labour laws. The need for reform of the labour laws has been recognised by the government and some indications have been given of the areas where the government regards changes to be most essential. In this chapter we examine the need for changes in the labour laws and make some recommendations in this regard.

1. Some Conceptual Issues

7.2 To begin with, it is necessary to consider the reasons why employer-employee relationships need to be regulated by law in the first place instead of leaving all such relations to be determined in the market place on the basis of voluntary contracts between the employer and the employee. The reasons why labour markets need to be regulated by law to a much greater extent than goods markets are well known. Workers are not commodities; they are human beings and citizens, and individual workers are also the weaker party in any employer-employee relationship. These considerations justify legislation aimed at protecting the rights of labour in a number of areas e.g. to form unions for purposes of collective bargaining, laying down minimum obligations which employers must meet with regard to social benefits, health and safety of workers, provision of special facilities for women workers, establishing grievance redressal mechanisms, etc. This is accepted practice in both developed and developing countries, though of course the nature of the law varies considerably across countries.

7.3 Having accepted the need to regulate employer-employee relations by law, it is also important to recognise that in a market economy the impact of labour legislation on labour market conditions may turn out to be quite different from what was intended. This is because decision to hire labour is an economic decision made by employers and laws which affect particular conditions to the employment of labour affect decision made by employers on employment. For example, if the minimum wage fixed by law is too high, it raises the cost of labour intensive activities and products in the organised sector (which is where the laws are enforced) relative to other products and activities and relative to the same products produced in the unorganised sector where the law cannot be enforced. Employers in the organised sector will tend to shift to more capital-intensive activities and products which implies that minimum wages may be effectively raised in the organised sector, but at the cost of lower levels of employment than would exist otherwise in these products in the organised sector. Similarly, laws designed to provide security of employment reduce the flexibility available to employers to adjust the labour force in response to changing circumstances and employers are likely to respond by shying away from labour using activities. Additional security for existing job opportunities is therefore obtained only at the cost of expansion of employment.

7.4 It is not easy to quantify the extent of the negative impact of labour market inflexibility. It can be argued that the extent of the negative impact is exaggerated. However a more reasonable conclusion is that it depends upon the economic environment. Rigid labour laws in a particular industry may have less impact on the level of employment if the industry is protected from competition from abroad because of high tariff walls and if technology choices and investment patterns are also controlled by the government making it more difficult for employers to shift to capital intensive products and activities. In such a controlled environment it could be argued that the high cost of labour resulting from labour market inflexibility can be passed on to consumers in the form of higher prices.[1] However, the negative effect of inflexible labour laws is obviously much greater in a world in which the domestic economy is liberalised and there is also competition from imports. Burdening domestic producers with labour laws that are much more inflexible than those prevailing in other countries reduces their ability to compete effectively with new domestic entrants, who can benefit from new technology and it also makes it difficult to compete with imports. It also limits their ability to compete internationally in export markets, especially in labour intensive products, an outcome which can be very costly in terms of employment opportunities foregone as is evident if we compare Indian exports performance in labour intensive manufactures with that of China. We note that labour rigidities are not the only factors reducing India's competitiveness vis-a-vis China. There are other factors which restrict our performance which need to be addressed. However rigid labour laws is definitely one of them.

7.5 To summarise, there is no doubt that we need labour legislation to protect legitimate labour interests, but the resulting legal framework must ensure a reasonable balance between the objective of protecting the legitimate rights of employees and the equally important objective of providing a framework which would encourage efficiency and create incentives to expand total employment. The laws, as well as the way they are implemented, must allow employers to create a structure of incentives which encourage labour productivity. This includes the flexibility to restructure and adjust the labour force to adapt to changing technology and changing market conditions. The need for such flexibility has increased because liberalisation and globalisation put a premium on flexibility.

2. Problems with Indian Labour Laws

7.6 India has a long tradition of labour legislation, dating from pre-independence times. A characteristic of the law is that the

---

1. It should be noted however that this is at best a static argument which ignores the dynamic efforts on employment arising from the efficiencies associated with such an extensively controlled system. Once dynamic effects are included labour market inflexibility could lead to lower growth and employment over time.

state is interposed between the employer and the employed in virtually every dispute. The original reason for this interposition, which dates from pre-independence times, was to enable the state to enforce labour discipline and avoid disruptions in production. In the post-independence period the emphasis shifted and the role of the state was seen primarily as protecting the rights of labour.

7.7 Since labour is included in the concurrent list in the Constitution, both the Centre and the State can legislate in this area and this has led to a multiplicity of laws. There are 47 labour related statutes enacted by the Central Government dealing with minimum wages, benefits in case of accident, death of worker, maternity, conditions of employment, dismissal, disciplinary action, formation of trade unions, industrial disputes, formation of trade unions, etc. In addition, there are a number of State statutes covering different aspects or segments of labour.

7.8 A comprehensive review of all these laws is definitely needed. They need to be simplified and brought in line with contemporary economic realities, including especially current international practice. At times, the problem is not so much with the law itself as with the lengthy almost interminable nature of legal proceedings which contribute greatly to the cost of hiring labour and the associated "hassle factor". There are also problems with the enforcement machinery i.e. the various inspectors responsible for enforcing the law. Complaints are frequently voiced by industry that this machinery uses the extensive powers at its disposal to harass employers with a view to extract bribes, a process which imposes especially heavy costs on small entrepreneurs. Equally, an opposite view is expressed by trade unions that the labour enforcement machinery needs to be further strengthened in the interest of better enforcement of labour laws.

7.9 These issues are beyond our terms of reference and they will no doubt receive the attention they deserve from the Second Labour Commission. For the purpose of this report, we wish to focus on some specific provisions which in our view are of particular importance for employment creation which need urgent attention. These relate to the Industrial Disputes Act (1947), the Trade Unions Act (1926), and the Contract Labour (Abolition and Regulation) Act, 1970.

i) Industrial Disputes Act 1947

7.10 The most frequently voiced complaint against Indian labour laws relates to the provisions governing retrenchment layoffs and closure in the Industrial Disputes Act (1948). Until 1976, the law in this respect was not very different from the position elsewhere and employers could retrench labour if the situation warranted provided they followed the "last come first go" rule in drawing up the list of workmen to be retrenched, gave a month's notice or pay in lieu of notice, paid half a months wages per year of service and informed the government. The Act was amended in 1976 to add a new Chapter V.B which made it mandatory for employers employing more than 300 workmen to seek the prior consent of government before effecting retrenchment or closure of a part of the enterprise.[2] The scope of this provision was further widened by an amendment in 1982 whereby all employers employing more than 100 persons were covered.

7.11 Although the legislation does not forbid retrenchment or closure but only requires prior permission of government, the Act has been interpreted in a manner which has made retrenchment virtually impossible. Furthermore, a large number of cases which were never intended to be treated as retrenchment because of court judgements have come to be viewed as retrenchment. For example, non-renewal of contract at the end of a contract period has been treated as retrenchment. Termination of employment during or at the end of a probation period has also been treated as retrenchment, even if the termination was because of failure to pass a test, which was a condition of employment. In fact, termination is now allowed only in cases of proven misconduct and this requires an elaborate process of enquiry before action can be taken.

7.12 The provision that retrenchment of labour or closure of a part of a unit requires prior provision is a unique provision of our labour markets which has the following negative effects:

- As pointed out earlier, it increases the perceived total cost of hiring labour and thus discourages investment in labour intensive products and activities. These activities

---

2. "Permission for closure or retrenchment has to be given by the appropriate government as defined under Chapter VB of the Industrial Disputes Act."

remain in the informal sector which has the effect of denying effective modernisation and technological upgradation in these areas which is essential to ensure competitiveness.

- Export industries are particularly disadvantaged because exporters face highly competitive markets and need the maximum flexibility to remain competitive. Since these export production areas are all labour intensive, the loss of export possibilities also means loss of potential high quality employment.
- Foreign investors, who have the option to invest in other countries, are deterred from investing in labour intensive industries. This may be the explanation why in many other countries foreign investment has gone into many labour intensive industries with a strong export orientation creating large amounts of high quality employment based on exports, but in India foreign investment has been largely in more capital-intensive industries, oriented towards the domestic market.

7.13 Employers can of course downsize the labour force through voluntary retirement schemes usually introduced with the consent of unions. This instrumentality has been used by many companies, but it is obviously much more costly. More importantly, this instrumentality can be used more easily by capital-intensive where labour costs are a relatively smaller part of total costs. In other words, the system makes it much more difficult to labour intensive units than for capital intensive ones. Closure of a unit as a whole is of course possible through the BIFR process, but this is extremely cumbersome and time consuming.

7.14 Apart the difficulty in retrenching labour, our labour laws in practice also make it very difficult to dismiss an employee. Dismissal is technically possible for malfeasance, non-performance or indiscipline provided due process has been followed. Unlike retrenchment, no prior approval of government is needed but, in practice, dismissal can be questioned by Trade Unions raising a dispute on this matter, and this can lead to protracted litigation. The problem in this case is not so much with the law as with the judicial and extra-judicial machinery, but the net effect is that employers are often unable to maintain discipline. These problems are particularly severe for industries which are labour intensive where large number of workers are involved and also for smaller entrepreneurs who cannot afford the heavy transactions cost imposed by such inflexibility.

7.15 The inflexibility introduced by our labour laws has not gone unrecognised by the judiciary. The following quotation from the Supreme Court's judgement in the case of Excel Wear vs Union of India AIR 1979 SC 25 says it all.

> "Gradually, the net was cast too wide and the freedom of the employer tightened to such an extent by introduction of the provisions that it has come to a breaking point from the point of view of the employers.... It is not quite correct to say that because compensation is not a substitute for the remedy of prevention of unemployment, the latter remedy must be the only one. If it were so, then in no case closure can be or should be allowed.... But, so long as the private ownership of an industry is recognised and governed on overwhelmingly large proportion of our economic structure, is it possible to say that principles of socialism and social justice can be pushed to such an extreme so as to ignore completely, or to a very large extent, the interest of another section of the public, viz. the private owners of the undertakings?"

7.16 Removal of these rigidities is now an urgent necessity. We recommend the following as items of for priority consideration if we are to achieve rapid growth of employment in the organised sector in the next ten years.

a. The requirement of prior permission of government for retrenchment, layoff or closure introduces a major inflexibility in the system. One solution which has been proposed is to amend the Industrial Disputes Act to make this provision applicable only to units having more than 1000 employees. While this approach would give additional flexibility to some units, it is clearly biased in favour of the more capital intensive areas. This is because the 1000 employee limit will cover many units in the capital intensive sectors which have relatively high investment while it will leave out units in labour intensive sectors with much lower levels of fixed investment precisely because they are labour intensive. Keeping in mind the need to provide the maximum incentive for investment and modernisation in labour intensive industries, a bolder approach is needed. We would therefore recommend a more radical step of deleting Chapter V-B from the Industrial Disputes Act completely and restoring the position prior to 1976. This was recommended in 1992 by the Inter-Ministerial Working Group on Industrial Restructuring and subsequently also by the Committee on Industrial Sickness (1993). As a balancing measure to improve protection of labour, the retrenchment compensation should be increased from the present level of half month's pay per year of service to one month atleast and possibly higher. A mechanism may also be devised to ensure that before effecting closure, the employer discharges in full the liabilities of the workers.

b. The provisions regarding dismissal after due process need to be simplified. Section 11A of the Industrial Disputes Act allows labour courts, Industrial Tribunals to interpose the state in matters that are best left to established internal processes.

c. The interpretation of the law to extend the provisions relating to retrenchment even to cases of termination of the service of a workman as a result of the non-renewal of a fixed term contract of employment between the employer and the workman concerned makes the law unduly rigid. A system of short-term employment contracts should be introduced under which workers hired on contract basis can be discharged at the end of the contract period without scope for dispute. In order to avoid legal challenge to this arrangement on the grounds of equal treatment with permanent labour doing the same job, provisions can be made for paying such labour a premium over the normal wage.

7.17 Another source of rigidity in our labour market arises from the provisions regarding service rules in the Industrial Disputes Act. Section 9a of the Act provides that the job content and the area and nature of work of an employee cannot be changed without giving notice to the employees of at least 21 days. In practice this provision actually requires the consent of each employee. This is applicable to all enterprises employing more than 100 workers and some States have made it applicable to firms with more than 50 employees. The requirement of a 21-day notice can present problems when units have to redeploy labour quickly to meet the requirement e.g. time bound export orders. More generally, the requirement of consent of workers means that employers cannot easily shift workers between different plants and locations, or even shift them to do new jobs within the same plant[3]. It is necessary to amend the Act to introduce much greater flexibility in this area. Restructuring and redeployment of labour, often involving retraining are essential features of a competitive industrial enterprise and India will not be able to achieve the high levels of efficiency needed in today's globalising world if such flexibility is not available to employer.

7.18 The Industrial Disputes Act provides for advance notice of a strike only in the case of industries notified as public utilities. No such notice is needed for other industries. The general practice in many countries is that some notice must be given. It would be desirable to amend the Act to make a reasonable notice mandatory in all cases. It would also be desirable to introduce the system of "strike ballot" whereby a strike can be called only if it is supported by a qualifying majority of the workers.

7.19 At present there is no time limit for filing disputes under the Industrial Disputes Act. This encourages piling up of old disputes leading to delays in courts. A time limit of 3 years should be stipulated within which a dispute could be referred for adjudication.

ii) Contract Labour (Regulation and Abolition) Act, 1970

7.20 The Contract Labour (Regulation and Abolition) Act was originally enacted to regulate the practice of contract labour to avoid exploitation of sweated labour. Section 10 of the Act empowers the Government to prohibit contract labour in certain

---

3. A firm wishing to introduce new technology could face a situation in which retrenchment could be avoided if redeployment were possible but it may not be able to obtain the consent of workers to the required change in job descriptions. It should be noted that these provisions are onerous because of the difficulty in implementing retrenchment since if retrenchments were more easily implementable workers would be much more willing to accept redeployment to avoid retrenchment.

situations at the discretion of the Government. In practice, the Act has been interpreted as requiring the abolition of contract labour for all services which are of a regular nature and performed on the factory premises. Two Supreme Court judgements in two different cases involving the Gujarat State Electricity Board and Air India have had the effect that employers using contract labour to perform regular services on the premises of the employer become liable to absorb such labour permanently on the rolls of the employer.

7.21 The role of contract labour has to be seen in the context of a growing trend towards unbundling of the production process into component parts and outsourcing supply of these components to different producing units. This practice will only increase with the growth of information technology. If such outsourcing leads to greater specialisation in the production of these services, with resulting gains in efficiency and reduced costs, it could stimulate a larger total demand for these services and therefore create employment. For example, outsourcing of security services could make the services more cost effective and therefore encourage a greater volume of demand. An important aspect of cost effectiveness is that the service can be discontinued or contracted on a reduced scale in difficult times. The present legal provisions introduce a disincentive to expansion of contractual services because enterprises can freely outsource those services which do not have to be performed on the premises (e.g. laundry) but for those services which are of a regular nature and have to be performed on the premises (e.g. waiters serving in workers canteens, cleaning, gardening, watch and ward services, loading and unloading etc.) employers outsourcing these services run the risk that the labour used in such services may be treated as contract labour, and may have to be absorbed permanently on the payroll. This obviously discourages employers from using such services to the extent that they otherwise might have done, with the net effect of reducing total employment. Alternatively, they are forced to resort to the expedient of insisting on frequent violation of staff so that none of the staff deputed to the unit serve for the minimum period when they can claim permanent status.

7.22 The Contract Labour (Regulation and Abolition) Act therefore needs to be suitably amended to allow all peripheral activities to be freely outsourced from specialised firms, even if it means employees of the specialised firms provide the services on the premises of the outsourcing units. The legitimate interests of workers engaged in these activities should be protected by defining minimum responsibilities of the outsourcing employer for health and safety of the workers employed on his/her premises while relying on extension of appropriate labour regulation to the companies or contractors from which these services are obtained to protect other rights of such labour.

iii) Trade Unions Act 1926

7.23 The Trade Unions Act 1926 allows any seven workers in an enterprise to form a trade union and register it. This has led to a multiplicity of unions which makes collective bargaining more difficult. It can also become a device on the part of employers to "divide and rule". It would be desirable to modify the Act and specify that at least 10% of the workers in an enterprise or 100 employees, whichever is less are necessary to form and register a union.

7.24 At present, the Trade Unions Act allows half the number of trade union office bearers to be outsiders. It is said that this does not encourage the development of internal union leadership which is more likely to be accountable and responsible. There is a case for amending Section 22 of the Act to reduce the number of outside officer bearers.

3. Parallel Reforms Needed in Other Areas

7.25 One of the problems in pressing for labour market reforms is the political sensitivity associated with anything that may be viewed as "anti-labour". In our view, far from being anti-labour, the proposed reforms will have the effect of expanding employment in the organised sector thus extending the many benefits that at present accrue only to labour in the organised sector to a much larger proportion of the working population. We have noted earlier in this report that expansion in the share of organised sector employment should be an important objective of the employment strategy and it may not be possible to achieve this objective unless labour laws are made more flexible.

7.26 Apart from building consensus on the potentially beneficial effect of reform of the labour laws it is also necessary to view labour law reform as an integral part of a broader package which will put pressure on both management and labour to increase efficiency and productivity, without which we cannot achieve our growth and employment objectives. In this context, it may be noted that some of the reforms in the product markets which are needed to put pressure on managements have already been implemented, e.g. increasing competition in domestic market and opening the economy to foreign trade. However, these need to be supplemented by reforms in the area of recovery of bank debts, bankruptcy procedures and corporate governance, all of which would put management under greater pressure to perform.

7.27 A market economy seeking high levels of efficiency must be able to put pressure on managements to improve efficiency and reduce costs, and impose penalties on those that are non-performing. Unfortunately the Indian financial and legal system does not achieve this objective. The lack of an effective system for enforcing recovery of debts through speedy bankruptcy procedures, with mechanisms that would allow inefficient firms failing to service loans to be speedily liquidated or taken over by new management. The present legal framework, consisting of the Sick Industrial Companies Act under which sick companies are referred to the BIFR, was originally designed to provide sick companies with assistance to allow them to restructure and be rehabilitated thus forestalling closure and loss of employment. It has proved to be almost completely ineffective. It has often provided unscrupulous managements with an extended period during which all recovery action is stayed and the time gained in the process is often used to siphon funds out of sick companies making them unrevivable. This ensures that companies that run into difficulties are inevitably driven into terminal sickness. At times promoters may even perceive a benefit in pushing a company into sickness.

7.28 We recommend that SICA be repealed and replaced by a new law modeled on the US Chapter 11 procedure under which default on debt payments due can trigger action by creditors. Promoters would then be given a minimum time period to negotiate a voluntary financial restructuring with creditors or bring in new capital or management, failing which creditors should be able to enforce speedy closure. It could be stipulated in the above process that dues of the workers would be fully discharged before effecting closure. This would introduce much needed market discipline on promoters which is visibly lacking today. It would also make it much easier to accept the need for labour market reforms as part of a balanced package in which both labour and management are seen as accepting the compulsion of the shift to a more competitive situation.

7.29 Another issue that has to be addressed in parallel with efforts at labour market reforms is the need for a social safety net in the form of unemployment compensation or insurance in the event of retrenchment. Industrialised countries, and even some developing countries, are able to provide employers with greater flexibility to hire and fire labour precisely because labour retrenched in the process of restructuring has the benefit of unemployment insurance.

7.30 A move to a system of unemployment insurance in the organised sector is in our view a desirable institutional development which should be expedited. The scheme should be strictly self-financing, based on compulsory deductions of contributions from wages, with a corresponding contribution from the employer and involving no liability on the part of the government. Employees retrenched or otherwise becoming unemployed should become eligible to receive support at a fraction (say 50%) of the wages drawn at the point of unemployment. The period for which such support would be available would depend upon the length of contributory service of the employee and the age. The extent of the contribution to be made by the workman and the employer for the effective functioning of such a scheme would have to be worked out on an actuarial basis. The employers contribution would be a tax on labour employed by them but it would give employers a degree of flexibility which they do not have at present.

7.31 It is important to emphasise that an unemployment insurance scheme of the type described above should be financed entirely from contributions by the employed and employers and it would also have to be compulsory. It would require statutory authority to introduce and would have to be regulated by the Government or some other suitable statutory agency. The feasibility of introducing such a scheme in the organised sector should be expeditiously examined.

8

Summary of Recommendations

The strategy for employment generation recommended by the Task Force is based on intervention in five major areas:

- Accelerating the rate of growth of GDP, with a particular emphasis on sectors likely to ensure the spread of income to the low income segments of the labour force.
- Pursuing appropriate sectoral policies in individual sectors which are particularly important for employment generation. These sector level policies must be broadly consistent with the overall objective of accelerating GDP growth.
- Implementing focused special programmes for creating additional employment of enhancing income generation from existing activities aimed at helping vulnerable groups that may not be sufficiently benefited by the more general growth promoting policies.
- Pursuing suitable policies for education and skill development, which would upgrade the quality of the labour force and make it capable of supporting a growth process which generates high quality jobs.
- Ensuring that the policy and legal environment governing the labour market encourages labour absorption, especially in the organized sector.

The individual recommendations for action in each of these areas presented in Chapters 3 to 7 are summarised below :

1. Policies for Accelerating Growth

8.2 Continuation of economic growth at an average of about 6.5% will not yield a significant improvement in the employment situation, especially the extent of open unemployment. The expected annual addition to the labour force is about 8.7 million per year over the next ten years. We need to accelerate GDP growth to a range between 8% and 9% to achieve our objective of generating enough additional employment to provide productive employment opportunities for the expansion and to ensure a sufficient tightening of labour markets in general to improve the quality of existing employment.

Increasing Aggregate Investment

8.3 To accelerate GDP growth to 8% and more requires a combination of a substantial increase in the rate of investment and an increase in efficiency of capital use (i.e., a reduction in ICORs). The rate of investment will have to be raised by at least 4.5 percentage points of GDP. This has to be financed by some combination of an increase in domestic savings and an increase in the foreign resource inflow.

8.4 Expanded levels of foreign direct investment could yield an additional 1.5 percentage points of GDP. The remaining 3 percentage points of GDP would have come from increased domestic savings. Since public sector savings have has deteriorated by this amount over the 1990s an increase in public sector savings of this order must be attempted.

8.5 The proposed improvement in public savings will require concerted efforts at reducing the revenue deficit in both the Centre and the States. This will require action on improving tax revenue realisation, reducing subsidies and raising user charges, trimming the government bureaucracy and eliminating losses in public sector enterprises by closing down loss making public sector enterprises or handing them over to the private sector. These are difficult decisions but we cannot expect the increase required in public savings if action is not taken.

8.6. The fiscal measures described above can be expected to have a negative effect on private savings as a percentage of GDP because they will reduce private disposable income but private consumption may not fall by the same amount. Private savings are therefore likely to be lower than they otherwise would be. Special efforts will therefore be needed to ensure that the private savings rate is maintained as a percentage of GDP, which implies an increase in private savings as a percentage of disposable income. It is particularly important to encourage long term contractual savings by the household sector. Reforms in the insurance sector are particularly important for this purpose.

Increasing Efficiency

8.7. The proposed acceleration in GDP growth cannot be achieved by the increase in investment envisaged above unless efficiency in all sectors is simultaneously increased. The most effective instrument to ensure efficiency is competition, which in today's world must be both domestic and international.

8.8. The reforms implemented since 1991 have created an environment where competition is much freer. However the process is still incomplete and needs to be extended to many sectors where controls are still extensive e.g. sugar, pharmaceuticals, dairying, coal mining etc.

8.9 The progress made thus far in opening the economy to international competition is commendable but it remains incomplete because of relatively high import tariffs. The process must be carried to its logical conclusion to achieve the stated target of lowering our import tariffs to the levels prevailing in East Asia over a three year period. The phased plan for tariff reduction promised in the Budget Speech should be released for discussion by September 2001.

Infrastructure Development

8.10 The state of our infrastructure is a critical constraint on our ability to achieve faster GDP growth. Our rural areas lack basic economic and social infrastructure for agricultural and other rural development e.g. a well functioning system for irrigation and water management and conservation, rural roads to provide basic connectivity, a reliable extension service to disseminate best agricultural practices, and adequate and reliable supply of electric power. Most of the infrastructure development in rural areas will have to come from the public sector and is therefore critically dependent on improvements in the fiscal position, especially of the States.

8.11 Infrastructure for the rest of the economy including power, roads, ports, railways and telecommunication also needs massive improvement to support 8% growth. It is possible to attract private investment in some of these areas. Given the severe resource constraints in the public sector, it is essential to evolve policies which will encourage public-private partnership in these areas. However the difficulty in devising the right policy framework for attracting private investment should not be under-estimated.

Finance and Banking

8.12. The development of a strong financial sector, encompassing both commercial banking and the capital markets, is a critical pre-condition for achieving rapid growth. The cost of credit from the banking system is still quite high with real interest rates varying between 6% and 10%. Much of this is not due to the inefficiency of intermediation but because of the high rates which banks have to pay for mobilizing deposits. This reflects the pressure on domestic interest rates arising from the high fiscal deficit and reduction in the fiscal deficit is therefore essential to move to lower interest rates.

8.13 There is also considerable room for improving the efficiency of the banking system. Competition among all categories of banks, including public sector banks, Indian private sector banks and foreign banks will lead to an improvement in the quality of banking sector services and this competition needs to be encouraged by following suitably liberal bank licensing policies which will allow qualified private banks (Indian and foreign) to expand their presence.

8.14 The banking system does not effectively service the needs of the informal sector and yet this sector is expected to provide much of the expansion in employment expected over the next ten years. Banking practices and procedures need to be reviewed to enable banks to adopt a more pro-active approach to lending for economically viable activities in the informal sector. The cooperative credit structure can play a major role in extending credit to the informal sector. This structure has become very weak in most States and there is an urgent need to strengthen the cooperative credit system. This may require legislative changes, which would free cooperatives from what at present is pervasive government control.

8.15 An important mechanism through which banks can meet the credit needs of the informal sector is by financing self-help groups (SHGs), which provide micro-credit for informal sector activities. Significant progress has been made in this area in recent years and the effort needs to be extended.

2. Sectoral Policies for Employment Promotion

Agriculture and Allied Activities

8.16 There is an urgent need to increase public investment in agriculture especially in irrigation and water management. The ability to do so is severely constrained by resource availability at the state level. Part of the solution lies in bringing about a general improvement in the resources position of the States. However this can be supplemented by restructuring the existing allocation of resources to agriculture by reducing subsidies and increasing user charges, (e.g. in power, irrigation and fertiliser) and devoting the resources thus mobilised to increasing public investment in this sector.

8.17 There is an urgent need to extend the benefit of decontrol to agriculture.

- The Essential Commodities Act should be repealed.
- Restrictions on marketing of agricultural produce through Agricultural Produce Marketing Committee (APMC) should be removed as they act as an impediment to development of a national market.
- Forward trading should be allowed in agricultural products.

8.18 Present laws regarding leasing of land should be liberalised to allow marginal land owners to lease out land to others to create operationally viable holdings. Degraded and wasteland, after detailed delimitation, can be taken out of the purview of tenancy laws and agro-companies allowed to buy, develop, cultivate and sell this land.

8.19 Agricultural exports are typically labour intensive, and their potential has not been adequately exploited in the past. Steps are needed to increase agricultural exports to support the diversification of agriculture, which is an important element in achieving faster agricultural growth in future. Export controls on agricultural products should be abolished and other instruments used to achieve domestic price objectives which are sought to be achieved through export controls.

Food Processing

8.20 Development of this sector is an ideal way to diversify the rural economy and expand high quality employment in non-agricultural sector. The generalised improvements in infrastructure such as assured electric power in rural areas, better road connectivity etc, discussed earlier will help this sector. In addition, the following sector specific policy initiatives are required.

i) The active involvement of larger industrial units, including MNCs and cooperatives where possible is essential. This is because successful food processing requires establishment of a chain from marketing at the one end to farming at the other. Major national and international food processing companies should be approached to ascertain the nature of the problems which limit their activities at present.

ii) There is a multiplicity of regulations related to food processing which needs to be integrated into a single Food Act and a single Food Regulatory Authority.

iii) An urgent review of the Prevention of Food Adulteration Act is required as its administration is extremely restrictive to the growth of this sector.

iv) Government should focus on R&D, information dissemination and development of rural industrial estates like food parks.

Small Scale Industry

8.21 SSI is an important source of employment as well as an important incubator for entrepreneurship. However, the objective of healthy development of this sector at this stage requires a shift in policy from protection to promotion. Some of the general policy measures needed for faster growth especially improvement in infrastructure, banking services or labour law reforms are crucial for the development of the small scale sector. In addition, the following policy support measures are especially important :

i) The benefits currently given to Small Scale industries should be extended to small scale enterprises in non-industrial sector, including those in services.

ii) Government should provide resources aimed at upgrading infrastructure for industry clusters where there is sufficient agglomeration of SSI units. A Centrally sponsored scheme for this purpose could be considered.

iii) State Governments must take concerted steps in consultation with industry representatives, to reduce the burden of inspector raj on small scale enterprises

8.22 The policy of reservation for SSI production only cannot be sustained in the face of the new import regime and the proposed lowering of tariffs. It is, therefore, necessary to implement a phased process of de-reservation which can be completed over the next four years. A scheme for such a phased dereservation is outlined in para 4.33 of the Report.

Employment in Services Sector

8.23 Almost 70% of the total employment opportunities generated over the next ten years is likely to be in the services sector. Some of the sector policy issues which constrain growth of services in critical sectors where growth could lead to faster growth in employment and improvement in the quality of employment are mentioned below in brief.

Travel and Tourism

8.24 India's potential for both domestic and international tourism is greatly under-utilised. Expansion in international tourism could contribute a substantial expansion in high quality employment opportunities in the years ahead. The following policy initiatives are especially important from the point of view of developing tourism :

i) Hotel room capacity in major Indian tourist centres (especially of the mid-price variety) is not adequate to support an expanded flow of tourists. Local authorities must take steps to earmark available land for hotel construction and expedite grant of necessary permissions for setting up of good quality hotels with reasonable price.

ii) Existing policy on bilateral air agreements needs to be urgently reviewed to ensure sufficient expansion in airline seat capacity to India. This capacity should not be limited by Air India's inability to utilise its bilateral rights.

iii) Combined effects of luxury tax and expenditure tax on hotels makes Indian hotels unduly expensive. These taxes need to be moderated

iv) Visa regime needs to be liberalised to allow tourists to obtain a tourist visa on arrival at the airport, as is the practice in many important tourist destinations.

Information Technology

8.25 Information Technology holds out very promising prospects for creation of high quality employment for skilled workers in software development and in a wide range of IT enabled services. The current slowdown in the IT sector is a negative short term development, but it should not weigh too heavily in evaluating medium term prospects. Government policy must give high priority to ensure that the environment facing this sector remains conducive to growth. High quality telecommunications and domestic and international connectivity with adequate band width is critical.

8.26 The government should continuously monitor developments in this sector and especially our performance against those of our emerging competitors internationally, to identify constraints in our competitiveness and the need for policy modifications if any.

Housing and Real Estate Development and Construction

8.27 Real Estate development, because of the construction activity it involves, is one of the most labour using sectors and can generate a large number of work opportunities. However, laws governing land development and rent control have pushed the market underground and restricted growth of this sector. The repeal of the urban land ceiling Act is a welcome step. However, State Governments must also follow the action of Central Government to free the land market. The Rent Control Act constitutes another major disincentive to construction of property for rent. Repeal of this Act is likely to unleash a construction boom.

8.28 The basic legislative steps mentioned above, would have to be accompanied by other policy reforms such as :

i) Ending the monopoly of urban development authorities like DDA over city land

ii) Freedom of conversion of rural land into urban usage

iii) Laws to facilitate private development of townships and Estates

iv) Reduction in Stamp duty on transfer of property

v) In the construction sector, present bias against large construction firms should be removed

Road Transport

8.29 The road transport sector, at present, is dominated by small operators. This is a sector where considerable economies of scale exists. Emergence of modern and large transport companies will not only improve the efficiency of the sector but also provide better working conditions to the workers in this sector and in associated road side activities like repair services and hotels etc.

8.30 Development of high quality roads and establishment of mechanised truck terminals are necessary to make this possible Also, the system of granting licenses and permits by State governments and the tax system to which road transport is subjected to needs to be reviewed as these militate against the development of an organised trucking industry.

Distributive Trade

8.31 Retail trade in India is characterised by small establishments and modernising retail trade involving large department stores is often considered detrimental to the employment objective. This may not be necessarily true The switch to modern retailing will certainly improve the quality of employment in the sector. It will also help to develop effective supply chains linking producers with potential consumers and provide quick feedback to producers on consumer tastes. This can bring many potential producers into the market without having to worry about marketing their output.

8.32 Distorted rental markets, ban on FDI in this sector and certain other regulations such as Essential Commodities Act have held back the development of modern retailing. Legislative changes in these areas recommended in the Report will help remove these barriers.

Education and Health Services

8.33 There is considerable scope for expansion of employment in provision of these services. Though much of the expansion is expected to come from public sector, there is also room to consider a combination of public and private sector. The experience of Kerala clearly demonstrates the role private sector can play in improving the reach of educational facilities. State Governments should encourage the role of private sector by replacing controls with a modern regulatory system that provides right atmosphere for private participation.

New Emerging Services

8.34 In addition to service sector activities discussed above, a host of new activities are likely to gain significance in future which will provide new opportunities for employment. An illustrative list of such services is given in the Appendix to chapter 4.

3. The Role Of Special Employment Programmes

8.35 Special employment programmes play an important role in providing supplementary employment to vulnerable sections of the population, especially in the seasonal lean period in rural areas. This helps in mitigating extreme poverty, and also to keep rural to urban migration under check. We, therefore, recommend that these schemes should continue, but their limitations as revealed in numerous evaluation should also be appreciated.

8.36 The functioning of the self-employment component in the restructured SGSY programme needs to be re-oriented as much as possible towards programmes supporting self-help groups with the assistance of NGOs with a good track record. Until there is clear evidence that the traditional IRDP type assistance produces results, it may not be desirable to expand the resources devoted to these types of schemes.

8.37 In view of the likely expansion in educated new entrants in the labour force in future, and the fact that self-employment has to play a major role in providing employment opportunities for this group, an expansion of PMRY scheme is desirable. However the provision of subsidy in such schemes is much less important than is generally made out. What is essential is that credit should be available to finance viable projects and that there should be effective means of training and providing advice on technology and marketing.

8.38 The KVIC programme needs to be restructured. The khadi programme suffers from some basic infirmities; costs are high and the product at the lower end of the quality range is not able to compete with mill-produced fabric available in the market. The village industries component however appears to have better prospects.

8.39 The recently launched REGP programme of KVIC, which is operated through the commercial banks, benefits from better financial supervision, and the production units are managed by entrepreneurs, as distinct from social workers. It therefore promises to offer a higher level of earnings per worker than in the erstwhile form of the KVIC programme. However, an objective evaluation of performance will be possible only after 2 to 3 years.

8.40 Wage employment programmes should be focused as much as possible on maximizing the development impact on rural areas through the creation of durable assets in the area of economic and social infrastructure. The restructuring of JGSY to give primacy to the creation of durable assets is therefore a step in the right direction. There is an urgent need to invest in such infrastructure, as the existing deficiencies in infrastructure especially in rural areas are glaring, and given the scarcity of resources it is desirable to use available resources for such investments even if the direct employment created is slightly lower. We would also recommend that in view of the fact that EAS has been universalized to all districts, there is merit in merging the EAS and the JGSY into a single employment programme in which funds devolve to panchayats.

8.41 Our ability to expand the total volume of resources devoted to special employment programmes in the years ahead will be limited because resources are severely constrained and there are several other demands on the system. Besides, a large expansion of the size of these programmes is difficult to justify given the mixed experience thus far. We would recommend that an independent assessment of the impact of these programmes as recently restructured should be commissioned by the Planning Commission before there is any increase in total resource allocation. Pending such a review, the total resources devoted to these programmes should be held constant at current levels though resources could be shifted from programmes perceived to be less effective to those perceived to be non effective on the basis of current monitoring and evaluations.

4. Labour Force Skills and Training

8.42 The system of specialised higher technical education needs to be strengthened if our technical manpower is to avail of the opportunities in the international labour market. I.I.Ts have demonstrated the capability of our manpower, if screened properly and then trained. I.I.Ts should be established in the each state. A role to private sector should be provided. Restrictions in the existing policy on charging of fees should be removed.

8.43 The present system of vocational training is inadequate to meet the skill requirements of rapid growth. A broad based effort is needed to reform the system. The existing ITI system will need to be restructured and additional resources provided to improve its output. Industry should be involved to a much greater extent in the management of ITIs and for this purpose, selected ITIs chosen for joint management with industry should be converted into autonomous bodies receiving government funds with a management structure in which industry representatives can be formally inducted on the governing boards and the institutions are also given sufficient autonomy to become effectively board managed.

8.44 It is necessary to review the present policy whereby training in Government ITIs has traditionally been provided free. It may be desirable to allow ITIs to charge fees, at least for the more specialised courses. A case can also be made for considering a small levy on companies to be contributed to a skill development fund which could be used to fund ITIs. The coverage of the levy, its amount and guidelines for the use of the fund would have to be worked out. To make industry perceive the benefits of the fund, 2/3rd of the collection in each district should be used to fund ITIs in the district. Industry associations should also have a voice in deciding allocations.

8.45 A Centrally sponsored scheme or an aid institution like the UGC should be set up for the ITI's. Barring certain exceptions, the ITI's have a physical environment, which is much inferior to the engineering college, diploma awarding polytechnics and the medical colleges. For the latter, there are UGC type schemes for up-gradation of buildings and equipments and even to run special training courses. Some parallel mechanism is needed for ITIs.

8.46 The problem of lack of demand for vocational training relative to higher level education, could be mitigated if graduates of ITIs and other vocational training institutions are eligible for entry into polytechnics and +2 level medical and engineering courses. Entry criteria and course curriculum should be redesigned for this purpose.

8.47 Development of entrepreneurship skills among the new self employed require "Mentors". Under the CII's entrepreneurship development project viz., Bhartiya Yuva Shakti Trust, the loan recovery rate is 94%, indicating strong economic viability. Such experiments need to be replicated on a much larger scale.

8.48 All enterprise, irrespective of size and status, small industries and tiny enterprises should be brought under the purview of Apprentices Act. However the payment of stipend to apprentices taken in by small establishments should be voluntary, and not mandatory, under the Apprentices Act. The law should also be amended to remove any obligation to provide employment to apprentices or even to give them preference.

8.49 The Department of Technical Education should be restructured to focus on vocational education and vocational training. A parallel institution is needed in State Governments to focus on vocational education in schools. At State Government level, Vocational Education, Vocational Training and Technical Education should be the responsibility of a single Department.

8.50 Private sector involvement in training has been discouraged because of highly subsidized training services provided by the public sector. There is also an undesirable nexus between public owned training delivery institutions and placement for jobs in public sector, excessive regulation in extending recognition to the institutions. This should change.

8.51 The Central Government should completely withdraw from delivery of vocational training services. It should foster autonomous professional bodies that give recognition to training institutes by declaring them as eligible training providers. The Government's role should be one of monitoring the institutions that set up standards of training, and evaluating and assigning rating to the private training establishments.

5. Reform of Labour Laws

8.52 India's labour laws have evolved in a manner which has greatly reduced the flexibility available to employers to adjust the labour force in the light of changing economic circumstances. In a globalised world, persisting with labour laws that are much more rigid than those prevailing in other countries only makes us uncompetitive not only in export markets but also in domestic markets. Some changes in the laws are therefore necessary if we want to see rapid growth.

8.53 The most important change needed is to abolish the requirement of prior permission of government for retrenchment, lay-offs or closure by deleting Chapter VB from the Industrial Disputes Act. This would restore the position to that prevailing prior to 1976. As a balancing measure, to improve protection of labour, the retrenchment compensation should be increased from ½ months pay per year of service to one months pay per year of service. This was recommended in 1992 by the Inter-Ministerial Working Group on Industrial Restructuring and subsequently also by the Committee on Industrial Sickness (1993).

8.54 The following other changes are also recommended:

- The provisions regarding dismissal after due process need to be streamlined. Section 11A of the Industrial Disputes Act which allows labour courts, Industrial Tribunals to interpose the state in matters that are best left to established internal processes.
- A system of short term employment contracts should be introduced under which workers hired on contract basis can be terminated at the end of the contract period without scope for dispute. In order to avoid legal challenge to this arrangement on the grounds of equal treatment with permanent labour doing the same job, provisions can be made for paying such labour a premium over the normal wage.
- The Industrial Disputes Act should be amended to make a reasonable notice mandatory in all cases. It would also be desirable to introduce the system of "strike ballot" whereby a strike can be called only if it is supported by a qualifying majority of the workers.
- At present there is no time limit for filing disputes under the Industrial Disputes Act. This encourages piling up of old disputes leading to delays in courts. A time limit of 3 years should be stipulated within which a dispute could be referred for adjudication.
- The Contract Labour (Regulation and Abolition) Act needs to be suitably amended to allow all peripheral activities to be freely outsourced from specialised firms, even if it means employees of the specialised firms provide the services on the premises of the outsourcing units.

APPENDIX

TASK FORCE ON EMPLOYMENT OPPORTUNITIES

The Task Force on Employment Opportunities was set up by the Planning Commission in January, 1999 vide Notification No. P-12099/15/98/LEM/ERS dated 21 January, 1999 under the chairmanship of Shri. Montek Singh Ahluwalia, Member, Planning Commission. Following are the terms of reference of the Task Force:

(i) To examine the existing employment and unemployment situation in the country.

(ii) To suggest strategies of employment generation for achieving the target of providing employment opportunities to ten crore people over the next ten years implying strategies for providing employment opportunities to one crore people per year on an average

(iii) To consider any other matter related with or incidental to the above Terms of Reference.

II. Members of the Task Force were notified as under:

Prof. Pravin Visaria, *Director*, Institute of Economic Growth, University Enclave, New Delhi; **Prof. Nirmala Banerjee**, Centre for Studies in Social Sciences, 10, lake Terrace, Calcutta; **Prof. K. Sundaram**, Delhi School of Economics, University of Delhi, New Delhi; **Prof. Subhashish Gangopadhyay**, Indian Statistical Institute, 7, S.J.S Sansanwal Marg, New Delhi; **Prof. S. Mahendra Dev**, Indira Gandhi Institute of Development Research, Gen. Vaidya Marg, Goregaon (E), Mumbai; **Secretary General**, FICCI, Federation House, Tansen Marg, New Delhi; **Director General**, Confederation of Indian Industries, 23, Institutional Area, Lodhi Road, New Delhi; **Secretary**, Department of Small Scale & Agro & Rural Industries, Udyog Bhavan, New Delhi; **Secretary**, Ministry of Labour, Shram Shakti Bhavan, Rafi Marg, New Delhi-110 001; **Secretary**, Department of Rural Employment & Poverty Alleviation, Krishi Bhavan, New Delhi; **Sr. Economic Adviser**, Department of Economic Affairs, Ministry of Finance, North Block, New Delhi; **Adviser** (LEM), (Member-Convener) Planning Commission, New Delhi-110 001

III. The Task Force invited in all its deliberations the following:

Dr. S. P. Gupta, *Member*, Planning Commission, New Delhi;

Prof. S. R. Hashim (upto February 2000), *Member* (Rural Development), Planning Commission, New Delhi; **Dr. N.C. Saxena**, *Secretary*, Planning Commission, New Delhi; **Shri R. P. Sinha**, *Pr. Adviser* (LEM), Planning Commission, New Delhi; **Prof. Ashoka Chandra**, *the then Director*, IAMR, New Delhi; **The Registrar General of India**, Office of the RGI, New Delhi and benefited from their perception of nature of employment problem.

IV. The Task Force set up the following Sub Groups:

	Sub Groups on	Chairman	Convenor ....
1.	Labour Force & Employment Projection	Prof. Pravin Visaria Director, IEG	Smt. Padmaja Mehta Director (LEM) Planning Commission
2.	Skill Development & Training	Prof. Ashoka Chandra Director, IAMR	Shri R.P. Upadhyay Joint Adviser (LEM) Planning Commission
3.	Special employment Programme	Prof. S. R. Hashim Member (RD) Planning Commission	Smt. Padmaja Mehta Director (LEM) Planning Commission
4.	Sectoral Policies	Dr. Amit Mitra Secretary General FICCI	Shri T.S. Krishnan Director (LEM) Planning Commission

V. The deliberations of the Task Force were formulated at the following meetings:

1st Meeting	16th February, 1999
2nd Meeting	26th April, 1999
3rd Meeting	13th July, 1999
4th Meeting	11th August, 1999
5th Meeting	11th October, 1999
6th Meeting	28th January, 2000
7th Meeting	12th September, 2000
8th & Final Meeting	24th May, 2001

VI. The eighth and final meeting of the Task Force authorised the Chairman to submit the report of the Task Force to Deputy Chairman, Planning Commission.

Report of the Steering Committee on Labour and Employment for the 10th Five Year Plan (2002-2007)

CONTENTS

1

Background

In the context of the preparation for the Tenth Five Year Plan (2002-07), a Steering Group on Labour and Employment was constituted under the Chairpersonship of Dr. S.P. Gupta, Member, Planning Commission with the following terms of references :

- *To review the projections of labour force and employment made by various studies and* agencies to firm up State-wise figures of projections of labour force and work opportunities that should from the basis of 10 h Plan exercise.
- To project State-wise unemployment among educated youth and suggest the strategies for providing work opportunities to the entrants to labour force.
- To take an overview of the existing framework of the Labour Policy and Social Security measures and to suggest appropriate strategy in the context of emerging needs of the market oriented economy so as to ensure healthy employer-employee relations and promote productivity.
- To review the role of Government in Labour relations with respect to workers in Public Sector and Government Sector.
- To propose a strategy to reduce the gap with regard to administered social security system and welfare measures between the organized and unorganized labour
- To review programmes for labour welfare so as to suggest a broad-based social security system for the labour and the unorganized self-employed persons.

- To suggest appropriate programmes for promoting occupational health and safety for the workers
- Any other issue concerning labour and employment policy, with the consent of Chairman of the Steering Committee

2. The Steering Committee has also set up 6 Working Groups to look into the various matters relating to labour, labour welfare and employment, in detail, in the Tenth Plan (2002-07):

i) Working Group on Employment, Planning and Policy.

ii) Working Group on Skill Development and Training;

iii) Working Group on Occupational Safety and Health;

iv) Working Group on Social Security;

v) Working Group on Labour Laws and Other Labour Regulations

vi) Working Group on Vulnerable Groups in Labour Force such as Child Labour, Bonded Labour, Migrant Labour, etc.; and

3 The Steering Committee met 4 times and deliberated upon the report of the Working Groups and their recommendations. Taking into consideration the suggestions and recommendations of the Working Groups, the Steering Committee prepared its final report and the same is presented below:

2

Employment :

Planning and Policies In the Tenth Plan

Labour Force and Employment Projections

The Steering Committee on Labour and Employment for the 10th Five Year Plan (2002-2007) would adopt the employment projections from the "Special Group on Targeting 10 Million Employment Opportunities per year over the 10th Plan Period." The Special Group under the Chairmanship of Dr. S.P. Gupta, Member, Planning Commission is using Current Daily Status (CDS) basis of employment as defined by the National Sample Survey Organization (NSSO) for estimating employment opportunities in the 10th Plan. The difference in the magnitude of unemployment is considerable if CDS and UPSS bases are compared. As per CDS concept, about 26.58 million person years are estimated as unemployed on an average working day in the year 1999-2000 (NSS 55th round). Incidence of unemployment on CDS basis is estimated at 7.3% in 1999-2000 in the country. Incidence of unemployment on CDS basis in 1993-94 (50th round) was estimated at 6%. Compared to 2.2% unemployment rate on Usual Principal and Subsidiary Status (UPSS) basis in 1999-2000, incidence of unemployment on CDS basis at 7.3% in 1999-2000 is very high.

Concept of Usual Principal Status (UPS) has been used in 8th Plan. Concept of Usual Principal and Subsidiary Status (UPSS) has been used in 9th Plan. However, UPSS has been criticized as most liberal approach because a large number of underemployed are included in the definition of employed in this concept. Current Daily Status (CDS) approach includes underemployed in the number of unemployed. In the 10th Plan, where gainful employment has been considered one of the primary objectives, CDS concept is considered better because it not only captures the unemployed persons but also captures underemployed to some extent. CDS is closer to the real situation prevalent in the country on unemployment. It is also closer to the level of poverty in the country.

State wise estimates of employment and unemployment are not compiled so far. State wise projections of labour force require age wise projections of population for the 10th Plan period. Technical Group constituted by Registrar General for the projections of population has not submitted its report so far. In the absence of State wise and age wise distribution of population, projections of labour force is difficult Similarly state wise projection of employment opportunities is difficult without projections of state wise Gross Domestic Product (GDP) by different sectors of the economy, which is being worked by the Planning Commission. So far Planning Commission has circulated projections of GDP for a few sectors only. For the purpose of projections of employment opportunities, projections for at least nine sectors are required.

For labour force projection, the available technical group projection on population has been used. Technical Group on Projection of Population has submitted its report in 1996. The results are a bit old now. As mentioned in the earlier paragraph, the new Technical Group formed under RGI is still working on its report. In the mean time, a set of alternative population and labour force projections to be used in the formulation of the 10th Plan are being worked out separately. The present projection on labour force will be replaced with the information on labour force obtained from the above committee whenever it is available.

Past trends for labour force, employment and unemployment are given in Table 1 for on CDS basis and Table 2 for on UPSS basis.

Table – 1

Estimates by Current Daily Status

(in million person years)

Estimated Persons	1983	1987-88	1993-94	1999-2000
Labour Force(in million)	261.33	290.50	335.98	363.33
Employed (in million)	239.56	272.32	315.84	336.75
Unemployment Rate* (%)	8.28	6.09	5.99	7.32
Number of Unemployed (in million)	21.77	18.18	20.14	26.58

* As percentage to labour force.

Table – 2

Estimates by Usual Principal & Subsidiary Status

(in million person years)

Estimated Persons	1983	1987-88	1993-94	1999-2000
Labour Force(in million)	308.63	333.49	381.46	406.85
Employed (in million)	302.75	324.29	374.27	397.88
Unemployment Rate* (%)	1.90	2.62	1.89	2.20
Number of Unemployed (in million)	5.88	9.20	7.19	8.97

* As percentage to labour force

Projections for Labour force, Employment and Unemployment on Current Daily Basis for the 10th Plan is estimated subject to all these limitations and is presented in the Table below. This is based on actual elasticity obtained during 1993-94 and 1999-2000.

Projections for Labour force, Employment and Unemployment on Current Daily Status (CDS) Basis

(in million person years)

	1999-2000	2001$	2002$	2007**
Labour force (1.8% p.a. growth)	363.33	371.52	378.21	413.50
Employment	336.75	340.82	343.36	373.03
Unemployment rate(%)	7.32	8.26	9.21	9.79
No. of Unemployed	26.58	30.70	34.85	40.47

* As on Ist April

** Based on 8% Growth in GDP during 2002-07

$ Based on 5.2% GDP Growth during 2000-01 and 2001-02.

According to a rough estimate made by the Special Group about 5.9 million work opportunities per year will be created by growth process itself. Rest of the employment opportunities will be generated through employment programmes under various Ministries and Departments adding to 10 million person year. It is estimated that about 7.1 million additional persons are expected to join the labour force every year during the 10th Plan period (2002-07), assuming labour force growth at about 1.8% per year.

3

Policies for Employment Generation

Growth and Employment Generation

Demand for labour or generation of employment opportunities is directly linked to the process of growth in economic activities. Faster growth is, therefore, necessary to productively employ the increase in the labour force and also for improving the quality of existing employment. An employment policy, therefore, must also consider the policies required for accelerating the overall growth in the economy. Some of the issue which need attention during the Tenth Plan and which are necessary for giving a fillip to the growth process in order to achieve the target of 8%, are :

- Increase in the aggregate investment levels by approximately 5% points through
  - Additional FDI inflows
  - Domestic Savings, especially public sector savings
- Policies to promote efficiency through domestic and international competition
- Infrastructure development
- Credit for informal unorganized sector

Sectoral Policies for Employment Generation

While improvement in the overall growth performance has a direct bearing for faster and better quality employment generation, equally important is the sectoral structure of the growth. To the extent a larger share of growth can be derived from labour intensive sectors/sub-sectors/ industries, the pace of generation of employment opportunities for any given overall rate of growth can be increased. The characteristics of the different segment of the labour force in terms of their skill base, residential status, aspirations from the job etc also have implications for the sectoral structure of growth which can most suitably and productively employ the labour force. The requirements of employment opportunities to be created for among the rural unskilled labour force on the one hand and among the educated youth on the other are different and this needs to be kept in mind.

Agriculture

Approximately 60% of the work force continues to be employed, though the share has declined sharply during 1993-94 to 1999-2000. The growth of this sector is important not only to support the high growth target for the Tenth Plan but also for the attainment of employment objectives. A large proportion of the labour force in the country is illiterate and does not possess any marketable skill. The chances of this class of labour force to find a decent job outside agriculture are very less. At the most, they can migrate to urban areas and land in urban informal sector where employment conditions are not good. Further such migration puts pressure on the urban civic infrastructure, which has more often than not failed to cope with such rural to urban migration. Therefore, though we may expect that share of agriculture in the total work force will continue to decline, the sector will continue to play the role of single largest employer for the incremental labour force. It is therefore only appropriate that adequate attention is paid to scope of productive employment generation in agriculture sector.

While it is true that incidence of underemployment in agriculture is significant, it is basically due to lack of diversification in this sector and concentration on crop production. It is possible to productively employ rural labour force in activities such as development of wasteland, watershed development, forestry, animal husbandry, sericulture, horticulture & floriculture, herbal & medicinal plants etc.

Within crop production activities in the rural areas, the crucial issue is improvement in the levels of productivity. The levels of per acre productivity is at a low level compared to international experience and there are also wide inter state and inter region differences in productivity. The improvement in productivity is necessary to improve the wage of workers and earnings of the self employed. Improvement in productivity and generation of employment, however, requires investment in areas such as irrigation, water conservation, land development, drainage etc. The slowing down of the public investment in real terms in agriculture needs to be reversed and also private investment needs to be encouraged. Such investments are specially needed in regions of the country where potential of agriculture sector has largely remained unexploited due to lack of such facilities.

Agro Processing Industries

Despite being the second largest producer of fruits and vegetable in the world, the food processing industry in India has not developed to its full potential. Food processing is a high value addition activity and is also very labour intensive. The likely fruits from development of this sector in terms of employment generation, diversification of rural economy and a general improvement in the rural economy is widely known.

The exploitation of the growth potential of this sector, however, has not been possible so far due to lack of general physical infrastructure facilities like roads, assured power supply and some of the facilities like establishment of cold chains, specifically essential for the sector.

The sector as it exists today is dominated by small and traditional producers, who are not able to make even the minimum necessary investments necessary for a sustainable and profitable unit. There is a need to evolve a comprehensive package to give boost to an organised growth of Food Processing Industry in the Tenth Plan. The elements of the package must include, among other things, promotion to R & D, promotion of a formal relationship between growers of farm produce and the industry, entry of larger units in the food processing activities, credit facilities and support for marketing. The role of cooperatives in development of post harvest preservation, silos & warehouses, cold storage facilities and air conditioned transport should also be encouraged.

Small Scale Industries

Promotion of SSIs has been one of the important strategies for employment generation since the early years of planned development process. Small Units have widely been acknowledged to employ more labour per unit of capital invested. However, the ability of the sector to stand upto the competition of more open economy has recently been in question. While the modern SSIs have by and large stood the test of the time, smaller and more traditional units have been facing problems of survival in the new environment. It is essential, therefore for the traditional units, to modernise in terms of technological improvement, managerial practices and quality improvement.

International experience suggests that the cluster approach provides the most enabling environment for growth of SSI sector. Government should therefore identify areas where there exists sufficient conglomeration of small scale units for developing common facilities for technical & marketing support, credit facilities etc. Such an approach is not only economical in delivery of the services to the entrepreneurs but also takes care of many obstacles of non economic nature faced by the entrepreneurs.

Construction

Construction is one the most labour intensive sector . Also, there exists large unmet demand for housing in both rural and urban areas. The National Building Organisation the urban housing shortage at 8.23 million units in 1991. Similarly in rural areas too there are such shortages. A boost to this sector is necessary to meet the housing demand, which constitute one of the basic necessities. In the process significant employment opportunities can be generated at different skill levels, though largely for unskilled labour.

A number of steps have been taken by the Government to promote construction sector. These include fiscal incentives in terms of benefit in personal income taxation and legislative steps like repeal of Urban Land Ceiling and Regulation Act. The repeal Act has, however, not yet been adopted by all States.

There is still a lot to be done to remove the constraints which are facing the sector and which need to be addressed to promote faster growth in this sector. Some of these include :

- Ending the monopoly of urban development authorities, like DDA, over city land
- Relaxation in rules regarding land use pattern
- Modernisation of municipal laws and planning practices to provide for private investment in supply of public utilities

Travel and Tourism

While Tourism and travel is one of the fastest growing industries in the world and employs close to 11% of the global workforce, yet it has not found its appropriate place in India's development agenda. This sector has enormous potential for employment generation. In terms of international tourist arrivals India is way behind countries like China or even smaller countries such as Turkey, Thailand, Malaysia and Indonesia.

Promotion of domestic as well as international tourism can contribute to substantial expansion in productive employment. Development of tourism industry is linked to provision of necessary facilities. Some of the initiatives required to encourage the growth of the sector are:

- Development of tourist circuits, covering all the infrastructural facilities required, as one investment project and in coordination with concerned agencies. Private sector should be motivated to invest in different types of allied activities.
- Necessary changes in the existing bilateral air service agreements, which are too restrictive in granting additional seats to foreign airlines. This is necessary to introduce competition, which would lead to cut in air travel costs and improved facilities for potential international tourists.
- Increasing the supply of hotel rooms of a reasonable standard, through public and private investment.

Employment Generation in Social Sectors

There is vast scope for improvement in the reach and quality of certain services is social sector especially in rural areas, such as -

- Elementary Education Services
- Vocational Training Services
- Skill Development Services
- Basic Health Services
- Drinking Water Supply
- Basis Municipal Services

Only about 60% of the children in the age group 6-14 years are in schools and net attendance in primary school is only 66 % of the enrolment. The objective of universalizing access to primary education will huge expansion in the basic infrastructure for education. Similarly there is a need to substantially expand the vocational training facilities. The proportion of vocationally trained among youth in labour force is very low in our country. Its 5% compared to 96% in Korea, 78% in Canada, 75% in Germany and 69% in France (World Employment Report). Even in countries such as Botswana and Columbia it is much higher at 22% and 28% respectively.

The reach of the general population to basic health services and access to primary health care facilities is also very narrow. Though substantial infrastructure for health care has been created over the years, large gaps exist between the requirement and the availability of such services. The requirements for health care infrastructure like number of Primary Health Care Centre, Sub Centres, Community Health Centres etc set for the year 1991 has not been achieved. In the years since 1991 requirements must have gone up. Even the infrastructure created over the years is functioning sub optimally; shortage of critical manpower being one of the reasons behind it. Filling the infrastructural gaps in provision of health care facilities and improving the functioning of existing centres will require the trained manpower in these areas. There exists critical shortage of the specialists and paramedical staff. Social sectors like primary education and basic health care has the potential of absorbing a large number of educated manpower, if the Government is committed to universalizing their access.

The manpower planning for health sector has not received adequate attention so far. Adopting a normative approach about the requirement of manpower in these areas (by adopting ratios on requirement of such manpower for per 1000 persons in population), it is possible to arrive at some estimates of employment potential in these sectors. This is also important from the point of view of manpower planning in the sense that it gives an idea of manpower requirements of different skills vis a vis the capacity of the existing system to generate such skills in required numbers. This is one of the reasons for dearth of para medical staff. The facilities for imparting training should be created to meet the manpower requirements of health sector.

Gaps exist in many of the municipal services for the population, which need to be expanded and strengthened. The crucial point here is to channelise investment in these areas and to determine the roles of public and private sector in provision of these services.

Employment in Organised Sector

More than 90% of the employment is in unorganized sector. The level of productivity and income in case of such workers is very low. One of the reasons for predominance of unorganized sector in total employment has been the inability of the organised sector to absorb the increase in the labour force.

Due to fiscal constraints facing the Governments at all levels, the growth of jobs in public sector declined sharply during the nineties. This led to an overall decline in the rate of growth of employment in the organized sector, despite a much improved performance in organized private sector employment growth..

The process of restructuring of economy in general and also within the public sector itself precludes any possibility for growth of employment in the public sector. It is, therefore, imperative to promote the growth of organized private sector to give further boost to momentum that it has picked up in the nineties so that over time the overall share of organised sector in total employment increases. But as of now, the private organized sector cater less than 2.55% of employment for meeting the demand of the labour force, dependence has to be on the growth of the informal sector and its improvement in productivity.

The incidence of unemployment among educated youth is very high and they also constitute a very large proportion of unemployed in the country. The growth of employment in the organized sector is very crucial to deal with the problem of unemployment among the educated youth as they have a preference for jobs in the organized sector, especially in the public sector. As the scope for any substantial expansion in public sector jobs is very limited, the private organized sector is required to grow fast to absorb the educated youth in the labour force. All specialized areas of self-employment which have high education requirement should be another thrust area. In this context it would be necessary to have a fresh look at some of the interventions in the labour market though various labour regulations.

Special Programmes for Employment Generation

Special wage employment programmes serve an important objective in the current employment strategy of the Government in terms of providing relief employment to those in distress. It has another important role of creating durable assets in the areas of implementation, which supports expansion in economic activities and employment generation. The contribution of wage employment programmes in the overall employment generation can at best be marginal. The recurring expenditure made on the wage employment programmes year after year are only able to maintain the same level of employment. The constraints on resources restrict any substantial expansion in the scope and coverage of these programmes.

Huge amount of public money is being spent by the Government on recurring annual basis to support wage employment programmes. A constant monitoring of these programmes is necessary to evaluate their contribution to employment generation vis-a-vis expenditure incurred on them. The quality of durable community assets created under these programmes need be assessed and monitored constantly as they are important for the development of the area in the long run as well as employment generation.

The employment created through the self employment programmes is more sustainable. Beneficiaries under these programmes get assistance for starting up their own ventures which gives him employment on a sustainable basis. The crucial point here is identification of beneficiaries and proper project formulation.

One of the problems facing the self employment programmes is the overlap between the programmes implemented by the Governments at the Central and State level. The targeted beneficiaries in most of the programmes are common. It has been the experience in some of the States that the same set of beneficiaries are being assisted under different and often competing programmes in terms of target groups and assistance offered. This has been happening primarily because of lack of proper identification of beneficiaries under different programmes at the household level and also due to lack of proper coordination between different programme administrators. To the extent possible the duplication of efforts by running competing programmes should be avoided. Also, there should be proper identification of beneficiaries in order to ensure proper utilization of subsidized funds made available to targeted households .

The problem of over-identification, in the sense of same set of beneficiaries being assisted under overlapping programmes, can be attributed to a large extent to lack of coordination between administering agencies for different programmes. A solution to the problem lies in setting up kind of a clearing house where all the agencies implementing the special employment programmes can share information on beneficiaries assisted under respective programmes. The District Employment Officers at the district level may be entrusted with this work.

Tenth Plan Approach and Strategy

The report states one of the important objectives of the Tenth Plan and beyond is to provide gainful high quality employment to the labour force. The main approach in the Tenth Plan would be to bring about a qualitative change in the structure and pattern of employment in terms of promoting growth of good quality work opportunities.

While improvement in the overall growth performance has a direct bearing for faster and better quality employment generation, equally important is the sectoral structure of the growth. To the extent a larger share of growth can be derived from labour intensive sectors/sub-sectors/industries, the pace of generation of employment opportunities for any given overall rate of growth can be increased. The characteristics of the different segment of the labour force in terms of their skill base, residential status, aspirations from the job etc also have implications for the sectoral structure of growth which can most suitably and productively employ the labour force. The requirements of employment opportunities to be created for among the rural unskilled labour force on the one hand and among the educated youth on the other are different and this needs to be kept in mind.

Creation of good quality work opportunities would be achieved by following a growth strategy in Tenth Plan, which would lay emphasis on rapid growth of those sectors, which are likely to create high quality employment opportunities and would deal with the policy constraints which discourage growth of employment. Particular attention would be paid to the policy environment influencing a wide range of economic activities which have a large employment potential. These include sectors such as construction, financial services, real estate and housing, transport, tourism & IT, crop based agriculture and allied sectors, agro forestry, non farm rural sector including the SSI, which need to be promoted through supportive policies. Emphasis would be laid on Tourism to ensure realization of full potential of this activity.

Employment strategy in the Tenth Plan would focus on employment growth and on the qualitative aspects of employment. In order to enable the poor to access the opportunities and to ensure consistency between the requirement and availability of skills, emphasis would be placed on skill development.

Keeping in view the above broad approaches for the Employment Planning and Policy. Some of the important recommendation of the Steering Committee are the following.

Recommendations

- Private Sector as well as all elements of social groups may be encouraged to invest in infrastructure, including rural infrastructure within a well defined parameters of public-private investments.

- The efficiency in the use of available resources in agriculture needs to be substantially improved by way of encouraging investment, in general, and private sector, in particular.
- Within agricultural activities other than crop production, certain unexploited areas viz., water shed and wasteland development, forestry, horticulture and floriculture, dairy product based activities, sericulture, etc. may be promoted.
- The State Governments may be encouraged to help in arranging credit facilities to the small scale industries either from the States exchequer or through the nationalized banks and create necessary forward linkages like marketing as well as create common facilities in areas where cluster of small scale industrial units are located
- An organized growth of Agro and Rural Industries may be encouraged for adequate participation of Private Sector.
- Research and Development in the area of food processing may be strengthened.
- To generate employment for skilled and semi-skilled persons, Private Sector's participation in social services such as health, education, basic municipal services, etc. may be expanded
- The existing programmes for infrastructure which have a very high labour intensity may have explicit physical targets for employment generation which may be monitored regularly.
- Clearing house arrangement at the District level may be set up for sharing of information by the different agencies administering different special employment programmes so as to avoid duplication.
- To promote absorption of labour in organized sector, some of the labour laws may be made more flexible
- To asses employment and unemployment situation on yearly basis, annual surveys of NSSO may be strengthened.
- Labour Bureau may put effort for faster processing of

data and its quick dissemination for wider use through a specially designed web-site and other IT assisted method.

- Policy and programmes should be undertaken to improve the productivity of informal sector.
- To equip the manpower with the right skills, more emphasis may be for skill development and training.
- To bridge the gap of unemployment, emphasis may be given to self-employment programmes. Necessary steps in this regard may be initiated for awareness generation regarding the prospects of self-employment in various areas, availability of credit and marketing facilities, etc.
- To meet the demand of the educated youth, necessary strategy may be worked out to create more high-quality jobs with higher levels of income.
- To bridge the gaps in collection/analysis and dissemination of labour and employment statistics, the computer technology and networking of the Labour Bureau may be strengthened.
- To build up a data-base, the Labour Bureau may continue to have regular interaction/dialogue with the State Govts. and organize annual workshops and meetings.

4

Skill Development & Training

Skill Development refers to develop the ability to pursue any job or service. Training is a part and parcel of the skill development process. Although both appears to be two different connotation it cannot be separated from each other. There is a wider gap between the skilled personnel and availability of job in the wider spectrum of labour market. According to NSSO survey on the basis of UPSS, 397 million persons are employed at a point of time whereas the total labour force as on 1.1.2000 is 406 million. It gives an indication that about 9 million persons have open unemployment which is a major concern for skill development and training. Besides, there is a large under employed labour force as revealed on the basis of unemployment estimates on CDS basis. They also need skill so that they can get into gainful productive employment.

Present Scenario

2. The skill level and education attainment of workforce determines the productivity as well as the adoptability of the working class in changing environment. Only 5% of the Indian labour force in the age group of 20-24 has vocational skills. The literate and illiterate upto the primary level of education constitute a very high proportion of the existing work force. While the level of educational attainment of the existing work force is very low, the educated without professional skill on the other hand constitute 69% of the total unemployment. The NSSO survey carried out in 1993-94 on employment and unemployment revealed that majority of the workforce in rural and urban areas does not possesses any identifiable marketable skill. In urban areas, about 19.6% of male

and 11.2% of female workers possess marketable skills, whereas in rural areas only about 10% of male and 6.3% of female possess marketable skill. Number of job seekers registered in the employment exchanges were 44.34 million till 31.12.2000. About 80% of the job seekers in employment exchanges are without any professional skills. The growth of labour force 1993-94 to 1999-2000 was 1.03% per annum as against the growth of employment in the same period was 0.98% per annum. 7-8% of the total employed are in the organized sector where additional employment generation is not significant and scope for additional wage employment is limited.

Vocational Training – Review of the Existing Programmes - Gaps & Weaknesses

3. Vocational training being a concurrent subject, Central Government and the State Governments share responsibilities. At the national level, Director General of Employment & Training (DGE&T), Ministry of Labour is the nodal Dept. for formulating policies, laying down standards, conducting trade testing and certification, etc. in the field of vocational training. A number of training institutions are also run by the DGE&T. At the State level, the State Govt. Departments are responsible for vocational training programmes. The Central Govt. is advised by National Commission for Vocational Training (NCVT), a tripartite body, to have representatives from employers, workers and Central / State Governments.

4. Starting from 54 ITIs in 1953, the number of training institutes functioning have gone upto 4274 (1654 are in the government sector and the remaining 2620 in the private sector) with the increased sitting capacity progressively raising from 10000 to 6.28 lakhs at present. To regulate the programme of Training of Apprentices in the industry, the Apprentice Act, which was enacted in 1961, was amended from time to time. Further, to advice the Government on laying down policies and prescribing norms and standards in respect of Apprentice Training Scheme, etc. the Central Apprenticeship Council has been in operation. The scope of Apprenticeship Training needs to be enlarged by covering more occupations in emerging high-tech areas in service sector and informal sector.

5. The Apprentices Act has essentially a dual purpose to serve – firstly, to regulate the programme of training apprentices in industry so as to conform to the prescribed syllabi, period of training, etc. prescribed by the Central Apprenticeship Council and secondly, to utilize fully the facilities available in industry for workers. As on 31.3.2001, in over 17,800 public / private sector establishments were covered under the Act and number of seats located were 2.20 lakh, out of which about 1.58 lakh seats were utilized. The Craftsmen Training relate to theoretical training on any craftsmen-ship with little exposure to practical utility. To reduce unemployment among educated youth by equipping with suitable skills for industrial employment, the Craftsmen training is imparted in 43 engineering and 24 non-engineering trades. In spite of this, a large number of employment in the unorganized sector continue to get their skill development in an unorganized manner. To develop capacity and meet skill development requirement in different disciplines for the unorganized sector, private partnership need to be encouraged. Some avenues and opportunities need to be articulate in consultation with private entrepreneurs and industrialists in the form of industry institute interaction. This arrangement could be able to spell out the requirement of trained personnel in desired trade and the institute would be in a better position to provide training facilities which will suit the industrial requirement.

6. Skill development and employment services, as in the past, continued to be provided to the special needs of the Vulnerable sections like, Women, Schedule Castes/Tribes, Persons with Disabilities and disabled ex-servicemen job seekers. To provide training facilities to women in employable skills, so as to enhance their participation in the industry as skilled workers and / or to help them in acquiring skills for taking up self-employment, income-generating activities. Training facilities, exclusively for women, are being imparted through a National Vocational Training Institute (NVTI) and 10 Regional Vocational Training Institute for Women(RVTI). The present training capacities of these Institutes is 2068. In the State sector there exists a network of 231 ITIs exclusively for women. In addition, there are 534 Special Wings for Women in general ITIs with the sitting capacity of 46,750, offering Craftsmen Training in various engineering and non-engineering trades. Vocational guidance and training are being

imparted for confidence building with improved skills and ability for preparing them to face competitive examinations conducted by Staff Selection Examination, Banking Service Recruitment Board, etc. for Group 'C' and equivalent posts. To enable the disabled to become economically independent and contributed to the national economic, 17 Vocational Rehabilitation Centres for Handicapped are functioning in various parts of the country.

7. In spite of infrastructure and facility available, skill development and training in the country is highly inadequate. To substantiate this fact, it may be pointed out that every year 55 lakh of students in the country pass out of Class X and out of which 33 lakh go to Class XI and thus, 22 lakhs are left out. Another category is dropouts after Class VIII i.e. about 190 lakh who do not pursue further studies. These are the people who look around for vocational training and self-employment. Therefore, every year, attention has to be paid around 210 lakh target groups. As against this, available formal training capacity of the country is only 23 lakhs. Therefore, the gap is about 187 lakhs. To fill up this gap to a certain extent, ITI system need to be revamped. Further, there is an urgent need to look into training of trainers as a large gap exist. Out of 55,000 instructors, only 40% have undergone a full instructed training course.

8. There are several other programmes and activities under the control of different Ministries and Departments. These include Vocational Education of Ministries Human Resource Development, Rural Areas and Employment and Dept. of Women & Child Development. Training activities of the Ministry of Industries and that of Khadi and Village Industry Commission, etc. All these programmes largely cater to the needs of the informal sector in a limited manner and are required to expanded to meet the emerging needs.

9. The vital issues for industrial, social and economic development of a country is the development of its human resources, which inter alia give due importance to education and training, and development of skills. In wider spectrum of skill requirement, liberalisation of economic policies together with globalization and technological changes bring change in occupational profile and skill requirement. In order to keep pace with accelerated development, it is essential to equip the labour

force with right skill and skill development is gradually assuming greater importance.

10. In the context of economic reforms and globalization of trades, structural adjustment in different organized and unorganized sector continue to have focus attention on technological up-gradation, skill development and training. Similarly, in the introduction of information technology and its skill development, several skills become obsolete in organized / unorganized sector which results in reduction of the structure, downsizing of employment etc and finally redundancy of skilled personnel in the organized and unorganized sectors. To tackle such situation, multi skill of such persons assures their sustainability in the sector and training in latest technology may also sustain their survival. Both de-novo training and multi skill call for additional infrastructure in different vocational training institutes. Merger of different skills in single programme may also deserve additional infrastructure either in the form of resource personnel or equipment and machineries.

11. In the context of better utility of Trainers, Trainers be trained in emerging areas of skill development. Trainers will keep themselves abreast of future skill requirement and discard them from obsolete trade in which they impart training. Age old equipment and machinery need for training may get discarded in the process and modern equipment take lace to meet future training need. Thus, the trainee acquire skill in latest trade.

Existing Gaps and weaknesses of NVTS

12. The effectiveness and efficiency of the system is slow because of various reasons viz. –

i) there is mismatch between skills requirement and skills produced by NVTS; ii) the unemployment rate of vocational training certificate holders is high; and iii) there is no reliable tracers studies. The infrastructure of ITIs is poorly maintained and many of the State Councils of Vocational Training are not functional or do not exist. The majority of the existing ITIs cater to the needs of traditional manufacturing center which represent less than 10% of the total workforce. The requirement of modern high-tech industries and service sector as well as those of unorganized sector have not been properly taken care of. The curriculum of ITIs are continuing for a long time. However, keeping in view the changing economic as well as technological scenario, there is a need for revision of curriculum.

Strengthening the Skill Development and Training

13. To strengthen the Industry - Institute interactions and assess the skill requirement, labour market information system need to be developed which inter alia will suggest future requirement of skill development. Small and medium industries should be encouraged according to their requirement to develop skill and training programme through their own resources. Similarly to improve governance and management of National Vocational Training Centres, All India Council of Vocational Training need to be established by emerging NCVT and Central Apprentice Council.

14. The capacity building, institution development and sustainability of programmes are crucial to improve effectiveness and relevance of the training programmes. To act as a role model for other institutions, some of the ITIs need to be revamped and attempt should be made to develop at least 1 ITI in each State as Centres of Excellence. Efforts should be made to provide vocational skills to all new entrants to the labour force by expanding skill training capacity especially for high technology and for other areas of employment.

15. To increase training capacity for in-service workers, regular skill up-gradation and training are needed to be organized for meeting the fast changing technology. The scope of apprenticeship training will have to be enlarged by covering more occupations in emerging hi-tech areas, service sector and informal sector. As the women vocational training plays an important role in the social as well as economical empowerment of women, efforts should be made to extend the existing facilities to a larger group of women and create a conducive atmosphere for their increasing participation in various skill training programmes. Likewise adequate participation of disadvantaged groups and disabled in vocational training will have to be ensured by holistically addressing problems of access to training, to employment

opportunities, difficulties in work place and if required, need-based programmes may be considered.

16. To strengthen the funding of the vocational training programmes, a Skill Development Fund may be considered to be set up. This would motivate the employer to pay adequate attention to the development of their employees and would benefit industries as a whole. Step in this regard can be initiated in consultation with the industries. Further, a study may be considered to be undertaken to institutionalize management, collection mechanism, contribution and utilization of skill development fund, etc.

Tenth Plan Approach & Strategy

17. While the initiatives taken through the earlier Plans, Policies and Programmes at the Centre and State level would strengthened, the following approach would be adopted during the Tenth Five Year Plan:

- Create adequate training facilities for organized sector and develop skill requirement according to demand in industry of use
- Create more avenues and opportunities for training need for informal sector as well
- Increase industry Institute interaction for demand driven skill development
- Create skill development fund mainly funded and managed by industry for improvement and effectiveness of training programme
- Improve governance and management by creating All India Council of Vocational Training
- Introduce Management Information system for labour market information
- Modernize and keep latest trade by introducing training for trainers
- Introduce multi-level skill training for sustainability of work force in job in the modern age of technological changes and globalization

18. In order to manage demand driven skill development, the strategy would be to strengthen the industry institute interaction and to assess the requirement of skill development. By introducing AICVT, governance and management of vocational training institutes would be managed. Introducing training for trainers and multi level skill in different institutes, latest technological change and its skill requirement, could be developed.

19. Keeping in view the above broad approaches for the Skill Development and Training, the Steering Committee recommends the following:

Recommendations

- *To increase literacy standards and production skills of persons in the informal sector,* facilities at the institutional and community based, may be utilized.
- *To strengthen the skill development, various associations in the informal sector may be* motivated to contribute funds.
- *Tax and credit incentives may be considered to be extended to the private sector companies* those who create training and skill development activities.
- *The scope of apprenticeship training may be enlarged by covering more occupations in* emerging high-tech areas, service sector and informal sector
- *In view of the fast changing technological scenario, the related curricula and skill areas* may be reviewed periodically for assessing the obsolescence and need for diversification in the various training areas.
- *A mechanism may be evolved to strengthen the inter-action between the industry and* industrial training institutes.
- *As the existing gaps for training and skill development cannot be filled in by single source,* efforts may be made to involve all stake holders i.e. employers, government, Voluntary organizations for sharing the cost of training.
- *Industry may be motivated to take responsibility of training and government may act as a* facilitator in the

implementation of vocational training programmes.

- *To enhance confidence building / entrepreneurship development and to give recognition of* existing skills, training programmes may be organized with a focus on skilled artisans / crafts persons.
- *A National Artisan Fund may be considered to be developed by pooling existing available* resources from various agencies.

5

Occupational Safety & Health

Occupational Safety and Health aspects occupy a very significant position in the policy frame work of Government of India. Although there is no national policy on Occupational Health and Safety, there are certain provisions under the Constitution of India which deals with matter regarding safety and health workers employed in various occupations. Due to proliferation and increase in severity of hazards in different works of economic activity, the declared objective of our Government is to keep pace with international trends and need for projecting a positive image internationally regarding health and safety concerns of working population. The Constitution of India contains specific provision on occupational safety and health of workers. The Directorate General of Mines Safety (DGMS) and Directorate General of Factory Advice Services and Labour Institutes (DGFASLI), the two field organizations of Ministry of Labour strive to achieve the principles enshrined in the area of occupational safety and health in mines, factories and ports.

Constitutional Provisions

2. The Constitution of India has specific provisions for ensuring OSH for workers in the form the three Article 24, 39 (e and f) and 42. The statues relating to OSH are broadly divided into three - statutes for safety at workplaces (e.g. Factories Act, 1948 and Mines Act, 1952), statutes for safety of substances (e.g. Indian Explosives Act, 1884), and statutes for safety of activities (e.g. Radiation Protection rules under the Atomic Energy Act). According to Article 24, no child below the age of 14 years, shall be employed to work in any factory or mines or engaged in any

other hazardous employment. Article 39 (e and f) deals with the policy towards securing - (e) that the health and strength of workers, men and women, and the tender age of children are not abused and that citizens are not forced by economic necessity to enter vocations unsuited to their age or strength; (f) that children are given opportunities and facilities to develop in a healthy manner and in conditions of freedom and dignity and that childhood and youth are protected against exploitation and against moral and material abandonment. Article 42 lays emphasis that the States shall make provision for securing just and humane conditions of work and for maternity relief.

3. The Seventh Schedule of the Constitution lists the jurisdiction of the Centre and the State Governments to legislate in particular subject matters. In terms of List–I, under this Schedule, the Central Govt. is exclusively authorized to make laws for regulation of labour and safety (Item No. 55 in the list) and for safety of workers employed in major Ports (Item No. 27 in the list). In the list of Concurrence subjects, welfare of labour (Item No. 24 in the list) and factories (Item No. 64 in the list) have been included. Thus under the Constitution, it is imperative that measures should be taken to ensure that all the workers irrespective of their place of employment are assured of Occupational Safety and Health.

ILO Conventions

4. Government of India, as one of the Founding Members of the International Labour Organization, derives conclusive guidelines from the conventions, recommendations and code of practices framed by ILO regarding OSH. The ILO has so far adopted 182 conventions and 190 recommendations. In the field of Occupational Safety, Health and Working Environment, ILO has framed 13 conventions and equal number of recommendations so far. Out of these, GOI has ratified 2 conventions viz., Radiation Protection Convention (No. 115), 1960 and Benzene Convention (No. 136), 1971. Some of the recent conventions and recommendations have a strong bearing on emerging occupational health and safety laws in the country. Convention No. 155 requires every member State to look into the policy which should aim at prevention of accidents and injury at work places by minimizing

the causes of hazards inherent in working environment. As per the Convention 161, Member country will have to adopt a National Policy on Occupational Health Services with particular reference to prevention of occupational diseases and health surveillance. Convention 174 and recommendation 181 define hazardous substance, major hazardous installation, major accident, etc. While Convention 176 imposes 3 key tasks relating to (i) adoption of a Policy on Safety & Health in Mines (ii) to pass laws for implementing the convention provision and (iii) create an inspectorate to enforce the laws, the Convention 152 of ILO deals with occupational health and safety in dock workers.

Review of the existing Programmes

5. The Mines Act, 1952 and Rules and Regulations framed there under, Factories Act, 1948 and Rules framed there under, Dock Workers (Safety, Health and Welfare) Act, 1986 and Regulations framed there under, Building and Other Construction Workers (Regulation of Employment and Conditions of Service) Act, 1996 and Rules framed there under, Dangerous Machines (Regulations) Act, 1983 and Rules framed there under, Insecticides Act, 1968 and Rules framed there under, Shops and Establishments Acts of State Governments, Beedi and Cigar Workers' (Conditions of Employment) Act, 1966, Municipal Solid Waste (management and Handling) Rules, 2000 notified under the Environment (Protection) Act, 1986, etc. are the important statutes covering OSH aspects of workers. At present, comprehensive safety and health statutes for regulating OSH of persons at work exists only in four sectors namely, mining, factories, ports and construction.

6. The Central Ministry of Labour and the Labour Department of the States are responsible for the safety and health of workers. DGMS and DGFASLI assist the Ministry in the technical aspects of occupational safety and health in Mines and Factories and Port Sector.

7. The DGFASLI functions as a technical arm of the Ministry in regards to matters connected with safety, health and welfare of workers in factories and ports/docks. It assists the Central Govt. in the formulation and review of policy and legislation on occupational safety and health in factories and ports, maintains a liaison with the Factory Inspectorate of States and Union

Territories in regard to the implementation and enforcement of Factories Act, 1948, renders advice on technical matters, enforces the Dock Workers Factories (Safety, Health and Welfare) Act, 1986, undertakes research in industrial safety, occupational health, industrial hygiene and industrial psychology, etc. It also provides training mainly in the field of industrial safety and health including one year Diploma courses in industrial safety and 3 months Post-Graduate Certificate Course in Industrial Health. With a view to reach at the practicable solutions to the various problems, the DGFASLI study the problem of safety and health in an integrated manner through its Labour Institutes. In addition, the organization also undertakes developmental activities as identified in various Plan schemes formulated and approved by the Ministry.

8. DGFASLI with its HQs in Bombay, has 5 National Labour Institutes and 11 Inspectorates of Dock Safety Offices in major Ports. The Central Labour Institute at Mumbai started working from 1959. The different division at the Institute undertakes activities such as carrying out studies and surveys, organizing training programmes, seminars and workshops, rendering services such as technical advice, safety audits, testing and issuance of performance reports for personal protecting equipments, etc. The Regional Labour Institutes located at Calcutta, Kanpur and Madras are serving the respective regions of the country. The Inspectorates of Dock Safety are established viz., at Chennai, Cochin, Jawaharlal Nehru Port, Khandala, Kolkata, Marmagoa, Mumbai, New Mangalore, Paradeep, Tuticorin, Vishakapatnam. Over the years, keeping pace with the industrial development and governmental policies, the Inspectorates of Dock Safety Offices have expanded rapidly.

9. The DGMS, through a variety of promotional initiatives and awareness programmes exercise preventive as well as educational influence over the mining industry, promotes the concept of self-regulation as well as workers participation in the safety management. One of the major responsibility of this organization is to draft appropriate legislation and set standards as well as its compliance through a variety of promotional initiatives and thereby creates an environment to give due priority to safety. The DGMS is a subordinate office of Ministry of Labour and has its HQs at Dhanbad with its Zonal, Regional and Sub-regional offices spread

all over mining area, is also entrusted with the responsibility of enforcing the provision of Mines Act, 1952, and the Rules and Regulations framed there under in Coal, Metalli Ferrous and Oil Mines. Apart from inspection of Mines, the DGMS also undertakes investigations into all fatal accidents and certain serious accidents and dangerous occurrences and makes recommendations to prevent recurrence of similar incidents.

10. To ensure enforcement necessary safety measures and mines, DGMS carried out inspections and enquiries. Under Sections 22 and 22A of the Mines Act, 1952, Regulation of 103 of Coal Mines Regulation, 1957 and Regulation 108 of the Metallic Ferrous Mines Regulations, 1961 the DGMS issues notices for improvement and prohibitory orders. With a view to keeping technical and professional competence of the inspecting officers updated and backing the regulatory, enforcemental, advisory and promotional roles, the DGMS implements plan schemes viz. Scientific and Technological Support (S&T), Survey of Accident from Mines and Identification of Corrective Measures, Development of Mine Safety Information System, Development of Mines Rescue Services, etc.

11. To generate, develop and sustain a voluntary movement of safety, health and environment at the national level, the National Safety Council (NSC) at Navi Mumbai, is functioning as an autonomous and self-supporting institution. To achieve its objective, the NSC conducts a variety of training, educational, promotional and consultancy activities. The Council regularly brings out periodicals on industrial safety and promotional materials like technical manuals, booklets, posters, etc. Chief Labour Commissioner (CLC) enforces the 'Building and Other Construction Workers (Regulation of Employment & Conditions of service) Act, 1996' and the central rules framed there under. DGFASLI provides technical support in drafting model rules, carrying out surveys and conducting training programmes in construction sector. The Directorate General, Labour Welfare under the Ministry of Labour deals with the welfare aspect or workers employed in beedi and cigar manufacturing. In spite of various agencies involved in regulating work place safety and health issues in the unorganised sector, the efforts are by no means comprehensive and unified. Besides, the Central Insecticides Board

under Ministry of Agricultural and Cooperation regulates safety aspects regarding manufacturing, packaging, labeling, distribution, handling and use of pesticides. The State Agriculture Departments are engaged in enforcing the Provisions of the Insecticides Act related to agricultural operation.

12. The unorganized sector which contributes about 92% of the total workforce in the country, despite its significance and contribution in the economy remained a neglected lot, especially for the safety and health during the course of their employment. Absence of comprehensive labour laws or ineffective enforcement of such laws expose the unorganized workers to exploitation. The most important and labour intensive unorganized sectors, which employs about 50-70% of the workforce of the unorganized sectors are from agriculture, construction, shops and establishments, beedi and cigarette manufacturing and home workers. Though these sectors have provided employment for many for a livelyhood no organized attempt has so far been made to improve their working conditions. The employees in some of the sectors have some protection for welfare but occupational safety and health measures are totally absent except for agriculture sector. Agriculture, being the major sector, number of enactments like Dangerous Machines (Regulation) Act, 1983, the Insecticide Act, 1968, the Plantation Labour Act, 1951, came into being from time to time. However, since the agriculture is a concurrent subject on par with the labour, the enactment part, though with the Government of India, the enforcement part is with the respective State machinery.

13. To provide for regulation of employment and conditions of services of building and other construction workers including fixing of hours of work, wages and overtime, dispute, resolutions and welfare amenities, the Building and Other Construction Workers, (Regulation of Employment and Condition of Services) Act, 1996 is in force. On safety aspects, constitution of Safety Committees in larger establishment, provision of notification of fatal accidents have been provided. In respect of the workers of Beedi and Cigar manufacturing Industry, the Beedi and Cigar Workers (Condition & Employment) Act, 1966 and the Factories Act, 1948 is applicable. The Act is for regulating the conditions of work in beedi and cigar manufacturing establishments and provide for welfare of workers employed therein. Likewise, the

Shops and Commercial Establishments (Central and State) Act are mainly related to payment of wages, overtime, holidays with pay, annual leave, etc. and the provision for other safety and health aspects are absent.

Existing Gaps and Weakness

14. Presently there is no agency or department of the Government of India exclusively for dealing with the matters of occupational safety and health. Comprehensive safety and health statutes for regulating safety and health of persons at work exists only in respect of 4 sectors viz. – Factories, Docks, Mines and Construction. In addition, there are a number of other statutes for regulating safety in particular activity, operations, sectors such as Transport, Storage and handling of Explosives, Petroleum, Insecticides, Radio-active materials, operations of Railways, Shipping and Aviation, etc. The approach in existing statutes for regulating safety at work is to lay down specific and detailed requirements to prevent risks of injuries in specific operations or circumstances. This approach lacks uniformity and well-coordinated approach to safety and health in all sectors of economy. In addition, there are many activities like software development units, hotels, handling of hazardous chemicals employing less than 10 workers are also outside the scope of safety and health legislations. There are also problems regarding procedures in amending the existing statutes. Further, the administrative procedures to effect the amendments to the existing statutes is so long drawn that quite often there is a time lag between the notification of the amendment and existence of the situation requiring such amendments.

15. Further, there is a lack of enforcement strategy through collective deliberations and analysis of the situation. Inspections have been generally left to the individual inspectors without much of guidelines and the major issues concerning a particular sector can be resolved only through the directions and initiatives of the enforcement agency from the highest level. In terms of administration of OSH legislation, there has been a lack of educational and awareness effort. However, super-specialization training activities for enhancing competence of inspectors of Mines are to some extent conducted by DGMS but there is no academics

for imparting such training. There is also a shortage of manpower for enforcement of statute in Mines. Mining activities of minor minerals have also increased and increasingly large workforce consisting of men and women are being deployed in such operation with very little concern on matters connected with the occupational safety and health. The challenges posed by mechanization and new technology will have to be addressed through upliftment of technical skill of inspectors and frequent inspections so that safety and health of workers get its due priority. The Mines Act has given major power to DGMS for ensuring compliance with the provisions statute. However, due to shortage of officers in the legal cell, the DGMS is not in a position to follow up all the cases. Small Mines growing into an important component in the mineral sector in the form of value of output, contribution to the economy and employment. However, the operational safety and health in such mines is a big problem because of lack of enforcement of legislation, inadequate number of inspecting officers in the DGMS, non-availability of documentary evidence, etc.

16. As far as factories, ports and docks are concerned, the manpower and enforcement are insufficient. New techniques are very important but lot of chemical industries, where risks are involved, have come up in the recent times. In the light of new hazards being introduced in the manufacturing sector with the use of modern technology, new products & new processes, there is no organized training programme for enhancing the competence of Inspectors of Factories. The functioning of safety officers in factories is also not very satisfactory. There are number of areas where studies are required for determining the problem of safety and health such as safety and health in export processing zones, software development units, ship breaking power generating units, multi-national enterprises, etc.

17. In the unorganized sector, very few sample surveys have been carried out to identify the occupational and health hazards. The Dangerous Machines (Regulation) Act, 1983 can not be effectively enforced in the agricultural sectors as it coverage extends besides the use of dangerous machines in agriculture, to production, supply and distribution which are carried out in factories and sales departments. In the area of construction

activities, very few State Governments have so far notified the rules and identified the Enforcement Agencies under the Building and Other Construction Workers Act, 1996. Further, inspection officials have not so far been given proper training for enforcement of the above statute. The Shops and Establishment Acts do not cover a variety of operations which pose safety and health hazards carried out in such premises. Similarly, safety and health aspects for the home-based workers, eating places, waste management are virtually insignificant and specific guidelines applicable to the hazards have not been developed.

Tenth Plan Approach & Strategy

18. The approach in the Tenth Plan (2002-07) would be to extend operational safety and health (OSH) to workers both in organized as well as unorganized sectors. While the existing safety and health statutes for regulating safety and health measures to persons at work in respect of factories, docks, mines and construction sectors would be strengthened, efforts will be made to improve OSH in the unorganized sectors in line with government's declared objectives. Taking the existing situation into consideration, a holistic approach needs to be adopted through a coherent National Policy on Occupational Health and Safety of Workers employed in all sectors of the economy.

19. The number of legislation which guide the operational safety and health aspects are applied only in the organized sectors and covered only 8% of the workforce. In this sector, a large number of operational safety and health are applicable in a fragmented manner and has been developed in a piecemeal manner resulting in duplication in some areas and gaps in others. At present, there is no single unified legislation which can take care the basic responsibility of operational safety and health in all sectors. In view of this, the Tenth Plan commits itself to bring a General Legislation (Umbrella) on OSH. This will help for reduction in multiplicity of enforcement agency and will have proper coordination among them with a view to provide a focus on OSH measures in industry.

20. Occupations and industries not covered by any mechanism of safety surveillance of workers include – dhaba workers, shop workers, road transport workers, unorganized mining, restaurants,

etc. The Tenth Plan approach would be to create awareness generation amongst the employer and workers regarding various occupational health hazards and accidents and the adverse effect and possible protective measures.

21. It is not appropriate to leave the large working population in the unorganized sectors unprotected. Most of the workers in the unorganized sectors are exposed to a variety of hazards and are compelled to accept employment for reasons of poverty. The enormity of task of applying OSH legislation to such a vast workforce spread far and wide is challenging and need a huge infrastructure and manpower for its effective implementation. Therefore, the approach of the Tenth Plan would be to provide short and long term measures required for OSH improvements in a steady and phased manner. On the other hand, a particular unorganized sector under the purview of a OSH legislation can not be brought without giving time to the employers, self-employed and employees in the concerned sector for shouldering such responsibilities. Therefore, one of the important and priority measures shall be to launch a well-designed awareness campaign.

22. In view of the increasing number of industries, it is not becoming possible to increase the number of inspectors who would be going around for checking safety aspects. Therefore, the responsibility of safety of units should be given to owners of the factories and some system of given accreditations who would be required to carry out safety audit at periodic intervals. The responsibility should be of owners of business units and be inspected by some agency, which would be a part of legal arrangement. Alternatively, a self-certification by the industries would be introduced. Further, to integrate occupational safety and health in the manufacturing/processing/service sector, an independent accreditation agency consisting of eminent professionals for establishment of national standard on OSH and development of an audit mechanism for assessing effectiveness of OSH industries, ports, mines and unorganized sectors through external safety audits, would be created.

23. To deal with the gaps arising out of changes in technology, introduction of new type of chemicals and sophisticated machinery, efforts would be made to equip the enforcement agency with latest techniques and skills that are required in the area of safety

measures. Likewise, knowledge of safety inspectors at State level would be updated through identified training of skill development and knowledge to the inspectors. Support of industry and technical expertise would be mobilized through awareness generation and ensure the participation of workers. To develop trained personnel in the area of OSH, efforts would be made to include occupational safety and health aspects in the professional courses like Engineering and Medical.

24. To meet the growing demand, mining activity of minor minerals has also increased and many new mines have been opened up. Accidents in Mines occur due to unsafe acts and unsafe conditions of work. Most of the accidents are preventable because directly or indirectly, these are due to human failures. To deal with the increasing mine accidents, effective measures should be taken for stringent enforcement of mines act. Further, the challenges posed by the mechanization and new technology would be addressed through upliftment of technical skill of inspectors and frequent inspections so that safety and health of workers gets due priority. DGMS, a specialized organization, engaged in the area of mines safety would be strengthened in terms of infrastructure facilities to enable it to provide better services towards operational safety aspects of the mines.

25. Keeping in view the above broad approaches for the occupational safety and health aspects, the Steering Committee recommends the following :

Recommendation

- *A coherent National Policy on Occupational Safety and Health of workers employed in* all sectors of economy may be formulated through tripartite consultation.
- *To reduce multiplicity of enforcement agencies and to have proper coordination among* them, a single unified General Legislation (Umbrella) on Occupational Safety and Health may be adopted. The enforcement of the provisions of legislations may be carried out by existing machinery available at Centre/States.
- *To assess effectiveness of OSH in industries, an independent national level* accreditations of eminent

professionals for establishment of national standards on OSH and development of an audit mechanisms, may be created.

- *The DGMS, DGFASLI, CIFs and State Agricultural Departments may be strengthened* for enhancing the technical skills of their personnel and exposing them to latest techniques in the field of OSH.
- *There is a need for constitution of an Apex Body at the national level to deal with the* matter connected with safety and health of workers in all sectors of economy.
- *To build up effective inter-ministerial coordination, a Core Group on OSH at work place* under the Ministry of Labour may be constituted.
- *To create universal awareness regarding OSH, responsibility may be left to the owner of* the business agency and also system of self-certification by the industries may be introduced.
- *Support of industry and technical expertise may be mobilized through awareness* generation and ensure the participation of workers.
- *To improve the existing occupational safety and health scenario in mines, factories,* ports, docks and unorganized sectors of economy, the government enforcement agencies and the management may jointly undertake substantial strengthening in the area of development of standard work procedure, public awareness about safety, safe work procedure, etc.
- *Syllabus of engineering and medical courses at college/university level should be* modified to include occupational safety and health as a compulsory subject.
- *Internal safety organizations of mining sector may be suitably strengthened and third* party safety audit system may be introduced for assessing status of safety in mines.
- *DGMS may be restructured for its effective functioning and optimal utilization of the* existing resources, replacement of human efforts through automation,

strengthening and planning and prioritization of inspections with the bear minimum increase in strength of inspectorate.

- *Considering the strength of enforcement agency with DGMS, the responsibility of* inspection of small mines may be delegated to the State Governments and the Mines Act may be amended.
- *To meet the challenges posed by latest technology effectively, the Labour Institutes under* DGFASLI may be granted autonomy in its functioning. Also they should generate their own resources under the principal of 'users pay'.
- *Factories employ 500 and above workers may appoint Safety Officer. Also factories* involving hazardous processes as defined under Section 2(cb) may conduct safety audit.
- *Inland container depots may be brought under the purview of Dock Workers (Safety,* Health and Welfare) Act.
- *A data-base may be created for various ports containing information on handling of* containers and dangerous goods, hazardous installations, inland containers depots, minor and intermediate ports, etc.
- *To provide safety and health cover, amendments to the Dangerous Machines* (Regulation) Act, 1983, amendments to the Section i36 of the Insecticides Act, 1968, may be made.
- *As a statutory obligations, Safety Officers for units employing 100 and above workers,* may be appointed by the employers.
- *To incorporate safety and occupational health aspects, amendments may be carried out* to the Beedi and Cigar Workers Act, 1966.
- *Material to awareness on OSH aspects may be developed in joint collaboration with the* professional bodies/ agencies concerned. The material thus developed in national and regional languages may be telecast on T.V.

channels and broadcast on radio for creating mass awareness on occupational safety and health to the persons involved in all the segments.

- *Video film, leaflets, safety posters etc. may be prepared as publicly material for* dissemination of occupational safety and health issues.
- *To over come the weaknesses in the enforcement of the statutes, wherever applicable, a* comprehensive enforcement strategy and guidelines on OSH aspects may be developed at the national level.
- *Central Board of Workers Education may be entrusted to organize training programmes of construction workers in the area of occupational safety and health in collaboration with professional independent institutes involved in construction safety.*

6

Social Security of Workers

Social Security in India was traditionally the responsibility of the family/community in general with the gradual process of industrialization/urbanization. Break up of the joint family set up and weakening of family bondage, the need for institutionalized and State-cum-society regulated social security arrangement to address the problem in a planned manner in wider social/economic interest at national level, has been felt necessary. Currently, ongoing measures towards transformation, process for trade and industry, increasing role of market forces and increase in longevity in general world over, have added a new dimension to the issue and enhanced the requirement further towards a planned and regulated institutionalized measure in the form of social security.

2. The concept of social security is to provide protection provided by the society to its members through a series of public resources against the economic and social distress that otherwise is caused by the stoppage or substantial reduction of earnings resulting from sickness, maternity, employment injury, occupational distress, unemployment, invalidity, old age and death.

3. The ILO concept of social security is based on the recognition of the fundamental social right guaranteed by law to all human beings who live from their own labour and who find themselves unable to work temporarily or permanently for reasons beyond their control. At the international level, the preamble of the Constitution of ILO also referred to the need and protection of workers from sickness, disease and injury arising out of their employment, pension for old age, protection of the interest of the workers who were employed in countries other than their own.

Constitutional Provision

4. Constitution of India is yet to recognize Social Security as a fundamental right. However, there are constitutional provisions for Right to an adequate means of livelyhood (Article 39(a) and under Article 41 of the Constitution, it requires that the State should within the limits of its economic capacity make effective provision for securing the right to work, to education and to public assistance in case of unemployment, old age, sickness and disablement. Article 42 requires that the State should make provision for securing just and human conditions of work and for maternity relief. Article 43 states that States shall endeavour to secure to all workers – agricultural, industrial or otherwise, a living wage, conditions of work, ensuring a decent standard of life . Article 47 requires that the State should raise the level of nutrition and the standard of living of its people and improvement of public health as among its primary duties.

Legislative Support

5. Presently, there are contributory and non-contributory social security laws in our country. The contributory laws are those which provide for financing of the Social Security programmes by contributions paid by workers and employers and in some cases supplemented by contribution / grants from the government. The important contributory schemes include the Employees State Insurance Act, 1948 and the Provident Fund, Pension and Deposit linked Insurance schemes framed under Employees Provident Funds and Miscellaneous Provisions Act, 1948. The major non-contributory laws are Workmen's Compensation Act, 1923, the Maternity Benefit Act, 1961 and the Payment of Gratuity Act, 1972. Because of the scattered and dispersed nature and high unemployment levels, the unorganized sector workers get low level of legislative protection.

Existing Social Security Schemes

6. The Social Security scheme in India cover only a very small segment of the organized work force. As per the Survey carried out by the National Sample Survey Organization in the year 1999-2000, the total employment both in the organized and unorganized in the country was in the order of 397 million. Out of this, 28

millions are in the organized sector and the balance 369 million in the unorganized sector. Only the organized sector workers are having the benefit of formal social security protection.

7. Our country, being the welfare State has taken upon extending various benefits of Social Security and Social Assistance to its workforce. The major Social Security mechanism are provided through – i) Workmen's Compensation Act, 1923; ii) Maternity Benefit Act, 1961; iii) Payment of Gratuity Act, 1972; iv) ESI Act, 1948; and v) EPF and M.P. Act, 1952, whereas the major Social Assistance are extended through – i) Welfare Funds of Mine Workers, Beedi Workers, Cine Workers and Construction Workers; ii) Welfare Fund of State Governments for the Unorganized Sector Workers; iii) Subsidized Insurance Scheme administered by LIC and GIC; iv) Other forms of Social Assistance like old age benefit, maternity benefit, survivors benefit, assistance for employment, training, education, etc. being administered and financed departmentally. Programme specific details of Social Security measures as exist today in the organized and unorganized sectors are as follows:

Programmes in the Organized Sector

8. Our country has enforced a few national laws for extending certain mandatory benefits. While some of them like provident fund, pension, insurance, medical care and sickness benefits are contributory either by employees or by both employees and employers and sometimes supplemented by the Government; the others like employment injury benefit, gratuity, maternity benefit are purely non-contributory and met by the employers alone.

Programmes in the Un-organized Sector

9. The Social Security for the unorganized sector is being provided through centrally funded Social Assistance Programmes Social Insurance Scheme, social assistance through welfare funds of Central and State Governments and public initiatives. The centrally funded Social Assistance programmes include a scheme called National Social Assistance Programme (NSAP) was launched through 3 Sub-schemes of - **i)** National Old Age Pension Scheme (NOAPS); **ii)** National Family Benefit Scheme; and **iii)** National Maternity Benefit Scheme. In providing social assistance

benefits to poor households, NSAP supplements the efforts of the State Governments with the objective of ensuring minimum national levels of well-being. To ensure creation of adequate employment opportunities to provide social security to the people in the unorganized sector, NSAP also provides opportunities for linking social assistance package to schemes for poverty alleviation and provision of basic minimum services. In this direction, the important schemes being implemented by the Government are - Employment Assurance Scheme (EAS); Swaran Jayanti Gram Swarozgar Yojana (SGSY); Jawahar Gram Samriti Yojana; etc.

Review of the Existing Programmes

10. Out of 397 million, only 28 million workforce enjoy worthwhile social security cover. Out of this, 25 million workers are covered by Employees Provident Fund (EPF) and the rest are covered either by Government or by Employees State Insurance Corporation (ESIC). This clearly brings out that about 90% of the workforce in the unorganized sector is unattended.

11. The Employees Provident Fund Act and Miscellaneous Provision (EPF & MP) Act, which was passed in 1952 is basically for security of workers. Presently, 3 schemes are in operation under the Act viz., i) The Employees Provident Fund Scheme, 1952; ii) The Employees Deposit Linked Insurance Scheme, 1976; and iii) Employees Pension Scheme, 1955. The Act initially apply to factories/establishments falling within 6 specified industries, which have completed 3 years of existence and employed 50 or more workers. The Act is now applicable to Factories/ establishments engaged in 177 industries/establishments employing 20 or more workers. The wage ceiling for covering under Employees Provident Fund was enhanced from Rs. 3500 to 5000 per month w.e.f. October, 1994. At the end of March, 2001, 3.26 lakh establishments with 24.53 million subscribers were covered under the Employees Provident Fund scheme. With the help of information technology, Employment Provident Fund Organization (EPFO) has taken up a very ambitious programme where they will use a smart card which will enable the subscriber to access to his account from any place of the country. Also, modernization of working facilities of EPFO and ESIC would help in a very big way in projecting a better image and confidence among the

members.

12. Employees Deposit Linked Insurance Scheme, 1976, which came into force w.e.f. August, 1976. All the employers who are members of the Provident Fund are members of this scheme also. Under the scheme, employers are required to pay contribution to the Insurance Fund @ 0.5% of the pay of the employees. During 1999-2000, there were 2550 claims settled and an amount of Rs. 42.25 crore dispersed. The Employees Pension Scheme is compulsory for all the persons who were members of the Family Pension Scheme, 1971. It is also compulsory for the persons who have become members of the Provident Fund from 16-11-1995 i.e. the date of introduction of the scheme. As on 31-12-2000, there were 2,99,640 widows, 1,62,096 children, 2497 orphans and 3,78,349 retired persons getting pension under the scheme.

13. The ESI Act, which provides for health care and cash benefit in the cases of sickness, maternity and injury during the work period, is applicable to non-seasonal factories using power and employing 10 or more persons and non-power using factories and certain other establishments employing 20 or more persons. The Act is being implemented area-wise in a phased manner. The ESI scheme is operated in 655 Centres situated in 22 States/UTs. As on 31-3-2000 there are 8.60 million employees and 33.37 million beneficiaries are covered under this scheme. The number of factories and establishments covered under the years has gone upto 2,25,076.

14. In the EPF & MP Act, there are constraints like wage ceiling limit, the threshold limit of employment, strength of the establishment and schedule of industries restrictions. In the case of Employees State Insurance scheme, also there is a wage ceiling limit as well as a cap on threshold of employment strength. Under the ESI Act, the responsibility for providing medical care is vested in with the respective State governments. The total expenditure incurred in administering the medical benefit in each State is shared by the respective State Govts. and respective Corporation in the ratio of 1:7. The Employees State Insurance Corporation (ESIC) has issued norms and guidelines both for staffing and equipping ESI hospitals under the scheme. Though the health delivery system is the responsibility of the State by way of ensuring availability of drugs, posting of specialists, medical

officers and paramedical staff in the ESI hospitals, the health delivery system has been found unsatisfactory.

15. The effective implementation of social security law viz., Workmen's Compensation Act, 1923, the Maternity Benefit Act, 1961, the Payment of Gratuity Act, 1972 and Minimum Wages Act, 1948 would lead to improvement of standard of living of the workers. The benefits available under the Employees State Insurance Act and those available under Workmen's Compensation Act for compensation due to injury at work as well as under Maternity Benefit Act are similar. Implementation of Workmen's Compensation Act, Maternity Benefit Act and Payment of Gratuity Act are not satisfactory due to the reason that implementations are the responsibility of the employers and the process of getting redressal for the beneficiaries is too complex and time consuming, whereas under ESI Act, ESIC assumes responsibility for paying the benefit. In case of Payment of Gratuity Act, 1972, an amendment was made and a new Section 4(A) has been inserted to make it obligatory on the part of the employer to obtain an insurance against his liability for payment towards the gratuity under the Act from the Life Insurance Corporation of India. However, this provision has not been given due effect from the appropriate government. In the case of Workmen's Compensation Act, 1923, workers in remote areas find it difficult to approach the Workmen Compensation Commissioner because of their locations.

16. The unorganized sector workers which comprise 90% of the total workforce are engaged as agricultural labour, cultivators, small traders and hawkers, porters, auto rickshaw drivers and other transport workers, etc. So far, an organized social sector coverage could not be extended to this sector because of their seasonal intermittent nature of work, low level irregular patterns of earning and employment, absence of employer-employee relationship and weak administrative structure at the rural areas. Under the Employees State Insurance Scheme and Employees Provident Fund Scheme, very small segment of workers in the unorganized sector workers are covered. Therefore, the huge gap in coverage in the unorganized sector would require a focused attention.

17. The Social Insurance Schemes available to the unorganized sector are operated through the LIC such as Social Security Group

Insurance Scheme. All persons in the age group of 18 to 60 years belonging to the 24 approved occupation groups i.e. Beedi Workers, Brick-Kiln Workers, Carpenters, Cobblers, Fishermen, Hamals, Handicraft Artisans, Handloom Weavers, Handloom & Khadi Weavers, Lady Tailors, Leather & Tannery Workers, Papad Workers attached to SEWA, Physically Handicapped Self-employed persons, Primary Milk Producers, Rickshaw Pullers/ Auto Drivers, Safai Karmcharis, Salt Growers, Tendu Leaf Collections, Urban Poor, Forest Workers, Sericulture, Toddy Tappers, Power-loom Workers, Women in Remote Rural Hilly Areas. The premium under the Social Security Group Insurance Scheme is Rs. 10 per thousand sum assured, of which 50% is paid out of Social Security Fund and rest 50% is paid by the beneficiaries or the nodal agency. The benefits available include payment of Rs. 25,000 in case of death or permanent total disability or loss of limbs and Rs. 12,500 in case of loss of one eye or one limb in an accident. During 1998-99, 1.28 lakh new lives were covcred and 47.72 lakh lives covered earlier were renewed under the Social Security Group Insurance Scheme.

18. At present, to provide social security to some of the unorganized sector workers, welfare funds for various target groups have been set up by the government without burden on the budget. The Central Government through the Ministry of Labour, also operates at present Five Welfare Funds for Beedi workers, Limestone & Dolomite Mine workers, Iron ore, Chrome ore & Manganese Ore Mine workers, Mica Mine workers, Cine workers. These welfare funds have been developed by way of collecting Cess from the persons who are selling the finished products. This type of welfare funds provide a good model for extending benefits to other areas like fish processing workers, salt workers etc. In respect of handloom workers, Ministry of Textiles extends financial assistance to handloom weavers and artisans under a Central Plan Scheme, the work shed-cum-housing scheme which is having subsidy, loan and beneficiaries contribution component. However, there is a need to take stock of the existing scheme and to ensure that some element of social security is brought for this group.

19. To extend social security to the rickshaw pullers in Jaipur, an experiment has been carried out by ESIC and if it gets

successful, throughout the country this group can get benefit. In addition to the Central Govt., a number State Govts. have also taken several initiatives to extend social security for unorganized sectors. Recently, the Government of West Bengal introduced State Assisted Scheme of Provident Fund for Unorganized Workers (SASPFUW). The scheme covers all wage employed and self-employed workers between the age of 18 to 55 years in the unorganized sector having an average family income of not more than Rs. 3500 per month. Each subscriber workers contribute a sum of Rs. 20 per month and equal matching amount contributed by the State Government. Similarly, the Govt. of Punjab has been implementing a Social Security scheme for farmers and labourers in case of death or injury on duty. To extend social security cover to manual worker, auto-rickshaws, washermen, tailoring workers, handcraft workers etc. the Govt. of Tamil Nadu has introduced a new Social Security and Welfare Scheme-2001. In addition to Governmental efforts, several public institutions and agencies are also providing various kinds of social security benefits to the selected groups of workers. Two of the outstanding examples are those of Self-Employed Women's Association (SEWA) and the Mathadi Workers Board in Maharashtra. These are some of the attempts where funds are being collected from outside the budgetary system for extending social security measures to unorganized sectors.

20. To provide Social Security to the Agricultural workers, the Government of India has launched a scheme viz. Krishi Shramik Samajik Suraksha Yojana, 2001 through the Life Insurance Corporation of India. This scheme envisage to cover 20,000 agricultural labourers from each of the selected 50 blocks/ districts, taking at least one from each State over a period of 3 years during the first phase. The benefits available under the scheme include Life-cum-Accident Insurance, Money-back and the superannuation benefit.

21. A sizeable number of workers engaged by various contractors for the purpose of loading/unloading, receiving canteen facilities, doing cleaning and sweeping of the premises, rendering security services etc. have removed out of the ambit of the ESI scheme on the ground that they are working in premises which are not covered by ESI scheme such as Railway stations, harbours,

point tourists etc. Steps should be taken to assess these number and to implement the various social security schemes in such areas so that these contract workers are able to deceive social security benefits.

22. At present, the money spent for the Social Security is very low. According to World Labour Report of 2000, expenditure on social security in India was 1.8% of GDP in 1996. Corresponding figures in other countries was - Sri Lanka 4.7%, China 3.6%, Malaysia 2..9%, Argentina 12.4% and Brazil 12.2%. This clearly indicates that whether it is organized or unorganized sector, focus attention has not been given. For e.g. there is no budgetary support from the budget for running ESIC. Even for EPFO, the Government's contribution of 1.16% is being met from the Non Plan only. At present, the Non-plan provision for this purpose is Rs. 600 crore, which is insufficient to cover all. Therefore, due to resource constraints, it is becoming difficult to enlarge the scope of this scheme. In view of this, it is desirable that to cover larger section of workers, plan funds may be provided to the EPFO subject to the availability of resources.

Tenth Plan Approach and Strategy

23. While the efforts made through earlier plans to extend the coverage of social security through various Acts and laws as well as through programmes viz. Social Insurance schemes, Centrally Funded Social Assistance Programmes, Social Welfare Funds, etc., would be consolidated, the approach of the Tenth Plan would be to provide social security to the organized as well as the unorganized sector workers on self-sustaining and self-financing basis without putting any additional pressure on the budget of the government. In this direction, Social security measures in association with Self-help Groups, Non-government Organizations, would be encouraged.

24. The agenda of liberalization and globalization adopted by our country over the last one decade underscore the need for comprehensive social security policy for a large section of the society including specific vulnerable groups like the aged, women, the disabled, tribal and scheduled caste. To provide social security cover to these vulnerable groups, the approach would be to integrate and converge the services of the existing schemes and

projects of various Ministries and Departments. To extend protection from illness, injury at the time of work and pension, basic minimum social security cover would be given in accordance with the availability of resources

25. An approach to the challenge of closing the coverage gap in social security provisions has to be developed at two levels. In order to remove existing inefficiencies, redundancies and existing gaps and weaknesses, the first level approach would be to strengthen the institutional arrangement in the organized sector. The second level would be to create a legislative and administrative frame work for significant penetration of social security cover in the unorganized sector. In this regard the strategy would be to motivate and encourage the State Governments for formulating and implementing schemes and programmes targeted to certain occupational groups in the unorganized sector as per their requirement and without putting any additional pressure on the budget.

26. In order to extend wider coverage of social security measures of the unorganized sector workers, the strategy would be to encourage the Cooperatives, Self-help Groups, Mutual Benefit Association set up, managed and financed by the occupational groups / workers of unorganized sectors and voluntary health insurance and pension scheme. Also focused attention would be paid towards alternative income generating activities with provision of credit arrangement for supply of raw materials, etc.

27. Awareness generation campaigns and dissemination of information to unorganized workers would be strengthened. To improve the efficiency of delivery mechanism of existing programmes to reach the workers in the unorganized sector, local institutions like Panchayati Raj Institutions, Civic Bodies, Municipalities would be involved for monitoring the social security programmes.

28. Keeping in view the above broad approaches for the social security measures for organized and unorganized sector workers, the Steering Committee recommends the following :

Recommendations

Common to both Organized and Unorganized Sectors

- *Considering the size of the massive workforce in the country, a Policy framework at the* national level on the provisions of social security to different groups of workers and employees in the country may be formulated and adopted.
- *The Minimum Wage Act may be amended enhancing the penalty so that the violation of* the provisions under the Act is made costly to the employers. A national minimum wage be pursued. Further, procedure of this Act should be strictly adhered to.
- *Presently, there are inter-state variations in the minimum wages. Even for the same* occupations, various in wages have been quite significant. To minimize such disparities, a National Policy on Minimum Wages may be evolved.
- *The enforcement machinery in the Central and the State Governments may be* strengthened and involvement of NGOs, Panchayati Raj Institutions and Cooperatives may be encouraged at the rural areas .
- *To prevent exploitation of workers in the unorganized sector, awareness generation may* be stepped up in close collaboration with the voluntary organizations, trade unions and other committed individuals. The work of awareness generation may be vigorously undertaken by the Central Board for Workers Education
- *A major coordinated thrust through planning processes may be made in the Tenth Plan.* This may be made through the labour sector of plan as distinct from Rural Development, Agriculture, Social Welfare, Backward Classes Welfare, Women & Child Development, etc.

Organized Sector

- *Employees Provident Fund Organization and the Employees Deposit Linked Insurance* Scheme may be strengthened to improve its efficiency and performance and streamline its operation for better customer services.

- *The delivery of services in Social Security instrument in Provident Fund and Employees* State Insurance Scheme (ESIS) may be improved and expanded by adopting information and communication technology in the over all interests of the workers.
- *To improve the health delivery system under ESIS, different options may be explored.* Whenever necessary, collaboration with Private Sector for running hospitals may be considered.

Unorganized Sector

- *Priority attention may be given to those Social Security cover for the unorganized sector* which can look after medical care, accident benefits and old age pension and maternity benefit.
- *Provident Fund Schemes and Employees State Insurance Schemes may be extended to* the workers in the unorganized sector through innovative approaches that would cater to the requirements of the workers in local conditions.
- *Innovative schemes under the Employees State Insurance Scheme may be launched on* experimental basis targeting groups like rickshaw puller, auto rickshaw driver, head loader, etc.
- *Emphasis may be given for the convergence of services for various social security* measures undertaken by Ministries/Departments, in an integrated manner
- *Community based and location specific social security measures may be encouraged* through Self-Help Groups, Voluntary Organizations, Panchayati Raj Institutions, etc.
- *Based on the experience of the existing welfare funds for Beedi, Mine and Cine workers,* efforts may be made to constitute similar welfare funds for fish processing, salt workers, etc.
- *In the case of Construction Workers Welfare Fund, in particular, only 2 States have* taken steps to create welfare fund as per the Act. A small CSS be considered to

motivate the States to set up such welfare funds for the construction workers.

- *State Governments may be motivated and encouraged to formulate and implement* social security schemes for the unorganized sector as per their requirements without putting burden on the budget.
- *Concerted efforts may be made to enhance the coverage under National Social* Assistance Programmes for providing old age pension, maternity and other benefits to the workers in the unorganized sector.

7

Labour Laws and Other Labour Regulations

Constitutional Framework

Labour is in the concurrent list of our Constitution allowing a limit autonomous to States to frame legislations for achieving their socio-economic objectives like employment generation. The Constitution of India contains reference to work in some articles relating to the Directive Principles of State Policies. These articles relate to rights to: adequate means of livelihood, equal pay for equal work, humane conditions of work, living wage for those who are and participation of workers in management. Some of the fundamental rights mentioned in the Constitution also make reference to work and a plethora of labour laws have been enacted in our country with their basis in the Directive Principles. It has been done with the projected objective of democratizing industrial relations as well as the wider society, has also to ensure certain minimum standards of employment for labour. Taking cue from the Directive Principles, a system of protective labour legislation has evolved. Most of the legislation are related to provide certain minimum standards of employment and social security to the working class. In plan after plan labour laws were emphasized as the means of social justice to the working class.

2. To safeguard some of the fundamental rights with reference to work as mentioned in the Constitution, a plethora of Labour Laws has been enacted in India with their basis in the Directive Principle. It has been done with a projected objective with democratizing industrialization as well as wider society, as also to ensure certain minimum standards of employment for labour.

Labour laws were expected to be supplemented by the instrumental role of an expanding labour bureaucracy. Most of the legislations related to provide to certain minimum standard of employment and social security to the working class apart from providing a State sponsored system of Industrial Disputes Resolution. In Plan after Plan, labour laws were emphasized as the means to secure social justice to the working class. However, over the years, the employers and workers have reacted differently to these laws and it is bound to be so in the nature of things. The feeling is that while employers have taken labour laws as so many impediments to different management of activities, the working class have seemingly remain critical of the government for not going for enough enumerating their sufferings and improving their standard of living. Often, this divergence of opinion has prevented clear thinking in the various issues. In that process, industry has failed to achieve the desired rate of growth.

Plan Dimensions

3. Reforms in the labour markets and especially labour laws must now be addressed urgently. Economists have long known that India's labour laws deny firms the flexibility they need to operate successfully in highly competitive markets. Enterprises do not have the flexibility to retrench labour or to close down a particular unit in the company in response to changing market conditions without getting prior government permission. The labour laws also specify the 'service rules' which govern employment and which cannot be changed very easily. This can make it difficult even to re-deploy workers to different activities when needed.

4. The intention behind these laws was to protect employment. However, in trying to protect existing employment they actually discourage growth of new employment. This was less of a problem in earlier years, when the economy was closed and even domestic competition was limited, and the additional costs could simply be passed on to consumers in the form of higher prices. This is no longer possible in an open economy, especially one subject to strong competition from imports. Indian industry needs flexibility to deal with the new and much more competitive situation. They need flexibility to downsize when needed and also to restructure

and reorganize business through sale acquisition and merger. The present labour laws are a serious impediment to this process. The resulting inflexibility discourages business from expanding freely, and also prevents restructuring which would improve efficiency and create a basis for future expansion of employment.

Implementation

5. The CLC(C) Organization also known as the Central Industrial Relation Machinery (CIRM) is responsible for prevention and settlement of industrial disputes and administration and enforcement of a number of enactments and rules framed there under in the industrial and other establishments for which the Central Government is the appropriate Government. The Important functions of CIRM are : i) Verification of Central Trade Union Organizations; ii) Enforcement of labour laws in organized sector; iii) Monitoring and reporting; and iv) Inspections.

6. Out of 50 labour related statutes enacted by the Central Government, there are 13 labour laws where Central Govt. is directly responsible for enforcement and in another 13 both Central and States are appropriate Governments. and for the rest, the State Governments. are solely responsible. As regards the feasibility of implementing the labour laws (as per the terms of the reference of the Working Group) such as Factories Act, Industrial Disputes Act, Central Labour (R&A) Act, the Workmen's Compensation Act, ESI Act, Employees Provident fund Act, etc. it is noted that the Factories Act and the Workman's Compensation Act are enforced exclusively by the State Governments. The Payment of Wages Act is also enforced by the State Governments except in respect of /Railways, Air Transport Services (ATS). Both the enactments in respect of Employees State Insurance (ESI) and Employees Provident Fund (EPF) Acts provide creation of an autonomous agency for implementation and administration of the ESI and EPF. The power to enforce and administer provisions of these enactments is with the State Governments and the Autonomous Agencies, created by the statutes. In respect of Industrial Disputes Act, the Central Govt. has delegated its powers to the State Governments in respect of 133 industrial establishments. However, no such provision for delegation of power exists under the Contract Labour (Regulation

and Abolition) Act. Various trade unions have endorsed the existing arrangement of administration and enforcement of labour laws in the central sphere establishments by the CIRM.

7. As regards the remaining enactments i.e. the Industrial Disputes Act and the Contract Labour (Regulation & Abolition) Act, it is stated that the Industrial Disputes Act contains a provision for delegation of power by the Central Government to the State Government. However, no such provision for delegation of power exists under the Contract Labour (Regulation & Abolition) Act. Thus, the Central Government has delegated its power to the State Governments under industrial Disputes Act in respect of 133 industrial establishments.

8. The State enforcement machinery is already over burdened since they have a huge number of establishments under them. In addition to industrial establishments the same State machinery also enforces laws pertaining to shops and establishments. The State Labour Departments and the officers have been entrusted with quasi-judicial work such as Presiding officers of Labour Courts, Commissioners for Workmen's Compensation, authorities under Payment of Wages Act and Minimum Wages Act, Registrar of trade unions, etc.

9. Although the Central Government has delegated its power to State Governments under Industrial Disputes Act in respect of about 133 industrial establishments, it has been observed that some State Governments namely, Maharashtra, Jharkhand etc. are not keen to exercise the power delegated to them under the Industrial Disputes Act. As a result CIRM officers are forced to handle the Industrial Disputes in respect of the establishments for which the power has been delegated to the State Governments. The existing arrangement of administration and enforcement of labour laws in the Central Sphere establishments by the Central Government i.e. LCIRM has proved to be quite useful. This has been endorsed by the trade union leaders of repute and CPSUs who are of the opinion that the quality of the services rendered by CIRM is far superior to the quality of services rendered by any State Governments.

Review of Labour Laws

10. There are large number of legislations to cover the subject

matter and over a period of time, depending upon the requirement, these legislations have been put in place. In the field of Industrial Relations, there are 3 major legislation viz. – i) Trade Union Act, 1926; ii) Industrial Employment (Standing Orders) Act, 1946; and iii) Industrial Disputes Act, 1947. In relation to Wages, there are 4 legislation viz., - Payment of Wages Act 1936; Minimum Wages Act, 1948; Working Journalist (Fixation of Rates of Wages) Act, 1958, Payment of Bonus Act, 1965. In the case of working journalists, the Govt. has taken up the responsibility for fixing wages to the journalists and non-journalists. There are about 16 legislation specifying the working hour conditions of services and employment and they cover large variety of situation from plantation, mines, ports and docks, motor transport, beedi, shops and establishments, construction workers and Factories Act, etc. Factories Act is a very important legislation which generally has maximum application to the length and breadth of industries in the country. This Act also lays down the safety requirements that need to be adhered to in the running of an industrial unit. In addition, there are 2 laws related quality and empowerment of women, 2 laws related deprived and disadvantaged sections of the society, 4 laws related social security, 2 laws related to employment and training, 10 laws related to others and 9 laws related labour welfare. The labour welfare laws mostly deal with certain welfare funds that have been put in place where some Cess is being collected and then utilized for the welfare of the workers without putting any burden on the government's budget.

11. The Government has constituted a second National Labour Commission (NLIC) and its report is awaited. The first term of reference given to Commission are to review the existing law, rationalize them and suggest simplification wherever required. The second term of reference is to suggest umbrella legislation for unorganized sector and ensure a certain minimum level of protection. The Commission has already made extensive consultation with the State Government and all the interested groups.

12. As regards implementation Labour Laws, it becomes difficult from the administrative point of view and both from the management side and workers side big demands are put forth and these laws are not being enforced properly. All these lead to a

very complicated system and therefore, for effective enforcement, simplification of laws are needed.

13. India is a Founder Member of ILO and our image is that we are very sensitive towards labour force. Out of 183 Convention that has been adopted, 39 have been ratified by India and Convention No. 89 which India has ratified enjoins that there will be a system of inspection which will be established for proper implementation of various laws and we require to submit report to the international body about the status of the inspection framework. The stand of the GOI before the ILO is that our Constitution itself, has given the similar kind of framework where freedom is available. There are 8 core conventions in the context of WTO controversy of linkages of trade with labour standards. Out of these 8, 2 of them are connected to freedom of association and collective bargaining. India has not ratified these conventions. India has ratified the convention of Bonded labour and Forced Labour and other 2 related to equality of opportunities and non-discrimination of work. 2 conventions (138 & 182), which have not been ratified, are related to Child Labour.

14. A number of laws have been enacted which need simplification. Keeping this in view, the GOI has constituted a Second National Labour Commission (NLC) and it is expected to give its report by 15-2-2002. The first terms of reference given to Commission are to review the existing law and rationalize them and suggest simplification wherever they require. The second important term of reference is to suggest umbrella legislation for unorganized sector for ensuring a certain minimum level of protection. The COMMISSION has made extensive consultations with State Govt. and all the interested groups.

15. There is a great need to amend various labor laws as many of these laws have become very old and they may have served for a particular purpose when they were enacted. Keeping in view the fast changing environment taking place all over the world and in our country, they have to be amended. The Jain Commission set up in 1998 by the Government of India for review of administrative laws, suggested that 18 laws. Major Acts, viz., Factories Act 1948, ESI Act, 1948, Minimum Wage Act 1948, Payment of Wages Act, 1936, Contract Labour Regulation and Abolition Act, 1970, Industrial Dispute Act, 1947, the Bonded

Labour System Act, 1976, the Equal Remuneration Act, 197. need to be amended immediately pending the views of the second NLC.

16. Though the Small Scale Industries (SSI) sector plays an important role in the economic development of the country and contributes significantly to its industrial output, employment and export, the various association of SSI are of the view that they are being unduly burdened with the maintenance of an unmanageable number of various forms and registers under different labour laws. In view of this, there is a need to evolve a different approach for the SSI as they are not in a position to undergo the process of so many inspections. The present inspection system is a big burden on the SSI, who does not have the capabilities to handle so many returns and inspectors. The inspection may be done only based on complaints. Some of the laws which can not be diluted, particularly, laws pertaining to safety of workers or payment of wages, a system of self certification may be considered to be introduced where units have to fill up simplified returns and system of random check should be evolved.

17. The Information Technology Sector and the Special Economic Zones (SEZ) are the fast growing sectors which have potential for further growth and investment. The growing demand is that the inspection procedure needs to be simplified, particularly, the IT Sector where people employed are fairly educated and large number of laws are not required. While simplification of the arrangements are required it should be seen that SEZ is not completely exempted from the purview of Labour Laws. SEZ / EPZ have been set up as enclaves separated from domestic tariff area by fiscal areas with a view to provide internationally duty free environment for export production. This has created a competitive environment both quality-wise and price-wise in the international market.

18. The State Governments. are coming forward to bring out amendments to many of the labour laws. They are demanding authorization to carry out amendments according to their specific requirements. As labour laws are in the concurrent list of Constitution of India, it may be appropriate to allow the State Government to make amendments to the labour laws as per their requirements.

19. National Renewal Fund (NRF) was created in 1992 with the objective of rehabilitating the VRS optees and to provide a safety network for such employees from the organized sector. The activities relating to retraining and redeployment of such employees were being administered by Dept. of Industrial Policy. Under NRF, Employees Assistance Centre was set up to provide counseling, retraining of rationalized workers to facilitate their deployment upto January, 2001. The number of workers counseled, number of workers retained and number of workers redeployed were 73194, 55374 and 19458 respectively. This position refers to the VRS optees in the organized sector comprising Central PSUs, State Sector PSUs and Private Sector Corporate bodies. In addition, Industrial Dispute Act has recently been proposed to be amended to make mandatory for corporates to pay higher compensation – 45 days wages for every year of service as against 15 days currently. It has also been proposed to allow companies and establishments employing less than 1000 workers to lay off employees or close down the company without seeking prior permission from the government. Government has recently introduced Ashraya Bima Yojana under which it provide compensation upto 30% of the last pay drawn (annual pay) for a period of one year to workers who lose their jobs and drawing salary Rs. 10000 p.m. This would help the process of reforming and improving industrial relations.

20. The existing laws apply only to the organized sector labour force, which constitutes only 8% of the total labour force. 92% of the labour population derives no benefit from these laws. In fact these laws actually discourage the growth of high quality employment in the organized sector and to that extent are against the interest of those who are seeking employment.

Tenth Plan Approach and Strategy

21. Law has some purpose and it must serve its purpose. Besides, law is not only the reflection of the society but it also acts as its educator. In a dynamic society, law and the social institutions mutually react on each other. It is necessary to know how far law has served the purpose for which they were enacted. Being a progressive society, we must continuously engage itself in modifying the existing laws and incorporating new ones

whenever such action is necessary. In this direction, it has been argued that many of our present labour laws and regulations are ineffective, anti-labour because, they innovate the growth of employment. While they may provide protection to the existing labour force, the inflexibility of laws hinders new employment. Therefore, to achieve sustainable growth and higher employment, to make Indian industries efficient, cost-effective and internationally competent in the face of globalization process, we need to modernize our labour laws for the largest benefit of our economy. While carrying out the requisite amendment, adequate safety net for the workers for sustainable growth will have to be kept in mind.

22. The SSI sector plays an important role in the economic development of the country and contributes significantly to its industrial output, employment and export. However, they are burdened with maintenance of unmanageable number of various firms and registers under the different labour laws. The approach during the Tenth Plan would be to exempt it from the rigor of the various labour laws and make it vibrant and efficient. In this regard, efforts will be made to conduct proper orientation and training programmes for the officers of the labour law enforcement machinery and create a positive climate for growth in this sector.

23. The enforcement of various labour laws pertaining to SSI units falls under the jurisdiction of State Governments. The entire onus of compliance for furnishing the returns and inspections falls on the SSI entrepreneur. Most of the SSI entrepreneur cannot afford to engage a person exclusively for this purpose. Therefore, the present system may be replaced by a system of Self-Certification wherein return submitted on various labour laws by SSI units are self-certified which may be treated as prima facie compliance. Alternatively, the approach may be to introduce a system of random inspection of certain percentage of units on annual basis with a well-defined criteria.

24. Labour laws are being implemented both by the Centre / State or by the State Govts. which has added to the dimension of labour law complexities. According to the situation and prevailing socio-economic conditions, the State Governments are in the better position to enforce the labour laws appropriately. Therefore, the approach of the Tenth Plan would be to authorize the State

Governments to make amendments to the labour laws as per their requirements.

25. In view of the increasing industrial disputes, Industrial Tribunals or Labour Courts are over burdened and the desired results of resolving the dispute within a time frame are becoming difficult. In view of this, for speedy and timely disposal, the approach would be to set up Lok Adalats, wherever necessary. In addition, the concept of social dialogue would be introduced where all concerned can participate for a meaningful discussion and amicable solution of major problems/issues involved in labour market reforms.

26. Keeping in view the above broad approaches for the Labour Laws and Other Labour Regulations, the Steering Committee suggests the following recommendations :

Recommendation

- *In the interest of the larger benefit of the economy, labour laws are to be modernized* through suitable amendments and make more harmonious;
- *As labour laws are in the concurrent list, the State Governments may be permitted to make* amendments to the labour laws as per their requirement.
- *While carrying out amendments, adequate safety net for the workers may be kept in mind.*
- *Scheme for pension and unemployment benefit for the unorganized sector workers may be* considered to be formulated depending upon the availability of resources
- *To avoid disproportionately regulatory burden on small scale units, the present system for* maintenance of various forms and registers under different labour laws may be replaced by a system of Self-Certification and treated as prima-facie compliance. In the case of default/ misinformation, provision may be made for stringent punishment
- *Inspection under the labour laws in SSI units may be conducted only on the basis of* complaints by stake holder like workers, neighbors etc. or when absolutely essentially

in the interest of safety of workers in industry.

- *Routine and periodic inspections of Information Technology Establishments may not be* necessary.
- *Special Quasi-judicial Tribunals meant by Departmental officers of Labour Dept. may* take up hearing of the dispute in the case of consolation talks fails.
- *Inspection of an establishment may be conducted at the level of an inspector. Superior* officer can inspect the establishments only when there are complaints against inspection and where question of safety of worker is involved.
- *Evolve a scheme so as to pull a part of VRS ex-gratia received by such restructured* employees to enable them to get regular monthly remuneration.
- *Health, safety and welfare of the workers may be given due importance while reviewing the* labour laws.
- *With a view to have wider coverage including workers in State PSUs and Private Sector,* National Renewal Fund may be reviewed.
- *Amend Contract Labour Act to introduce greater flexibility in hiring labour, and at the* same time assuring quality of employment.

8

Vulnerable Groups in Labour Force

The unorganized sectors which comprises 90% of the workforce have several vulnerable groups within this such as Child Labour, Bonded Labour and Migrant Labour, etc.. Migrant labourers are scattered, highly unorganized and prone to migration and on occasion migrant labourers are compelled to work as bonded labours. This chapter deals with the magnitude of the problems, various on-going programmes and their gaps and weaknesses as well as approach and strategy to eliminate the Child Labour and Bonded Labour and also to improve the working conditions and other benefits of the migrant workers.

I. Child Labour

2. A working child is a child of age between 5 to 14 years who is doing labour either paid or unpaid and is kept working at any hour of the day within or outside the family, i.e. a child who is deprived of the right to education and childhood. In a stricter sense, those children who are doing paid or unpaid work in factories, workshops, establishments, and mines and in the service sector such as domestic labour is child labour. The most vulnerable among these children are those who work in hazardous activities.

3. The concern for children and the problem of child labour continues to pose challenges in our country. According to the 1991 census, the estimated figure of working children in our country was 11.28 million as against the 13.4 million in 1981 census. As per the 55th Round of NSSO Survey, the number of working children is 10.5 million. Although Government's

interventions have been able to tackle the problem of child labour significantly, particularly, the organized sector, efforts are required to address the problem in the unorganized sectors. The State with the highest child labour population in the country is Andhra Pradesh, which according to the 1991 census had 1.66 million working children. Other States where the child labour population is more than one million are Madhya Pradesh, Maharashtra and Uttar Pradesh. More than 90% of child labour is engaged in rural areas, in agriculture and allied activities.

Constitutional Provision

4. There are Constitutional guarantee under Articles 24 and 39 and legal provisions under Child Labour (Prohibition and Regulation) Act, 1986 and various other Acts, such as the Factories Act, 1948; the Mines Act, 1951; the Beedi and Cigar Workers (Condition of Employment) Act, 1960 etc. to stop child work. However, for millions of working children, these Acts have no meaning. Acts and Directives already exist at present. Some of them are described below. Article 24 provides that children below the age of 14 years shall not be employed to work in any factory, mine or any other hazardous employment. Article 39 (i) lays down that no one would be forced by economic necessity to enter into a vocation unsuited to health or strength of a child. In spite of all these, children are employed in industries, which are legally prohibited to employ children. The real issue is implementation of various Acts. At present, there is no need for any further enactment on Child Labour.

Programmes for Rehabilitation

5. The programme continuing for rehabilitation of child labour is the National Child Labour Project (NCLP). This followed from a National Policy on Child Labour announced in 1987. The action plan under the National Child Labour Policy comprises:

(i) A legislative action plan;

(ii) Focusing of general development programmes for benefiting children wherever possible; and

(iii) Project based action plans in areas of higher concentration of child labour engaged in wage/quasi-wage employment.

6. Accordingly, the scheme of NCLP was formed in 1988 for rehabilitation of child labour a few hazardous industries like carpet industry, lock industry etc. The Cabinet approved NCLP on 25.1.99 and permitted the Ministry of Labour to expand the existing number of projects up to 100.

7. As a follow up, a series of steps have been taken by the Government. A high powered body, the National Authority for the Elimination of Child Labour (NAECL) was constituted on 26th September, 1994 under the Chairmanship of Labour Minister. The functions of NAECL are:-

(i) to lay down policies and programmes for elimination of child labour particularly in hazardous industries;

(ii) to monitor the progress of implementation of programmes, projects and schemes for elimination of child labour;

(iii) to coordinate implementation of child labour related projects of the various sister Ministries of the Government of India (to ensure convergence of services for the benefit of the families of child labour).

8. Secretaries to Government of India in the Ministry of labour Information & Broadcasting, Welfare, Rural Development, Textiles and the Departments of Expenditure, Education, Health, Family Welfare and Women & Child Development are members of the National Authority for the Elimination of Child Labour. The NAECL in their meeting on 16th January,1995 adopted a programme of securing convergence of services of the Ministries of Government of India and Departments of the State Governments which implement child related programmes at the national, state and filed levels. The purpose of securing convergence of services is to provide education, health, and other inputs to children taken out of schools in a cost effective manner by pooling the resources of various ministries.

9. A major activity undertaken under this scheme is the establishment of special schools to provide non-formal education, vocational training, supplementary nutrition, stipend, health care, etc. to children withdrawn from employment. The broad features of the revised scheme are given below:

i) Child Labour Rehabilitation-Cum-Welfare Centres - These centres act as a bridge institution to enable children withdrawn from work to join mainstream education.

ii) Awareness Generation - A sustained awareness generation campaign will continue.

iii) Convergence of Services - Benefits available to poor parents of working children from all other scheme should be converged.

10. Under the scheme, target groups are the children below 14 years of age and working in occupations/processes listed in the schedule to the Child Labour (Prohibition & Regulation) Act; or occupation which adversely affects their health and psyche. In the later category, the hazardous nature of the employment for the children should be reasonably established.

Review of Existing Policy and Programmes

11. As a follow up, a series of steps were taken by the Government including setting up a National Authority for Elimination of Child Labour and sanctioning 64 additional area based projects (in addition to 12 continuing project) under the scheme of NCLP. As on date, there are 100 National Child Labour Projects in 13 child labour endemic states for rehabilitation of about 2.13 lakh working children.

12. Apart from NCLP, the Government has been implementing a Grant-in-aid scheme for assisting NGOs/voluntary organisation for taking up action-oriented programmes in the field of child labour since 1979-80. Under the scheme voluntary agencies are given financial assistance directly by the Ministry of Labour to the extent of 75% of the project cost for the rehabilitation of working children.

13. The main thrust of the National Child Labour Project is to reduce the incidence of child labour in the project areas, thereby, encouraging the progressive and sequential elimination of child labour. It was envisaged that the project activities would include:

- Stepping up enforcement of child labour laws
- Non-formal education

- Income and employment generation
- Raising public awareness, and
- Survey and evaluation

14. In terms of operationalisation of the projects, the main objective of the National Child Labour Project was to withdraw children working in hazardous occupations and reducing the incidence of child labour in areas of known concentration of child labour. It was envisaged that all children withdrawn from work would be put into NCLP rehabilitation schools/centers for a maximum period of three years and thereafter mainstreamed into the formal primary school system.

15. Under the Grant-in-Aid scheme, Voluntary Organisations are being financially assisted to the extent of 75% of the project cost for taking up welfare projects for rehabilitation of working children. The projects are monitored through field visits, periodic reports, etc.. The National Resource Centre on Child Labour set up in V.V. Giri National Labour Institute in Noida, UP in March, 1993, continued to extend support to create data bank on child labour, research and training, documentation, media management and technical support, etc

16. In addition, India is participating in the ILO's International Programme for the Elimination of Child Labour (IPEC). Altogether 165 action programmes have been taken up for implementation under IPEC during 1992-2001. While the programme initially focused on small initiatives through NGOs and other social partners, an area based approach through the National Child Labour Project (NCL) is being implemented. Along with these 6 projects, a total of 11 projects are currently under implementation in the country. The long-term objective of the IPEC is to contribute to the effective abolition of child labour through enhancement of the capability of ILO constituents and non-government organizations to design, implement and evaluate programmes as well as to create awareness and social mobilization for securing elimination of child labour.

17. **Existing Gaps and Weaknesses**

i) Non-availability of accurate, authentic and up-to-date data on child labour has been major handicap in planned intervention for eradication of this social evil.

ii) A scheme like National Child Labour Project (NCLP) cannot solve all the problems relating to child labour. The basic solution lies in education for all the children

iii) 83rd Constitutional Amendment Act is still in the Bill form. Only upto 81st Amendment is passed into Acts. This 83rd Bill is relating to compulsory education as mentioned in Directive Principles. The Bill seeks provision of compulsory education at the age of 6-14 years for all (primary education).

iv) Poverty has been identified as a major factor compelling parents to send their children to work. An integrated approach, which is needed to tackle the problem, is almost absent.

vi) Lack of awareness and educational opportunities and ineffective enforcement of child labour related laws has failed to combat the problem as envisaged in the Policy.

Tenth Plan Approach and Strategy

18. To eliminate the problem of child labour while policies and programmes initiated during the previous Plans, particularly, during the Ninth Plan would be continued in a more focused and holistic manner, the approach for the Tenth Plan would be universalization of primary education thereby reducing the occurrence of child labour. Also, effective implementation of minimum wages would be ensured. In addition to the universalization of primary education, an effective area-based methodology for pre-vocational education would be worked out and the existing technical training institutions would be utilized to impart vocational skills to all students before they attain 14 years of age. To achieve this, an appropriate area-based curricula for pre-vocational / skill training in the NCLP schools would be adopted / developed.

19. To eradicate the child labour from the hazardous occupation and progressively move towards complete elimination of child labour, the strategy would be to effectively implement the existing scheme of National Child Labour Project. In order to formulate suitable project as well as strengthen the on-going projects, a

continuous survey would be carried out to assess the number of working children including those who are working in hazardous occupations and children working for a wage.

20. At present there is no legislation for compulsory education in our country. Further, the quality of school available for children, particularly, schools in villages are in poor condition and most of the buildings are in a very dilapidated condition with no provision for drinking water etc. The strategy during the Tenth Five Year Plan would be focused on improvement of schooling, adult wages, poverty reduction, etc. Also complimentary strategies and involvement of all sections of society i.e. Government, Non Governmental Organizations, Trade Unions, Media, employer's organization, etc. would be pursued.

21. To ensure that the project is able to attain objectives within the time frame, an effective monitoring system would be established. Utmost effort would be made to effectively implement the Child Labour Act by propagating strong awareness generation programmes at various levels, particularly, in rural areas and urban slums.

22. Keeping in view of the above broad approaches for elimination of child labour, the Steering Committee recommends the following:

Recommendations

I. Central Plan

- *As NCLP is the back-bone for elimination of child labour activities, an effective* convergence may be established with the schemes of Dept. of Education, Rural Development, Ministry of Social Justice & Empowerment and other related programmes of various Ministries / Departments.
- *The NCLPs may be expanded to cover all child labour endemic districts.*
- *The NCLP Society may be made more broad based to include representatives of employers,* Trade Unions, all concerned Government Departments – Education, Rural Development, Health, social welfare and Non-

governmental Organisations with an effective gross root presence. The meetings of the NCLP society may be held at least once every quarter.

- *During the Tenth Five Year Plan, the NCPL may be continued with the target to eliminate* child labour from hazardous occupations by 2005.
- *To ensure effective delivery in a time bound manner, focus may be given on important* components of the project.
- *NCLP schools / centers may attempt to target only those children who have been* withdrawn from hazardous occupations in the age of 9 to 14 years.
- *The District Administration may ensure that children from NCLP schools are given* priority in admission to Government run schools as soon as they are ready to take the examination.
- *The Project Society may maintain complete details of the children mainstreamed to formal* schools and those who have joined the vocational programmes after completing their education in the NCLP centers.
- *NCLP center may provide a nutritious cooked Mid Day Meal to all children, which should* be better than the normal schools. The amount currently provided for nutrition needs to be upscaled. The helper provided for each center could be used for cooking/serving the meal in addition to the regular duties.
- *To ensure that the project is able to attain its objectives within the given period, an* effective monitoring system may be established.
- *To avoid children entering the workforce and encourage them to go to school, awareness* generation through print media, electronic media, etc. may be given top priority.
- *Necessary steps at the Centre / State level may be taken to free all the districts hazardous* occupation child labour
- *To facilitate concerted action by all concerned, Union Ministry of Labour may identify and* announce for each year of Tenth Plan, the names of districts which may be

declared, as having all children working in hazardous occupation at home or elsewhere, placed in school

II. State Plan

- At present, there is no effort from the States / UTs regarding elimination of child labour. To motivate the States / UTs, a CSS on Child Labour may be considered

II. Bonded Labour

23. The system of debt bondage in India is an outcome of certain categories of indebtedness, which are prevailing since long involving certain economically exploited, helpless and weaker sections of the society. The system of bonded labour originated from the uneven social structure characterized by feudal and semi-feudal conditions. Bonded labourers constitute the most vulnerable section of rural poor.

Constitutional provisions

24. The constitution of India guarantees all its citizens – justice, social, economic and political freedom of thought, expression, belief, faith and worship, equity of status and opportunity and fraternity. Under Article 23 of the Constitution, Traffic in human beings and other similar forms of forced labour are prohibited and any contravention of this provision, shall be an offence, punishable in accordance with the law. Under the Bonded Labour System (Abolition) Act, 1976, identification and release of bonded labourers and rehabilitation of freed bonded labourers is the direct responsibility of the State Government concerned. The Act dose away with every obligation of the bonded labourer to repay any bonded debt; and also dispenses with future liability of repaying a bonded debt.

Programmes for Rehabilitation

25. To assist the States for rehabilitation of released bonded labourers, a Centrally Sponsored Scheme (50:50) basis viz. Rehabilitation of Bonded Labour is in operation since 1978. Over the year, the scheme has undergone a lot of qualitative changes from time to time, procedures for operating the scheme have been simplified. The rehabilitation assistance has been enhanced to Rs.

20,000/- for bonded labourer w.e.f. May, 2000 and in the case of 7 North Eastern States, the assistance is upto 100%. Under the modified scheme, provision has been made for grant to the State Govt. for conducting district-wise survey, evaluatory studies, awareness generation activities, monitoring and review of implementation of the Bonded Labour System (Abolition) Act, 1976.

26. The existing scheme for rehabilitation of bonded labourers which was modified in May 2000 to enlarge its scope for covering activities relating to survey of bonded labourers, awareness generation and evaluation studies, would continue during the 10th Five Year Plan. The task of identification, release and rehabilitation of the freed bonded labourers has to be simultaneous. The Panchayati Raj institutions would need to be actively involved in rehabilitation efforts. The rehabilitation programme should be such as to meet the need of the whole family, integrating the poverty alleviation and employment generation programmes. The rehabilitation programmes need to be effective, multi-dimensional covering a wide range of items such as:

- Allotment of homestead and agricultural land
- Provision of low cost dwelling units
- Provision of input and back-up services for agricultural and allied activities
- Easy access to credit for meeting ceremonial, consumption and developmental needs.

Review of Existing Policy and Programmes

27. Since the enactment of Bonded Labour System (Abolition) Act, 1976 as many as 2,80,411 bonded labourers have been identified upto March, 2001 in 13 States. Out of these, 2,56,825 bonded labourers have reportedly been rehabilitated by the State Governments under the Centrally Sponsored Scheme. All concerned State Governments have Constituted Vigilance Committees which are meeting periodically as per Section 13 of the Bonded Labour System (Abolition) Act, 1976.

28. The implementation of the Bonded Labour System (Abolition) Act, 1976 and Centrally Sponsored Scheme for

Rehabilitation of Bonded Labour are being monitored by the Central Government. A compendium of Guidelines and instructions for identification, release and rehabilitation of bonded labour have been issued to the State Governments for their guidance. It has been emphasized that the rehabilitation process should have 2 components – i) Psychological rehabilitation; ii) Physical and economic rehabilitation. In so far as psychological rehabilitation is concerned, the released bonded labourers, who had been used to the world of domination and bondage, need to be made aware / educated and assured that they are entitled to earn their economic livelihood and decent living. To pull the resources for meaningful rehabilitation of bonded labourer, the State Govts. have been advised to integrate and dovetail the Centrally Sponsored Scheme for rehabilitation of bonded labourer with other on-going poverty alleviation scheme Swaran Jayanti Swa Rojgar Yojana (SJSRY), special component plan for Scheduled Caste, Tribal Sub-plan etc.

29. **Existing Gaps & weaknesses**

i) The Bonded Labour System (Abolition) Act, 1976 do not have any provision relating to identification of bonded labourers. Acts and Rules are silent on the methodology for conducting surveys for identification of bonded labour system. As a result, the State Governments are following an approach according to their conditions.

ii) Vigilance Committees in District and Sub-Division in various States have not been reconstituted.

iii) The long term solution to complete eradication of bonded labour system is linked with effective steps to eradicate poverty in the country. However, there is no coordinated effort amongst the various Depts / Ministries in the State/ Central Government to implement the poverty alleviation programme effectively.

iv) There is no arrangement to rehabilitate migrant workers, who are identified as bonded labourers.

v) Infrastructure at the village level is highly inadequate to deal with the implementation of asset based programmes. Rehabilitation effort can not be successful in the absence of proper infrastructure and with the existence of the net work of mal-functional middle-man who operates like parasites to take away the fruits and benefits of rehabilitation to their advantage.

vi) The freed bonded labour who comc from the lowest strata of the society and represent the extremes of poverty and destitution are unable to exercise the choice of a particular scheme, which may be more suitable for his economic independence and livelihood.

vii) To withstand the organized on-slaughts against bonded labour, community approach to rehabilitation is absent in the present scheme

Tenth Plan Approach & Strategy

30. While the strategy for effective implementation of the Bonded Labour (Abolition) System Act, 1976 and Centrally Sponsored Scheme for Rehabilitation of the Bonded Labour would be continued to be implemented effectively, the Tenth Plan Approach would be to enlarge the scope for covering activities relating to survey of bonded labourers, awareness generation and evaluation studies. The scheme for Rehabilitation would be taken up in consultation with the beneficiary. Effective management of the project and training programme would be encouraged to be implemented through the self-help groups comprised of beneficiaries.

31. Priority would be given to identify the drought prone and poverty stricken areas where the incidence of bonded labour system had taken place. Also, a survey would be undertaken on selective basis to identify the bonded labour system. Special efforts should be made to rehabilitate these labourers on priority basis and remove the general economic backwardness of such area by focused integration of various ongoing plan programmes through inter-Ministerial /Departmental coordination and convergence of services.

32. The institutional mechanism in the shape of Vigilance Committee is important. The Vigilance Committee would be improved to make it broad-based so as to boost up its effectiveness. To ensure the proper functioning, all Vigilance Committees would be reconstituted by inducting a few thinking and progressive

minded individuals as well as representatives from Trade Union organizations and local NGOs.

33. To ascertain the actual figure of bonded labour, the strategy would be to undertake a comprehensive survey using valid statistical methodology to identify the bonded labour system on regular basis in all the sensitive districts. The bonded labour so identified would be released and rehabilitated on priority basis. Besides special efforts would be made to remove the general economic backwardness of such area by focused integration of various ongoing plan programmes. No new initiative has been taken recently. The scheme for bonded labour needs to be well implemented and if need be, reformulated.

34. Keeping in view the above broad approaches for rehabilitation of bonded labour, the Steering Committee recommends the following:

Recommendations

- *The effectiveness of the Bonded Labour Act primarily depends upon the identification of* bonded labourers. Except in terms of the functions of the Vigilance Committee, there is no inherent provision in the Act to force identification of bonded labourer. Therefore, the intuitional mechanism in the shape of Vigilance Committee would improve considerably if these bodies were broad based. Accordingly, it would be appropriate to induct a few right thinking and progressive minded individuals including representatives from trade union organizations and local NGOs as co-opted members in these committees. In order to ensure their proper functioning, all Vigilance Committees should be reconstituted once in two years.
- *Complete documentation of all bonded labourers identified and released, as also those who* have been fully rehabilitated and who are awaiting rehabilitation is necessary. This is particularly important in the case of migrant bonded laborers, who on their identification are in some cases repatriated to their home state. On their repatriation, their name may be included in the list of released bonded labourers being maintained in the home

state, so that necessary follow up action can be taken for their rehabilitation & as the feed back to improve design of the Centrally Sponsored Scheme.

- *The formal credit delivery system has not been able to keep pace with the actual demand* for small credit. Therefore, the micro credit, which provides a broad range of financial services such as deposits, loans, repayment services, money transfer and insurance to poor and low income house holds including micro enterprises, has been considered as an effective and viable tool for eradication of poverty as also for elimination of debt bondage. In this regard, the State can take the primary initiative by enlisting the involvement and support of reliable and committed NGOs and providing a conducive to the self help groups.
- *There is a need for strengthening and activating the machinery for ventilation and* redressal of grievances of the aggrieved. The Camp Approach adopted by the Government of Rajasthan in 1980s was an excellent example of a proper mechanism and procedure for ventilation and redressal of complaints by an aggrieved person in a totally open and transparent manner. Such an approach may be revived and applied all over the country. There is a need for continuous surveillance over the functioning of such mechanisms at appropriate levels.
- *Priority may be given in developmental efforts to the pockets in different parts of the* country which are dry, drought prone and poverty stricken, prone to other natural calamities, migration, indebtedness and from where the incidence of bonded labour system have been reported on one time or the other.
- *Locational differentiation in design and implementation of Centrally Sponsored Scheme* may, therefore, be necessary.
- *The existing Centrally Sponsored Scheme of Rehabilitation of Bonded Labour should continue in the Tenth Plan.*
- *To assess the progress and effectiveness of the*

implementation of Rehabilitation of the Bonded Labour scheme, the Ministry of Labour may carry out evaluation through leading socio-economic research establishments viz. Prograttion Evaluation Organization, Planning Commission, Indian Institute of Public Administration, NCAER, etc. and also through the State Governments.

- *The Central Government may take up awareness generation programme for* familiarization, orientation and sensitization of functionaries dealing with the identification, release and rehabilitation of bonded labour at all levels through periodic training programmes / workshops

III. Migrant Labour:

35. The concern for vulnerable condition of migrant labour continues to pose challenges before the developing nations including India. Labour migration affects the socio-economic development of the country. Migrant labourers are marginalized landless farmers who leave rural areas to come to urban cities to get work. They are deprived section of the economy and needs attention.

Magnitude of Migration

36. Migration has been a regular phenomena in recent times involving people within a given geographical area or beyond the boundaries of a State or nation. According to 1961 Census, 144.8 million persons were enumerated at places other than their birth places. 1971 Census 166.8 million persons were counted as migrants. The number of migrant labour during 1981 Census, rose to 204.2 million. According to 1991 Census 226 million persons have changed their places of residence within the country. According to National Commission on Rural Labour (1991) there are more than 10 million circular migrants in the rural areas alone out of which, 4 million are inter-state migrants and 6 million are intra-state million.

Existing Legislation

37. The Inter-State Migrant Workmen (Regulation of Employment and Condition of Service) Act, 1979 is the existing

Legislation. The Act aims at regulating the employment of Inter-State Migrant Workmen and to provide for their conditions of services and other related matters. It applies to every establishment in which 5 or more inter-state migrant workmen are employed or were employed on any day of the preceding 12 months and to every contractor who employees or who employed 5 or more inter-state migrant workmen on any day of the preceding 12 months.

Principal steps being taken through planning process

38. Presently there is no scheme for the benefit of migrant labour. However, the Migration Act which safeguard the interest of the migrant labour is being implemented effectively. The responsibility for enforcement of the provisions of the Act in establishment where the Central Government is the appropriate government lies with the Office of the Chief Labour Commissioner (Central) and the responsibility for enforcement of the provisions of the Act in establishments located under the State sphere lies with the respective State governments.

Tenth Plan Approach & Strategy

39. To reduce the vulnerability of the migrant labourers and protect them from conditions of extreme exploitation, the Tenth Plan approach would be to tackle the problem through a multi-dimensional course of action like effective implementation of various employment generation rural development programmes, provision of improved infrastructure facility, land reforms, universalization of education, etc.

40. Key actions are required both at the destination as well as at the point of origin of migration in order to reduce vulnerability and increase the capacities of the targeted social groups. During the Tenth Plan, concerted efforts would be made to generate data base of migrant workers

41. Most of the migrant workers being poor and illiterate are not aware of their rights under the law. The vast majority of migrants do not obtain adequate shelter or even toilet facilities. They do not have the access to the Public Distribution System and other municipal services. Lack of information about labour

market conditions and the basic rights as per the provision of the constitutions lead them to more vulnerable. To deal with such problems the strategy would be to create strong awareness generation amongst the migrant labourer and to ensure effective implementation of the Inter-State Migrant Workmen Act, 1979.

42. Keeping in view of the above broad approaches for migrant labour, the Steering Committee recommends the following :

Recommendations

- *The first and foremost requirement for effective action lies in the creation of a reliable* information system for labour migration, as macro level data is often inadequate to capture the flow and pattern of migration. Apart from estimating the magnitude of migration, the database may cover the vital aspects like: causes of migration; processes of recruitment; occupational profile of migrants; working and living conditions of migrant workers; skill profile of migrants; expenditure and remittance patterns of migrant workers; status of enforcement of legislations like the Minimum Wages Act, Equal enumeration Act etc. Initially such survey may be undertaken in the major lending and borrowing districts in the States and thereafter in other districts during the Tenth Plan. At least Rs.10.0 crore may be provided for this purpose during the Tenth Plan.
- *Awareness generation programme on the need to provide equal treatment to migrant* workers may be taken to protect the interests of migrant workers. This will include incentive to the NGOs and Trade Unions to focus attention on migrant workers' problem at the destination. The Government may provide financial assistance to the State Governments, Trade Unions, NGOs and other agencies to organize awareness camps in the areas of origin and destination of migrant workers so that they are familiar with various labour laws and protection available to them. A scheme may be prepared and some provision may be kept for this purpose during the Tenth Plan. Concerted efforts may be made towards enforcement of ISMW Act, 1979: more vigorously so that the interests of the migrant workers are protected.

- *Emphasis may be made for creation of awareness generation regarding the social and* living conditions of migrants in various parts of the country, particularly, to those origin districts from where most migration takes place.
- *Key actions are required both at the destination as well as at the point of origin of* migration in order to reduce vulnerability and increase the capacities of the targeted social groups. During the 10th Plan, concerted efforts may be made to generate database of migrant workers, generate awareness among the workers about the legal and other measures available to them.
- *Concerted efforts may be made to generate and strengthen data base of migrant workers,* generate awareness among the workers about the legal and other measures available to them, focused approach on implementation of employment generating programmes in the areas of origin and emphasis on enforcement of Inter State Migrant Workmen Act.

IV. Building and Other Construction Workers

Magnitude of Construction Workers

43. The construction workers constitute the second largest category of workers in the unorganized sector. There are more than 17.62 million building and other construction workers in India as per estimates of National Sample Survey (1999-2000). A large number of multi-national, national and local company employing lakhs of workers in construction and allied activities like white washing, painting, plumbing and fixing of electrical fixtures.

Present Scenario

44. The environment of construction is subjected to vagaries of nature such as rains, floods, elevations and depressions, uncertainties of geological and soil conditions and exposure to extreme temperatures and weather. Construction jobs are highly labour-intensive and also highly mechanized. The entire activity is mobile, seasonal, intermittent and mostly inter-connected. The

completion period of projects ranges widely and calls for engagement of labour from various trades, skills and professions. The duration of employment, quantum of work (work pressure) and arduousness differs from one extreme to another.

45. Construction labour is basically unskilled, more often than not, migrant with high turnover and frequently seasonal, drawn from agriculture. The workers are usually socially backward and uneducated with low bargaining power. One of the major features of construction industry is that it is prone to risks of accidents. Although it is difficult to obtain accurate statistics due to non-detection and non-reporting, the number of such accidents in most countries, frequently exceeds that in manufacturing industry. Factors contributing to this include:

- The high proportion of small firms and of self employed workers;
- The variety and comparatively short-life of construction sites;
- The high turnover of workers;
- The large numbers of seasonal and migrant workers many of whom are unfamiliar with construction processes;
- Exposure to the vagaries of the weather;
- Too many different trades and occupation

Existing Legislation

46. No doubt, the provisions of various labour laws i.e. the Workmen's Compensation Act, 1923, the Contract Labour (Regulation & Abolition) Act, 1970 and the Inter-State Migrant Workers (Regulation of Employment and Conditions of Service) Act, 1979, Minimum Wages Act, 1948, Industrial Disputes Act, 1947 etc. are applicable to the building and other construction workers. Two more Central legislations viz., i) the Building and other Construction Workers (Regulation of Employment and conditions of Service) Act, 1996; and ii) The Building and Other Construction Workers' Welfare Cess Act, 1996, were enacted.

Principal Steps through legislation

47. The legislation provides for regulating the employment

and conditions of service, safety and health and welfare measures for the construction workers. In respect of safety provisions. The legislation conforms to ILO Convention No. 167 concerning Safety and Health in construction work. The Act also provides for creation of Welfare Fund at State level to be financed by contribution made by beneficiaries, levy of cess on all construction works at rates from 1-2 % of the construction cost incurred by an employer and non mandatory grants/loans by the State / Central Governments. The Act also provides certain other welfare amenities like temporary accommodation at or near work sites, crèches, canteen, first-aid, etc.

48. Enforcement of this legislation is the responsibility of the appropriate government as per the distribution of functions between unions and States. A Monitoring mechanism by the Central Ministry of Labour, has been set up to oversee the implementation of the provisions of law by the State Governments. who are required to frame necessary States Rules and set up Building and Other Construction Welfare Board. These legislations are expected to improve the living conditions of workers engaged in the construction activities.

Tenth Plan Approach and Strategy

49. The approach of the Tenth Plan would be to create a strong awareness generation amongst the building and other construction workers regarding their protection of rights and provisions made in various labour laws and schemes for their welfare. This awareness generation may also include the provisions in the legislations regarding conditions of services, safety, health and welfare measures for them. The strategy of the Tenth Plan would be to create a strong data base regarding the number of building and construction workers, welfare measures, social security measures, etc. and to strengthen the enforcement of the 2 enactments viz., i) Building and Other Construction Workers (Regulation of Employment and Other Conditions of Service) Act, 1976; and ii) The Building and Other Construction Workers Welfare Cess Act, 1996.

50. Keeping in view the above broad approaches for building and other construction workers, the Steering Committee recommends the following:

Recommendations

- Most of the workers employed in the construction work are illiterates, migrants and are not aware about various labour laws/welfare schemes available to them. For this, awareness generation camps/seminars, publicity through electronic and print media may be undertaken. Reputed Research Institutes, State Governments, NGOs, trade unions may be entrusted with the responsibility of undertaking the relevant advocacy and awareness generation campaign.
- Concerted efforts may be made to motivate the State Governments to implement the provisions of the Building and Other Construction Workers (RECS) Act, 1996 so that Construction Workers Welfare Fund is constituted and various schemes and programmes are put in place for the benefit of the construction workers.
- Emphasis may be given on skill upgradation of the manpower engaged in the construction works to enhance competitiveness of the sector, productivity and thereby income of the workman.

V. Landless Agricultural Workers

Present Scenario

51. Landless agricultural workers constitute a very significant percentage of the total workforce in India. Out of 397 million total workforce as per survey conducted by the NSSO in 1999-2000, about 237 million workers are employed in the agriculture sector alone. Marginalized social and economic existence and the resultant weak bargaining power denies them stable and durable employment opportunities. Their indigent and poor economic condition many a time forces them to take loans at usurious rate of interest leading to bonded labour situation. The Green Revolution, which has made our country self sufficient in food production, however, has not contributed much towards the betterment of the social and economic conditions of the agricultural workers. Betterment of living for landless agricultural labourers is, therefore, a planning issue.

Existing Legislation

52. Various labour laws such as Minimum Wages Act, 1948; Bonded Labour System (Abolition) Act, 1976, Workmen's Compensation Act, 1923; Inter-state Migrant Workers (Regulation of Employment & Conditions of Service) Act, 1979, etc. have not been able to adequately safeguard the interests of agricultural workers and provide any specific welfare measure to them.

Present Plans and Programmes

53. The Government of India and many State Governments have implemented various promotional social development schemes as well as protective social security schemes for the families below the poverty line and people in low-income brackets. Some of the promotional schemes are Swarna Jayanti Gram Swarojgar Yojana, Jawahar Gram Samridhi Yojana, Indira Awas Yojana etc. and protective social security schemes are Janshree Bima Yojana by LIC, National Social Assistance Pogramme (includes the earlier National Old Age Pension Scheme and National Maternity Benefit Scheme) and various financial assistance schemes being run by the State Governments.

54. In order to specifically address the needs of agricultural workers, the Government of India has launched a new Pilot scheme viz. 'Krishi Shramik Samajik Suraksha Yojana – 2001' for agricultural workers, the largest segment in the unorganized sector. The main provisions of social security under the scheme are as under:

(a) Life-cum-accident insurance

(b) Money back, and

(c) Pension and superannuation benefits.

The Pilot scheme will cover 1 million landless rural labour in 100 districts. Government of India's matching contribution of premium/contribution risk coverage/pension is paid from LIC's Social Security Fund.

Tenth Plan Approach and Strategy

55. To eradicate poverty amongst the landless agricultural labourers, the Tenth Plan Approach would be to converge various

services like education, employment generation etc. Implementation of programmes of the Dept. of Rural Development would be strengthened based on approaches and method which involve the poor themselves in the process of poverty eradication and economic growth. Also a strong awareness generation would be created amongst the landless agricultural workers regarding the scope of various welfare and employment generation schemes being implemented by the Government.

56. To provide social security to landless agricultural workers, the Tenth Plan approach would be to motivate the State Governments to initiate programme, which would be focused on economic up-liftment of landless agricultural workers.

57. Keeping in view of the above broad approaches for landless Agricultural workers, the steering group recommends the following:

Recommendations

- *To assess the magnitude of the problem of agricultural landless workers, a periodical survey* and building up of data base would be necessary. Further, to arrest this problem, there is a need to ensure the effective implementation of Minimum Wages Act, up-gradation of skill development, creation of awareness generation and introduction of social security measures without putting burden to the government budget and introduction of legislative measures for ***compulsory education for all.***
- To assess the effectiveness and functioning the Pilot scheme Krishi Shramik Samajik Suraksha Yojana, 2001 may be evaluated.
- The State Governments may be motivated to formulate and launch schemes to provide social security benefits to the agricultural landless workers. The possibility to share the contribution on account of the State Governments by the Central Government at initial stage and then reducing it on tapering basis in a phased manner, may be explored.

9

Financial Implications

Allocation of Plan resources for the Labour and Employment Sector in the past, although not very substantial in terms of size and percentage to the total Public Sector outlay, yet it has been progressively increasing from Plan to Plan. In a way, allocation of resources for the Labour and Employment Sector has been responding to the emerging needs of its target groups as is evident from the data given below:

Rs. in million

	Total Public Sector Outlay	Outlay for Labour & Emp. Sector	%age
Fifth Plan (1974-79)	388532	501	0.13
Sixth Plan (1980-85)	975000	1996	0.20
Seventh Plan (1985-90)	1800000	3337	0.19
Eighth Plan (1992-97)	4341000	13140	0.30
Ninth Plan (1997-2002)	8592000	20793	0.24

Source: Five Year Plan Document, Planning Commission.

2. Taking into consideration of the expansion of the on-going programmes and new starts in the Tenth Five Year Plan, the following Working Groups have recommended outlay as detailed below:

Outlay for the Labour & Employment Sector

(Rs. in lakhs)

Sl. No.	Name of the Working Group	Funding Pattern	Outlay recommended for 10th Plan by Respective Working Groups		
			For Cont. Schemes	For New Schemes	Total
1.	**Employment Plg. & Policy**				
2.	**Skill Development & Trg.**	CS CSS	15315 10000	26630 211974	41945 221974
3.	**Occupational Safety & Health**				
	i) DGMS	CS	4150	1500	5650
	ii) DG(FASLI)	CS	3680	1150	4830
	iii) Unorganized Sector	CS	0	900	900
4.	**Social Security**				
	i) Krishi Shramik Samajik Suraksha Yojana, 2001		300000	-	300000
5.	**Labour Laws & Other Regulations**	-	-	-	
6.	**Vulnerable Groups in Labour Force**				
	i) National Child Labour Project (NCLP)	CS	66082	-	66082
	ii) Rehabilitation of Bonded] Labour]	CS CSS	50] 5880]	-	5930
	Total		**405157**	**242154**	**646311**

3. Keeping in view the likely level of achievement by the end of the Ninth Five Year Plan for the continuing schemes and also taking into account the outlays recommended by the Working Groups for their expansion in the Tenth Plan plus the new starts, the Steering Committee recommends an amount of Rs. 3500.0 crore for the Labour and Employment sector as against the total recommended outlay of Rs. 5742.99 crore, by the various groups.

ANNEXURE

Constitution of Steering Committee on Labour and Employment

In the context of the formulation of the Tenth Five-Year Plan (2002-2007), it has been decided to set up a Steering Committee on Labour and Employment. The terms of reference and composition of the Steering Committee will be as follows:

1.	Dr. S.P. Gupta, Member, Planning Commission	Chairman
2.	Principal Adviser (LEM) Planning Commission	Member
3.	Secretary, Labour	Member
4.	Secretary, Rural Development	Member
5.	Secretary, Urban Employment & Poverty Alleviation	Member
6.	Secretary, Small Scale and Agro and Rural Industries	Member
7.	Secretary, Social Justice and Empowerment	Member
8.	Director General, National Sample Survey Organisation (NSSO)	Member
9.	Secretary, Labour (Assam)	Member
10.	Secretary, Labour (West Bengal)	Member
11.	Secretary, Labour (Uttar Pradesh)	Member
12.	Secretary, Labour (Gujarat)	Member
13.	Secretary, Labour (Kerala)	Member
14.	Director General, FICCI	Member
15.	Secretary General, CII	Member
16.	Shri Umraomal Purohit	Member
17.	Shri I.P. Anand, Permanent Member of ILO Governing Board. (or Sh. Vineet Virmani, Council of Indian Employers, 15, Golf Links, New Delhi, as an alternate)	Member
18.	Prof. K. Sundaram, Delhi School of Economics	Member
19.	Chairman, KVIC	Member
20.	Adviser (LEM) Planning Commission	Member-Secretary

The Steering Committee will be taking an overview and giving general guidance for working out the actual plans, programmes and policy guidelines for the 10th Plan. The terms of reference of the Steering Committee are as follows:

a) To review the projections of labour force and employment made by various studies and agencies to firm up Statewise figures of projections of labour force and work opportunities that should form the basis of 10th Plan exercises; b) To project State-wise unemployment among educated youth and suggest the strategies for providing work opportunities to the entrants to labour force; c) To take an overview of the existing framework of the Labour Policy and Social Security measures and to suggest appropriate strategy in the context of emerging needs of the market-oriented economy so as to ensure healthy employer-employee relations and promote productivity; d) To review the role of Government in Labour relations with respect to workers in Public Sector and Government Sector; e) To propose a strategy to reduce the gap with regard to administered social security system and welfare measures between the organized and unorganized labour; f) To review programmes for labour welfare so as to suggest a broad-based social security system for the labour and the unorganized self-employed persons; g) To suggest appropriate programmes for promoting occupational health and safety for the workers; h) Any other issue concerning labour and employment policy, with the consent of Chairman of the Steering Group.

The Steering Committee may co-opt such official(s) or non-official(s) as member(s) of the Committee as may be considered necessary. The Steering Committee may also constitute Working Group(s), if so desired.

The Steering Committee, will work through a set of Working Groups which will be given 3 to 4 months' time to report on the respective areas. The Steering Committee, after considering the reports of the Working Groups, will submit its report to Planning Commission by the end of November 2001.

Report of the Special Group on Targeting Ten Million Employment Opportunities per year over the 10th Plan Period

Contents

...Contd...

...Contd...

..Contd...

Foreword

The generation of adequate work opportunities for our growing labour force has been one of the central objectives of Indian development planning since its very inception. We have long recognised that productive employment is not merely a means to the ultimate ends of economic well-being and poverty reduction, but is an important end in itself. It is a basic source of human dignity and self-respect. It is also an important means for nurturing national identity and social cohesion. On the whole, we have been reasonably successful in our efforts, and open unemployment in India has been kept quite low over an extended period of time.

In recent years, however, two trends have become apparent, which dictate a reappraisal of our approach to development and employment generation. First, demographic trends indicate that the rate of growth of population in the working age group is accelerating due to the high birth rates experienced in the late 1970s and early 1980s, and is likely to attain its peak during the current decade. Second, the pace of creation of work opportunities has not kept pace with the growing requirement during the 1990s, despite an acceleration in the growth rate of the economy. Taken together, these trends imply that if nothing is done, the country will face the spectre of rising unemployment with all its attendant economic, social and political consequences. There is also a growing recognition that the commonly cited unemployment figures mask the high incidence of underemployment in the country. Too many of our people do not have sufficient work to engage them round the year, while others work long hours at low levels of productivity and with little remuneration.

It is in recognition of these facts that the Prime Minister announced to the nation that the government is committed to "create ten crore employment opportunities over a period of ten years". The Planning Commission was entrusted with the responsibility of giving shape to this vision. To this end, the Planning Commission constituted a Task Force on Employment Opportunities in January 1999 under the chairmanship of Shri Montek S. Ahluwalia, then Member, Planning Commission. The Task Force submitted its report in July 2001, which has been placed in the public domain for wider debate and discussion.

The Task Force assumed that the recently observed trend in labour intensities in the various sectors of the economy would continue to prevail, and concentrated primarily on the major macroeconomic policy changes that would be required to increase the growth rate of the economy sufficiently in order to generate the requisite employment opportunities to absorb the projected increases in the labour force. The Task Force assessed the requirement of job creation to be lower than ten million per year.

However, in its deliberations, the Task Force had not paid adequate attention to the issue of the large backlog of underemployment, which is perhaps as pernicious a problem as open unemployment. Once this is taken into account, the target of ten million job opportunities per year becomes essential, and consideration needs to be given as to how this can be met. It is certainly true that an acceleration of the growth rate is essential to tackling the employment issue, and the Task Force has made many valuable suggestions in this regard. However, we cannot entirely disregard the possibility of increasing employment intensities through appropriate policy interventions at the sectoral and regional levels. It was felt by the Planning Commission that the Task Force report needed to be augmented in at least these two dimensions.

In order to address these issues, among others, the Planning Commission constituted the Special Group on Targeting Ten Million Employment Opportunities per Year under the chairmanship of Dr. S.P. Gupta, Member, Planning Commission. It is a source of satisfaction that this report of the Special Group has met our expectations. It clearly indicates that it is possible to increase labour intensities in the economy and to reduce underemployment through well-designed policy and programme interventions which take into account sectoral and regional specificities.

The Special Group has laboured hard to discharge the onerous responsibility assigned to it. Its breadth of consultations and its transparency have ensured consideration of a wide range of views. I would like to take this opportunity to place on record my appreciation of the efforts put in by the Special Group, and especially by Dr. S.P. Gupta. I am certain that the findings of this report, along with the growth- augmenting macroeconomic policy recommendations of the Task Force, should pave the way for us to devise a more employment-sensitive development strategy and public policy.

— **K. C. Pant**

May 21, 2002

Preface

The Special Group on "Targeting Ten Million Employment Opportunities per year over the Tenth Plan Period" has been constituted by the Planning Commission by drawing experts from the Steering Committee on Labour and Employment for the Tenth Plan of the Planning Commission and co-opting experts and specialists from within the Government, and from academics and practitioners in this area. The Terms of Reference of this Group is given in Annexure "C" of this Report.

The Report has attempted to analyse all the recent major sources of information and their findings covering this area. The Special Group felt that there is a need for much detailed disaggregated data and information in this area than what is available at the moment. For example, information regarding the unorganised or informal sector, which provides nearly 92 per cent of employment in the country, is extremely sketchy. Besides, whatever is available from different sources is not strictly comparable because of their differences in definition, coverage and terms of reference. Keeping all the limitations in view, the Group chose a set of data and information base, which have been properly examined and can be used with reasonable degree of confidence. In preparing this database, it took the help of Central Statistical Organisation and other relevant governmental statistical bodies who have been kind enough to make some special tabulation of relevant data for the Report. Further, the Group expresses its concern about the lack of awareness on the need for generating employment capacity from different programmes and policies formulated and implemented by many of the Central Ministries and other Government agencies. Even their understanding of the need for exploring potential areas of new jobs is often seen to be absent. In their programmes or project preparation, they are too much obsessed by setting the target for financial outlays and their disbursement patterns and are little concerned about their physical performance including employment generation. Information regarding the labour market is also very poor. The knowledge regarding interactions between education, health, other infrastructures, technology and employment need to be improved. Employment, effectively, is treated as the end product of any selected production strategy and no serious attempt is made to see how the production strategy can be geared with the available profile of manpower, their skill, knowledge and their potential areas of development. Labour is regarded only as a necessary input in production and often forgotten that they are also the final consumers and the final recipients of all the development benefits.

The employment strategy, in fact, should be formulated mainly from the grassroot level and it cannot be totally replicated from the experience of other countries, other than drawing lessons on broader dimensions. Since the labour and employment policies are largely in the domain of the States, any recommendation of the Group to be implementable must be in tune with the policies of the States. For this, the Group could solicit the views of the representative members of the States in the Steering Committee on Tenth Plan, constituted by the Planning Commission under my chairmanship. The Report in its findings emphasised the need for undertaking suitable policies and programmes in reversing the trends observed in the late nineties, of a significant slow down of the growth of employment, aggravated by a near jobless growth in many sectors. Care has been taken accordingly not to allow this trend to be extrapolated in future by depending exclusively on growth on a "business as usual" basis. It identified large areas of potential employment opportunities rather overlooked in the early phase of our reforms, especially in the rural sector and also those assessable as a benefit of the present increased deregulation of the economy and by the expansion of its demand and technology market from its opening up with the rest of the world. Accordingly, the Group suggested several policy changes and new innovative schemes to exploit the employment potentialities in these new areas. The Group placed high priority on the growth of the unorganised sector as the main employment provider (at present, it contributes nearly 92 per cent of the country's employment) and recommended appropriate policies to ensure a level-playing field to this sector, so that its production may be viable in the new globalised open economy setting. The target of 50 million jobs is considered to be achievable, which will comply with all the Plan employment targets, subject to an overall growth of 8 per cent per annum, supplemented by the recommended policies and programmes including those given in this Report to encourage labour-intensive activities and technologies.

I am indeed indebted to all the Members of this Group for their valuable suggestions and help. I am especially indebted to Dr.Mahesh Sharma, Chairman, KVIC and all the Secretaries of Central Ministries who have consistently advised and helped in giving directions, policy suggestions and information in their respective areas. I am also extremely grateful to Professor Amitabh K. Kundu, of JNU, Professor Ruddar Dutt, of Delhi University; Dr.Garry Jacobs, Member, Mother's Service Society, Pondicherry; Dr.D.K. Trehan, Economic and Statistical Adviser, Ministry of Agriculture and Cooperation; Dr.H. Ramachandran, Director, IAMR; Dr. N.S. Sastry, Former DG, NSSO; and all our colleagues in the Planning Commission, Shri R.P .Sinha, former Principal Adviser (LEM), Smt. Jyotsna Khanna, Principal Adviser (LEM), and especially to Shri Shailendra Sharma, Member-Secretary of this Group and Adviser (LEM), Smt. Padmaja Mehta, Director (LEM), Shri Raj Kumar, Senior Research Officer (LEM) for giving technical, informative and analytical inputs in preparing this document. I also highly appreciate the editorial help provided by Dr. Nandita Khadria of IAMR and the committed and efficient secretarial support rendered by S/Shri Govind Sharma, P .Sankar, Hemant Gaba, Ms. Neelam Khanduri and all others in my office and in the LEM Division in completing the Report. I had the great opportunity to have consultation with other esteemed members of the Planning Commission, who had given their valuable suggestions and alternatives for generation of employment in various sectors. I would like to mention specific contributions by Dr. D. N. Tewari, Member, Planning Commission in the areas of forest and wasteland development. Finally, but foremost, my great gratitude to Shri K.C. Pant, Deputy Chairman, Planning Commission, for giving me this opportunity to study this very important area of concern not only in India but in most of the emerging economies, and for his constant encouragement and guidance.

— S. P. Gupta

21 May, 2002

Summary and Overview

I. The Task Given

The Special Group on targeting ten million employment opportunities per year over the Tenth Plan period has been constituted by the Planning Commission to explore appropriate policies and programmes for generating targeted gainful employment for 50 million persons over the Tenth Plan. The composition and details of the Terms of Reference are given in Annexure "C". The Special Group accordingly examined all the relevant studies and sources of information for assessing the present status of employment and unemployment in India and by interacting with relevant Ministries and agencies, has attempted to recommend appropriate macro and sectoral policies and "programmes in specific areas" needed to generate the aforesaid employment opportunities over the Tenth Plan. In addition, it assessed the implications of creation of fifty million job opportunities over the Tenth Plan vis-à-vis the employment targets stipulated in the Approach Paper of the Tenth Plan. The objectives stipulated in the Approach Paper are :

(i) To absorb all new entrants to the labour force over the Tenth Plan period by gainful, high quality employment; and

(ii) To remove unemployment by the turn of this decade.

The Group, to meet these requirements, first analysed the present employment and unemployment situation to assess the likely future employment scenario over the Tenth Plan on a macro and disaggregated basis, and subsequently came out with policy recommendations and suggestions for launching appropriate programmes in specific areas to meet the Plan's employment goals.

II. The Present Status and the Emerging Trends

The examination of the major sources of information revealed that the unemployment rate in India has increased significantly since 1993-94 and was above 7.3 per cent in 1999-2000 compared to 6.0 per cent in 1993-94 on Current Daily Status basis. For Scheduled Castes, the corresponding unemployment rates were 9.6 per cent and 8.3 per cent in 1999-2000 and 1993-94 respectively. It is apprehended that now these rates have increased further. The total volume in terms of person years unemployed has touched about 27 million in 1999-2000. Nearly 74 per cent of them are in the rural sector and 60 per cent among them educated. In some States and in certain sections of labour force, the unemployment rate has increased to more than 25 per cent. To give a specific example, the unemployment rate in Kerala among youths (age 15-29 years) is above 35 per cent as against the national average of around 13 per cent. This situation has placed a big challenge before the nation, the policy makers, entrepreneurs and people in general, asking for remedial action. At the same time, increased globalisation, advent of new technology and frontiers of knowledge along with the revival of many traditional technologies and the benefit of increased deregulation and many key economic reforms have opened up, along with several initial challenges, tremendous new opportunities for higher growth and additional job opportunities. Now, in the Tenth Plan it is time to meet the challenges and make use of these new opportunities.

The present rising unemployment is primarily an outcome of a declining job creating capacity of growth, observed since 1993-94. The employment growth fell to 1.07 per cent per annum (between 1993-94 and 1999-2000) from 2.7 per cent per annum in the past (between 1983 and 1993-94) in spite of acceleration in GDP growth from 5.2 per cent between 1983 and 1993-94 to 6.7 per cent between 1993-94 and 1999-2000. It means that the capacity of job creation per unit of output went down about three times compared to that in the 80s and early 90s. For example, the employment elasticity of the 80s and early 90s of 0.52 went down to 0.16 in the late nineties. The organised sector's employment generating capacity (measured in terms of employment elasticity) came down to near zero and in the public sector has been negative in most cases. This is primarily because of

(i) the present policy of shedding excess labour that this sector is carrying in order to meet the growing market competition, often known as rightsizing;

(ii) the trend towards increasing capital intensity per unit of output; and

(iii) the pattern of growth moving in favour of capital intensive sectors.

Among the sectors outside the organised ones, agriculture, which was the major employment-generating sector in the past, has almost stopped absorbing any more labour in the later period. As a result, in spite of a higher overall GDP and agriculture growth in the 90s compared to the 80s, the overall growth of employment fell from 2.7 per cent per annum observed between 1983 and 1993-94 to 1.07 between 1993-94 and 1999-2000. In fact, the incidence of unemployment today would have been much higher but for the slowing down of the labour force growth significantly in the recent past. The labour force growth was 2.43 per cent between 1983 and 1993-94 and it came down to 1.31 per cent per annum between 1993-94 and 1999-2000. This trend of a slowdown in the employment growth and increase in the incidence of unemployment is of greater concern, especially when one considers the backward regions, Schedule Castes and Schedule Tribes, other weaker sections of the population including females, youths and educated.

Along with the above unfavourable trends indicating possible rise of unemployment in future, several healthy trends were also observed in the late 90's suggesting that the workforce in India is slowly getting tuned to meet the present needs in the context of growing competition and globalisation. As for example, the composition of the work and the labour force in the late 1990s, indicating that it is becoming more skill and education oriented. It should be noted, however, that on the average the skilled labour force at present is hardly around 6-8 per cent of the total, compared to more than 60 per cent in most of the developed and emerging developing countries. Also, the labour productivity in general in this period is seen to be increasing faster, both in the organised and unorganised sectors. The growth of the rural non-farm sector is seen to be much higher than that of the agricultural one, which has helped absorption of the excess labour from agriculture in the rural non-farm sector. The real wages of casual labour are also seen to be increasing faster than in the past, both among agricultural and industrial workers. But this is accompanied by increasing casualisation of labour. It is however difficult to establish the extent of benefits in terms of net average earnings accruing to the workers and whether the quality of their jobs has improved. Considering both the pluses and minuses of the emerging trends in the employment situation, the Group views that to reach the country's development target both in output and employment, in a viable and equitable fashion, several major changes from the past economic policies and launching of innovative pro-employment programmes will be needed in the immediate future-failing which the level of unemployment as also the quality of employment may deteriorate significantly below the present level.

The above observations are also supported by the findings of several other recent reports like (a) the Task Force on Employment Opportunities constituted by the Planning Commission, (b) the latest, Population Census of India 2001, (c) the Economic Census of 1998 (CSO), (d) data produced by the employment exchanges in India and, lastly (e) the McKinsey Report, by using different methods of calculation of employment and unemployment like UPS, UPSS, CDS, CWS recommended by NSSO and those defined differently by other Reports. All these Reports bring out a common message that if the experiences of the late nineties are extrapolated i.e., repeated in future, then India is going to face increasingly higher incidence of unemployment, with an ever-increasing gap between the demand for jobs and supply of job opportunities. Some of the Reports explicitly bring out that even with a high growth rate of 8 per cent per annum over the next decade, implying significant acceleration over the achievement of 5.5 per cent GDP growth of the Ninth Plan, the unemployment rate is going to increase further, reaching upto more than double by the end of the Tenth Plan. A comparative study of the findings of these reports has been attempted in Annexure B.

III. The Future Strategy

The employment strategy of the Tenth Plan has to be formulated against this backdrop in order to reach the goals set by the Approach Paper of the Plan and to fulfill the terms of reference given to this Group. Accordingly, the first task of the Group was to examine, in broad macro terms, activity sectors of high potential for generating employment in the future. For this, the necessary data has been collected and analysed, estimating the employment intensity of the selected sectors, their recent trends in terms of the changes in the employment intensities (commonly known as employment elasticity, measured as percentage changes in employment to percentage change in output) and the contribution of these sectors as percentage to total employment, at the beginning of the Plan period. The sectors have been broadly divided into organised and unorganised. The present paucity of data has been a major constraint in this exercise. With the help of the Central Statistical Organisation and the relevant Ministries and the practice followed in different employment Reports, a rough classification of the economy into the "organised" and the "unorganised" sectors has been done, which in the opinion of this Group is reliable enough to lay down, on a broad basis, the employment strategy for India for the future. Table (A) gives the detailed estimates. The estimates show that (i) unorganised sector has the highest labour content of output with high employment elasticity whereas (ii) organised private sector has the lowest. The public sector (belonging exclusively in the organised sector), which was a major employment provider in the past, has recently by heavy shedding of excess labour become the lowest potential employment generator. Indeed in some cases, its employment elasticity has become even negative. In the unorganised sector, the employment elasticity was as high as 0.213 in 1999-2000 whereas in the organised sector, it was as low as 0.066, i.e., almost a jobless growth.

In the year 1999-2000, the total contribution to employment by the organised sector was only 8 per cent of which private sector segment's contribution was hardly 2.5 per cent. Rest 92 per cent came from the unorganised sector. On this basis, one can see even if the organised sector grows at 20 per cent per annum and the private organised sector at 30 per cent per annum, their contribution to total employment will increase hardly by 1.5 to 2 per cent of the total over the Tenth Plan. This proposition however remains hypothetical since given the capital intensity in this sector as of today (above 5.5), this high growth will not be sustainable because of the saving /investment constraint of the economy. On the basis of this ground reality, the Group concluded that exclusively for generating the desirable high level of employment, we have to target the unorganised sector, including small and medium enterprises, which also cover a large part of the services sector of the economy.

Going into the detailed sector basis, i.e., dealing separately with agriculture, mining, manufacturing, electricity, gas and water, construction, trade, tourism and hotels, transport and communication, including information technology, financial sector and community services sector, we notice that the ranking of prioritisation vis-à-vis employment potential, will almost remain the same as done on the basis of macro classifications i.e., in favour of the unorganised sector, with the single exception of the community, personal and social services sectors where the public sector has a better employment generation capacity than the private one. The sub-sectors identified in this Group are mainly the education and the health services. The detailed parameters, sector-wise, are given in Table 1 (a) and discussions in detail in Chapter II and Chapter III. But the selected strategies, identifying the unorganised sector as the main source for employment generation need to be supported by the test of viability and feasibility. At present, the unorganised sector is contributing nearly 59 per cent in GDP, 92 per cent to employment and also substantially to the exports of the country. In certain areas, in the unorganised sector e.g., in the manufacturing, its growth rate was consistently 2-3 per cent points above the organised manufacturing. Such growth gives confidence about this sector's sustainability. But of late, because of the opening up of the economy with deregulation and market orientation including withdrawal of several key subsidies, the unorganised sector in general and especially some of its components are meeting with growing sickness and slowing down of activities. Some other macro economic changes including removal of quantitative restrictions and reduction of tariffs have also affected their competitiveness in the recent past, leading to some economists putting questions about the very viability of these sectors in the new economic surroundings. This Group does not agree with the view, especially because the percentages of sickness in the unorganised sector in terms of outstanding debts is much lower than the organized sector. But at the same time it realised that the unorganised sector, to be made viable and competitive under the new circumstances, suitable policies and programmes have to be recommended so that the sectors become more productive and quality conscious. It will also have to be ensured that the rule of level playing field is applied for this sector.

The problems and the solutions in terms of selected policies and programmes are all given in detail in the main body of the Report. The Group, however, felt that because the private organised sector has become highly capital intensive and the capital input going to the unorganised sector is relatively declining fast (Table A), appropriate programmes and policies should be devised for suitable reallocation of capital in favour of the labour intensive industries and economising the use of capital in the highly capital intensive organised sector (appropriate for a labour surplus, capital scarce economy) to boost the growth and to make 8 per cent growth feasible. This is corroborated by the fact that the capital efficiency in the unorganised sector is estimated to be much higher than in the organised sector[1].

The other dimension referred to in the Plan's employment policy is regarding the improvement in the quality of jobs available to the people. On this count, the organised sector is in a much better position where the productivity of labour is higher, the wages given are more and the job security is better provided by a separate legislation for the organised sector.

These considerations have led some economists to consider that on the above count, the future strategy on employment should be to encourage only the growth of the organised sector and slowly allow the unorganised sector to wither away gradually. But all the world over, even in the most developed countries, the experience is otherwise. Everywhere, the unorganised sector is contributing substantially to employment and is producing goods in a viable environment. The same is likely to happen in India.

1. SIDBI Annual Report 2002.

The employment strategy that is developed in detail in this Report provides for suitable legislation for improving job quality in the unorganised sector. All policy incentives needed for this purpose for the unorganised sector, however, should be compatible with the present market system and WTO rules. The Report drew lessons from the experiences of several developed and advanced countries, in selecting proper incentive packages and policies before making recommendations in this Report. To sum up, the employment strategy for future, to meet the Plan's employment goals is to encourage the use of labour intensive and capital saving technology, in general and to rejuvenate the growth of the unorganised sector in particular, which at present contributes 92 per cent to the country's employment and enjoys more than seven times labour intensity per unit of production, as compared to the organized sector. However, the unorganised sector needs to be made more productive to sustain itself against the domestic and international competition by proper choice of programmes and policies compatible with India's economic reforms and the WTO rules.

IV. Inter-country Experiences: The Co-existence of the Large and Small Business in Synergy

There is a view among several economists that the organised sector with its better productivity and competitiveness and high job quality is going to replace unorganised small business totally to provide higher growth, better quality of life and employment in the economy. But if we look across the world among some of the most developed and emerging countries, we notice that even under most competitive conditions, it is the unorganised, small business, which is providing major employment opportunities and also surviving alongside with the highly organised large sector. For example, in the U.S. all firms under the Small Business Act contribute nearly 50 per cent of the private workforce along with more than half of GDP[2]. Similarly, in Japan[3], of the total 54.16 million people engaged nationwide (excluding those in primary industries), 42.27 million, i.e., 78 per cent employment is in small and medium enterprises and the total value in manufacturing from

2 US Small Business Administration (SBA)

3 Small Business Cooperation (JSBC)

SMEs is 51 per cent, in wholesale 64 per cent and in retail 78 per cent. In Germany also, 64 per cent of all employeds have their jobs in small and medium firms, which (produces) contributed at least 48 per cent to the Gross National Product and 27 per cent to exports for the year 1990. Lastly, in Korea[4], there are nearly 96,000 small and medium manufacturing enterprises, which employ 1 to 300 persons each. They represent 99.1 per cent of all manufacturing enterprises and account for 69.2 per cent of total employment in this sector. In this context, it may also be noted that most active companies amongst small and medium manufacturing enterprises in Korea employ 5 to 30 persons per unit. Similarly, it is observed that nearly 60 per cent of US small business have 4 employees or less, 18 per cent have 5-9 employees, 11 percent have 10-19, 9 per cent have 20-99, and only 1.4 per cent have above 100-499 – the traditional high-end demarcation in qualifying in the small business segment. In Japan, the SME is also defined as one that employ less than 100 in wholesale and less than 15 in retail and services sector. Similarly, in China SMEs provide nearly 75 per cent of urban job opportunities and their number of units has exceeded 8 million, being 99 per cent of total enterprises in China. A large number of these enterprises are employing around 4 persons per unit under the SME sectors in China. All these suggest that although the definition of SSEs in India and SMEs in some of the most developed countries may not be the same, but at the same time it would be wrong to presume that they are not at all comparable as a large percentage of SME units in these countries employ persons less than fifteen, close to that observed among small enterprises in India. Further, they also enjoy special financial and fiscal privileges as in India. The SB Act in US is one of the notable examples.

IV(a). Incentives Given:

In Korea, as in India, there are the Credit Guarantee programmes which help small enterprises to have access to bank loans without collateral support. Also, like India, Korea has set up a special technology development fund and other programmes for supporting venture capital. On the marketing side, the Central Government, local autonomous authorities and State-run

4 Small and Medium Business Administration (SMBA)

Table – A

Output, Employment & Productivity of Organised, Unorganised and Public Sector

Employment in million #
GDP in crores at 1993-94 prices

	Organised			Un-Organised	Grand Total	% composition		Public	Private
	Total	Public	Private			Organised (a+b)	Un-organised	Sector (a)	Organised (b)
Value added (GDP) (NET)									
1993-94	256849	180343	76006	441143	697992	36.80	63.20	25.9	10.89
1999-2000	418920	266519	152401	600425	1019345	41.10	58.9	26.1	15.0
Growth in per cent	8.50	6.68	12.30	5.27	6.52				
Outstanding Bank Credit of scheduled commercial Banks									
(Rs. thousand crores)*									
1993-94	80.8	28.1	52.7	94.9	175.7	46.0	54.0	16.0	30.0
1999-2000	247.4	66.8	180.6	145.9	393.3	62.9	37.1	17.0	45.9
Growth in per cent	20.5	15.5	22.8	7.4	14.4				

(Contd...)

(...Contd...)

	Organised			Un-	Grand	% composition		Public	Private
	Total	Public	Private	Organised	Total	Organised (a+b)	Un-organised	Sector (a)	Organised (b)
Employment									
1993-94	27.18	19.3	7.88	288.66	315.84	8.61	91.39	6.1	2.51
1999-2000	28.11	19.42	8.69	308.64	336.75	8.34	91.66	5.8	2.54
Growth in per cent	0.56	0.10	1.64	1.12	1.074				
Employment Elasticity	0.066	0.015	0.133	0.213	0.165				
Labour Productivity growth per annum (%) (1993-94 to 1999-2000)	7.88	6.67	8.38	4.10	5.38				
Relative Labour Intensity organised/unorg. (1999-2000)	0.1305								

* EPW, Feb 2-8, 2002. EPW Foundation, Table 10. # Person years

Source:
1. For organised employment, classified by DGE&T, reported in the Economic Survey of Government of India.
2. Organised sector GDP is as classified by CSO.
3. For Bank Credit, Private Corporate sector including Public Sector is equated with organised sector. (March 2000 and March 1994)
4. Unorganised sector is by residual.

NB: The classifications of the economy by value added and employment are not strictly comparable. But even with reasonable margin of error, the dimensional differences in the features of the two sectors – organised and unorganised – are so significantly large as to give enough confidence about the robustness of the findings of this Table.

corporations in Korea are encouraged to extend procurements from SMEs, besides special incentives to increase exports.

In Germany also, special privileges and special incentives are provided for the Small and Medium firms. For example, in the "Equity support programme" earmarked for the small and medium industries, special support is given to young entrepreneurs and new starters. This programme includes, among many, two years free of interest, a comparatively low interest rate, 10-year grace period and 20-year repayment period.

In Japan, there is the Small and Medium Enterprise Basic Law which stipulates that the government must implement necessary measures in a comprehensive manner in the following areas in the SME sectors.

(i) Modernisation of equipment;

(ii) Improvement of technology;

(iii) Rationalisation of management;

(iv) Structural upgrading of small and medium enterprises;

(v) Prevention of excessive competition and establishment of proper sub-contracting; and

(vi) Stimulation of demand.

China has also launched a pilot project to introduce credit guarantee schemes for SMEs, covering 30 provinces. As per estimates, a corpus of around 7.6 billion Yuan (Rs 61 billion) has been raised. Like India, China also has the National Technological Innovation Fund to supplement technology upgradation among SMEs

These are only a few examples which show that in most of the developed and successful Newly Industrialising Economies, SMEs are surviving with selective incentives and making substantial contribution to employment, output and exports.

Therefore, the question of easying out of the SMEs by large organised sector in India in foreseeable future is ruled out. The organised and unorganised sectors are to coexist satisfying the different needs of development and growth, as have happened in most of the developed and newly industrialised economies.

V. *Identification of Areas of New Employment Opportunities and Issues regarding their Viability and Quality*

Of late, the small enterprises growth in the unorganised sector in India has been slower than the growth of the organised sector, especially compared to the private organised sector, in contrast to the eighties when its growth was consistently higher than the organised sector. The potential for higher growth in the unorganised sector both in terms of output and employment remains very high; especially when many segments of this sector are carrying high idle capacity. As to the organised sector, at the moment, its contribution to employment is hardly eight per cent of the total. The public sector which contributes 5.8 per cent of total jobs, at present, is not likely to add to any significant employment generation in the short and medium term because it has excess labour and the future is likely to see more retrenchment than recruitment of new labour in this sector. This Special Group interviewed the public sector executives and came to an assessment that nearly four million excess labour is likely to be shed during the Tenth Plan. The case for encouraging the growth of the organised sector is certainly supported by its capacity to invest in major infrastructure (in most cases, they are capital intensive) to give support systems to the rest of the economy, but for generation of employment, their growth cannot be regarded as the answer. The private organised sector has an employment base of 2.58 per cent to the total. This sector in the second half of 90s grew much faster (nearly 12.3 per cent per annum) and produced high quality jobs compared to the other sectors of the economy. However, because of its low base and comparatively low employment elasticity, it has been estimated that even if it grows at 30 per cent per annum over the Tenth Plan, its contribution to total employment will increase hardly from 2.58 per cent to 3.5 per cent of the total employment.

It is sometimes argued that if the legal conditions for hiring and firing of labour force are relaxed (referring to the present Industrial Disputes Act, 1956), the organised sector could be made more employment-friendly and the employment generation in this sector can be improved. But given the fact that this sector (especially the public sector segment) is already carrying excess labour, the immediate effect will be more firing than hiring. With the already existing high unemployment rate, this can be made socially acceptable only if it is preceded by appropriate social security measures. While in the long run, this relaxation of the 'exit-entry rule' of labour may lead to more hiring of labour per unit of output by the large organised sector, given its present employment elasticity of near zero and its very low employment intensity per unit of output, any improvement in its contribution to jobs in the total employment of the economy will be very marginal, by a few decimal points from the present level of 8-9 per cent of the workforce by the end of the Tenth Plan. Therefore, purely on the ground of employment generation, the favourable effect of any change in this legislation is marginal, at least in the short term. Gradual withdrawal of the Act could be considered, observing the net impact on employment at every phase. Along with it, the social security coverage may be increased and care should be taken of the retrenched labour. As the Labour Commission is looking at all issues in relation to Labour Laws, the Group decided not to deliberate on this issue in this Report.

Even in the services sector where the employment elasticity is high and increasing, the contributions to employment from the organised segment of this sector and their employment elasticities are again very low. Therefore, the importance of the small and medium sector activities for employment generation all across the economy comes to the forefront. However, the viability of a large segment of the unorganised sector against the present ever increasing competition from the domestic and global market is likely to be of great concern in the future. Until now, it has withstood the pressure from major competition and contributed to more than 40 per cent of our exports. But now new challenges are coming from more deregulation and globalisation.

The only answer to this situation is to increase productivity and job quality of the unorganised sector. It means that all attempts should be made to implement those policies, which will release the basic growth constraints and by ensuring a level playing field for this sector. All available studies show that the growth and the quality of jobs in the unorganised sector has been very much affected by the absence of timely low cost credit, improved technology, good infrastructure, quality consciousness, modern marketing, proper organisation and a synergy with the large organised industries. No reliable data is available as to the flow of total credit going in to the unorganised vis-à-vis the organised sector. But in a limited way if we look at the outstanding bank credit of scheduled commercial banks, we notice that the flow has increased significantly in favour of the organised sector from 46.2 per cent in 1993–94 to 62.9 per cent in 1999-2000 whereas in the unorganised sector, it fell from 53.8 per cent to 37.1 per cent during the same period. In other words, bank credit grew by 20.5 per cent per annum in organised sector as against 7.5 per cent in the unorganised sector. This is against a marginal increase in the organised sector as a percentage of GDP to the total. This trend must be reversed. Similarly, percentage of Net Bank Credit to the total credit going to SSI sector came down from 17.5 per cent in 1998 to 14.2 per cent in 2001. Therefore, a higher allocation of credit is needed to the unorganised sector by reducing say the high transaction cost in its credit market when the capital efficiency in the unorganised sector is expected to be much higher than the organised sector. Besides, all measures should be taken to improve its technology, quality and productivity by vocational and other training, skill development, organizational changes like cluster development etc. Indeed hardly 5.3 per cent of Indian youth in the labour force in the age group of 19-24 in 1999-2000 are trained in vocational skills through formal training as against nearly 30 per cent in selected LDC's and above 70 per cent in developed countries. Further, as the strong point of the unorganised small sectors vis-à-vis employment generation is its high employment elasticity, its employment intensive character should be protected by selecting proper labour-intensive technology drawn from all sources including from the grassroots indigenous level and proper rules and regulations should be laid down so that benefits of higher growth get translated in the form of increased earnings of the workers. This is needed because traditionally this sector is vulnerable to exploitation. As has already been mentioned, because the major portion of the poor are in the unorganised sector, a faster growth and productivity in this sector will also reduce poverty. In the attempt to increase the labour productivity, more emphasis should be on the growth of this sector rather than for substituting labour by capital. Further, to improve the job quality and its security, major changes in legislation will be needed regarding basic social security measures, working conditions, minimum wages and protection of labour interests. They have all been discussed in the main body of the Report.

VI. Employment Generation: 50 Million Job Opportunities over the Tenth Plan

In order to formulate the necessary programmes and policies sector-wise and occupation-wise for generating the additional employment opportunities for the future, the Group felt that there is a need for assessing the gaps between the demand and supply of labour i.e., unemployment over the Tenth Plan in the aggregate and in separate categories. The purpose of this report is to formulate policies and programmes in order to fill these gaps. In earlier paragraphs, the potential areas of new employment creation and the broad policies needed for that have been discussed. In this Section, the report attempts to quantify the number of job opportunities to be created, given the Tenth Plan target of 8 per cent growth of GDP and the employment targets of absorbing all the new entrants to the labour force during next 5 years and removing unemployment by the end of the decade. Finally, this has to be assessed against the terms of reference given to this Group: the creation of a minimum ten million gainful employment on an average per year over the Tenth Plan period. For this, the Group decided that the method of estimation of employment and unemployment on the basis of the usual and subsidiary status (UPSS) used during the Ninth Plan formulation would not be of help to get any realistic estimate of the quantum of generating gainful employment in order to fulfill the Tenth Plan targets, especially given the promise for gainful nature of employment, as per the Group's terms of reference. This is because on the basis of UPSS calculation, the volume of unemployment shown is always under-estimated since it excludes a large number who are significantly under-employed or unemployed over a major part of the referred period. Hence, we switched over to what is called the Current Daily Status (CDS), which is conveniently one of the other options provided by the National Sample Survey Organisation for measurement of employment and unemployment. If the gainfully employed are defined as those who are near full-time employed, then the CDS definition on employment given by the NSSO will give more realistic estimate at least directionally.

Most countries across the globe use the concept close to weekly status, which again is closer to that of CDS used in this report. Within India almost all other reports from alternate sources agree that the CDS concept of unemployment is the most realistic. All these issues have been explained in Chapter I of this Report in detail.

On this basis (i.e., CDS), the Group's exercise shows that given an 8 per cent growth per annum and an unchanged pattern of growth as well as the continuance of the increased capital intensity in production, especially in the organised sector which was observed in the late 1990s, the maximum job opportunities that will be generated will be around 5-6 million a year on the average, much below the ten million target given. This will also fail even to absorb the new entrants to the labour force over this period, which will be around seven million a year, with the optimistic assumption of the labour force growth of 1.8 per cent per annum against working age growth of 2.3 percent per annum over the Tenth Plan. On the top of it, the base period (2001-02) unemployment pool of 35.0 million will remain untouched. This led to the view that given the present economic parameters in India, growth per se will not be able to provide the required job opportunities. This placed a big policy challenge before the planners as to how to change the pattern of growth by reforming the macro and sectoral policies, supplemented by developing appropriate programmes and schemes in specific sectors so that the new job opportunities could be created. Some economists provide an alternative approach that the Plan's growth target should be raised to above 10 per cent to satisfy the Plan's target of employment. This is based on the assessment that given a low employment generation capacity of output and the increasing capital intensity of the economy, a higher growth rate is the only answer. But the Group's view is that at present even the target of 8 per cent growth is under heavy financial constraints. The proposed alternative of 10 per cent growth rate will need more than 36-37 per cent of investment rate, raising from the present 24 percent, which seems to be rather infeasible. Therefore, according to the Group, the only alternative left is to economise the use of capital and adopt more labour intensive pattern of production so that within a feasible growth rate, the employment target can be fulfilled. Accordingly, the Group interacted and examined all the programmes and schemes of respective Ministries and agencies and the policy changes undergone in the reform process and came to the view that even at an 8 per cent growth per annum, only by proper selection of programmes and policies and technology, it is possible to generate ten million job opportunities per year which will help to absorb all new entrants to the labour force and reduce unemployment to near-zero by the end of the present decade. It identified the activities where there is a major potential of large new job opportunities as in agriculture, including social forestry, animal husbandry, fishing, horticulture and related areas and small and medium industries, construction, tourism, information technology, financial sector, education and health. A major portion of these activities is in the unorganised sector. This sector also includes a large number of self-employed and artisans. The details are given in Chapter V and Annexure A. For exploiting their potentialities, the recommended policy initiatives have been discussed in detail in Chapter V. In many instances, these proposed changes in policies and programmes would not entail any significant additional finance. They would ask for involvement of grassroot enterprise, skills, institutions and often even indigenous technology. This should be further supported by creation of an enabling environment by removing all legislative hurdles and bureaucratic interference. Besides, it is realized that there is a need for launching specific employment generating programmes in some areas where aggregate growth is having little impact. This includes, the Prime Minister's Rozgar Yojana (PMRY) in the small scale sector and the Rural Employment Generation Programme (REGP) in the KVIC, the Sampoorna Gram Rozgar Yojana (SGRY), the Pradhan Mantri Gram Sadak Yojana (PMGSY), Swarnajayanti Gram Swarojgar Yojana (SGSY) and many other specific programmes in Agriculture, Horticulture, Fishing, Forestry, Animal Husbandry, small business and certain areas of social services targeting employment and income generation in general and in the rural sector in particular as well as in specific target groups and regions. Grassroot institutions and appropriate NGOs and voluntary organisations should be made partners in the implementation of most of these programmes.

The needs for employment vary across age groups, education level, skill possessed, social group, and place of residence – rural or urban. Indeed such characteristics come out in much sharper contrast across regions. Expectations from a job also vary with the general level of economic development at a location. In this context the most backward or distressed locations and social groups deserve higher priority. In the Tenth Plan a new scheme to guarantee employment to all those in the need of work is to be launched in selected most distressed districts in the country.

All these special programmes have been discussed in detail in the Annexure A and the broad macro sectoral policies in Chapter V. Conceptually, the potential job creation has been decomposed into (i) mainly from the growth buoyancy; and (ii) from specific employment generation programmes and programmes for changing the patterns of growth between sectors and sub-sectors, regions and occupational groups.

According to the Group's exercise, of the proposed 50 million job opportunities to be generated over the Tenth Plan, nearly 20 million should come from specific employment generation programmes and 30 million from growth buoyancy. Most of the selected specific programmes are based on creating tangible assets and hence they are supposed to generate a continuous employment stream. Care should be taken to avoid programmes or schemes, which generate one time employment only. As has already been mentioned, nearly 90 per cent of the new job opportunities will come from the growth of small and medium enterprises and self-employeds. The estimated composition of job opportunities is given in the following (Table-B).

Table – B

The Estimates of Potential Job Opportunities in Different Sectors (in millions)

	Total Additional Job opportunities created over the Tenth Plan (Million)		Total Incremental (Million)	Total Employment Terminal year of Tenth Plan (Million)
	Growth based (a)	Programme based (b)	(a+b)	
Agriculture*Including National Watershed Development Project for Rainfed Areas (NWDPRA), Farm Management Programme, Agro Clinics, Greening India Programme, Watershed and Wasteland Development, Medicinal Plant, Bamboo Development and Energy Plantation like Ethanol etc.	0.41	9.06	9.47	200.48
Mining & Minerals	-0.20		-0.21	2.01
Manufacturing (Excl. Prime Minister's Rozgar Yojana (PMRY) & Rural Employment Generation Programme (REGP).	1.42 (large Manufacturer)		1.42	49.51
	6.0 (SSI)		6.0	
Electricity, Gas & Water	-0.21		-0.21	0.88
Construction	6.30		6.30	22.46
Trade, Hotels & Restaurants	11.23		11.23	52.22
Transport, Storage & Communications	5.51		5.51	20.43
Financial Sector	1.93		1.93	7.25
Community Sector	-2.71	3.2	0.49	30.06

(Contd...)

Special Programmes *				
Prime Minister's Rozgar Yojana				
(PMRY) (SSI) REGP (KVIC)		2.2	2.2	
		2.0	2.0	
Sampoorna Gramin Rozgar Yojana (SGRY)		1.29	1.29	
Pradhan Mantri Gram				7.06
Sadak Yojana (PMGSY)		0.77	0.77	
& Swarna Jayanti Gram Swarozgar Yojana (SGSY)		0.80	0.80	
Total	**29.67**	**19.32**	**48.99** (Approx. 49-50)	392.35

* Details are given in Table 5& 7 & Annexure (A)

VII. Attainment of Plan Employment Objectives and the Supportive Policies

Table B shows that the employment generated from the targeted high rate of growth of eight per cent per annum over the Tenth Plan needs to be supplemented by schemes and programmes for generating additional employment opportunities of around 65 per cent more in order to satisfy the employment generation target of the Tenth Plan. In total, it asks for nearly 49-50 million additional employment generation to cover the substantial gap between the demand for and supply of labour (i.e., unemployment over the Tenth Plan), thereby fulfilling the objectives set out in the Approach Paper of the Tenth Plan. The likely composition will be around 60 per cent from growth and 40 per cent from policy-based programmes and schemes to be launched over the Tenth Plan. For accelerating growth from the present level of 8 per cent per annum, several key macro and other sectoral policies need be changed with further reform and deregulation in a wide range of activities. In addition, accelerated investment programmes mainly covering the key social and physical infrastructure areas are recommended. All these have been spelt out in Chapter V and Annexure A of this Report. The recommended policy changes are spread over a large canvass, covering at one end hi-tech large organised industries and services and at the other end pertaining to those in the small and medium business including even the tiny industries in the unorganised sector. However, the general message is that the unorganised sector initially will need more support and incentives from the Government as compared to the organised sector. The percentage share of the three broad sectors in incremental terms (refer to the Table C) in generating employment is estimated as (i) 19 per cent from primary, (ii) 29 per cent from secondary sector and (iii) 52 per cent from services sector. In total (i) 52 per cent from agriculture, (ii) 14 per cent from secondary sector and (iii) 34 per cent from services sector in terms of employment in the terminal year of the Tenth Plan.

Table – C

Employment Generation Broad Sector Wise (10 th Plan)

Sectors	2001-02 (million)	% age	In million Incremental over 10th Plan	% age	2006-2007 (million)	% age
Primary	193.2	56.3	9.26	18.9	202.46	51.6
Secondary sector	42.09	12.5	14.48	29.52	56.57	14.43
Services Sector	108.06	31.5	25.26	51.6	133.32	33.98
Total	343.35	100.00	49.00	100.00	392.35	100.00

Table D shows that given the pattern of generation of additional employment opportunities (presented in Table C), the unemployment rate will go down by nearly 44 per cent over the Tenth Plan period and will almost be eliminated by the end of the Eleventh Plan. The additional employment generation over the Tenth Plan will be around 49-50 million persons i.e. a rate of growth of 2.7 per cent per annum over the Tenth Plan against a labour force growth of 1.8 per cent per annum. This scenario will satisfy the stipulated employment target of the Tenth Plan and generate 10 million job opportunities every year.

Table – D

Employment Scenario based on 8% Growth per Annum and Changed Industrial Structure on the Basis of Proposed Policy and Programmes in the Tenth Plan*

	Unit	1999-2000	2001-2002	2006-2007	2011-2012	Growth over 10th Plan percentage per annum
Labour Force	million	363.33	378.21	413.50	453.52	1.8
Employment	million	336.75	343.36	392.35	451.53	2.7
No. of unemployeds	million	26.58	34.85	21.15	1.99	-9.5
Unemployment rate	(%)	7.32	9.21	5.11	0.44	

Special group estimates

* on CDS basis

VIII. Quality Labour Supply

The manpower planning for the future needs be programmed separately for each occupation so that the increased demand for skilled and educated persons should be matched by corresponding increase in the supply of skilled and educated persons over the Tenth Plan. It is observed at present that the unemployment among educated and skilled workers is very high nearly touching 25 per cent (three times more than the national average of unemployment rate) and at the same time in contrast, there are shortages, in certain sectors. This may be partly because of the fact that most of the education and skill development in the past have been geared to satisfy the need of the organised sector, which provided higher remuneration and better job quality and security. But in future, because of the limit in the absorbing capacity for additional employment in the organised sector, education and skills need to be orientated primarily towards the needs of the unorganised sector like agriculture, small industry, services and self-employed as also the new areas like IT, tourism and financial sectors. There is a danger that otherwise the economy will be experiencing growing unemployment among high skilled "formally trained" personnel and at the same time it will suffer from shortages in low level skilled and vocationally trained people in the labour market, inhibiting the improvement in productivity and a sustainable growth in the unorganised sector. Lastly, the complimentarity of the development needs between the large and small unorganised sectors has to be properly revived as only then a sustainable growth in employment could be achieved fulfilling the Plan target, creating 10 million jobs a year. The Report in Chapter V spells out the policies and programmes needed to build the required targeted manpower and employment.

It is however worth mentioning that unless for every programme/scheme, appropriate delivery systems are developed, most of the above employment generation targets may not materialize. All these will result in poor governance, which the Mid Term Review of the Ninth Plan so eloquently pointed out, happening all across many other sectors of the economy. For correcting this gap, among many other necessary measures, the key one is to launch an ambitious civil service renewal programme aimed at strengthening of the delivery institutions, direct administration and the panchayats.

The Report has concluded by giving a caution that unless the cause of employment is taken up on a high priority and not on "business as usual" basis, the unemployment at the end of the Tenth Plan will reach around 40 million i.e., nearly ten per cent of the labour force, with severe socio-economic implications, especially in certain areas and among certain sections of the population.

1

Introduction

This special group on "generation of employment opportunities for creating 10 million jobs per annum over the Tenth Plan" has been constituted by the Planning Commission under the chairmanship of Dr. S.P. Gupta, Member, Planning Commission, on 5.9.2001. Its objectives are: (i) to explore avenues for fulfilling the Tenth Plan targets of providing gainful employment to all additions to the labour force over the Tenth Plan period (2001-02 to 2006-07) and (ii) to create opportunities for gainful employment of around 10 million per annum, on the average, so that the rate of unemployment is reduced significantly by the end of 10th Plan period and almost eliminated by the Eleventh Plan period. (For detailed terms of reference see Annexure).

In preparing this report, the special group has examined all the studies/reports recently available in this field including the one brought out by the Task Force on Employment Opportunities appointed by the Planning Commission on 21.1.99 and released on 1.7.2001. Besides, it felt the urgent need for updating all available information and to probe into the problem of measurement of employment and unemployment in order to understand the nature and extent of unemployment and structure of employment for the year 2001-02, which is the base year of the 10th Plan.

While exploring the avenues for employment generation, the group had to take cognizance of the fact that the GDP growth in the late 90s is seen not to be accompanied by a commensurate expansion in employment. Further, in future, public sector employment is expected to decline more as it is carrying excess labour at present and is also physically withdrawing from several areas. There are fears that the process of internal liberalization and global competition, though inevitable, may increase the capital intensity of production and more of labour substitution resulting in job losses or even negative growth in many areas. For example, the existing industrial units in the organised sector are already shedding excess labour in order to remain competitive and for that they are adopting new technologies, which are typically more automated and therefore not job creating. This problem is further aggravated by the downsizing of the public sector undertakings. Most of the public sector undertakings are now going in for Voluntary Retirement Schemes through which it is roughly estimated that nearly 10 per cent to 15 per cent of their workforce, i.e., around 3.88 million can be retrenched over the medium term period. The net result of these forces could be a very slow growth of employment in the organised sector. Besides, the weightage of the organised private sector at present is hardly around 3% of total employment. One has therefore to look necessarily into the possibilities of generating more jobs in the unorganised sector. But many innovative policies and programmes will be needed to generate "gainful" employment in the unorganised sector.

A new look to the future employment strategy is, therefore needed to ensure its "quality and gainful nature" and to work out appropriate policies and programmes so that the objectives of the Tenth Plan employment target of absorbing all increase in the labour force and eliminating unemployment by the end of the Eleventh Plan are achieved.

Concepts and Sources

There has been a continuing debate regarding the appropriate method of measurement of employment and unemployment in an economy. It is well known that just as very few can afford to remain unemployed from the labour force in a poor country like India for all the days of the year, so also, not many can get employment all the days of the year. Hence one has to decide as to who will be regarded as employed in terms of days they work during the year and its intensity in terms of hours of work they undergo. Here some cut off point is needed. Similarly, about "Quality" of employment, we have to decide whether we should relate it to the earning capacity of labour, setting a floor like the minimum wage or to the extent of security the labour enjoys in the work surroundings or to the labour's contribution to production. Here also some precise definition is needed. All these we have tried to take into consideration in this report on the basis of the existing information covering several major sources.

Sources: There are four major sources chosen providing inter-temporal and spatial data on work force and unemployment: (i) National Sample Survey of the Government of India (NSSO) (ii) Employment Exchange registers at different centres, run by the government (iii) Census of population and (iv) the Economic Census by CSO. The first one is the most comprehensive one, which we have mainly used in this report and the others we have used at times for comparisons within their known limitations and non-comparability. The 1999-2000 NSS covers rural and urban sectors of 509779 and 309234 persons respectively.

The employment and unemployment rates are generally available from the estimates made, based on NSSO's surveys, every five years. However, these estimates are not related to the remuneration or productivity of the employeds. No available indicators are recorded in the NSSO Survey to get estimates of the productivity of employeds so that they can be related directly with the concept of gainful employment. It provides only a measurement of people who are not sitting idle for certain days of the year. NSS also provides estimates of employment on the basis of time disposition of the person.

The NSSO provides four different measures of employment and unemployment, which capture different facets of employment/unemployment situation following the recommendations of the Expert (Dantwala) Committee on Unemployment.

- Usual Principal Status (UPS): A person is counted as being in the labour force on principal usual activity basis if he was either engaged in economic activity (work) or reported seeking/being available for work for the major part of the preceding 365 days. Those classified as being in the labour on this basis are further unemployed depending on whether the majority of the days in labour force was spent in economic activity or in seeking/being available for work. The Usual Principal Status unemployment rate is the proportion of those classified as unemployed on this basis expressed as a percentage of those classified as being in the labour force. On this criterion, persons can be counted as being employed even if they were unemployed (or were outside the labour force) for a significant part of the year. Equally, a person can be counted as unemployed even though he may have been employed for part of the year.

- Usual Principal and Subsidiary Status (UPSS): This provides a more inclusive measure covering, in addition, the participation in economic activity on a more or less regular basis of those classified as unemployed on the Usual Principal Status as also of those classified as being outside the labour force on the same criterion. This would result in a larger proportion of the population as being in the labour force with a higher proportion of workers and lower unemployment rates relative to the UPS criterion.
- Current Weekly Status (CWS) : The reference period here is the week, i.e., the 7 days preceding the interview. A person is counted as employed if he was engaged in economic activity for at least one hour on any day during the reference week. A person not being engaged in economic activity even for one hour on any day but reporting seeking/being available for work during the reference week is classified as unemployed. To the extent that employment varies seasonally over the year, the labour force participation rates on the Current Weekly Status would tend to be lower. However, reflecting the unemployment during the current week of those classified as being employed on the UPS (and the UPSS) criterion, the Current Weekly Status unemployment rates would tend to be the higher. The difference between the unemployment rates on the Current Weekly and that on the Usual Status would provide one measure of seasonal unemployment.
- Current Daily Status (CDS): Based on the reported time disposition of the person on each day of the reference week (in units of half day where needed by the presence of multiple activities within a day), person-days in

> employment (unemployment) are aggregated to generate estimates of person days in employment/unemployment. The person day unemployment rate is derived as the ratio of person days in labour force (i.e. person day in employment plus person days in unemployment). This measure captures the within-week unemployment of those classified as employed on the Weekly Status. The CDS measure of unemployment is widely agreed to be the one that most fully captures open unemployment in the country.

In the earlier report of the Task Force on Employment Opportunities, the recommendations were based on calculations of employment and unemployment on Usual Principal and Subsidiary Status basis (UPSS). It was viewed in this present report that CDS is a better measure to capture unemployment than the usual status and therefore the CDS basis bas been used in this report for estimation purpose. For this a special Tabulation has been done by NSSO.

The rationale for using CDS as measuring employment and unemployment is the following. The terms of reference of the Report is to find out the unemployment gap in terms of absence of gainful employment opportunities and to work out policies and programmes to fill the gap. At the moment, there is a large unemployed and under-employed workforce i.e., not having any gainful employment, although by using the measurement on UPSS basis, several of them are declared employed. This results in over-estimation of the level of employment. To avoid this, largely, we have estimated the extent of employment and unemployment on CDS basis.

To support this choice, we quote from NSSO employment and unemployment report of 1999-2000 "the usual status approach adopted for classification of the population is unable to capture the changes in the activity pattern caused by seasonal fluctuations. But the estimate obtained by adopting the current weekly or current daily status approaches are expected to reflect the overall effect caused by the intermittent changes in the activity pattern during the year. The latter (CDS) reflects also the changes which take place even during the week. The estimate of the employed based on current daily status gives average daily picture of employment".

Thus, we regard in this report CDS measurement as the most appropriate because we want to have an estimate of the gap i.e., that is jobs to be created on gainful basis in order to bring out recommendations as to how they can be filled up by changes in policies and programmes.

The NSSO Report also provides estimates of the likely under-employment that is hidden in the number of employed category calculated by the usual and subsidiary status approach when they are compared with current daily status. The activity pattern of the usual employment during the days within the reference week is indicated by the distribution of their days by current daily status. The relevant results for rural and urban India are presented in the following (Table E). It is observed that the proportion of person days of the usually employed, utilised for work, is lower for females as compared to the males throughout the period 1987-88 to 1999-2000. During 1999-2000 this proportion was estimated at about 68 per cent and 79 per cent for females in the rural and urban India respectively as against 90 per cent and 94 per cent for males in rural and urban India respectively. Once again, it is observed that if the work is not available, large portion of the females withdrew from the labour force rather than report themselves as unemployed. The distribution obtained from the present survey is presented in Table E.

Table E

Per 1000 Distribution of Persons-days of Usually Employed (principal and subsidiary status taken together) by their Broad Current Daily Status

Current daily status	Rural						Urban					
	Male			Female			Male			Female		
	1999-00	1993-94	1987-88	1999-00	1993-94	1987-88	1999-00	1993-94	1987-88	1999-00	1993-94	1987-88
(1)	(2)	(3)	(4)	(5)	(6)	(7)	(8)	(9)	(10)	(11)	(12)	(13)
Employed	897	909	926	676	663	638	942	949	938	791	766	716
Unemployed	53	40	27	41	30	26	27	27	37	22	24	37
Not in labour force	51	51	47	283	306	336	31	25	25	187	210	247
All	1000	1000	1000	1000	1000	1000	1000	1000	1000	1000	1000	1000

There are three other major sources providing information on employment and unemployment and their present status. They are: the latest population census of 2001 and the employment exchange information of the government. The population census provides decadal growth of the main workers and also of the marginal workers. Main workers are defined as those who have work for the major part of the reference period (i.e., 6 months or more). The marginal workers are those who had not worked for the major part of the reference period. The estimates of workforce as percentage to population are available on all-India basis, also state-wise and in the union territories. In this Census Report, however, the concepts of employment and unemployment are different from one given in the NSSO Report. Therefore, a strict comparison should not be attempted; only their broad trends can be used.

The third source is the data given by employment exchanges. There are nearly 958 employment exchanges spread all over India which record registration for jobs in the live register on a time series basis; but there are major problems in using the information from this source, because of the following reasons.

(i) All the job seekers registered with the employment exchange are not necessarily unemployed.

(ii) All job seekers or unemployed do not register themselves with the employment exchange.

(iii) In some exceptional cases, there is a chance of duplication in the register.

(iv) The job seekers who find employment through agencies other than employment exchanges do not always report to the employment exchanges for deletion of their names.

(v) Employers also do not intimate the employment exchanges when selections are done from the employment exchanges' list.

(vi) There are cases when a default to renew the cards results in deletion of their names.

The fourth source is the Economic Census of 1998 brought out by India's Central Statistical Organisation. This census provides, among several others, the data on the growth of the workforce. Here of course the farm sector (i.e., the crop production and plantation) is excluded. To quote "The census included all enterprises engaged in economic activity, both agricultural and non-agricultural, whether employing hired work or not except in crop production and plantation". The definition of workers in the Economic Census, however, is not comparable with the NSSO definition. Therefore, the data can be used only to have a broad comparison in trends on employment with the NSSO data.

2

Present Employment and Unemployment Situation

The Table 1, 1(b) and 9 to 19 provide the present employment and unemployment scenario in India based on the latest data from The National Sample Survey Organisation for 1999-2000. The estimates on employment and unemployment have been made on the basis of current daily status (CDS); the rationale for choosing CDS basis has already been discussed in the earlier chapter. From the analysis of these tables, the following conclusions are drawn:

(1) There has been a deceleration in the population growth between 1983 to 1993-94 and 1993-94 to 1999-2000 from two per cent per annum to 1.9 per cent per annum [Table 1(b)].

(2) There has been a significant deceleration in the labour force growth from 2.43 per cent per annum to 1.3 per cent per annum, between the two periods [Table 1(b)].

(3) There has been a significant acceleration in GDP growth between 1983-84 to 1993-94 and 1993-94 to 1999-2000 from 5.2 per cent to 6.7 per cent per annum [Table 23].

(4) There is a significant decline in the labour intensity in production in almost all the sectors barring a few and also in the aggregate, declining from 0.52 to 0.16 measured as employment elasticity to value added [Table 1].

(5) Because of this, in spite of a higher growth in GDP over the second period, employment growth declined

from 2.7 per cent to 1.07 per cent per annum [Table 1(b)].

(6) As a result, the number of unemployed has increased from 20.13 million in 1993-94 to 26.58 million in 1999-2000. In 1983, it was also as high as 21.8 million [Table 1(b)]. In fact it would have been much higher but for the very heavy deceleration in the growth of the labour force from 2.43 per cent to 1.3 per cent per annum. This deceleration in the labour force has happened in spite of the fact that the working age population (15-59 years) increased more than 2.5 per cent per annum over this period.

(7) Consequently, the unemployment rate i.e., unemployed as percentage of labour force increased from 5.99 per cent in 1993-94 to 7.32 per cent in 1999-2000 [Table 1(b)].

(8) Inter-state unemployment rates are also showing increasing regional disparity in the year 1999-2000 compared to 1993-94. In the later year, the highest unemployment is noticed in Kerala of 20.97 per cent of labour force and lowest in Himachal Pradesh of 2.96 per cent of the labour force (Table 9).

(9) The unemployment rate is much higher in the lower consumption classes than in the upper ones; the lowest consumption classes having nearly 100 per cent more unemployment rate than the higher ones. This has significant implication for households below the poverty line. (Table 12).

9(a) Similarly, the percentage of casual labour to total labour has increased significantly since 1977-78 and mainly at the expense of self-employed. The regular salaried labour in proportion has almost remained the same over time. This increased casualisation of labour has been of some concern vis-à-vis the job quality and security of employment. In the Report's policy recommendations to improve the job quality of labour, especially in the unorganised sector, where casual labour is more concentrated, proper care has been taken by developing corresponding social security measures (safety nets) and changes in legislation so that this sector is not heavily exploited. In the recent Population Census of 2001, it is seen that there also is a heavy increase in the marginal workforce as against the main workforce. [Table 30]

(10) In terms of employment elasticity of output, as has already been mentioned, it has gone down from 0.52 over the years 1983 to 1993-94 to 0.16 over 1993-94 to 1999-2000. This means that over this period, there has been a reduction in the labour intensity of output of the order of 31 per cent i.e., 5.5 per cent per annum. This is indeed much higher than the reduction in the labour intensity at the rate of 2.20 per cent per annum in the earlier period i.e., between 1983 and 1993-94. This trend in the decline of the labour use in output (i.e., employment elasticity) is observed not only in the aggregate, but also in most sectors with two exceptions (a) transport and (b) financial services and real estate (Table 1). The overall decline in the employment elasticity is to a large extent due not only to the changes in the broad 9 sector composition of output, but also in the intra-sectoral composition and technology impacts of labour capital substitution. A separate study shows that the capital intensity in Indian economy in almost all the sectors, including even the small unorganised sectors and services, is increasing over time. The aggregate ICOR has increased from previous 3.4 (over 1991-92 to 1996-97) to nearly 4.4 since 1996-97. Over the Ninth Plan it touched over 5.0.

(11) Employment in organised sector had been hardly 8.34 per cent, of which public sector accounts for 5.77 per cent and private sector only 2.58 per cent in the total employment generated (Table 1).

(12) The organised sector is dominated by public sector by contributing nearly 70 per cent of employment of the organised sector. This is mainly in (i) mining, (ii)

electricity and water and (iii) community and social services. These three constitute nearly 60 per cent of the public sector employment and unfortunately all of them are showing negative employment elasticity. All these show that the public sector (which are all in the organised sector) contributed to a very small extent in the total employment generation during this period (1993-94 to 1999-2000). Of the remaining, the "public sector transport" in contrast, has contributed sizeably to organised sector employment during this period although the employment elasticity is much lower than the unorganised segment Table 1(a). Thus this sector has a comparatively high potential in the organised group for employment generation in the future provided it increases its employment elasticity. So far as community and social services are concerned, nearly 85 per cent of the employment in the organised group are in the public sector although they showed a very low employment elasticity in the past. But the Group viewed that they have large employment generation potentiality for the future, especially in some of their sub-sectors like education and health; However, the Public Sector in aggregate (between 1993-94 and 1999-2000) has shown almost a jobless growth, when its employment elasticity was 0.015 (Table A). Further, in future a large part of this sector's potential growth may be negated by the impending downsizing policy (often called as right sizing) of the government, which affects this sector significantly.

(13) Another sector in the organised public group is the construction. This sector as a whole has a high employment elasticity and high output potential; but the weightage of the organised sector in general and public sector in particular is very low and its observed employment elasticity is around zero. Indeed for generating employment, the private sector, especially the unorganised private sector should be targetted.

(14) Of the organised manufacturing, the employment generation potential of the private sector is seen to be

higher than the public sector manufacturing (the former contributing more than 75 per cent of total organised manufacturing output), but it hardly constitutes 1.5 per cent against the total employment of the country and 16.5 per cent of total manufacturing employment. The remaining 83.5 per cent of employment is generated in the informal/ unorganised manufacturing where the labour intensity of output seems to be nearly 10 times more [Table 2].

(15) Thus, to summarise, although the quality of employment in organised sector is high, its contribution to employment is likely to be rather limited and moreover confined only to few sectors like financial services, manufacturing and potentially in the social services like education and health. Of course, although sectors like electricity and water have a low direct employment generation potentiality, their indirect employment effects may be considerable, helping employment generation in many other sectors of the economy.

(16) The major source of employment generation is the unorganised sector of the economy including self-employment and small business where the present employment weightage is as high as 92 per cent of the total employed labour force.

(17) Its main employment generating activities are (a) agriculture and allied, (b) trade, restaurant and hotels including tourism, (c) some of the social sectors like education and health, (d) the small and medium enterprises, mainly in the rural non-farm sector (e) transport & construction. For example, the small and medium manufacturing enterprises contribute to nearly 80 per cent of the manufacturing employment and its employment elasticity is 2.9 times more than the organised sector (Table 2). We can, therefore, consider that to achieve a more favourable effect on employment, what is needed is a shift in the percentage composition of manufacturing in favour of SSI and medium units. Indeed, the past experience shows that the small and medium units in the unorganised sector

are growing much faster compared to the organised industries, helping the desired shift.

(18) Even as of today, the agriculture including allied activities, comprises 57 per cent of India's total employment. Between 1983 and 1993-94, its employment elasticity was as high as 0.70 and now in the later period of 1993-94 to 1999-2000, it has come down to 0.01. This decline is largely due to changes in the intra-sectoral composition within this sector when most of the labour-intensive sub-sectors grew comparatively slower, along with some significant mechanization in other sub-sectors. This decline might also be reflecting some reduction in under-employment in the agriculture sector; when there is a shift of labour from agriculture to non-farm rural activities and migration to urban areas. But given an appropriate policy, this sector can still be a gold mine for generating faster employment by changes in the sectoral composition of agriculture in favour of labour intensive high value areas like horticulture, floriculture, agro-forestry, minor irrigation, watersheds etc. Details are given in Chapter III of the Report.

(19) The other major employment generating areas in the unorganised sector that have already been identified are trade, restaurant and tourism, and information technology (IT). They are all witnessing a high growth of above 9.0 per cent per annum and are having very high employment elasticities. The transport, construction and the other services sectors are also equally equipped for their high growth and employment intensiveness.

(20) To sum up, with some changes in the inter and intra sectoral composition and adopting appropriate labour intensive technology, growth in the unorganised sector can be significantly raised. The organised sector, especially its public sector component, has a rather low employment generating potential, being handicapped by a negative employment elasticity with the exception of the financial sectors and potentiality in certain parts of social sector like education, health etc. But these two

have as low a weightage as 3.3 per cent to the total employment. The community and social services need a major change in the composition in favour of health, education etc., and only then can it substantially contribute to the growth. Already a significant increase in the weightage of this sector in this group is in sight. It was 25.8 per cent in 1993-94 and 33.3 per cent now. These two sub-sectors together are showing a growth rate of around 4.5 per cent per annum compared to this sector's growth of 0.2 per cent per annum between 1993-94 and 1999-2000. Given the Tenth Plan's target on education, literacy and health standard, the scope of its growth and potential employment generation is very high.

(21) In terms of contributing to incremental employment growth between 1993-94 and 1999- 2000, the organised component has done better than the unorganised component in mining, minerals, electricity and social services. Interestingly, all these sectors are almost wholly under the public sector domain. In the organised transport, public sector's growth is higher than private sector and also its weights. Therefore, so far as organised transport is concerned, public sector shows greater growth potential. For the remaining sectors like agriculture, manufacturing, construction, wholesale trade, transport and financial services sector, performance in employment generation of the unorganised sector is far better.

(22) Regarding the growth of workforce in the occupational category, it is noticed that the highest growth in this period is observed in administrative, executive and managerial personnel, followed by service workers and production related workers including transport equipment operators and labourers. The growth of the managerial personnel increased from around 4 per cent per annum between 1961 and 1993-94 to 9 per cent per annum between 1993-94 and 1999-2000 on UPSS basis. Similarly, the service workers growth also doubled in the later period. All these increases are primarily at the

expense of farmers, fishermen, hunters, loggers and related workers where hardly a growth of -0.21 is observed. (Sundaram-Employment and Poverty in India in the Nineties, Golden Jubilee Seminar of NSSO, May 2001 – Table 6). Similarly, we notice high growths among (i) the professionals, nurses and medical and health technicians (6.86 per cent), (ii) launders, hairdressers, beauticians (4.4 per cent), (iii) transport operators (6.53 per cent) and (iv) brick and other construction workers (nearly 7.92 per cent per annum) during the latter period (1993-94 to 1999-2000) which are much higher than the aggregate growth of the workforce during this period. This suggests that the composition of the labour force is becoming more and more skill-oriented with better training and education. Implicitly, it also means that the skill component of the production process is increasing with better technology resulting in higher productivity to meet the present compulsion of market competition. The percentage composition for technical and skilled personnel to total manpower in the organised sector is much higher, as this sector uses comparatively hi-tech production. But because of its low employment elasticity and contribution of hardly 5 – 7 per cent to total employment in the year 1999-2000, the scope of job opportunity for educated and skilled manpower in the sector will be marginal. The major absorption of educated and skilled labour over 1993-94 and 1999-2000 indeed came from the unorganised sector. This is a very good omen for future signaling that the labour productivity and skill base of the unorganised sector has increased over this period. It has been estimated that the contribution of skilled and educated manpower in India over this late 90's was hardly 7 to 8 per cent of the total labour force (Prof. Sundaram's Paper, as referred). This means that there is a tremendous potential for increase in demand for the educated and skilled, providing opportunities for new jobs in the future. The extent of potentials for jobs in this area will be further appreciated if we notice that in most of the developed countries, the technical and educated job component of workforce is as high as or more than 50 per cent. Now the challenge is how to increase the supply of labour force of better skill and better quality to match the potential demand visualized in the Tenth Plan. But the planner should note that although the unemployment rate among the educated and skilled are now showing signs of marginal decrease, still it is very high on average and especially in certain areas and in certain types of professional skills (Table 29). For example, at the aggregate level the unemployment rate among educated and especially among skilled workers are nearly two to three times more than the all India aggregate unemployment rate. As educated unemployeds are more vocal, all steps need to be taken to see that the supply of skilled labour must match the demand for them and the existing pool of educated and skilled unemployed (with proper training) should be absorbed first. At the same time in certain areas immediate action should be taken to plan for increasing the supply of personnel, to avoid bottleneck in future, hampering the growth of the economy. For example, at this moment the supply of teachers, trainers and technicians is showing little increase. Indeed, the teacher supply in this period was hardly one per cent per annum. All efforts should be made in future employment policy to increase the supply of teachers and trainers immediately, especially in the vocational area and appropriate programmes should be launched to increase entrepreneurial capabilities and skill for self-employment. But in this context appropriate policies should be taken to make jobs in these sectors attractive. Hence the whole concept of improving job quality comes. As the absorption capacity for high skill jobs has its own limit in the organised sector, the future plan for education and training should keep in mind the type of skill needed for many newly emerging activity sectors like IT, tourism, financial services and the vast unorganised SSI and services sector including the new area in agriculture and the non-farm rural activities. All these have been discussed in detail in

Chapter V of this Report.

(23) As an alternative source, we get the estimates of the growth of work force over the 1990s from the 2001 Census. Table 14, Section A gives the decadal growth rate of the workforce over the 1990s. Here again we notice the growth of workforce comprising the main workers (we have taken the main workers separating the marginal workers since it is closer to the concept of the workforce measured on the CDS basis) has decelerated significantly from the 1980s of around 2.34 per cent to 0.81 per cent in the1990s. These estimates are not strictly comparable with NSSO estimates because of their differences in the concept and measurement used for the workforce. But both the NSSO and the Census clearly demonstrate that there has been a significant deceleration in the growth of workforce (from the eighties to the nineties). As to the rate of growth of the marginal workers in the Census they grew much faster compared to the main workers; this is corroborated also by the fast growth of casual workers in the NSSO Survey. But here again one should be careful in trying any strict comparisons between the two sets of estimates.

As already mentioned, the "employment exchange" data is another source for estimating the incidence of unemployment in the country. Here also, we notice, on an annual basis, the number in the live register of the employment exchange is increasing over time and it has reached a level of 41.3 million persons in the year 2000. Keeping in mind the limitations of this source, it can only be loosely compared with the unemployment figures derived by the CDS method, based on NSSO data. The latter gives an unemployment level of 27 million person years. Both figures are very large. Therefore, they warrant special attention in preparing the Tenth Plan's programmes, policies and fund allocations.

Finally, a comparison of the unemployment rates estimated by UPSS, UPS, CWS and CDS methods of the NSSO are given in Table 10 and 11. It is clear from these tables that UPSS gives the lowest unemployment rate and CDS the highest. Obviously, therefore, the UPSS estimates of employment includes large number of under-employed and even unemployed measured on weekly or daily status basis and provide a comparatively comfortable picture regarding the employment situation in the country. A large number employed according to this criterion will be below the poverty line. Properly measured, the level of unemployment is seen to have a strong correlation with the number of people below the poverty line. In this perspective another feature of the nineties' employment situation needs special notice. Table 12 clearly shows that the incidence of unemployment among the lower consumption classes is much higher than among the rich. Indeed it shows that, per household, the dependency ratio measured as 'one minus the number employed deflated by the total number in the households' is much higher than the richer classes. Under the circumstances, unless the average earnings of the poor increase faster enough to compensate the rise in the dependency ratio, the per capita income/consumption of the poor people cannot increase. The policy for future is, therefore, how to increase job opportunities for these consumption classes: either by increasing the rate of growth of activities in these sectors, increasing their productivity or by proper policy of education and training to shift the labour force from their traditional occupation to areas of higher growth and productivity. It is of great relief to see that the real wages of casual labour in agriculture and non-agriculture has increased from 2.51 per cent to 3.59 per cent in rural males and almost stagnant in rural females. But compared to the average real income of the population, the relative real wages increase is relatively much lower in the 90s compared to the 80s.

The Regional Scenario:

The concern for the present high rate of unemployment needs to be taken more seriously given the large inter-state differentials (See Table 9). The unemployment rate (on the CDS basis) has reached a figure as high as 20.97 per cent in Kerala; next is West Bengal with 14.99 per cent, followed by Tamil Nadu 11.78 per cent of their respective labour force. At the lower end, the lowest unemployment rate is observed in Himachal Pradesh of 2.96 per cent, next higher up is in Rajasthan at 3.13 per cent followed by Punjab at 4.03 per cent and Uttar Pradesh 4.08 per cent. But in general, the ranking of States according to their respective unemployment rates remained almost the same between 1993-94 and 1999-2000. However, the coefficient of variation between them increased significantly, in the 1990s compared to the 1980s. Besides, no strong correlation is observed between the inter-state SDP growth and the employment growth. Further, it is of interest to see that of the 16 States in Table 9, there are three States with very high and increasing unemployment rate. They are Kerala, Tamil Nadu and West Bengal. Of them, Kerala has comparatively lower growth rate of GDP but higher employment elasticity, whereas Tamil Nadu and West Bengal have a very high growth above seven per cent but with very low employment elasticity. These results show that GDP growth rate or high labour intensity in production exclusively will not reduce unemployment. For reducing unemployment, the challenge is to combine a high growth rate with high employment elasticity (i.e., labour intensity in production) by proper sectoral and technology choice. It is supported by the fact that there are only three States among the 16 – Gujarat, Karnataka and Haryana – who could combine high growth and high employment elasticity and achieve significant decline in the unemployment rate. All these suggest that region-based employment policy and programme will be needed in addition to the overall growth strategy, to reduce the growing disparity in the rate of unemployment between the States.

In Table 17, the incidence of unemployment has been examined in a more disaggregated form, for each State, separated between males and females. It is found that the incidences are very high in some groups; for example, in Kerala, the rural female unemployment rate is as high as 26.1 per cent as compared to a lower unemployment rate of 20 per cent among the males (Table 17). In West Bengal, the rural female unemployment is near as high as among the Kerala females, of 25.1 per cent. For States with high literacy rate like Kerala and a high growth rate like West Bengal, this high unemployment scenario will be of great concern. Examination is needed in detail on the nature and composition of their growth, in order to isolate the features responsible for this demand-supply imbalance in the labour market.

Other than the regional disparity and gender differences in some States, we also notice other features, which will be of equal concern. Table 16 shows that the unemployment rate among youths

(15-29 years) is increasing significantly in 1999-2000 over 1993-94 with the sole exception of females in the urban sector. In contrast, among the female youths of the rural sector, unemployment rate is increasing significantly. For males, both in rural and urban sector, the unemployment rate is increasing and in general in all cases, the youth unemployment is observed to be higher compared to the national aggregates [Table 18 & 19].

Similarly, when we examine on a regional basis, we notice that the States like Kerala or West Bengal again, give a disappointing picture regarding the level of unemployment among youths (Table 18 & 19). Among the female youth in rural Kerala; the unemployment rate is as high as 45.8 per cent; in West Bengal it is 39.1 per cent and nearly as high in Tamil Nadu. Among urban female, the incidence of unemployment is still higher. For example, in Kerala, among urban female youths, the unemployment rate is 50.4 per cent; West Bengal and Tamil Nadu also give a high figure. Altogether, nearly seven or eight States have a very high unemployment rate. The unemployment among youths in the urban sector for example, is also very high in Bihar, Himachal Pradesh, Karnataka, Madhya Pradesh, Maharashtra and Orissa. This high youth unemployment in a way cuts across all the States, especially in the urban sectors. This shows that apart from the genuine problem of employment for the rural sector, positive policies are needed to generate employment in the urban sector and especially among the youth, educated and skilled (Table 29 on usual status). This is especially needed because the organized activity, which dominates the urban sector, is suffering from a near jobless growth. However, the Table 15 shows that in 1999-2000, unemployment among educated females in the urban area has significantly fallen. This is a highly positive feature showing the effect of increasing female literacy and work participation. But the level is still very high and increasing among females with higher education. For other groups, they are almost the same, with a marginal decline in most cases. Here, a synergy is needed between the job demand and the education and skill formation. All these show that unless job opportunities in matching areas increase, the unemployment among youth and educated may increase significantly in future. As to the incidence of unemployment among special sections of population, e.g. BPL population, their labour force are seen to be growing faster than the employment opportunities, resulting in an unemployment rate nearly double from that among the upper classes. This has a very adverse effect in the poverty reduction among poor sections. Finally, with reference to Table 1 (b), one can see that the unemployment rates among Scheduled Castes and Scheduled Tribes are higher and the number of unemployeds is increasing at a much faster rate within the rest of the population. They are the weaker sections of the society and, therefore, special employment generation programmes and policies for them will be warranted. In our policy recommendation, attempt has been made to consider all these.

3

Future Employment Scenario:

The Need for Creating 50 Million Person Years of Gainful Employment Opportunities in the Tenth Plan

The Table I (b) clearly demonstrates that as per the nineties' development pattern, the growth of workforce in India exhibited a deceleration from 2.7 per cent per annum to hardly 1.07 per cent per annum between the periods 1983 to 1993-94 and 1993-94 to 1999-2000, according to the NSSO Survey. Comparatively, the deceleration in the labour force is much slower, declining from 2.43 per cent per annum to 1.31 per annum, all measured on CDS (Current daily status) basis. As a result, given these trends, the future will witness a growing gap between the labour force and the work force i.e., the number of unemployeds. Already the number of unemployed has increased from 20.13 million to 26.58 million between 1993-94 and 1999-2000. The decline in the growth of work force was sharper in the rural areas falling from 2.5 per cent per annum from the earlier period (roughly in the eighties) to 0.70 per cent per annum in the later period (roughly in the nineties). In the urban areas, however, the decline was less, from 3.9 per cent per annum to 2.32 per cent per annum. [Table 1(b)]. This indicates a faster growth of unemployment in the Rural areas as compared with the Urban areas. This is to be judged against a much slower growth of urbanization observed compared to our earlier projection, given now by the latest Census of 2001. It brings out the need for a special focus on generating employment in the rural sector. Evidently, the declining trend in agricultural employment in this period at 0.02 per cent per annum has not been amply compensated by the growth of employment in the Rural non-farm sector over this period. Table 1(b) shows that the growth rate of the Rural Sector as a whole was hardly 0.7 per cent per annum over this period.

Tenth Plan Projections

The Tenth Plan covers a five-year period 2002-2007. Its base is 2001-02. Accordingly, estimates for employment and labour force are attempted in this report for the year 2001-02. Two major assumptions have been made for this:

1. The labour force growth will be around 1.8 per cent per annum since 1999-2000, covering the whole of the Tenth Plan period, an assumption that has been made by the Report of the Task Force on Employment Opportunities constituted by the Planning Commission. According to the above Report, this is largely explained by the increase in the net enrolment rate for education when a large number went out of the labour force during this period. However, the estimates based on the net enrolment rate between 1993-94 and 1999-2000 given by the Ministry of Human Resource Development covering all government, government aided, government recognised schools and institutions including 1-10 classes covering primary and secondary and the gross enrolment in the higher secondary (10+2 new pattern) and intermediate/ pre degree/ pre university, junior colleges, show that this very low increase in the enrolment rate (0.58 per cent per annum between 1993-94 and 1999-2000), could hardly explain the 0.10 per cent decline in the labour force in this period (Table 25). Therefore, the heavy decline from 2.43 per cent to 1.31 per cent observed between 1993-94 and 1999-2000 still remains largely unexplained. There may be another explanation noted by the Special Group as given by the NSSO Report that because of the very low employment opportunities over this period, probably a large number, especially among the rural females voluntarily dropped out of the labour force. More probe will be needed to get an answer to this heavy decline in

the labour force during this period. For estimating the labour force for 2001-02, minor correction has been made for switching over from NSSO agriculture year to the standard fiscal year of the plan.

2. The average rate of growth of GDP estimated for this period is 5.2 per cent per annum for 2000-01 and 2001-02. The sectoral break-up of these two years has been given in Table 3 A.

3. The sectoral employment growth will be determined by their respective employment elasticities observed over the recent past i.e., between 1993-94 and 1999-2000 (NSSO 55th round).

As has already been mentioned the labour force growth between 1993-94 and 1999-2000 has been estimated at 1.3 per cent per annum (on CDS basis), a fall from 2.43 per cent per annum of the earlier period. Such a heavy decline on a sustainable basis is not corroborated by most inter-country experiences. Indeed from available inter-country comparisons, one sees that in most countries with their slowing down of the population growth and an increase in per capita income, there has been a comparatively faster growth of labour force compared to the growth of population. In the latest Census, India's population growth has been seen to come down to 1.95 per cent per annum over the nineties. The provisional projection by the Planning Commission over the Tenth Plan puts growth at 1.63/1.64 per cent per annum. Given the projected age distribution and assuming the labour force participation rates per each age group unchanged, the growth rate of labour force will be around 2.66 per cent. Therefore, assuming that the decline in participation rate of late 90s given by NSSO may continue, the assumption of 1.8 per cent growth in the labour force if at all is on the lower side. Regarding the GDP growth and its sectoral break-downs over the Tenth Plan, they have been done on the basis of all information available at this point of time. The Central Statistical Organisation has recently brought out the quick estimates of sectoral growth for the year 2000-01 and advanced estimates for 2001-02 of GDP. These estimates show a GDP growth much lower at 4 per cent per annum for 2000-01 and 5.4 per cent for 2001-02 and the break up of sectoral growths marginally different from the one used in this exercise given in Table 3 (a). Judged against the quick and advance estimate of CSO, an error factor of 0.03 per cent in our employment calculations can be worked out. But as per past experience, both the quick and advance estimates may further change. Considering this, the Special Group decided to continue with the existing estimates [See Table 3(a)].

The estimates of employment and unemployment of the Tenth Plan's base year (2001-02) are given in Table 3. The estimates of unemployed for the year 2001-02 have been given around 34.85 million person years (defined on CDS basis) when the unemployment rate went up around 9.21 per cent. It also provides the estimates of addition to labour force over the Tenth Plan period as 35.29 million person years. Thus, over the Tenth Plan, we have to deal with the problem of creating job opportunities against a potential job demand of more than 70.14 million person years (i.e., 34.85 million base period unemployment and 35.29 million new labour entry). Against this perspective, the employment objective of the Approach Paper of the Tenth Plan has to be addressed. The Approach Paper recommends providing employment opportunities to all the additions in the labour force over the 5-year period and reducing significantly the rate of unemployment over the Tenth Plan, so that by the end of the Eleventh Plan, the per cent unemployment will be near zero.

The Tenth Plan visualized a substantially higher growth rate of 8 per cent per annum. The tentative break-up of the aggregate growth rate has been attempted in consultation with the Tenth Plan work, which is given in Table 3 (a). Given this growth pattern and assuming the present sectoral employment elasticities, an estimate has been made of the level of employment and unemployment over the Tenth Plan. Accordingly, a case for providing increased employment opportunities of around 29.67 million person years (i.e., an increase from the base figure of 343.36 million to 373.03 million) has been put forward, with the help of a 8 per cent per annum growth over the next five-year period. This means, an employment growth of 1.7 per cent per annum as against a labour force growth of 1.8 per cent per annum. The result: even with as high a growth, the objective of providing employment opportunities to all addition to labour force will not be achieved; an additional 5.47 million employment opportunities will have to be created. This, added to the base period stock unemployment of 34.85 million, will give an unemployment rate of 9.79 per cent at the end of the Tenth Plan, an increase from 9.21 per cent at the base. This arises largely due to the near jobless growth character in many sectors of the economy especially in the organised sector and a growing capital intensity in many of the organised sectors and even in some of the unorganised sectors including some small scale industries. The unemployment rate at the end of the Tenth Plan can even go up by a minimum one percentage point (adding 4 million more unemployment) if the labour force growth increases to 2.0 percentage per annum. The answer is, therefore, to look for a development strategy, which will revamp the activities in those sectors where the comparative advantage lies in a labour-intensive nature of production. But as the economy is now operating under globalisation, all care should be taken in the reallocation of activities between sectors and sub-sectors so that every sector can meet the open market competition. To give a simple example, without the changes in the overall growth rate of agriculture, the sub-sector compositions can be changed by changing the cropping patterns and resources allocated between food and non-food, from less to more labour intensive sectors. Even this strategy may not always need additional investment resources. In fact, it is often said that a change in favour of labour intensive activities is accompanied by saving of capital by substitution of capital by labour and knowledge/ technology. Specific programmes and projects are to be identified and launched keeping this goal in view. In this effort, extensive discussions with Ministries and sector specialists have been undergone. In doing so, we noticed to our disappointment that the awareness for the need for employment generation is generally very poor while formulating the plan programmes/policies. This applies to most of the concerned ministries and authorities. In its findings, it has been the view of this Special Group on Employment Generation that agriculture and allied sector activities have a very large employment generating potentiality. This is to be achieved not necessarily by heavy additional investment, but by reallocation of funds and choice of appropriate technologies. But to be sustainable under the present globalised system, this should be supported by appropriate policies to increase their productivity and competitiveness which would make them viable.

Tables 3 and 4 present the scenario of employment generation, separating those emanating from growth per se without any change in the existing employment elasticities, i.e. implicitly assuming a "business-as-usual" scene (with no changes in intra-sectoral composition of labour intensity of output) and from those with selective changes in policies and programmes in favour of more labour use. The sectoral estimates of these are given in Table 5. As Table 7 shows, the maximum addition to generation of employment from special programmes will come from (i) agriculture and allied activities, (ii) small and medium enterprises, broad-based rural non-farm activities and some of the social services sectors like education and health. Besides, appropriate policy changes have been identified for the fast development of sectors of high labour intensity like construction, tourism, communication and information technology and financial services. There are many potential areas in the informal sectors and especially in the self-employment area, which can provide high employment, and therefore should also be developed.

The next chapter (Chapter IV) would provide detailed identification of areas with potential employment opportunities along with the schemes and programmes (most of them being considered in the Tenth Plan) to harness this potential. Subsequently, attempts are made to quantify the person years of employment to be created from all these programmes and policies. However, it should be remembered that there are many activities, which although not contributing to direct employment, have high multiplier in generating indirect employment like power, and organised manufacturing, and therefore need to be considered with high priority.

Finally, Table 5 gives the final summary table. This Table shows that with suitable programmes and policy changes, the same eight per cent growth rate, can generate additional 19.32 million person years of employment opportunities over the Tenth Plan period, giving a total of 50 million person years of employment opportunities over the Tenth Plan. This recommended scenario will not only absorb all additions to labour force generated over the Tenth Plan, but also reduce the level of unemployment by nearly half and will eliminate it completely by the end of the Eleventh Plan. The percentage unemployed will go down from

9.21 per cent to 5.11 per cent by the end of the Tenth Plan and unemployment will be eliminated completely by the end of Eleventh Plan. To summarize, nearly 20 million person years of employment opportunities have to be created by selective innovative programmes and policies leading to a changed pattern of growth in favour of labour intensive sectors; the remaining 30 million will come from the normal buoyancy of growth as perceived over the recent past (1993-94 to 1999-2000), giving a total of 50 million person years over the Tenth Plan.

Before concluding, we would like to give some rationale for presenting the alternative employment growth rate against the baseline growth of GDP of 6.5 per cent assumed in the Tenth Plan Approach Paper. Table 6 gives the employment perspective using these estimates. This scenario shows that on the "business as usual basis" (i.e., with the present employment elasticity) the percentage unemployed will grow up to 11.0 million at the end of the Tenth Plan, giving a total unemployed labour force of 45.56 million person years. This picture is not acceptable on any socio-economic or political ground. The picture can be partly ameliorated by initiating proper employment generating programmes/policies to alter the patterns of growth towards labour-intensive sectors. In that case, as the Table 6 (B) shows, the unemployment rate can be contained at the base level, by the end of the Tenth Plan. The additional employment to be created by the selected innovative programmes and policies will be to the extent of 7.5 million person years. But at the same time, one should remember even this scenario will show that at the end of the Tenth Plan, 38.5 million person years will be unemployed almost the same as in the base year. Considering these two alternative scenarios, one can conclude that a much higher growth rate (around 8 per cent) is needed for the future along with positive policies and programmes for changing the sectoral pattern and technology in favour of labour-intensive production if unemployment is to be tackled.

There have been two other major Reports :

1. The Task Force for Creating Employment Opportunities, constituted by the Planning Commission.
2. The Growth Imperatives and Employment Generation in India by McKinsey Global Institute, working in

collaboration with McKinsey India office on the economic performance in India.

They also provide the future projections of employment and unemployment in India.

The first report estimated employment and unemployment and their projections on the basis of usual status along with subsidiary employment (UPSS). It arrived at an unemployment rate of 4.55 per cent at the end of 2012 with 1999-2000 as base and with an assumed growth rate of 8 per cent per annum, i.e., nearly double in the terminal year from the base of 2.23 per cent, which means 22.97 million unemployeds in 2012 rising from the 9 million at the base with all changes in policies prescribed. Similarly, for the year 2007, it gives an unemployment rate of 4.27 per cent i.e., near double from the base (1999-2000). But it has not recommended the need for identifications of sectors and activities where direct employment generating programmes and policies will be needed. In general it emphasized the role of the organised sector, especially the services sector to give more than 70 per cent of additional employment and almost ruled out any contribution from primary sectors. In our estimate, the services sector contributes upto 30 per cent of total employment generation at the base year of which 5.3 per cent only in the organised sector in 1999-2000. The present special group report on the other hand has given its reason, to identify a different set of sectors as potential employment generating activities for the future over the medium term. A detailed comparison is given in Annexe B of this report.

The second report provides an estimate of employment for the year 2010, based on a growth rate of 10 per cent per annum, supported by an exhaustive reform package; but it also ends with an unemployment rate even after a 10 year period of almost the same level, as in the base: This exercise of ours has used the measurement of unemployment on CDS basis. This report therefore clearly fails to give answer to India's problem of unemployment.

The Tenth Plan scenario on business as usual that has been attempted in this special group report, assumed a per annum growth rate of productivity of labour of 6.2 per cent as compared to 5.6 per cent in the 55th round of NSSO (1993-94 to 1999-2000) and the long term trend growth of 3.5 per cent per annum between 1983 and 1999-2000. Further, in the modified 10th Plan scenario (where special efforts on employment generation have been attempted by appropriate policy changes and sector-wise programmes in order to meet the 10th Plan objective of reducing unemployment significantly and generating 10 million job opportunities every year), an assumption has been made of increasing the labour productivity at 5.2 per cent per annum, much higher than the past productivity increase of 3.5 per cent per annum between 1983 and 1999-2000. The task force report for creating employment opportunities assumed implicitly 5.6 per cent per annum growth in the labour productivity, very close to that assumed in our report, and the McKinsey report assumed a growth of 8 per cent per annum.

4

Identification and Quantification of Employment Potentials

I. Agriculture & Allied

Agriculture and allied activities grew at a moderate rate of 3.1 per cent per annum between 1993-94 and 1999-2000 as against 2.9 per cent between 1983 and 1993-94, in terms of value added. But in spite of this, employment growth touched near zero i.e., the number of persons employed remained static over this period. This is partly due to the shedding of excess labour. It is also due, to a large extent, to the slowing down of the agricultural investment and a change in the pattern of agricultural growth with comparatively lesser activities in the labour-intensive value added areas of agriculture like watershed development, wasteland development, minor irrigation, development of forestry and animal husbandry. Over the Tenth Plan to reverse this trend, the following programmes with higher labour intensity in products have been identified:

1. A substantial potential area for employment generation could be achieved, by bringing additional acreage switching from cereals under cultivation to oilseeds and pulses. By this, the potential of generating additional employment has been estimated by the Ministry of Agriculture to be around 139 million man-days per annum on a non-cumulative basis i.e. 0.46 million person years in the last year of the Tenth Plan. This has been done by deflating the man-days by 300 to get person years, so that it comes close to the concept of the CDS basis of

measurement. The assumption of 300 days work a year is regarded by many as too high. If we take less number of days work per year, the employment potentialities in person year will increase further. However, as some of these production will come after the land is shifted from other crops grown, the net addition to employment will not be more than 0.35 million person years [See Annexure A (a) Table 2].

2. Under the programme National Watershed Development Programme for Rainfed Areas (NWDPRA) it has been estimated that 30 million additional man-days more every year on a cumulative basis can be generated which comes to nearly 0.50 million person years by the end of the Tenth Plan [Annexure A (a) Table A3].

3. The horticulture sector, is estimated to have a potential of creating employment opportunities of 1800 million man-days over the Tenth Plan, i.e., 360 million man-days each year which is, 1.20 million person years, approximately [See annexure A (a) Para 11(iii)]. This is however subjected to an additional outlay of around Rs. 10,000 crores.

4. Besides, from the farm management programmes, nearly 112.5 lakh jobs are likely to be created by bringing in 75 lakh ha. additional net sown area under the scheme. Together with the increase in cropping intensity, 1.25 million person years of employment opportunities will be added during the Tenth Plan. [See Annexure A (a) Para 14 and Table A4].

5. Proposed Tenth Plan programmes on Agricultural clinics and the seed production are likely to generate 0.15 million person years and the tractors etc. another 0.1 million person years at the end of the Tenth Plan [See Annexure A (a) Para 15, 16 and 17].

Therefore at the aggregate the total potential of additional employment generation from different programmes and schemes already formulated by the Ministry comes to 3.55 million person years by the end of the Tenth Plan.

II. Greening the Country through Agro Forestry

Forestry & Agro Forestry

The "Task Force" on greening the country set up by the Planning Commission has recommended the following programmes, over the Tenth Plan, which will give substantial additional employment from this sector.

Ten million hectare of degraded forest can easily be regenerated and afforested which on the yearly basis means approximately two million hectares to be greened, on watershed development basis involving around two million people. In the present Report, a conservative estimate of 1.5 million person years employment opportunities over the 10th Plan to be created has been provided. Details are given in Annexure A (b) Para 2 (i).

Development of medicinal plants

India has been identified as one of the eight global centres for plant diversity. This sector opens fresh opportunities for the production of a whole range of theraptics as also food supplement, cosmetics, toiletries and nutraceuticals and veterinary medicine. According to the Task Force on Medicinal Plants set up by the Planning Commission, nearly one million people will get productive employment besides one lakh on pharmacy, health, tourism and manufacturing and various products. Our present Report has assumed a minimum of 0.5 million jobs from this area at the end of the Tenth Plan [See A(b) Para 2 (iii)].

Bamboo development

The Task Force on Greening India estimated that a potential of generating two million jobs is there over the Tenth Plan for bamboo development. In our present Report, we have assumed 1.5 million persons as the minimum at the end of the Tenth Plan [See Annexure A (b), (iv) and Table 6].

III. Energy Plantations

Table – F

Employment Potential through Energy Plantations

Project	Area (Ha)	Income generation (Rs.crores)	Jobs (million)	Gestation Period
(a) Energy plantation				
Prosopis	5 million	6500		3 years
Casurina	5 million wasteland	13500	7.5 m	5 years
(b) Ethanol Plantations	800,000 irrigated	12,000	2.5 m	1 year

Of which from Project (a), because of its long gestation, we estimated that hardly 1.22 million person years employment is likely to be generated during the Tenth Plan. From Project (b) of the 2.5 million job potential, this Report has assumed a conservative estimate of 0.79 million. The details are given in Annexure A(c).

IV. Rural Sectors and SME's

Sampoorna Gramin Rozgar Yojana (SGRY)

The Prime Minister has announced this programme with an annual outlay of Rs.10,000 crore on the Independence Day of India 2001 with a job potentiality of 100 crore man days per annum i.e., 3.33 million person years. This outlay amounts to an addition nearly of Rs.6,000 crore annually. This programme integrates a number of special programmes (mainly EAS and JGSY) implemented until now. On the basis of the present norm of employment generation per unit outlay, it is estimated that these special programmes have generated approximately 1.67 million jobs annually in the past. Assuming that of the 100 crores of mandays at least 90 crores will be achieved, the same norm will give an additional job of 1.29 million person years over the Tenth Plan [See Annexure A(d)].

Pradhan Mantri Gram Sadak Yojana (PMGSY)

The allocation for rural roads was about Rs.500 crore in the year 1999-2000. Now it has been raised to Rs. 2,500 crore under the present programme. Assuming that the overall norm of employment to output relation as observed in construction industry over the year 1999-2000 is to continue, the employment generation per year in the Tenth Plan under the programme on a non-cumulative basis will be around 0.98 million person years. That means an additional employment of approximately 0.77 million person years to be generated over the Tenth Plan [See Annexure A(d)].

Swarnjayanti Gram Swarozgar Yojana (SGSY)

The new approach to self employment in rural areas is forming self help groups (SHG) to run micro enterprises supported by micro credit. By 2004, 14 Lakh SHG will be set up. Present average of 8.5 lakh sustainable jobs creation a year, will be raised to 43 to 45 lakh persons in five years i.e. an average increment of 0.8 million per year.

Small and Medium Enterprises & KVIC

Under manufacturing, nearly 37 per cent of the output and 83 per cent of employment have been generated in the unorganized informal sector in 1999. According to our estimates, 4.2 million additional jobs can be created by specific programmes e.g., Prime Minister's Rozgar Yojana (PMRY) and Rural Employment Generation Programme (REGP) and the proposed Cluster Development Programme in the small and medium industries including KVIC, on top of employment generation from the general growth of this sector derived on the basis of extrapolated employment parameters of around 5.99 million. KVIC submitted a plan of creating additional two million jobs from different special programmes including REGP [See Annexure A(e)]. The break up of job opportunities in SSI including KVIC are the following:

Table – G

Job Opportunities Creation in SSI including KVIC

I.	Programme based KVIC in	
	KVIC in REGP	2.00 m
	PMRY (SSI)	1.65 m
	SSI Clusters	0.55 m
	Sub total	**4.20 m**
II.	Growth based	
	SSI	3.86 m
	Coir	0.10 m
	Handloom	0.40 m
	Powerloom	0.10 m
	Handicraft	0.93 m
	Sericulture	0.50 m
	Wool (unorganised)	0.10 m
	Sub total	**5.99 m**

Note : In addition, 1.43 million will come from the growth of large manufacturing (net of SSI)

V. Community Services – Social and Personnel Services

Education and Literacy

This sector has experienced a large downsizing of labour between 1993-94 and 1999-2000. It is significantly dominated by the organised sector (36% of total), of which 85% are in the public sector. This is the sector where excess labour is expected to be shed significantly over the Tenth Plan. However, there are certain sectors like education and health, which have tremendous potentialities of generating high employment because of present shortage of teachers and trainers, nurses and doctors. By this an additional employment of 1.7 million in the elementary education [See Annex A(f)] and for training the teachers and trainers, and 0.8 million from health and self-employment programmes [See Annex A(f)] have been provided. The high potentiality of Jobs for teachers with vocational and other trainings can be assessed when we see that in India hardly 5.3 per cent of youths in the labour force are trained whereas in the developed countries they are as high as 65 to 70 per cent (see Table 26). Besides, there are several other broad sectors like construction, transport, and communication, trade and hotel, tourism, finance, other miscellaneous services where employment generating potentials are very high. Most of them have been captured by the effect of the overall GDP growth of those sectors. A significantly higher GDP growth in all these sectors have been assumed in the Tenth Plan.

Information & Communication Technology

Two sectors among them need special mention : Information Technology (IT) and Tourism. The IT sector which is just now emerging has a substantial potential in generating employment both direct and indirect. Admittedly, it also replaces some labour in several sectors, but its net contribution is very positive. Chapter V shows that its direct employment generation potentiality is as high as 0.4 million over the Tenth Plan. Indirect employment generated by this sector however, would appear in other sectors. However, they should not be counted as employment creation in this sector in order to avoid any double counting.

Tourism

The second one, tourism, is very labour intensive and provides high quality jobs; it is capable of being primarily focused on rural areas with appropriate and low cost programmes and it has extensive forward and backward linkages. The note submitted by the Ministry to the Group estimates around 3.6 million jobs per year over the Tenth Plan taking direct and indirect employment into consideration. No separate estimates of direct employment have been provided. The group estimates on the basis of input-output parameters a rough contribution of 0.3 million of direct employment per year which is included in the overall employment generation by the services sector. For detailed policies for these sectors, refer to Chapter V.

Programmes & Policy Based Efforts

The Special Group therefore assessed that if the policies and programmes outlined in the above five areas can be included in the Tenth Five year Plan, 19 to 20 million additional employment opportunities can be created.

5

Policy Reform for Employment Generation in Selected Key Areas

The earlier chapters assessed the dimensions of the employment generation opportunities which need to be created in order to attain the Tenth Plan employment target. The potential areas for additional employment generation have been identified and a rough estimate of the employment generation possibilities have been worked out. Specific major work programmes for that purpose have also been proposed. Most of them have been included in the respective Ministries' Tenth Plan programmes. In this section the supportive policies, both macro and sectoral, to arrive at the targeted growth rate and the desired patterns of the growth in selective priority areas on employment considerations, with appropriate technology backup to increase employment intensity in production have been spelt out. It has been broadly estimated that the attainment of an eight per cent growth per annum per se over the Tenth Plan, assuming the past sectoral break up and employment elasticities, will be able to provide nearly 30 million additional employment opportunities which is slightly more than half of what is needed to absorb all additions to the labour force over this period and to eliminate unemployment over a decade. For the rest (nearly 20 million employment opportunities) policies and programmes need to be identified so that the patterns of sectoral growth can move in favour of labour intensive areas, thereby improving overall employment elasticities

However, any strict separation of the two sets of policies is difficult to comprehend. Any change in the sectoral growth or use of factor proportion in production by appropriate technology choice will also affect the overall growth along with an increase in employment generation. For example, any growth pattern which makes more use of the availability of surplus labour in India and its skill and less of capital will increase the potentiality of higher growth because India is a labour surplus and capital short economy. For this to happen various segments of the unorganised sector in India, which has a large employment base and also high employment elasticity, need to grow faster. But as the Indian economy is now operating in a globalised competitive situation, the productivity and the job quality of these sectors along side needs to be improved. Therefore, appropriate policies and programmes have to be instituted so that this objective is fulfilled. In general, the organised sector has comparatively higher productivity and job quality both in terms of earning rate and security of job. But their contribution to employment at the base year of the Tenth Plan is very low, less than 8 per cent, of which the public sector has a weight of more than five per cent of the total in terms of employment generation and shows a negative employment elasticity, being loaded with excess labour over time and consciously pursuing a downsizing policy. Therefore, the importance of the unorganised sector in generating employment and their productivity comes as the key policy issue. This is a challenge the unorganised sector has to face. At the same time, the unorganised sector has practically no job security and given an excess of labour in the unorganised market, the labour in this market is very much prone to be exploited, and until now only marginally protected by less than satisfactory implementation of the provision of Minimum Wages. The labour productivity of the unorganised sector could be increased by putting more capital and knowledge inputs, using appropriate technology, properly developed more at the grassroots level. It is observed that the flow of capital per unit to the unorganised sector is much lower compared to the organised sector. This means the capital efficiency is likely to be much higher in the unorganised sector compared to the organised sector.

Therefore, in this Chapter we consider apart from macro policies for growth, the sectoral policies for influencing growth patterns in favour of employment generation, and the policies on supply side of labour.

I. MACRO POLICIES FOR GROWTH

This has been discussed extensively in the Tenth Plan Approach Paper. At the risk of too much of simplification, one can say that the growth potential in the Indian economy is estimated mostly on the basis of the "Harrod Domar model" which prescribes a higher investment as a percentage of GDP and a lower incremental capital output ratio (i.e., capital efficiency) to generate higher growth.

All policies, which encourage investment and sources of finance of investment i.e., domestic and external sector, and improve capital efficiency are relevant for boosting the overall growth. Thanks to globalisation, demand is most unlikely to be a constraint if India's exports have the competitiveness (price, quality and prompt services) to penetrate the world market where her share is now very small.

For sustainability of this growth path in a free market economy, all policies, which lead to a decrease in unit price and improved quality competitiveness, have to be pursued. To achieve this, the creation of a competitive and free market both for goods and factors with perfect mobility is essential.

II. SECTORAL POLICY

Sectoral Policies for influencing growth patterns in favour of employment generation

(a) Agriculture

To increase growth in agriculture all policies for better utilization of land and water should be pursued. For example, policies on utilization of all types of hitherto unutilized lands, especially the cultivable and afforestable lands owned by the Governments need to be given priority. Rough estimates suggest that 80 million hectares may be allotted on 99 years lease or ownership basis to the following categories of individuals in order of priority for agriculture and / or afforestation.

a) Landless labourers

b) Small and marginal farmers

c) Medium size farmers

d) Educated unemployed youth including agricultural and technical graduates

e) Ex-servicemen

f) Co-operative societies

g) NGOs

h) Corporate bodies

Consolidation of land holdings has been a major factor responsible for improving land management and enhancing productivity in northern states, e.g., Punjab, Haryana, Rajasthan and Western U.P. The Central Government may offer to bear all administrative expenses incurred by the States on consolidation plus an equal amount as incentive bonus to the States.

A back-ended beneficiary oriented subsidy scheme for reclamation of degraded lands like ravines, un-levelled lands, saline, sodic, alkaline and water-logged lands, has been contemplated by the Agriculture Ministry.

Acquisition of land for public works is to be strictly restricted to infrastructure needs only.

Some incentive for computerizing land records and lowering stamp duties to a maximum of 5 per cent can go a long way in avoiding pseudo legal and illegal conveyance systems as well as avoidable litigation in rural areas.

Legalising the land leasing-in and leasing-out systems and promotion of contract farming through standardized contract formats enforceable on both parties will help in increasing the size of holdings and improving the viability of agri-units.

Similarly, for water investment in irrigation is to be given a big push both for major and minor irrigation and watershed management in the rainfed areas. ICOR in irrigation especially in minor irrigation is the most favourable even within the agriculture sector and has the most immediate and tangible impact on improving productivity, increasing rural incomes and removing poverty. Besides being labour intensive, expansion in minor irrigation and watershed development will increase employment generating capacity of Agriculture.

For the agricultural sector, a change in the sectoral policy for increasing the growth has been recommended in the Tenth Plan Approach Paper. To quote, "agricultural output increased in the 1990s because of higher output support prices and input subsidies. Now, it must come from higher investments in irrigation, seeds, power and roads".

Public investment in irrigation, power and roads should be sufficiently stepped up by reducing subsidies on fertilizers, water and power. Canal systems are in poor shape for lack of operations and maintenance outlay. These should be improved by stepping up plan allocations for maintenance, involving users growth in management and appropriate pricing of water to cover operation and maintenance cost.

The semi-arid and rain fed areas of the Central regions, which have higher potential for increasing productivity, would be the focus of attention given in the Tenth Plan. These measures selected for the Tenth Plan can accelerate agricultural growth as well as trigger growth in other sectors, besides reducing poverty. Also, policies to reduce control and regulatory measures are recommended to increase incentives in agricultural growth. For this review, amendment and even repeal of the Essential Commodities Act, 1955, Milk and Milk Products Control Order (MMPO), the small scale reservation in producing agricultural equipments, decanalising of the export of agricultural commodities and extension of future/forward trading will be needed. The Essential Commodities Act may be converted into an emergency legislation to be invoked only for a limited number of commodities and a limited period with due approval of the Central Government.

All restrictions on movement of agricultural produce should be removed through a Central legislation, making it a fundamental right.

All limits on stock of foodgrains and agricultural products must go.

All restrictions on institutional finance against agri-stocks must be removed.

Farmers and traders may be allowed to take loans from financial institutions by pledging their stocks.

Corporate sector may be allowed to buy directly all agricultural produce in open market and requirement of routing commodities through mandies may be abrogated.

All restrictions and licensing of processing of agricultural produce may be removed.

Forward trading in all agri-commodities may be permitted and promoted within this year.

Many of these measures have been initiated in the present Budget 2002. Besides, further action is needed regarding the management of "Agricultural Produce Marketing Act", and the "Credit Link Subsidy System" for construction of cold storages and the rural godowns.

Similarly, linkages between research and extension service need to be strengthened to improve quality and effectiveness of the research and extension system. Again several policies in this direction are spelt out in the present Budget (2002-03), which will change the patterns of agricultural growth, to improve its employment intensiveness.

The Minimum Support Price for foodgrains and other commodities needs to be so adjusted as to promote diversification of agriculture. This should be done both geographically and over time. For food and nutritional requirement of our people for leading healthy lives, a wider range of food products is needed than are presently consumed on the average. It also calls for increasing the production of pulses and oilseeds. Most of the non-foodgrain products are however perishable in nature. In order to encourage this diversification through minimization of wastages considerable focus on post-harvest technologies and improved marketing infrastructure will be required. As the new areas like pulses and oilseeds are more labour-intensive these shifts will boost employment generation per unit of output.

An important component in agricultural diversification is animal husbandry, including dairying and poultry which hold immense promise for increasing not only rural livelihoods, but urban as well. Proper development of this sector will require attention not only to technology processing and marketing arrangements, but also to issues of animal welfare.

Greater attention should be given to rain water harvesting and increasing the irrigation potential through scientific watershed development. These are highly employment-intensive activities. There is also a considerable scope to improve the efficiency of our existing irrigation infrastructure through better and more participative management practices.

All these issues in terms of specific programmes have already been discussed in Chapter 4 of the Report. NSSO survey results show that there is high female unemployment in the rural sector. Therefore, the Tenth Plan must also focus on programmes for increasing the work opportunities and productivity of female farmers. Increasing women's access to productive land by regularizing leasing and share cropping of uncultivated agricultural land by women's groups, encouraging collective efforts in bringing wastelands under cultivation and providing policy incentives to women in low input subsistence agriculture will have immediate benefits in terms of the household's food security and women's empowerment along with additional employment generation.

As has already been mentioned, animal husbandry, fisheries, floriculture and horticulture and extended areas of agriculture have very high employment potentialities and their growth has comparatively gone down in the 1990s. Therefore, favourable policies should be made to boost their growth. In this context, focus of farm forestry should be revived which has been surprisingly diluted despite its enormous potential especially in agriculturally backward areas. There are better social returns in promoting agro-forestry models in the rain fed or semi-arid regions which contain most of India's marginal lands. It is in this context that we need to have a big incentive. Similarly, tree plantations and wastelands belonging to the poor need be encouraged. The details of these policies are available in a Planning Commission Task Force Report on Greening India.

(b) Food Processing

Food Processing is an important employment generating activity within the agricultural sector. While India is the second largest producer of fruits and vegetables in the world, its food processing industry remains under-developed. Due to perishable nature of goods and low percentage of processing, the wastage in this sector is very high. The major constraints in the development of food processing industry are the absence of assured electric power in rural areas coupled with high cost of power and poor road connectivity from the rural producer to the urban markets. At present, the food processing industry is dominated by small scale producers including traditional village industries with very little assistance from or linkage to the organised industries. It is now time to restructure the food chain from production to consumption keeping in mind the special requirements of the industry. Corporations or modern cooperative organisations are needed to develop and manage the chain from farming to food processing to marketing. They must develop modern storage facilities at the processing stage including measures for handling of produce to minimize damage. Identification of varieties that meet the market requirement of the consumers' taste is also important. Specific issues needing attention are:

- The National Agriculture Policy has emphasised the need to facilitate contract farming with its backward and forward linkages, especially in the hinterland of proposed food parks, to be set up in the 10th Plan period. This would enable greater value addition and consolidation of operations.
- Synergies between the Food Parks and the Agriculture Export Zones need to be developed so that facilities/ provisions set up for one zone may be considered for the others.
- There is an urgent need to provide post-harvest infrastructure facilities in the hinterland of the food parks. These could be in the form of harvesting equipment, sorting, grading, packing, pre-cooling, washing operation, etc. Setting up of these facilities would improve the level of food processing, reduce post harvest losses, contribute to value addition and generate new jobs in rural areas.
- There is an urgent need to strengthen the Mandies to enhance (a) transparency, (b) trading in varieties more appropriate for processing, (c) trading in graded varieties of raw material and (d) proper incentives for production of raw materials, suitable for processing.

- Convergence of programmes under the Agriculture Export Zone, Ministry of Agriculture, Ministry of Commerce and Industry, etc, is necessary so that market linkage developments could be utilised by farmers and food processing units.
- It has been recommended that as far as possible Value Added Centres (VACs) may be set up in all Food Parks as well as areas of concentration of horticultural/ agricultural produce with road connections, which are proposed under the Pradhan Mantri Sadak Yojana.
- For reduction of the post-harvest losses which are estimated at Rs.50,000 crore annually, it is necessary to take urgent steps to set up irradiation plants, cold storages based on vapour absorption technologies, pre-cooling, etc. It is estimated that cold storage capacities of 15 million tons would be required to be set up in the 10th Plan period. To enable private entrepreneurs to set up cold storages/cold chains, it would be imperative to provide subsidy during the initial period of the 10th Plan, say for a period of three years, as private entrepreneurs are not coming forward in this area. At least five irradiation plants across the country would be required to be set up for enhancing shelf life for diverse products like fisheries, horticulture, cereals, spices, etc.
- To bring our food products at par conforming to international safety and quality standards, it would be necessary to set up a network of quality testing/ certification laboratories across the country. Encouragement would need to be given for taking up Hazard Analysis and Critical Control Point (HACCP), ISO-9000 and harmonised standards for good food hygiene and quality under Food Product Order (FPO). Facilitation of Bar Coding, as prevalent in developed countries, would promote standard products and systematic marketing. The efforts of adoption of CODEX standards for Indian food products need to be studied in line with the requirements of the World Trade Organisation.
- There is an urgent need to harmonise provisions of various laws/regulations for the food processing sector to

encourage high quality of food products and at the same time to reduce hassles faced at present by the industry.

- There is an urgent need to set up retail chain for distribution of quality food products, to help in creating sustained demand for quality food products to cater to the needs of customers by supplying standard and hygienic food products. Private sector may be encouraged to set up such retail chains by giving suitable financial incentives.
- There is also need for rationalisation of the administrative structure controlling the food processing industry sector. The functional departments fall under different ministries. For example, the Ministry of Agriculture deals with the entire post-harvest infrastructure for all agricultural, horticultural, animal husbandry operations, while FPO is under the Essential Commodities Act and dealt by the Ministry of Food Processing Industries, and meat and meat products and milk products are administered by the Dept. of Animal Husbandry and Dairying. The Marine Products and Agriculture Products exports are dealt by the export promotion authorities like MPEDA, APEDA, etc, under the Ministry of Commerce. Similarly, the National Horticulture Board (NHB) is under the Ministry of Agriculture. The Department of Food is looking after the Directorate of Vanaspati and Oils. Sugar, edible oil, pulses, etc, are also looked after by the Department of Food.
- There is an urgent need to solve the problem of rationalisation of tax structure for food processing industries. The agriculture sector has been exempted from all taxes (like excise and income tax). But the agriculture produces attract a number of levies like infrastructure cess, market cess, sales tax, mandi tax, turnover tax, inter state transfer regulations, etc. At the point of conversion, i.e., value addition, excise, income tax and other taxes are levied. The packaging material used is also subject to heavy taxation. All these taxes increase the cost of food products and it becomes a food/commodity for the rich, thereby reducing its demand.

(c) Small and Medium Enterprises

One of the other high potential groups among the unorganised enterprises is that of skilled and semi-skilled artisans who play a very significant role in rural economy in both and manufacturing and maintenance services. The condition of these artisans numbering around 25 million has become vulnerable in the fast changing scenario. To protect and promote employment among this section, agencies like KVIC, DC (Handicrafts), DC (Handlooms) have to play a well-defined pro-active role during the Tenth Plan period.

The next and the most important area of generation of additional employment is the small and medium enterprises especially in the unorganised sector. Their employment generating capacity is very high and boosting of growth in these sectors in the context of overall increase in GDP will improve the employment generation per unit of output. But as has already been mentioned, for sustenance and viability of this sector in the globalised economy, improvement in their productivity and job quality will be the key policy concern.

The labour productivity of this unorganised segment is seven times less than the organised sector and nine to ten times less than the organised private sector. This indicates the extent of the challenge that this sector has to face to catch up with the productivity levels of the organised sector and also with those of the rest of the world. Since the QR regime has been dismantled and the tariff rates are coming down, this sector is facing hard competition from abroad say from countries like China by increased imports mainly because of its lower productivity and high unit cost. This is true both for the organised and unorganised sector though in different degree. The encouraging thing is that even though the growth of the labour productivity in the unorganised sector is less as compared to the organised sector, and the gap is increasing, at the same time the unorganised sector has improved its labour productivity by nearly 4 per cent per annum between 1993-94 and 1999-2000. This is not a bad performance since the Indian economy as a whole is improving labour productivity by a marginally high rate of 5.4 per cent per annum. Indeed, in certain parts of the unorganised sector, the labour productivity is already very high and these sectors have high growth possibilities. It is also to be considered that the small industries in India have been able to contribute nearly 40 per cent of India's exports and, therefore, have shown their ability to compete with the rest of the world.

As a supporting evidence of the improvement in labour productivity in some parts of this sector, the Sample Survey conducted by the office of the Development Commissioner whose results have been released only a few months ago reveal that for SSI, the per unit employment has decreased from 6.3 persons in 1987-88 (Second Census) to 3.6 persons in 1999-2000 (last Census). The average production per unit was Rs.31.31 lakh in 1999-2000 as against Rs.7.38 lakh in the Second Census. This gives a clear indication of increasing productivity per labour through adoption of improved technologies. This also suggests an increase in the capital intensity of these units and an improvement in technology and product quality. For example, the fixed investment per registered unit in this sector has gone up from Rs.1.60 lakh in 1987-88 to Rs.2.76 lakh in 1999-2000. Similarly, the investment per unit in plant and machinery has gone up from Rs.0.93 lakh to Rs.1.62 lakh during the same period. Evidently the small producers are improving their productivity and technology and are growing in size. Indeed a shift of credit allocation in favour of the unorganised sector and economizing of capital in the organised sector is a must in a labour surplus and capital short economy. The capital efficiency in the unorganised sector is obviously higher than in the organised sector. Although, detailed data on flow of funds is not available, the RBI Report indicates that while the unorganised sector produces 63 per cent of GDP, the net outstanding credit of Scheduled Commercial Banks to this sector is only 37.1 per cent of total Bank credit. More disturbing is the fact that this allocation ratio has come down from 54 per cent in 1993-94 (Table A, Summary and Overview Chapter).

There is another problem that the unorganised small and medium enterprises will be facing. With the pressure of high degree of unemployment, which is largely concentrated in the unorganised sector and especially in the rural non-farm sector, exploitation of workforce in this sector by the employers has become easier. Therefore the attempt to improve the quality of labour, one of the Group's Terms of Reference in this sector, in terms of better average earnings and work conditions will be easier if the present unemployment gap is reduced first by increasing the demand for labour for this sector. Thus the problems of quality of labour and the problem of quantity i.e., job availability have to be tackled simultaneously. The lack of economic activity in rural areas and consequent unemployment acting as a push factor increased migration from rural areas to towns resulting in paucity of basic minimum services including sewage, drinking water, health and others in the urban areas. The earnings of these migrants are also low due to their lack of skills and little economic strength.

Constraints in growth in the SSE sector

The constraints to growth in this sector are mainly in the form of finance and infrastructure availability, and lack of skill and marketing. Thus various such constraints limit the scope of business operation of this sector. One of these is poor resource base because of poor economic conditions. There is the problem of financial assistance to meet its working capital and fixed capital requirements. Premises are required for operating business at reasonable rent. For this credit is necessary and availability of credit at reasonable rate of interest is a must for the unorganised sector. While this credit constraint could be same for organised and unorganised sector, organised sector because of its bargaining strength and official patronage and support it enjoys in the shape of development assistance of various forms, is relatively in a better position to overcome this constraint. Unorganised sector enterprises, on the other hand, are left to fend for themselves, because of their less bargaining power. Therefore, institutional arrangements for meeting their genuine need for credit for development of activities should be found. Micro credit facilities may also be developed for them. If necessary, Self Help Group (SHG) could be organised to provide a proper credit channel for urban unorganised sector.

Skill Development

The people engaged here often have very low skill. Training and technology upgradation are two important tools for increasing productivity in the unorganised sector. Training is required for both the new entrants and the existing workers. Training should focus on the bottom end of this sector, which is much larger in size than the middle and top levels. On the technology front, there should be more linkages between laboratories and entrepreneurs in the unorganised sector. This technology upgradation should improve productivity. Facilities should also be available for skill upgradation to work with new technologies.

Another important question is how a certain degree of social protection or social security could be made available to the unorganised sector workers. Today, the workers in the unorganised sector have no protection. Efforts should be made to introduce social security for them. The nature of social security should cover minimum benefits in terms of wage, health, maternity, old age, death etc. Provision of some compensation in illness and other exigencies is required for the workers in the unorganised sector.

For promotion of micro enterprises, technological development is a must. Technology, for decentralised production and centralised marketing, centralised designing and centralised quality control should be followed.

Regarding the working conditions and other problems faced by the workers in this unorganised sector - some institutional support is essential. Evolution of an institution will be necessary which will help to create a sense of oneness among the people who face similar problems. This will create a support base mutually strengthening each other in this sector. Empowerment of the workers will also be necessary. Information, inculcation of awareness among the poor of his/ her capacity, rights, capabilities, and organisation should be available to unorganised sector workers. It is necessary to recognise the existence of an unorganised sector because self-employment is likely to be the key to employment generation and it is the unorganised sector, which provides scope for self-employment.

Technology Development

For promotion of micro enterprises, technological development is essential. Technological advances must focus on rural areas. India now needs to focus on technologies that will change the way of the two-thirds of the country's rural population employed in the unorganised sector. There is a necessity to catalyse industrial and technological development through research industry interface, which will develop new areas of research and reinvent many old and traditional technologies. Without technological development in the unorganised sector, the disparities between the organised and the unorganised sector will increase and the latter will not be able to survive in this competitive world.

Micro Finance

The rural poor in the unorganised sector has yet not been able to come out of the clutches of moneylenders charging usurious interest rates. The credit needs of the rural poor are characterised by the absence of any clear distinction between production and consumption purposes. The needs are small, but often arise at unpredictable times and are usually of an emergent nature. Meeting these credit needs as and when they arise is crucial, if their dependence on unorganised credit agents is to be reduced. However, it is a fact that borrowing from informal agents is very convenient, though the terms are harsh. The credit needs of the rural poor are at present only partially met by the formal credit agencies and a majority of the rural poor continues to depend on the informal sources of credit. A study conducted by Price-Water house, a firm of Chartered Accountants, reveals the following pattern of credit usage by the rural poor.

- 63 per cent of total credit availed by the rural poor is used for consumption purposes
- Only 37 per cent of the total credit availed by the rural poor is for productive use
- The overall share of organised sector in credit flow to the rural poor is around 16 per cent.

The study gave the following reasons for this distortion:

- Non-availability of credit for consumption needs from the organised sector.
- Very high transaction cost to the borrowers from the organised sector.
- Rigidity of terms and conditions for a loan from organised sector.
- Delay in sanction of loans by the organised sector.

- Very high rate of defaults under the Government Sponsored Programmes has led to reluctance on the part of the banks to extend credit to rural poor.

Non-availability of credit from organised sector like commercial banks and developmental banks limits the credit flows to the unorganised sector and accordingly limits the productivity improvement in this sector.

Projects developed under Prime Minister's Rozgar Yojana (PMRY), over the period 1996-1999 have been evaluated rigorously by the financial establishments, which provided credit for these ventures. The rate of activities supported included manufacturing, business (shops, retail trade etc) and services (repairs shops, PCOs, auto-rickshaws etc). A study of 16,000 units by Programme Evaluation Organisation of the Planning Commission showed that 80 per cent of the units were functioning, of which 83 per cent were reporting profits and 34 per cent of them were able to fulfill their obligations for repayment of loan and interest on a regular basis. The others were also able to repay loans but required some re-scheduling. Independent assessment by RBI has also established that the recovery rate of the units set up under PMRY is around 45 per cent.

Job Quality in the unorganised sector - Small, Medium and Micro Enterprises

There is a considerable scope for improving the quality of employment in this sector. In particular, the urban unorganised sector has some promising segments where technological improvement and labour absorption can move in tandem through effective policy interventions and improvement in productivity and earning levels can take place through suitable institutional and market adjustments, and working conditions can improve with decent job creation becoming a definite reality. The present competitive economic regime that has already taken root in the Indian economy and is likely to become fiercer in the near future will not permit the unorganised sector to sustain in the present manner. The policy approach to the unorganised sector must undergo a drastic reformulation wherein, instead of looking at the sector as an economic drag on the rest of the economy the government put in place macro economic policy measures which will promote growth in the sector, which in turn, will enhance its working efficiently and ultimately lead on to the goal of improving the quality of employment and the earnings of people engaged in the sector.

In this context one should explore the potentiality of development of clusters. Our micro enterprises specialize in specific commodities. There are locations where, over a long period in the past, this specialization has taken place, for example, brassware in Moradabad, gem cutting and polishing at Jaipur and Surat, and fine garments (chikan-work kurtas) at Lucknow. The turnovers are large, and being labour intensive activities, the number of those who work in these activities is of the order of thousands. Level of productivity must be competitive because only then can such a large volume of activity be sustained. However, the quality of employment of many workers may not be of an acceptable standard. This happens because highly labour intensive means of production are practised. While this affords work to many, the level of income per worker continues to be low. One of the reasons for this is that age-old practices of production continue. Occupational health of workers gets affected because the work places are not designed on the principles of ergonomics while often a scientific study of the work practice can yield suggestions to improve the occupational conditions. This may require some marginal investments in relatively less expensive capital equipment. For example, at Moradabad, the brassware town, as shown by an ILO study, the health of workers in the household brass foundry, their productive work-time and hence their output can improve very substantially, if a properly designed Chimney is installed in the room to facilitate escape of fumes. Such equipment is well within the reach of saving capability of the foundry establishments. But it is necessary to study the operations and make the equipment available. The workers themselves are busy in day-to-day work and are left with little time to invest into innovation. The capital equipment manufacturers, by themselves, would not see much return. The buyers of the output of such establishments, who are normally the traders–exporters or the wholesale domestic merchants, would generally not have any financial incentive to facilitate improvement in the work practices. The intensive competition among the large number of micro enterprises is able to keep the cost of procurement low and profit of traders high. Efforts are not being made to attract the designers and manufacturers of relevant capital equipment to take interest in producing and marketing the kind of equipment that can create a healthier work place. In other words, the market driven practices, if not tampered with by certain minimum standard of occupational health and practice, can lead to a highly adverse work environment. This point can be further developed in the context of the infrastructure that is available at locations where many micro enterprises are concentrated. Normally, there is too much pressure on the little scarce facilities of water, electricity, civic amenities, and local roads, again contributing to an adverse work environment.

It is not feasible to enforce them merely through regulations like Factories Act, minimum safe and healthy production practices. In the past, the approach was to develop industrial estates at green-field locations and a number of new enterprises got created there over a period of time. However, the bigger challenge is to improve the lot of the already functioning micro enterprises. For this purpose, in the Tenth Plan, a major push to development of clusters will be given so that, wherever there is already a high intensity of micro enterprises, concerted efforts to improve the infrastructure, technology, and surveillance of health of workers are made. One has to demonstrate the returns to workers and to the micro enterprise from marginal investments made in work practices.

At this stage four clusters have been identified – toy industry (Delhi and Mumbai), stone industry (Rajasthan and Andhra Pradesh), lock industry (Aligarh and Dindigal) and special purpose machine tools for lock industry (Aligarh). There exist a number of programmes for benefit of small and micro enterprises. These include:

- Credit for modernization
- Credit guarantee for tiny units without collateral
- Market development assistance through industry associations
- Local infrastructure development through industry associations

- Testing laboratories for product quality

Besides these enterprise-specific programmes, the general programmes aimed at the households are:

- Housing for low-income groups
- Micro finance
- Skill Development
- Health care

If all these programmes could be focused at a particular cluster, the returns in terms of better productivity, income of workers and a better quality of job will be immense. In other words, rather than having multiple programmes each having a spread over a large area, the Tenth Plan may emphasize these micro development programmes at specific cluster.

Specific measures have already been taken by the government in the light of the recommendations of the Report of the Study Group of Development of Small Enterprises set up by the Planning Commission under the Chairmanship of Dr. S. P. Gupta, Member, Planning Commission. The major developments that have taken place in 2001-02 in pursuance of the Comprehensive Policy Package announced in August, 2000 for the SSI sector are briefly outlined below:

1. A Credit Linked Capital Subsidy Scheme for adoption of New/Improved Technology was launched with an aim to provide 12 per cent capital subsidy on projects of technology upgradation in specified sub-sectors. At present, 14 sub-sectors are covered. Duration of the Scheme is from 1st October 2000 to 30th September 2005.
2. A Market Development Assistance (MDA) Scheme was launched for the Small Scale sector envisaging financial assistance to SSI Association for their participation in International Fairs. Financial assistance is also being provided for commissioning market study reports. Assistance is also extended for initiating/contesting anti-dumping cases etc.
3. A Cluster Development Programme which aims at development of clusters by providing infrastructure

facilities and support services including technological upgradation for strengthening their competitive position, has also been launched. These Clusters would serve as a common facility for technological know-how, testing and certification facilities including development of international market. 4 Clusters are being developed with assistance from UNIDO. These are:

(i) National Programme for development of Toy industry.

(ii) National Programme for development of Stone Industry.

(iii) National Programme for development of Indian Lock Industry.

(iv) National Programme for development of Indian Machine Tool Industry.

4. A Scheme for setting up Testing Centres/Laboratories by Industries' Associations is being implemented. The objective of the Scheme is to promote setting up of Testing Centres to offer facilities mainly to Industrial units including SSI units located in the States for testing the quality of raw materials, components and the end products as per the relevant standard specifications. The maximum amount of Government of India Grant-in-aid under this Scheme is 50 per cent of the cost of testing equipment and machinery installed in the laboratory of the Testing Centre subject to a maximum of Rs. 50 lakh as one time grant.

5. Technology Development and Modernisation Fund Scheme (TDMF): SIDBI is operating the TDMF scheme with a corpus of Rs.300 crore to encourage existing industrial SSI units for modernization of their production facilities and adoption of improved and updated technology. The Scheme initiated in 1995 has been extended up to the financial year 2003. The direct assistance is provided by SIDBI at its PLR and refinance is at 2 per cent below PLR. No upfront fee is levied as against 1 per cent under other schemes. Since inception,

Rs. 154.15 crores have been disbursed up to March, 2001.

6. Technology Upgradation Scheme for Textile and Jute Industries (TUFS) of the Ministry of Textile for technology upgradation of textile and jute industries was launched on April 1, 1999 for a period of 5 years. Interest reimbursement of 5 per cent on the interest actually charged is allowed. Since inception, Rs. 72.58 crores have been disbursed.
7. The office of DC (SSI) have introduced the Incentive Scheme of ISO-9000 Quality System aimed at encouraging technology upgradation and Quality improvement in SSI sector to prepare them to face global competition. The Scheme provides reimbursement of 75 per cent of the amount spent for acquiring ISO-9000 Certification (or its equivalent) up to Rs. 75,000/- to each unit.
8. The Government of India is concerned about the sickness in the small scale sector and have taken a number of measures from time to time. As a result the incidence of sickness has been reducing consistently in the past few years. Now the sickness in small scale sector is much lower than in large industry. A major step taken by the Government in tackling the problem of sickness is to adopt a revised definition of sickness based on Kohli Committee Report. The revised definition would enable banks to take action at an early stage for revival of sick SSI units.

(d) Employment Generation in Khadi & Village Industries

KVIC and VSI are the key integral parts of small scale enterprises. In this section, a separate discussion of their objective and policies is presented. The Khadi and Village Industries programmes which operate in the most decentralized manner in the rural sector, can function as an effective instrument of rural employment generation in the country. In view of the ever-increasing need for employment generation in rural areas, the present era of openness and economic liberalization has thrown new challenges before the KVI sector.

In the above backdrop, this Group suggests following broad objectives of KVI programmes for the Tenth Five Year Plan.

Objectives:

The approach paper of the Tenth Five Year Plan highlighted the role of Khadi and Village Industries sector in promoting non-farm employment in rural areas. The KVI Sector possesses immense potential in generating additional employment in the non-farm sector with low per capita investment. This inbuilt potential needs to be tapped fully during the Tenth Five Year Plan by giving due priority to this sector in our national programme for employment generation.

Though keeping past trend in mind, this sector can very well achieve an annual average employment growth rate of 6 per cent, this growth can be accelerated to higher rate provided the necessary fiscal and policy support are extended during the Tenth Five Year Plan period for the conducive development of KVI programmes.

The achievements of the KVI sector during the second half of Ninth Five Year Plan, more specifically under its REGP being implemented through banks and financial institutions, inspires a great hope and evokes ample expectation for higher growth rate of KVI sector in terms of employment as well as production (value addition) during the Tenth Five Year Plan. The State KVI Boards, which are functioning as important vehicles for implementing KVI programme, need to be strengthened adequately in order to deliver the added task envisaged for this sector in the Tenth Plan. In this direction, though, it is necessary to get enhanced support from the respective State Governments.

While giving focussed attention to the expansion of KVI programme in larger number of villages during the Tenth Five Year Plan, due priority to the coverage for remote villages need to be given. Coverage should be extended to more and more backward panchayats and blocks by devising a separate liberalized package for the development of hill, border and other backward regions.

The entire effort to accelerate the growth rate of the KVI Sector needs to be directed with a combination of efforts by expanding coverage of Margin Money Scheme, continuation of pattern of financial assistance to traditional Village Industries activities and involvement of Self Help Groups (SHGs) in maximum possible ways.

The Group is also of the view that while working towards achieving various targets set for the Tenth Five Year Plan, the recommendations made by the High Powered Committee (HPC) for the accelerated development of KVI programme, but left unfulfilled over the years, are also to be considered. Recently the Government of India has announced a package for development of Khadi and Village Industries. as per recommendations of the Committee constituted under the Chairmanship of Shri K. C. Pant, Dy. Chairman, Planning Commission, which is to be taken into consideration during the Tenth Plan.

Though KVI programme is generally meant for rural artisans/ entrepreneurs, the recent evaluation study conducted by the Programme Evaluation Organisation (PEO) of the Planning Commission, brought out the fact that to a considerable extent, the people living below poverty line have been benefited/helped to earn additional income from KVI sources and crossed the poverty line up-wards. The study revealed that about 71 per cent of sample households have actually crossed the poverty line with the help of additional income from KVIC programme. This indicates the inherent qualities of the KVI programme which can be used as an effective tool to help the downtrodden. The Group enlists following major objectives:-

i) To achieve an overall growth rate of above 6 per cent in terms of employment by the terminal year of the Tenth Plan period.

ii) To focus on the sustainability of past employment and make it more remunerative.

iii) To enhance productivity and earnings of artisans by ensuring access to better inputs.

iv) To utilize the existing infrastructure in a more effective and optimum way and to strengthen the same.

v) To widen the scope, coverage and reach of KVI programme and explore new strategies for quality assurance and marketability of products.

TARGET

KVIC has worked out following targets for the Tenth Plan period:–

i) To generate additional employment to the level of 20.00 lakhs i.e., 18.10 lakhs under Village Industries and 1.90 lakhs under Khadi by the terminal year of Tenth Plan, thereby achieving a rate of 6 per cent growth (3 percent in Khadi and 7 per cent in Village Industries) per annum under Khadi and Village Industries respectively.

ii) To enhance Khadi production to the level of 134.00 million Sq.m in terms quantity with corresponding production value of Rs. 917.16 crores.

iii) To generate Village Industries production worth Rs. 12488.98 crore by the terminal year of Tenth Five Year Plan.

STRATEGIES ON RURAL NON FARM INDUSTRIES/ ACTIVITIES

In order to accomplish the above objectives, there is a need to reprioritize the programme and policies and KVIC has suggested following strategies in this regard.

1. Targeted approach towards the traditional artisan based activites within the KVI sector.

The present coverage of traditional artisans under KVIC's fold is very small. There is an imperative need to ascertain the total all India size of traditional artisans and work out strategies for their coverage.

2. Special emphasis on development of KVI programme in North Eastern, Backward, Hilly and Border areas.

Due to various geographical disadvantages, the North Eastern part of our country has remained industrially backward. Apparently, it is difficult to develop this region through large-sale industrialization. KVI activities can play a predominant role in the development process of this region during the years ahead. Therefore, it is proposed that during the course of expansion of KVI programme in virgin areas, priorities may be accorded to hilly, border and other backwards areas. During the Tenth Five

Year Plan special initiatives are to be launched for integrating North Eastern Region, Hilly and Border areas with its activities by taking up a special Action Plan. Special incentives or liberalized approach towards such Action Plan will be much desired to achieve such an objective.

3. Involvement of Self Help Groups (SHGs) under KVI sector in order to widen the programme at the grass root level.

The process of expansion of KVI programme in uncovered areas cannot be successfully implemented without the involvement of grass root level agencies. The Self Help Groups (SHGs), mostly formed by rural women folk, have already acquired commendable position in micro credit system, apart from generating the spirit of Self Help and Self reliance among the rural people. However, it is observed that so far SHGs have not been involved in the implementation of KVI programme. During the Tenth Five Year Plan, it is proposed to actively involve SHGs for the promotion of KVI programme, and widening the coverage. SHGs in turn may establish linkages with the NGOs already working under the purview of KVI sector, in order to ensure sustainability. Micro-Finance Institutions are to be promoted. KVIC's leading NGO would be considered for taking up micro-financing activities also.

4. Involvement of Beneficiaries in the Planning process.

For smooth implementation of various schemes of KVIC, it is suggested that the beneficiary organisations like State Khadi and Village Industries Boards, other institutions, co-operative societies etc. working for the sector need to be involved at the planning stage itself, so that much more benefits of large network of these agencies and their production and market network is available to the sector. The NGO working under KVIC/KVIB should be actively involved in the implementation of Margin Money Scheme.

5. Budgetary support for traditional artisans in place of institutional finance.

At present, KVIC provides assistance to the village industry programme based on the project finance, for which the REGP has been introduced. It is observed that though this new approach has considerably helped to inculcate certain financial discipline and banking habit among the rural entrepreneurs, the fact remains that there are a large number of traditional rural activities, under the purview of KVI programme which are not in a position to fulfill the stringent viability criteria being adopted by the banking sector, while appraising projects. This Group is of the view that unless the interest of this needy target group is protected adequately, they would be left at the mercy of local money lenders. During the Ninth Plan period, the Government of India has considerably reduced the budgetary support of Village Industries Loan fund discontinuing the Village Industries Loan from budgetary provision. The Group feels that this decision is detrimental to the growth of the Village Industries Sector in general and traditional artisans in particular. In this context, this Group strongly recommends continuation of the budgetary support under Village Industries Loan head. This fund may be mainly utilized to meet the requirement of traditional Village Industries Activities, which are not able to avail Bank Finance under Margin Money Scheme. This budgetary support is also necessary to meet the requirement of funds in North Eastern States, identified hill border remote and inaccessible areas which can be liberalized pattern of assistance.

6. Establishing backward and forward linkages by adopting cluster development approach.

Implementation of any programme in an isolated manner can not bring the desired results. This is particularly when the programme is implemented in a decentralized manner.

This Group noted that considerable efforts have been made in developing village industries clusters during the Ninth Five Year Plan. However, a lot more needs to be done to make this programme reach new areas and develop artisan clusters. Development of cluster needs supply of needy inputs and common facilities. Therefore, a Common Facility Scheme is essential to develop such identified clusters. We suggest that it should continue its efforts with greater emphasis on clusters during the Tenth Five Year Plan and identify at least 25 clusters every year, so that atleast 100 additional clusters can be made functional by the terminal year of Tenth Plan.

7. Focus on Research and Development.

One of the primary objectives of KVI sector proposed for the Tenth Plan is to enhance the productivity of artisans. This can be better done by taking up extensive research and development activities under Khadi and Village Industries Sector. In a market driven economy, continuous innovation in product design, process and packaging are sine-qua-non for sustainability. During the Tenth Five Year Plan while continuing with the ongoing efforts at in-house and sponsored R&D centres, as a measure of economy in this regard, a few best functioning R&D institutions may be identified and motivated to undertake extensive Research & Development activities in Khadi and Village Industries Programme with suitable tie-up arrangements. It is also suggested that while augmenting designs, packaging etc. there is need to consolidate the efforts made so far and establish better liaison with nodal agencies like IITs, National Institute of Design (NID), National Institute of Fashion Technology (NIFT) etc.

8. Better monitoring and data system including Information Technology

While expanding coverage and programme during the 10th Five Year Plan, it is essential to strengthen its monitoring system by introducing greater use of modern information technology. Alongwith the data bank of its assisted units, it should maintain a data bank of all rural industry units in the country so that their contribution to economy is established. The existing monitoring mechanism and data collection system also requires strengthening. It is necessary to conduct concurrent evaluation of the programmes to take remedial measures timely. It should undertake special studies on problems of khadi and village industries on regular basis. The Group noted that it has started computerization of its activities and is in the process of creating data base in electronic form, linking with zonal offices, regional offices, state offices, etc. It is suggested that a network should connect all aided agencies for smooth flow of information.

9. Better marketing strategy

Expansion of domestic market as well as tapping potential export market are essential requirements in the fast changing market scenario, so as to ensure sustainability of KVI activities. In this context, this Group feels that there is an urgent need to intensify its marketing activities by establishing widespread objective and efficient sales network supported by improved Management Information System. The existing marketing system and policies require a thorough reorientation and revamping so that it can rise to the occasion in today's market sensitive economy. This Group also suggests introduction of a common logo for KVI products as a part of quality assurance and sales promotion.

In the wake of competition and market oriented production process, it has to work out appropriate marketing strategies so that its products can sustain while competing with other similar products from the organised sector. Equally essential is the cost competitiveness of products, which will pave the way for better acceptability of these products. In a market driven economy without developing a system to gather market intelligence and prompt services it will be extremely difficult to survive even for a short while. It is high time to take stock of the policies and approaches followed hitherto to capitalize on the efforts already initiated in bringing common brand name, renovation of sales outlets, improving quality, packaging, design etc.

The KVI products hold various inherent qualities, which need to be highlighted for making the market more conductive to these products of the rural tiny sector. Qualities like ethnic value, natural character, purity, originality, eco-friendliness, human touch, being handmade products etc., are to be capitalized by adopting suitable strategies.

Policy Support to Village Industries

No doubt, the ultimate objective of it is to make the rural entrepreneurs/artisans self-reliant. But it is apparent that during the course of working for the socio-economic causes, this sector often faces various odds and unhealthy competition from various quarters. KVI activities being decentralized in nature and traditional in techniques, are labour intensive, which make them unique on the one hand but add to the cost of production on the other. Hence, this Group is unanimous in its opinion that this sector deserves due protection of Central as well as State Governments. While dealing with various segments of KVI programme like Khadi, Village Industries, HRD, R&D, Marketing etc. in this report, we have pleaded for detailed policy support in relation to each of them. This Group recommends following policy supports, which are general in nature, for pushing up the growth of this sector during the Tenth Five Year Plan:–

(i) Enhanced budgetary support from the Government of India.

(ii) KVI programme represents a tiny sector of Indian economy. However, at present for all policy formulations this sector has been tied up with SSI sector and Government of India's policies are generally formulated keeping the agro and small industries sector in view. Therefore, there is a need for adopting a different policy approach for the exclusive development of KVI programme.

(iii) KVIC need to be recognized and nominated as the nodal agency for the development of total village industry sector in the country. This is more relevant since there are large number of rural artisans functioning in isolated manner without any organizational cover.

(iv) The country has entered an era of economic liberalization, which in turn is bound to trigger a series of competition right from the procurement of raw materials to marketing of finished products. It is necessary to insulate this tiny sector against challenges from the organized sector. So there is a need for protection of the sector from the onslaught of cut throat competition, posed by large scale industries and organized sector.

(v) In view of the social objectives of Khadi programme, various subsidies/ concessions extended to this sector in the form of rebate, MDA, ISEC may be continued.

(vi) Various concessions being provided to SSI sector may be extended to KVI sector too. This is necessary mainly because for availing such concessions, normally units are to be registered with the Directorates of Industry of concerned State, whereas KVIC units are registered with either State KVI Boards or KVIC so they are unable to avail of many of these concessions. Hence, it is suggested that units registered with KVIC or State KVIBs may be treated as registered units with State Industry Departments and extended all benefits and facilities available to such units.

(vii) Fiscal concessions are to be made applicable to KVI sector in all States and Union Territories in a uniform manner.

(viii) Agencies/Departments under Central/State Governments may extend purchase and price preference to this sector while procuring their stores.

(ix) KVIC may be given the status of export promotion council as varieties of products under KVI sector are exported and many more have increasing export potential. This will help to avoid cumbersome procedures involved in export of multiple products.

Services Sectors – Community, Social & Personal

(e) Health

Improvement in the health status of the population has been one of the major thrust areas in social development programmes of the country. This was to be achieved through improving the access to and utilization of Health, Family Welfare and Nutrition Services with special focus on underserved and underprivileged segments of population. Technological improvements and increased access to health care have resulted in steep fall in mortality but disease burden due to communicable diseases, non-communicable diseases and nutritional problems continue to be high. In spite of the fact that norms for creation of health care infrastructure and manpower are similar throughout the country, there remain substantial inter-state/inter-district variations in availability and utilization of health care services and health indices of the population.

The areas of attention in the Tenth Plan include the reorganization and restructuring of existing health care infrastructure, including the infrastructure for delivering ISM&H services at primary, secondary and tertiary care levels, so that they have the responsibility of serving population residing in well defined geographical areas, and have appropriate referral linkages with each other. One of the major factors responsible for poor performance in hospitals is the absence of personnel of all categories who are posted there. It is essential to ensure that there is appropriate delegation of powers to Panchayati Raj Institutions

(PRIs) so that there is local accountability of the public health care and problems relating to poor performance can be sorted out locally.

There is a need for horizontal integration of all aspects of the current vertical disease control programmes including supplies, monitoring, IEC, training and administrative arrangements; so that they become an integral part of health care. In order to facilitate this the states may speedly implement the recommendation regarding horizontal integration of on-going vertical programmes, including the suggestion that there should be a single health and family welfare society at state and district levels.

There are six lakh practitioners in Indian System of Medicine and Homeopathy in the country. They will be provided with appropriate orientation/skill upgradation through CME programmes, mainstreamed and utilised in improving access to health care coverage under the national programmes. Efforts will be made to fully implement the recommendations of the Planning Commission's Task Force on preservation, promotion and cultivation of medicinal plants and herbs, ensure availability of good quality ISM&H drugs at affordable prices within the country and fully realize the export potential for these drugs and formulations.

There will have to be continued commitment to provide essential primary health care, emergency life saving services under the National disease control programmes and the National Family Welfare programme free of cost to individuals based on their needs and not on their ability to pay. At the same time, suitable strategies will have to be evolved, tested and implemented for levying and collecting user charges from people above poverty line and utilizing funds obtained for improving the quality of health care services.

Data from NSSO indicate that escalating health care costs is one of the reasons for indebtedness not only among the poor but also in the middle-income group. It is therefore essential that appropriate mechanisms by which costs of severe illness and hospitalization can be borne by individual/Organisation/State are explored and affordable appropriate choice made. Global and Indian experience in this area, including efforts at risk pooling, cross-subsidy at local drives, social insurance, health insurance/ health maintenance organisation will have to be reviewed and appropriate steps initiated. If the Plan Target for education given in the Plan document is to be fulfilled there is the need for providing much large number of doctors, nurses and other medical professionals. This has been given in the Annexure.

(f) Nutrition

Currently, the major nutrition-related public health problems are chronic energy deficiency, micronutrient deficiencies, such as anaemia due to iron and folic acid deficiency, Vitamin A deficiency, Iodine deficiency disorders, chronic energy excess and obesity and associated health hazards.

Nutritional problems need to be tackled across a broad front. There needs to be continued increased in food grain production to meet the needs of the growing population. This increase should be more in the case of coarse grain production to meet the energy requirements of the BPL families at lower cost. Efforts have to be made to check the sluggish trend in per capita availability of pulses, and increase pulse production, improve affordability of pulses and increase consumption. Similarly, increased availability of vegetables at affordable cost throughout the year in urban and rural areas is desirable to address nutritional needs of the population.

As a Tenth Plan strategy, efforts have to be made to move from un-targeted food supplementation to fully operationalising growth monitoring, including screening pre-natal women, in order to identify onset under nutrition and initiate appropriate health and nutritional interventions. Another necessary step is to move from treatment from infection when children are brought, to prevention, early detection and management of infections through improved access to health care, which would prevent any deterioration in the nutritional status of children

(g) Education

Our performance in the field of education is much behind our expectation. Out of approximately 200 million children in the age group 6-14 years, only 120 million are in schools and net attendance in the primary level is only 66 per cent of enrolment.

This is completely unacceptable and the Tenth Plan should aim at a radical transformation in this situation. Education for all must be one the primary objectives of the Tenth Plan. The Sarva Shiksha Abhiyan, which has been launched to achieve this objective, indicates a strong reiteration of the country's resolve to give the highest priority to achieve this goal during the Plan period. It should also be our resolve that the process of integrating our educational system with the economic needs of the people and of the nation must begin at the primary school stage itself. Assertion of the dignity of labour and vocationalisation of curricula are essential to ensure that a disjunction does not take place between the educational system and the work place.

Universalizing access to primary education and improvement of basic school infrastructure must be a core objective of the Tenth Plan. This would mean targeting the provision of one teacher for every group of 40 children for primary and upper primary schools, opening of a primary/alternate schooling facility within 1 km of every habitation, provision of free textbooks to all SCs/STs children and girls at the primary and upper primary school, management and repair of school buildings through school management committees, provision of opportunities for Non-Formal and Alternative Education for out of school children in the most backward areas and from unreached segments of the population in response to local needs and demands articulated at the grass root level.

Mere establishment of schools without hiring teachers happens in many parts of the country, especially in rural areas. It is therefore essential that control over schools and teachers be transferred to local bodies which have a direct interest in teacher performance. States should be encouraged to implement the 73rd and 74th Amendments of the Constitution, which facilitate the transfer of management of primary and upper primary schools to panchayats/local bodies. Planning, supervision and management of education would have to be through local bodies at district, block and village levels. Efforts should also be made for social mobilization of local communities for adult literacy campaigns and for promotion of primary education.

Concerned users of public services have a self-interest in monitoring and improving public services. Where panchayats and other local bodies are not effective, it may prove more productive to set up parents groups with representatives of the local bodies and teachers to monitor the delivery of basic education to the rural areas. These parent-teacher groups must be empowered to do this monitoring and enforcing accountability on absentee teachers and disappearing school supplies.

Steps would have to be initiated to fill up all the existing vacancies of the teachers in a time bound manner, with defined responsibility to local bodies and communities, and to remove legal impediments in the recruitment of para-teachers. For quality education, provision of adequate academic support/training to all the teachers will be necessary. In this connection, the use of IT needs to be explored in terms of teacher's capacity building, as also for spread of literacy through TV, media.

The Mid-Day Meal Programme has made a difference in attendance and retention wherever a proper cooked meal is served. The practice of only providing grains followed by some State Governments, and that also not according to the prescribed norms in all cases, is vitiating the very purpose of the scheme. The State Governments must make efforts to provide hot cooked meals. If it is not possible to cover all the primary schools, efforts must be made to cover all schools in the backward and tribal areas, so that at least the children who badly need this extra nutrition are covered.

The University and Higher Education Sector also needs attention. Although the number of universities has expanded, and many of the universities continue to maintain high standards of education, it is a matter of serious concern that the expansion in quantity has been accompanied by a fall in quality. Modernization of syllabi, examination reforms and greater attention to issues of governance of universities and colleges, all require urgent attention. Part of the problem facing universities is the inadequate provision of budgetary resources from the government. Since budget resources are limited, and such resources as are available need to be allocated to expanding primary education, it is important to recognize that the universities must make greater efforts to supplement resources from the government. University fees are unrealistically low and in many universities have not been raised in decades. This policy is only starving the universities of the minimum resources needed to ensure quality education and is not in the interest of the students. A substantial hike in university fees is essential. Resources raised through adjustment of fees can be supplemented by contributions from industry, constituting funds/trusts like the Bharat Shiksha Kosh, etc. It is also necessary to encourage the establishment of private universities.

Laws, rules and procedures regarding facilitation of educational institutions must be modernized and simplified so that honest and sincere individuals and organisations can set up universities, colleges and schools. Controls on fees, teacher salaries, infrastructure, staff strength must be eliminated. The regulatory system must also put the greatest emphasis on fraud detection and punishment while letting normal individuals to function more freely.

These considerations apply with even greater force to the technical education system. Both technical and management education need to be managed strategically in order to provide broad-based multi-disciplinary education incorporating composite skills and knowledge to meet the challenges posed by globalisation. In view of the spurt in demand for education in information technology and other new and emerging technology areas, suitable courses at the degree level need to be given a boost. The challenges posed by faculty shortage and resource limitations have to be tackled through rationalization and networking. If the above policies are to be implemented we have to increase the supply of trained teachers and their availability in remote areas. For this the incentive structure of teachers in the late nineties need to be reviewed. The growth of teachers are much below the visualized need to fulfill the education target of the Tenth Plan. Proper programmes need to be chalked out for generating teachers at all levels matching with the likely demand pattern for the future.

(h) Information Technology

The potential contribution of information technology to employment generation is both direct and indirect. Directly, the growth of the computer hardware and software industries is generating new job opportunities in India. Indirectly, the adoption of computer technology by other industries expands the range of services they provide and can stimulate more rapid growth of these sectors. The indirect impact of IT is far larger than the direct impact. In the USA, it is estimated that for every direct job created in the IT industry, 3-4 jobs are created by indirect ones. This does not include the non-IT jobs created by the growth of other sectors of the economy under the stimulus of information technology.

IT is both a labour creating and labour saving technology. As the introduction of automated machines replaced manual labour in factories and on fields, it was once believed that the spread of computer technology would result in massive job destruction. However, two decades of experience has demonstrated that the reverse is actually the case. Surely specific types of jobs are eliminated, but overall computerization creates far more than it destroys. The spread of computerization acts as a catalyst for the growth of many types of businesses. This is not only true of businesses directly related to the computer industry, such as research and development, computer education, computer repair and maintenance. In fact, every sector of the economy is being energized by the adoption of computer technology. Studies by the National Research Council in the USA have found that IT has a stimulating effect on the growth of a wide range of service industries. IT has demonstrable benefits for employment and skill levels. Evidence indicates that IT contributes to growth in demand for labour, as well as an overall skill upgrading in the workplace.

The IT sector will be defined in a narrower sense as those businesses that are directly related to the manufacture of computer hardware and software, the training of personnel for the manufacture and operation of computer equipment, use of computers in education and the utilization of computer technology for IT enabled services such as call centers, medical transcription services etc.

In 1990 India's IT industry generated \$7.7 billion in revenues, 15 times the level in 1980. Exports rose from \$150 million in 1990s to nearly \$4 billion in 1999. With a compounded annual growth rate of more than 50 per cent between 1991 and 2001, the India IT software and services sector has expanded almost twice so fast as the US software sector though from a smaller base. No other country has consistently grown by more than 50 per cent every year in the past 10 years.

The global market for software services spurs growth of India's IT sector. The global outsourcing market is worth more than $100 billion. In 2000-01, software exports accounted for 13 per cent of India's total exports. By 2003, software exports from India are expected to account for almost 23 per cent of India's total exports. India has already acquired a substantial market share in the global customized software development market. In 1991, according to a World Bank study, India's share was about 11.9 per cent of the global market. In 2000, it was 19.5 per cent. Last year 266 of the Fortune 1000 companies sourced out their software requirements to India, with more than 1250 companies exporting software.

India's success can be attributed to a combination of factors, such as Resource endowments, availability of cheap skilled labour, favourable government policies, such as investments in higher education, and presence of large number of Indians working in US firms who played an important role in matching US buyers with Indian suppliers with low level of investment required to launch software services.

In 1999, NASSCOM engaged McKinsey, the international consulting firm, to conduct an in-depth study of India's potential in IT related industries. McKinsey projected that India could generate 2 million additional jobs in this sector by 2008 and contribute US$ 87 billion to national income. According to the McKinsey study, direct employment in India's software industry is expected to rise from 1,80,000 in 1998 to 2.2 million in 2008.

Table H

Projection of Additional Employment in IT Sector

Year	Additional Workforce requirements
2001	90,000
2002	115,000
2003	150,000
2004	195,000
2005	250.000
2006	300,000
2007	340,000
2008	370,000

Estimation of growth of employment opportunities in the IT industry is complicated by the fact that more than any other industry IT is international in character and dependent on global trends, which have been subject to wide fluctuations in recent years. Following the publication of the McKinsey study in 1999, the global IT sector actually grew faster than had been anticipated due to the explosive growth of the internet and dot com companies. Then, abruptly the bubble and the euphoria about IT and internet subsided.

In assessing India's potential in this industry over the next decade, we must try to avoid both unrealistic euphoria and unrealistic pessimism that result from relying on short-term performance to extrapolate long-term trends. The fact is that even now at a time when the newspapers are full of news about lower growth estimates and falling share values for India's premier IT companies, the IT industry in India is still growing and generating additional jobs, admittedly it is not growing as rapidly as it was a year ago or as it was projected to continue at that time. The assessment of the group is that it will contribute to approximately 0.2 million per year and around one million at the end of the Tenth Plan giving additional employment generation as direct employment.

The real employment potential of ICT will be realised when such services support the community, social and personal services required by the Indian masses. This is the issue of Digital Divide, on which the Special Group is constrained to observe adequate policy attention has not so far been focussed in India. Whatever efforts at use of ICT in Education, Health, Nutrition, Housing, Real Estate, Banking, Insurance and other personal services have been made, have not been designed with the perspective of low budget consumer. The cost of research on Technology peeps the cost high. But the real purpose of planning for ICT is to narrow and eliminate the digital divide.

Policies to Meet the Problem of Digital Divide

Having said that, the mere existence of a gap in levels of ICT services between rich and poor within the country does not imply that ICTs should be priority for government action; after all, poor countries also have fewer factories, fewer cars, fewer doctors and nurses. Threshold effects are at work.

However, if the opportunities for improved income generation and access to services provided by the new ICTs are limited to the wealthy, this will perpetuate and strengthen a number of disparities, including gender inequality and the inequalities faced by the disabled.

The first step to begin fulfilling the communications needs of the poor is to leverage the full potential of market mechanisms in reaching out to poor communities, by allowing the establishment of a competitive, private sector-led market. A range of studies suggest that there can be dramatic increases in access to telephone and Internet services, through a telecommunications-sector reform programme based on three pillars: privatisation, completion, and independent regulation, but all should lead to lower cost of the service.

Gaining full benefit from private-sector participation and liberalization also requires the regulatory environment of the communications industry to be conducive to a well functioning competitive market. In the telecommunications sector, this can be achieved through legal and regulatory mechanisms that promote, among other things: fair interconnection and revenue-sharing arrangements between telecommunications operators; moving toward cost-oriented tariffs and the elimination of internal cross-subsidies, with the limited exception of carefully designed subsidies to ensure access and use for the poor; as well as recourse to a strong and truly independent regulatory agency, capable of enforcing rules.

Moving to private competitive markets is unlikely to be enough to ensure that the poor have access to ICTs, however. A combination of regulatory requirements, carefully designed privatisation and license contracts, and bidding procedures and financial support for private provision of public access will be required to meet the goal.

Using regulatory and policy support for public access, be it to a telephone line, to a radio, TV screen, or to an Internet terminal, countries can aggregate demand so that a large number of people benefit from one or a few connection.

In a competitive environment, the costs of providing public access in environments where private returns to provision are likely to be low can be financed through special funds. These funds are set up a transitory mechanism to help partially defray the initial investment costs of network expansion in rural and poor areas.

The choice of a funding strategy can also support a level playing field among operators so that none of the operators is overly compensated or unfairly burdened by the funding mechanism.

It should be noted that the ICT movement is still in its early stages in out country.

(i) Tourism

Tourism is a priority sector because, among others, it is able to maximise the productivity of India's natural, human, cultural and technical resources; it is labour intensive and cottage or small industry based providing employment, that is of a high quality; it is capable of being primarily focused on rural areas with appropriate and relatively low cost programme and it has extensive forward and backward economic linkages that build overall income and employment, especially for women, youth and disabled persons. The objective of the tourism policy is to position tourism as a major engine of economic growth and to harness its direct and multiplier effects for employment and poverty eradication in an environmentally sustainable manner. These objectives will be achieved through the following strategies:

1. Positioning and maintaining tourism development as a national priority activity;
2. Enhancing and maintaining the competitiveness of India as a tourism destination.
3. Improving India's existing tourism products and expanding these to meet new market requirements.
4. Creation of world class infrastructure.
5. Developing sustained and effective marketing plans and programs.

The focus of the Ministry of Tourism during the Tenth Five Year Plan will be on encouraging private public partnership in which the government would be the active facilitator and catalyst with the ultimate goal of creating world-class infrastructure and innovative products. Marketing of destinations and brand building will be the strategies for promotion of tourism. The specific components of the development activities to be undertaken during the Tenth Plan will include infrastructure development, product development of Mega tourism resorts, targeted approach towards development of tourism circuits, entrepreneurship development and promotion of self employment opportunities, enhanced tourist facilitation, human resources development, research and computerization, promotion and marketing, environmental protection and cultural preservation, and provision of incentives. Major policy initiatives such as liberalization in aviation sector, Aviation Turbine Fuel pricing policy which influences internal air fares, rationalisation in tax rates in the hospitality sector, tourist friendly visa regime, and procedural changes in making available land for construction of hotels etc., which do not come directly under the purview of the Ministry of Tourism, Government of India, but under the other Ministries and State Governments will be vigorously pursued.

With appropriate public investment (estimates placed before the Planning Commission) and commensurate investment by the private sector and the implementation of the policies mentioned in the previous paragraph, it is expected that the international and domestic tourism will get a boost and India's share in the world tourism will increase from the present 0.38 per cent to 0.50 per cent by 2004 and 0.62 per cent by 2007. Correspondingly, the direct and indirect employment from tourism is expected to increase from the present 41 million to 54 million by 2004 and to 66 million by 2007, i.e., an increase of 3.6 million jobs per year.

(j) Construction

The construction activities are very much influenced by the real estate development. The recent repeal of the Land Ceiling Act, likely to be followed by the States to free land market will largely boost the real estate activities. The proposed repeal of Rent Control Act will further encourage the growth of this sector.

In a package proposed in the Tenth Plan to give incentives to the cities and States for urban sector development, there has been a proposal for recommending selective freedom to convert rural land for urban use, reduction of stamp duty on transfer of property and laws facilitating private development of township – all these will increase the real estate growth, and thereby generate increased demand for construction. It is noticed that in the organised and mechanized segment, there has been a very low employment elasticity and at this point of time very little contribution to the employment generation in this sector, whereas in the unorganised segment employment elasticity is very high. But unfortunately, their wage rates are very low because of the low productivity in this unorganised segment along with heavy exploitation of labour by the employers in the absence of proper legislative safeguards. If for generating additional employment this segment has to be developed, then proper schemes are needed to improve their technology by putting additional funds and also necessary legislation so that the construction labour will not be exploited. Let only small construction companies use migrant labour that move from one construction sight to another with their spouses and children. These migrant labourers obviously find their occupation more remunerative than the alternatives available in the villages from which they come. But their mode of daily existence around the work imposes the constraint on the urban areas to which they migrate. Hence, to repeat, the unorganised segment of the construction sector needs specific legislation and also programmes for developing their productivity by infusing more technology and credit.

The Group feels that both the large mechanised activities and the small and medium ones have their own respective roles and will survive alongside. In the area of bridges, major irrigation and dam construction, high rise buildings etc., the large mechanized construction activities will be unavoidable. But at the same time, in the areas like rural road building, low cost housing, minor irrigation etc, the small construction units with minimum improvement in mechanization can serve the purpose and fulfill the need for generating more jobs.

III. POLICIES ON SUPPLY SIDE OF LABOUR

Specific welfare measures for Building and Construction Workers are enumerated in this chapter later. However, the nature of (i) labour administration and (ii) Pro-employment measures required in this sector are not the same as for organised sector. Hence construction industry employers, contractors etc., have to be given the same preferences as the micro and small enterprises

In this section, policies and programmes are discussed which will enable the skill/competence level of labour force to match with those required for satisfying the new jobs to be created for the Tenth Plan. For example, over the late nineties, (1993-94 to 1999-2000) it is observed that:

(i) The percentage of the skilled and educated employment is increasing in the total employment generated.

(ii) The absorption of this increased supply of skilled and educated manpower has been significantly more in the unorganised sector because of the near saturation of new recruitment observed in the organised sector. The major absorbing sectors were the agriculture, small and medium enterprises, and non-farm rural sector and the services sector (especially its fast growing areas like tourism, information technology, road transport, financial services etc.).

(iii) The unemployment rates among the educated and skilled labour force are observed to be very high, two to three times more than the average unemployment rate in the labour force.

All these suggest that the policy implications of these trends are :

- To reduce unemployment among the skilled and educated labour, early redeploying by proper training and skill development by formal or informal method should be initiated.
- Development of institutions for skill development and training, either in the public sector or private sector, should be expedited by mutual partnership and also on

regional basis in order to meet the likely nature of skill demand in future.

All these are the responsibilities of the Ministries of labour, HRD and many other agencies in the public and private sector where a coordinated approach among them will be needed. Of course, the principal responsibility is at the State Government level for vocational training. As the major labour absorption is likely to be in the unorganised sector where the job quality now is very unsatisfactory, proper programmes should be developed to improve the productivity in this sector, with necessary legislation to prevent exploitation. Specific programmes have been identified in the Report and presented in the following section.

(a) Skill Building and Training

As we have already mentioned, our focus needs be more on the unorganized sector, as distinct from the capital-intensive corporate sector, since this is the sector that is identified as the main job giver in future, and also where viability is at stake under global competition. The answer is therefore, to increase the productivity of labour in this sector and to make it attractive to improve its job quality.

Given our terms of reference, our task is to achieve creation of employment opportunities of better quality in a short to medium term framework of 5 years. Therefore, quick yielding measures for improvement of skills of entrants to labour force become an important instrument of planning. The task is by no means easy because development of human capital (HRD) is necessarily an activity with a long gestation period. (And is becoming all the more difficult as public sector, which has capital- and hence technology, with a well structured training programme for its fresh recruits, cuts down drastically on its intake.)

Issues, Strategy for improving Vocational Training

The Group, after its deliberation, and also considering recommendations of relevant committees includes the one by MOL as following.

- Expansion of vocational training facilities
- Improvement in effectiveness, Efficiency and Relevance

of existing training programmes of DGE & T (Ministry of Labour)

- Improvement in Governance and Management of National Vocational Training System (NVTS under the Ministry of Labour)
- Suggestions of/for other Ministries/ Departments to augment various Skill Development Programmes
- Training for Informal Sector

(i) Expansion of vocational training facilities –the suggested measures

- Greater involvement of private providers of training and NGOs
- Adequate resources (earmarking of funds) in States' plan budget
- Increase in training capacity for in-service workers
- Enlarge scope of Apprenticeship Training by covering more occupations in emerging high-tech areas, service sector and informal sector
- Adoption of new training delivery mechanisms (like distance learning)
- Sufficient in-built component/ outlay for training under all schemes funded by the Central or State Governments related to poverty alleviation/ employment promotion/ social welfare etc.
- Strengthening of Skill Development Programme for Women and disadvantaged groups.

(ii) Improvement in effectiveness, Efficiency and Relevance of existing training programmes of DGE & T (Ministry of Labour)

- Setting up of a Skill Development Fund (SDF) on partnership basis between the industry and the Government, with major voluntary contribution coming from industry

- Strengthening of interaction between industry and ITIs and developing some ITI's as Centres for Excellence
- Vertical mobility of craftsmen and apprentices (across levels of proficiency and education)
- Staff development and motivation
- Strengthening of monitoring mechanism and joint inspections
- Vocational guidance & counseling and assistance in placement
- Strengthening of research capabilities
- Modularisation and multi-skilling
- Competency based certification system for workers without formal qualifications
- Development of a formal policy for vocational training

(iii) Improvement in Governance and Management of National Vocational Training System (NVTS under the Ministry of Labour)

The Problem

- After the manifold growth of ITIs/ITCs, and continuance of 3 to 4 decades old system of governance and management of vocational training, the NVTS still remains to be upgraded and modernized
- Weak links between State level (wherever, they are at all existing) and the National Councils
- Separate national level councils for 'Vocational' (NCVT) and 'Apprenticeship Training'(CAC)
- No State level forum to design and promote 'Apprenticeship Training'
- No link across multiple Departments of Central Government rendering training (as exists for higher technical education)

Suggested Approach

- Merger of National Council for Vocational Training (NCVT) and Central Apprenticeship Council (CAC) into an All India Council of Vocational Training (AICVT).
- Formation of State level corresponding bodies (Functions of National level and State level bodies should not be the same; the State level bodies to do field level functions of recognition of ITIs etc, and National level body to set guidelines, and assign performance ratings).
- AICVT and corresponding State level bodies to take on board a number of other vocational training providers in ministries/ departments other than Labour.
- AICVT and corresponding State level bodies to have mandatory representation of the major actors involved in vocational training in the various economic activities.

(iv) Suggestions of/for Ministries/ Departments, other than Labour, to augment various Skill Development Programmes

(a) Housing and Urban Development Corporation (HUDCO) – ITIs to provide both in-service and pre-service training

(b) Council for Advancement of People's Action and Rural Technology (CAPART) – to set up more technology resource centres across country

(c) Secondary Education – to earmarked funds for vocationalisation of secondary education.

(d) Community Polytechnics – to reorient training to demand driven output.

(e) Khadi Village Industries Corporation (KVIC) – to identify new target groups, involve NGOs

(f) Associated Chamber of Commerce (ASSOCHAM) –

- Autonomous bodies with full autonomy to manage ITIs on experimental basis
- Incentives by Government to private sector to establish ITIs

(v) Training for Informal Sector – the Recommended Strategy

Training activity, for entrants to organised sector has always received a highly preferential treatment in access to resources, in contrast to those who enter the world of work through the unorganized sector. Market processes in the phase of economic reforms have accentuated this tendency further. Consider the exorbitant capitation fees for training in medicine, high private establishments fees for newly emerging areas of employment-I.T. and I.T. enabled services, engineering, hotel and catering, etc. The problem had already got compounded even before reforms, because the formal training certificates became a screening parameter, for recruitment to public sector/Government. And within the HRD activity, literacy and general education always received greater attention of Central and State Governments than training of prospective entrants to labour force. In short, we have not had a policy for skill building for bulk of the new entrants to labour force, who have to find a job in the unorganized and the informal sector. The suggestion in this respect, therefore, are:

- Government to articulate a policy framework for support of informal sector training
- Use all available methods to increase literacy standard and production skills of persons in the informal sector
- Detailed surveys on training needs and existing arrangements for training in informal sector
- Motivate associations in the informal sector to help develop skills and entrepreneurship
- International agencies such as UNICEF and World Bank to act in collaboration with Government at grass root level for administration and distribution of aid to informal sector
- Opening training-cum-production centers in informal sector to enable individuals to earn while they learn e.g., handicrafts sector
- Common identity cards by local bodies and Police to those working in informal sector clearly specifying the places where informal sector activity is not wanted

- Refinancing for urban micro-credit that creates training facilities for this sector to open up entrepreneurship in this area
- Private sector companies to be enabled to create foundations to finance community-based programmes which include training and business support to micro-enterprises, coupled with tax and credit incentives
- Identify organisations through which action programmes can be developed – trade based guilds, trade unions (including the smaller ones) and self-help groups
- Government not to enter into curriculum development except for the high return, high technology areas

Construction Sector

- An Act enables levy of a cess to generate funds for welfare of construction workers. A part of this to be utilised for financing training of informal sector construction workers.

Reform of Vocational Training Establishments in the States

Mode of Administration of Training Services operated by Government

The services for training are rendered through the Central and State Governments. Most of the ITIs in the state sector, and the institutes for advanced training, and training of instructors under the Ministry of Labour are organised as subordinate offices of Government. In contrast, similar establishments under other departments, Ministry of Information Technology, for example, are organised as autonomous bodies. Administering these establishments by using the normal rules of Governments for personnel and financial matters greatly reduces the flexibility, which a specialised institution should have. Such institutional structures also preclude the possibility of raising any resources from the trainees towards financing at least a part of the cost of the services rendered. Thus, the discipline of a consumer-server relationship that accrues from claims against payments made is not easily possible in the existing departmental set up of the services rendered. These training and training related establishments should therefore be restructured as "autonomous bodies". As autonomous bodies they would be required to publish their 'accounts' and place them as well as a review of their performance before the relevant legislatures. This is more transparent than the operation of an attached office of Government whose details of operations and accounts get submerged in the voluminous accounts of the main Ministry/Department.

As a first step in restructuring of Industrial Training Institutes, one of the prerequisites for extending Central financial assistance for developing 100 State run ITIs as institutes of excellence during the Tenth Plan period will be that the identified ITI (i) be registered as an autonomous body, and (ii) have a formal tie up with industry.

Motivating States by taking up Centrally Sponsored Schemes

- Developing at least one ITI in each district as a centre of excellence
- Model Instructor training institutes; financial implications to be worked out including the contribution possible by the State Governments
- ITIs in the North East
- ITIs in J & K

Attracting Investment into Skill Building Activities

Vocational skill building needs to be developed as an entrepreneurial activity in which the private sector would be willing to invest. Income tax incentives are available to higher technical and medical education establishments. Such establishments can draw in resources from market because of higher returns on such education. Vocational skill building establishments need better income tax incentives than the higher education establishments.

The Tenth Plan Working Group on Skill Building recommends a study to institutionalize management, collection mechanism, contributions and utilization of skill development fund. The purpose is to attract resources from the beneficiaries from training including the employers and the trade unions. This study should be done on priority basis, and should also explore the possibility of extending income tax incentives to the contributions made.

Under Section 37(1) of Income Tax Act, benefit for providing apprenticeship training is available to employers employing 500 or more workers. This benefit should be available to all establishments registered under Factories Act, Shops and Establishment Act, or any other relevant Act that enables setting up of institutions.

Equipment donated to vocational training institutes should be exempt from customs duties.

The group concluded with the caution: unless proper action is taken because the organised sector's remuneration and job quality are very high, all students will move to high-tech centres for skill development. The result is, because of low rate of new recruits in the organised sector, they will end in increasing the unemployment pool.

Information base for Planning for Skill Building – the National Classification of Occupants.

Skills are required for occupations. Manpower planning exercise is linked with the occupation profile of workers. Therefore, any programme for skill building has to take note of the emerging structure of occupations in the economy. This requires a system of classification of occupations. At present, the available classification is the National Classification of Occupations, which was prepared in the year 1968 (NCO, 1968). Thereafter a radical change in the occupational profile of Indian workers has occurred. With urbanization, changes in technology, and radical changes in work practices in agriculture, many of traditional occupations should have vanished, and new occupations emerged.

The Ministry of Labour, in consultation with the Department of Statistics, had taken an initiative to develop a new classification of occupations. This was around the year 1996, i.e., at the commencement of the Ninth Plan. However, due to certain practical problems, the work could not proceed. Now, in the year 2001, the Ministry of Labour had decided to pursue the exercise with in-house efforts.

(b) Occupational Safety and Health (OSH)

A number of laws which guide the occupational safety and health aspects are applied only in the organized sectors and cover only 8% of the workforce. In this sector, a large number of occupational safety and health measures are applicable in a fragmented manner as regulations have been developed in a piecemeal manner resulting in duplication in some areas and gaps in others. At present, there is no single unified legislation, which can take care of the basic responsibility of occupational safety and health in all sectors. In view of this, the Tenth Plan commits itself to introducing a General Legislation (Umbrella) on OSH. This will help reduce the multiplicity of enforcement agencies and will have proper coordination among them with a view to providing a focus on OSH measures in industry.

Many occupations and industries which include dhaba workers, shop workers, road transport workers, unorganized mining, restaurants, etc., are not covered by any mechanism of safety surveillance of workers. The Tenth Plan approach would be to create awareness amongst the employers and workers regarding various occupational health hazards and accidents and the adverse effects and possible protective measures.

It is not appropriate to leave the large working population in the unorganized sectors unprotected. Most of the workers in the unorganized sectors are exposed to a variety of hazards and are compelled to accept employment for reasons of poverty. The enormity of the task of applying OSH legislation to such a vast workforce spread far and wide is challenging, and needs a huge infrastructure and manpower for its effective implementation. Therefore, the approach of the Tenth Plan would be to provide short and long term measures required for OSH improvements in a steady and phased manner. On the other hand, a particular unorganized sector cannot be brought under the purview of an OSH legislation without giving time to the employers, self-employed and employees in the concerned sector for shouldering such responsibilities. Therefore, one of the important and priority measures would be to launch a well-designed awareness campaign.

To deal with the gaps arising out of changes in technology, introduction of new types of chemicals and sophisticated machinery, efforts would be made to equip the enforcement agency with latest techniques and skills that are required in the area of safety measures. Likewise, knowledge of safety inspectors at State level would be updated through identification of training needs of skill development and imparting knowledge to the inspectors. Support of industry and technical expertise would be mobilized through awareness generation and ensuring the participation of workers. To develop trained personnel in the area of OSH, efforts would be made to include occupational safety and health aspects in the professional courses like Engineering and Medical.

To meet the growing demand, mining activity of minor minerals has also increased and many new mines have been opened up. Accidents in Mines occur due to unsafe acts and unsafe conditions of work. Most of the accidents are preventable because, directly or indirectly, these are due to human failures. To deal with the increasing mine accidents, effective measures would be taken for stringent enforcement of Mines Act. Further, the challenges posed by the mechanization and new technology would be addressed through upliftment of technical skill of inspectors and frequent inspections so that safety and health of workers gets due priority. DGMS, a specialized organization, engaged in the area of mines safety would be strengthened in terms of infrastructure facilities to enable it to provide better services towards operational safety aspects of the mines. Some suggestions in this context are:

- A coherent National Policy on Occupational Safety and Health of workers employed in all sectors of economy may be formulated through tri-partite consultation.
- To reduce multiplicity of enforcement agencies and to have proper coordination among them, a single unified General Legislation (Umbrella) on Occupational Safety and Health may be adopted. The enforcement of the provisions of legislations may be carried out by existing machinery available at Centre/States.
- Support of industry and technical expertise may be mobilized through awareness generation and ensuring the participation of workers.
- To improve the existing occupational safety and health scenario in mines, factories, ports, docks and unorganized

sectors of the economy, the government enforcement agencies and the managements may jointly undertake substantial strengthening in the area of development of standard work procedure, public awareness about safety, safe work procedure, etc.

- To incorporate safety and occupational health aspects, amendments may be carried out to the Beedi and Cigar Workers Act, 1966.
- Reading material to create awareness on OHS aspects may be developed in collaboration with the professional bodies/ agencies concerned. The material thus developed in national and regional languages may be telecast on T.V. channels and broadcast on radio for creating mass awareness on occupational safety and health to the persons involved in all these segments.

(c) Social Security

The agenda of liberalization and globalization adopted by our country over the last one decade underscores the need for comprehensive social security policy for a large section of the society including specific vulnerable groups like the aged, women, the disabled, tribal and scheduled castes. To provide social security cover to these vulnerable groups, the approach would be to integrate and converge the services of the existing schemes and projects of various Ministries and Departments. To extend assistance during illness and injury at the time of work and pension, basic minimum social security cover would be given in accordance with the availability of resources.

An approach to the challenge of closing the coverage gap in social security provisions has to be developed at two levels. In order to remove existing inefficiencies, redundancies and existing gaps and weaknesses, the first level approach would be to strengthen the institutional arrangement in the organized sector. The second level would be to create a legislative and administrative framework for significant penetration of social security cover in the unorganized sector. In this regard the strategy would be to motivate and encourage the State Governments for formulating and implementing schemes and programmes targeted at certain occupational groups in the unorganized sector as per their requirement and without putting any additional pressure on the budget.

In order to extend the coverage of social security measures for the unorganized sector workers, the strategy would be to encourage setting up of the Cooperatives, Self-help Groups, Mutual Benefit Associations, managed and financed by the occupational groups / workers of unorganized sectors and voluntary health insurance and pension schemes. Also, focused attention would be paid towards alternative income generating activities with provision of credit arrangement for supply of raw materials, etc.

Awareness generation campaigns and dissemination of information to unorganized workers would be strengthened. To improve the efficiency of the delivery mechanism of existing programmes to reach the workers in the unorganized sector, local institutions like Panchayati Raj Institutions, Civic Bodies, Municipalities would be involved for monitoring the social security programmes. The specific recommendations are:

- Considering the size of the large workforce in the country, a policy framework at the national level on the provisions of social security to different groups of workers and employees in the country may be formulated and adopted.
- The Minimum Wages Act may be amended enhancing the penalty so that the violation of the provisions under the Act is made costly to the employers.
- Presently, there are inter-state variations in the minimum wages. Even for the same occupations, variations in wages have been quite significant. To minimize such disparities, a National Policy on Minimum Wages may be evolved.
- The enforcement machinery in the Central and the State Governments may be strengthened and involvement of NGOs, Panchayati Raj Institutions and Cooperatives may be encouraged.
- To prevent exploitation of workers in the unorganized sector, awareness generation may be stepped up in close collaboration with the voluntary organizations, trade unions and other committed individuals. The work of

awareness generation may be vigorously undertaken by the Central Board for Workers Education.

- The delivery of services in Social Security through Provident Fund and Employees State Insurance Scheme (ESIS) may be improved by adopting information and communication technology in the overall interests of the workers.
- Priority attention may be given to those Social Security covers for the unorganized sector which can look after medical care, accident benefits, old age pension and maternity benefit.
- Provident Fund Schemes and Employees State Insurance Schemes may be extended to the workers in the unorganized sector through innovative approaches that would cater to the requirements of the workers in local conditions.
- Innovative schemes under the Employees State Insurance Scheme may be launched on experimental basis targeting groups like rickshaw puller, auto rickshaw driver, head loader, etc.
- Emphasis may be given to the convergence of services for various social security measures undertaken by Ministries/Departments, in an integrated manner.
- Community based and location specific social security measures may be encouraged through Self-Help Groups, Voluntary Organizations, Panchayati Raj Institutions, etc.
- Based on the experience of the existing welfare funds for Beedi, Mine and Cine workers, efforts may be made to constitute similar welfare funds for fish processing, salt workers, etc.
- State Governments may be motivated and encouraged to formulate and implement social security schemes for the unorganized sector as per their requirements with minimum burden on their budget.
- Concerted efforts may be made to enhance the coverage under National Social Assistance Programmes for

providing old age pension, maternity and other benefits to the workers in the unorganized sector.

(d) Labour Laws and Other Labour Regulations

The Tenth Plan approach will be to take a fresh look at the structure of labour laws. Our present laws are far too rigid since they do not allow firms mainly in the organised sector to retrench labour or downsize without the permission of the appropriate government, which in most cases is the State Government. This permission is very difficult to secure. Unfortunately, these provisions, which were meant to protect employment, might have actually served to discourage growth of employment. The inability to shed labour in times of difficulty encourages entrepreneurs to avoid hiring labour. This problem, to a large extent, is relevant for the organised sector. Therefore, the labour force involved vis-à-vis the Industrial Disputes Act that provides conditions and rules for retrenchment of labour, has to be reviewed. However, it affects only eight per cent of the total employed labour force. This should be kept in mind while approaching the remaining 92 per cent of the jobs in the country.

The changes proposed in the Industrial Disputes Act are to provide more flexibility in the hiring and firing of labour in order to increase productivity, efficiency and adjustment process in the changing demand market at national and international levels. Also, this is proposed to ease the closure process of the sick units, which have become an economic burden on the society. This Group views that with considerable excess labour being carried by the public sector in the organised segment and a jobless nature of growth in the organised sector as a whole, the immediate effect may turn out to be net labour shedding. This should be assessed against the present high level of unemployment. In this context, one should also remember that the social security support in India is much below the standard provided in the developed countries, because of which their tolerance level of unemployment is very high. No doubt, in some organised establishments, it will be easy to recruit more labour by the relaxation of this legislation, but the net effect by a rough calculation over the next three or four years is likely to be insignificant in either way. One should remember that the contribution of total employment by the organised private sector is hardly 3.5 per cent and, therefore, the potential of generating sizeable employment in this sector, even by changing the law will be insignificant over the Tenth Plan period. The Labour Commission is also examining this issue. This issue, therefore, is to be sorted out in a long-term perspective and not for immediate generation of employment in the country. The Group suggests that one alternative is to relax the Act gradually and ensuring full security of the retrenched labour. So far as the repeal of the Contract Labour Act is concerned, the experience shows that it will help giving more flexibility in recruiting labour without putting a long-term financial commitment on the employer and, therefore, a change in the Contract Labour will encourage more recruitment. But given the present Group's recommended strategy in upgrading the job quality and security of the workforce, proper care should be taken so that in this process, more casualisation of labour not take place by increased exploitation by the recruiting agencies. Already, the growth of casual labour in the 1990s is very high. A proper social security measure and a regulatory body to oversee the function of the recruiting agencies should accompany any change in this Act to safeguard the minimum quality of the job provided.

One of the reasons for rigidity in labour laws is that the 'employer' is expected to provide, individually, for security of employment (i.e. guarding against risks of loss of job, family sickness) retirement benefits and bear the costs of accidents and other occupation related risks compensations. This happens because the labour market institutions, which are designed to provide social security to workers, have narrow reach, are almost exclusively administered by Central Government, provide security at a high cost, are highly specific to individual employers, and lack the concepts of 'shared risk'. Therefore, a more innovative and broad-based social security system for workers is needed to smoothen the process of labour reforms and enable rationalization of labour laws.

The SSI sector plays an important role in the economic development of the country and contributes significantly to its industrial output, employment and export. However, they are burdened with maintenance of unmanageable number of various forms and registers under the different labour laws. The approach during the Tenth Plan would be to exempt it from the rigor of the various labour laws and make it vibrant and efficient. In this regard, efforts will be made to conduct proper orientation and training programmes for the officers of the labour law enforcement machinery and create a positive climate for growth in this sector.

The enforcement of various labour laws pertaining to SSI units falls under the jurisdiction of State Governments. The entire onus of compliance in furnishing the returns and inspections falls on the SSI entrepreneur. Most of the SSI entrepreneurs cannot afford to engage a person exclusively for this purpose. Therefore, the present system may be replaced by a system of Self-Certification wherein return submitted on various labour laws by SSI units are self-certified which may be treated as prima facie compliance. Alternatively, the approach may be to introduce a system of random inspection of certain percentage of units on annual basis with well-defined criteria. Labour laws are being implemented both by the Centre and by the State Governments, which has added to the dimension of labour law complexities. To carry out amendments in the labour laws according to specific requirements, various State Governments were demanding authorization for carrying out the amendments. The State Governments are in the best position to enforce the labour laws appropriately, according to the situation and prevailing socio-economic conditions of the States. As the labour laws are in the concurrent list of the Constitution, the approach to Tenth Plan would be to authorize the State Governments to make amendments to the labour laws as per their requirements.

In view of the increasing industrial disputes, Industrial Tribunals or Labour Courts are over burdened and the desired results of resolving the dispute within a time frame are not forthcoming. In view of this, for speedy and timely disposal, the approach would be to set up Lok Adalats, wherever necessary. In addition, the concept of social dialogue would be introduced where all concerned can participate for a meaningful discussion and amicable solution of major problems/ issues involved in labour market reforms.

Recommendations on labour laws, framework of procedures, administrators and related services

- As labour laws are in the concurrent list, the State Governments may be permitted to make amendments to the labour laws as per their requirement.
- While carrying out amendments, adequate safety net for the workers may be kept in mind.
- Formulation of schemes for pension and unemployment benefit for the unorganized sector workers may be considered, depending upon the availability of resources.
- To avoid disproportionate regulatory burden on small scale units, the present system of maintenance of various forms and registers under different labour laws may be replaced by a system of Self-Certification and treated as prima-facie compliance.
- Inspection under the labour laws in SSI units may be conducted only on the basis of complaints by stake holders like workers, neighbours etc., or when absolutely essential in the interest of safety of workers in industry.
- Routine and periodic inspections of Information Technology Establishments may not be necessary.
- Special Quasi-judicial Tribunals manned by Departmental officers of Labour Department may take up hearing of the dispute in case the conciliation talks fails.
- Health, safety and welfare of the workers may be given due importance while reviewing the labour laws.

(e) Vulnerable Groups In Labour Force

To eliminate the problem of child labour, while policies and programmes initiated during the previous Plans, particularly, during the Ninth Plan would be continued in a more focused and holistic manner, the approach for the Tenth Plan would be universalization of primary education, thereby reducing the occurrence of, child labour. Also, effective implementation of minimum wages would be ensured. In addition to the universalization of primary education, an effective area-based methodology for pre-vocational education would be worked out and the existing technical training institutions would be utilized to impart vocational skills to all students before they attain 14 years of age. To achieve this, appropriate area-based curricula for pre-vocational/skill training in the NCLP schools would be adopted/developed.

To eradicate child labour from the hazardous occupations and progressively move towards complete elimination of child labour, the strategy would be to effectively implement the existing scheme of National Child Labour Project. In order to formulate suitable projects as well as to strengthen the on-going projects, a continuous survey would be carried out to assess the number of working children including those who are working in hazardous occupations.

At present there is no legislation for compulsory education in our country. Further, the schools available for children, particularly, schools in villages are in poor condition and most of the buildings are in a very dilapidated condition with no provision for drinking water etc. The strategy during the Tenth Five Year Plan would be focused on improvement of schooling, adult wages, poverty reduction, etc. Also, complimentary strategies and involvement of all sections of society, i.e., Government, Non Governmental Organizations, Trade Unions, Media, employers' organization, etc., would be pursued.

To ensure that the project is able to attain objectives within the time frame, an effective monitoring system would be established. Utmost effort would be made to effectively implement the Child Labour Act by propagating strong awareness generation programmes at various levels, particularly, in rural areas and urban slums.

(i) Bonded Labour

Tenth Plan Approach & Strategy

While the strategy for effective implementation of the Bonded Labour (Abolition) System Act, 1976 and Centrally Sponsored Scheme for Rehabilitation of the Bonded Labour would be continued, the Tenth Plan Approach would be to enlarge the scope for covering activities relating to survey of bonded labourers, awareness generation and evaluation studies. The scheme for Rehabilitation would be taken up in consultation with the beneficiaries. Effective management of the project and training programmes would be encouraged for implementation through the self-help groups comprising of beneficiaries.

Priority would be given to identify the drought prone and poverty stricken areas where the incidence of bonded labour system is greater. Also, a survey would be undertaken on selective basis to identify the bonded labour. Special efforts would be made to rehabilitate these labourers on priority basis and remove the general economic backwardness of such areas by focussed integration of various ongoing plan programmes through inter-Ministerial / Departmental coordination and convergence of services.

The institutional mechanism in the shape of Vigilance Committee is important. The Vigilance Committee would be improved to make it broad-based so as to boost up its effectiveness. To ensure proper functioning, all Vigilance Committees would be reconstituted by inducting a few progressive minded individuals as well as representatives from Trade Union organizations and local NGOs.

To ascertain the actual figure of bonded labour, the strategy would be to undertake a comprehensive survey, using valid statistical methodology to identify the bonded labour system on regular basis in all the sensitive districts. The bonded labour so identified would be released and rehabilitated on priority basis. Besides, special efforts would be made to remove the general economic backwardness of such areas by focused integration of various ongoing plan programmes. No new initiative has been taken recently. The scheme for bonded labour needs to be implemented well, and if need be, improved.

Recommendations

- The effectiveness of the Bonded Labour Act primarily depends upon the identification of bonded labourers. Except in terms of the functions of the Vigilance Committee, there is no inherent provision in the Act to force identification of bonded labourer. Therefore, the institutional mechanism in the shape of Vigilance Committee would improve considerably if these bodies were broad based. Accordingly, it would be appropriate to induct a few right thinking and progressive minded individuals including representatives from trade union organizations and local NGOs as co-opted members in these committees. In order to ensure their proper functioning, all Vigilance Committees should be reconstituted once in two years.

(ii) Migrant Labour

Tenth Plan Approach & Strategy

To reduce the vulnerability of the migrant labourers and protect them from conditions of extreme exploitation, the Tenth Plan approach would be to tackle the problem through a multi-dimensional course of action like effective implementation of various employment generating rural development programmes, provision of improved infrastructure facility, land reforms, universalization of education, etc.

Key actions are required both at the destination as well as at the point of origin of migration in order to reduce vulnerability and increase the capacities of the targeted social groups. During the Tenth Plan, concerted efforts would be made to generate database of migrant workers.

Most of the migrant workers being poor and illiterate are not aware of their rights under the law. The vast majority of migrants do not get adequate shelter or even toilet facilities. They do not have access to the Public Distribution System and other municipal services. Lack of information about labour market conditions and their basic rights under the Constitution increases their vulnerability. To deal with such problems the strategy would be to create strong awareness generation amongst the migrant labourers and to ensure effective implementation of the Inter-State Migrant Workmen Act, 1979.

Recommendations

- The first and foremost requirement for effective action lies in the creation of a reliable information system for labour migration, as macro level data is often inadequate to capture the flow and pattern of migration. Apart from estimating the magnitude of migration, the database may cover the vital aspects like: causes of migration; processes of recruitment; occupational profile of migrants; working and living conditions of migrant workers; skill profile of migrants; expenditure and remittance patterns of migrant workers; status of enforcement of legislations like the Minimum Wages Act, Equal Remuneration Act etc. Initially such a survey may be undertaken in the major lending and borrowing districts in the States and thereafter in other districts during the Tenth Plan. At least Rs.10.0 crore may be provided for this purpose during the Tenth Plan.

(iii) Building and Other Construction Workers

Tenth Plan Approach and Strategy

The approach of the Tenth Plan would be to create a strong awareness generation amongst the building and other construction workers regarding protection of their rights and provisions made in various labour laws and schemes for their welfare. This awareness generation may also include the provisions in the legislations regarding conditions of service safety, and health and welfare measures for them. The strategy of the Tenth Plan would be to create a strong data base regarding the number of building and construction workers, welfare measures, social security measures, etc. and to strengthen the enforcement of the two enactments viz., i) Building and Other Construction Workers (Regulation of Employment and Other Conditions of Service) Act, 1976; and ii) The Building and Other Construction Workers Welfare Cess Act, 1996.

Recommendations

– Most of the workers employed in the construction work are illiterates, migrants and are not aware about various labour laws/welfare schemes available to them. For this, awareness generation camps/seminars, publicity through electronic and print media may be undertaken. Reputed Research Institutes, State Governments, NGOs, trade unions may be entrusted with the responsibility of undertaking the relevant advocacy and awareness generation campaign.

(iv) Landless Agricultural Workers

Tenth Plan Approach and Strategy

To eradicate poverty amongst the landless agricultural labourers, the Tenth Plan Approach would be to converge various services, like education, employment generation etc. Implementation of programmes of the Department of Rural Development would be strengthened, based on approaches and methods, which involves the poor themselves in the process of poverty eradication and economic growth. Also, a strong awareness generation would be created amongst the landless agricultural workers regarding the scope of various welfare and employment generation schemes being implemented by the Government.

The Government of India has launched a new scheme viz., Krishi Shramik Samajik Suraksha Yojana, 2001 on a pilot basis through the Life Insurance Corporation of India for providing social security to agricultural workers including the landless agricultural workers. The benefits available under the scheme include Life-cum-Accident Insurance, Money-back and the superannuation benefit. The Tenth Plan Approach would be to motivate the State Governments to initiate programmes, which would be focused on economic upliftment of landless agricultural workers.

Recommendations

- To assess the magnitude of the problem of agricultural landless workers, a periodical survey and building up of database would be necessary. Further, to arrest this problem, there is a need to ensure the effective implementation of the Minimum Wages Act, up-gradation of skill development, creation of awareness generation and introduction of social security measures without putting serious burden on the government budget and introduction of legislative measures for compulsory education for all.

Annexures – (a-f)

Sectoral Programmes

Agriculture and allied including Horticulture, Farm Management, Watershed, Wasteland Development, Medicinal Plants and Energy Plantations, special programmes on Rural Development and Employment Generation, Small Scale Industries including KVIC covering PMRY, REGP and Cluster Development, Education and Health

Annexures – A(a)

In the Annexure, only specific programmes and schemes have been discussed which have been identified for generating additional employment opportunities over the Tenth Plan. Their corresponding investments are supposed to come partly by reallocation of the existing investment allocations and thereby changing the patterns of growth in respective sectors for increased employment generation, and partly as an additional sum, which is to be provided in the Tenth Plan allocation in respective sectors. However, in case of a shortfall in the stipulated allocation, the employment generation target accordingly may have to be scaled down. The Special Group in anticipation has made adjustments by selectively reducing the employment generation targets of different programmes/schemes suggested by respective Ministries and agencies.

Agriculture

1. The Ministry of Agriculture has estimated the potential of generating additional employment in agriculture during the Tenth Plan, based on certain assumptions. This is because of non-availability of precise data about actual employment being generated in various schemes in agriculture. The assumptions are:

(a) The average man-hours used for producing one quintal of a particular crop based on the results of "Comprehensive Scheme for Cost of Cultivation" will be applicable to the additional production, as a result of additional area to be brought under certain agricultural crops during the Tenth Plan.

(b) Each ha. of additional irrigated area covered under "On farm Management Scheme" will generate 1.5 additional jobs.

(c) The average real wage rate during the Tenth Plan period will remain Rs.60 per day per worker.

(d) Further employment potential has been worked out for the five years of the Tenth Plan as a whole. Year-wise details could be worked out by dividing the information by the number five.

2. The average number of man-hours used for producing one quintal of crop in the year 1998-99 was as follows:

Table – A1

Crops	Average number of man-hours used for producing one quintal
Groundnut	69.3
Soya bean	34.4
Rapeseed & Mustard	34.7
Tur	72.4
Gram	31.2

3. Based on the above ratios the additional employment in various sectors of crops husbandry in agriculture has been determined as follows:

(i) It is planned that additional area under *Groundnut* during Tenth Plan shall be to the extent of 5.6 lakh ha. giving an additional production of 6.8 lakh tonnes. Since approximately 690 man-hours are required to produce one tonne of groundnut, for 6.8 lakh tonnes, the total additional man-hours needed would be 4692 lakh man-hours.

(ii) Under *Rapeseed and mustard,* it is planned to bring an additional 5.80 lakh ha. area, which will give an additional production of 5.50 lakh tonnes. Since approximately 347 man-hours are needed to produce one tonne of rapeseed and mustard, additional 5.50 lakh tonnes would require 1908 lakh man-hours.

(iii) In respect of Soyabean, it is planned to bring additional 9.6 lakh ha. under cultivation, which will give an additional production of 10.4 lakhs tonnes. Since in the case of Soyabean approximately 344 man-hours are needed to produce one tonne, the additional production of 10.4 lakh tonnes of soyabean would require approximately 3577 lakh man-hours.

(iv) As per the Department's programme, it is expected to bring an additional area of 0.47 ha. under *Arhar,* which will give an additional production of 0.40 lakh tonnes. A total of approximately 724 man-hours are needed for producing one tonne of Arhar. On this basis the additional production of 0.40 lakh tonnes would require approximately 289 lakh man-hours of employment.

(v) In the case of Gram, it is estimated that an additional area of 2.29 lakh ha. would be brought under cultivation giving an additional production of 2 lakh tonnes during the Tenth Plan. Since one tonne of production of Gram requires approximately 312 man-hours, the additional 2-lakh tonnes of production would need 624 lakh man hours.

4. The above programmes will generate 11009 million man-hours or approximately 139 million mandays of employment during the Tenth Plan as can be seen from Table A2 below.

Table – A2

Additional Employment Generation

No.	Crop	Additional Area (Lakh ha)	Additional Production (Lakh tones)	Additional Man hours (lakh Man Hours)
1.	Groundnut	5.6	6.8	4692
2.	Rapeseed and Mustard	5.8	5.5	1908
3.	Soyabean	9.6	10.4	3577
4.	Arhar	0.47	0.40	289
5.	Gram	2.29	2.20	624
	Total			11090 or 139 million mandays*

* 11090 lakh man-hours or 1109 million man-hours is equal to 139 million man-days assuming that 8 man-hours constitute one manday.

5. The estimated additional employment (from Table 2) by the Ministry of Agriculture is 139 million mandays per annum on a non-cumulative basis i.e. 0.46 million person years in the last

year of the Tenth Plan. However, some of these productions will come after the land is shifted from other crops grown. Therefore, the assessment made by the Ministry may not come true and this may be ambitious. Corrections may be made to lower the estimate of employment to be generated from these programmes. The net addition to employment as assumed by the Special Group will not be more than 0.35 million person years.

6. During the Eighth Five Year Plan, the average production of food grains was 187 million tonnes. The average production of foodgrains during the Ninth Five Year Plan is expected to be around 205 million tonnes. This gives an average increase of about 18 million tonnes. Stocks of cereals with the FCI as on 1st June 2001 were estimated to be 60 million tonnes. There will be a procurement of about 20 million tonnes during the current Kharif season. This means that a very large portion of additional production of cereals/foodgrains is going into stocks.

7. The normative requirement has been calculated by the norm of food requirement given by the National Institute of Nutrition, Hyderabad which gives a figure of 182.5 Kgs. of foodgrains needed per capita, per annum for maintaining good health. The total population figure given by the Population Census is converted into consumption unit by dividing the population figure by a factor of 1.06 and adding to this the requirement for seed, feed and wastage, which is assumed to be 12.5% of the total foodgrains production. The total requirement of foodgrains as assessed by normative approach is always less than the total production of foodgrains. *Therefore, there is every reason to move away from production* of cereals to horticulture and non-commercial crops. This diversification will be a major policy thrust for agriculture during the Tenth Five Year Plan.

8. The Department is implementing the National Watershed Development Project for Rainfed Areas (NWDPRA) since the Eighth Plan. The programme follows an area approach and is not an employment generation programme. However, it provides employment opportunities to small and marginal farmers and agricultural labourers both directly and indirectly. The direct employment is generated mostly in the activities relating to conservation and development of land and water resources such as bunding, check dams, water harvesting structures, nurseries,

afforestation etc. The indirect employment is generated as a result of multiplier effect of natural resource conservation and diversification of farming system, livelihood support activities leading to higher production and higher income. Keeping this in view, a calculation has been made for direct employment opportunities based on the Ninth Five Year Plan experience. To assess employment generation, it has been assumed that a wage rate of Rs.60 per day will be paid to the workers during the Tenth Plan. Estimated employment potential in NWDPRA during the Tenth Plan will be 30 million in a year as given in Table A3 below:

Table – A3

Estimated Employment Potential in NWDPRA during Tenth Plan

Year	Area to be treated (ha.)	Average Daily Wage Rate	No.of labour days (millions)
2002-03	10 lakhs	60/day	30
2003-04	10 lakhs	60/day	30
2004-05	10 lakhs	60/day	30
2005-06	10 lakhs	60/day	30
2006-07	10 lakhs	60/day	30
	50 lakhs		

9. The Working Group on Horticulture constituted by the Planning Commission has estimated that by the end of the Tenth Plan period, horticulture production is required to be increased to 268 million tonnes from existing 148 tonnes. The additional production of 120 million tonnes would require investment of Rs.12394 crore which will also bring additional private investment and generate additional employment to the tune of 1200 million mandays at farm level and 600 million mandays in allied activities like grading, packaging and post-harvest management.

10. The employment generation, as per standard package and practices of Horticultural operations, though is expected to be 3200 million mandays at farm level only by the end of Tenth Plan. The figure of 1800 million mandays has been cited as a most conservative assessment of employment over the Tenth Plan.

11. As per the standard norms of labour requirement in horticulture crops, the following is the assessment of the

employment opportunities.

i) Average requirement of labour for replacement of old orchards and bringing in new areas under horticulture crops is 800 mandays per ha. per year.

During the Ninth Five Year Plan, an additional area of 31 lakh ha. was brought under horticulture crops through replacement of old orchards and new areas. The area under horticulture increased from 132 lakh hec. to 163 lakh hec. during this period. As per the estimates of the Tenth Plan Working Group on Horticulture, an additional area of 40 lakh hec. will be brought under horticulture through replacement and new areas. Taking into account a conservative requirement of 800 mandays per hec. per year, 3200 million mandays will be generated only through this activity.

ii) The additional production of 1 tonne would require for post-harvest management activities such as grading, packaging, processing and handling etc., labour of 5 mandays. To reach the targeted 120 million tonnes of additional production during the Tenth Five Year Plan, this would generate 600 million mandays.

iii) Thus, the total mandays employment creation potential of horticulture sector is to be of the order of 3800 million mandays. However, on the very conservative side, the Horticulture Division of Ministry of Agriculture has projected generation of only 1800 million mandays during this Plan period. For each year the mandays generation would be 360 million.

12. The Department of Agriculture and Cooperation would implement a new Scheme "On Farm Water Management" during the Plan period. The scheme will be implemented only in the Eastern States and has following components:

(i) Assistance for installation of Shallow Tube wells with Pump-sets

(ii) Assistance for diesel pump sets

(iii) Assistance for low lift irrigation points

(iv) Assistance for dug wells in the plateau region

13. During the Tenth Plan period, it is targeted to cover 75 lakh ha. net area under the scheme. Assuming that each ha. of additional irrigated area covered under the scheme would give 1.5 jobs, additional jobs of a total of 112.5 lakh will be created during the entire Tenth Plan period as given in Table A4.

Table – A4

Employment Opportunities in On Farm Water Management Scheme

Nature of Schemes	Plan Period	Employment Opportunities Expected ('000 Nos.)
On-Farm Water Management Scheme	**9th Plan**	
	2001-02	1050
	Tenth Plan	
	2002-03	2250
	2003-04	2250
	2004-05	2250
	2005-06	2250
	2006-07	2250
	Total 10th Plan	11250

14. The assumption that each hectare of additional irrigated area would give additional 1.5 jobs is based on the present statistics of existing irrigated area and jobs created therein. Irrigation will result in increase in intensity of cultivation. Implicit in this is the assumption that the farmers will grow more than one crop, which will result in higher employment generation. The Group, however, decided to take a conservative estimate of 1.25 million person years at the end of the Tenth Plan as against 2.3 m targeted.

15. Another new scheme on Agri-clinics will be implemented during the Tenth Plan. Under this scheme, 25000 agri-clinics will be set up during the Plan period. Assuming that each clinic will employ at least three persons, a total of 75000 jobs will be created under the Scheme.

16. It is planned that during the Tenth Five Year Plan, an additional 40-lakh quintals of certified seeds would be produced for distribution to the farmers. This additional quantity would

result in generation of 75,000 additional jobs, out of which 68,000 jobs will be created on the field and the remaining 7,000 jobs would be created for processing, cleaning, tagging and bagging of seeds.

17. There are four Farm Machinery Training and Testing Institutes working under the control of the Ministry of Agriculture, imparting training on agricultural implements and machinery to various groups of persons such as farmers, rural youth, mechanics etc. Around 2000 such persons are trained every year by these institutes. About 50 per cent of these 1000 persons get wage employment, while other 50 per cent engage themselves in self-employment. Further about 1-lakh tractors are added every year to the total population of tractors in the country. Each tractor generates several jobs, but at least one job of a Driver can be attributed directly to the agriculture. Therefore, one-lakh jobs of tractor drivers will be generated in the agriculture on farm machinery.

18. Therefore, at the aggregate level the total potential of additional employment generation from different programmes and schemes already formulated by the Ministry of Agriculture comes to 3.55 million man years by the end of the Tenth Plan, after taking a conservative approach. The Special Group is of the view that this much employment generation in agriculture and allied activities will be possible in the Tenth Plan. This is shown in Table A5.

Table – A5

Total Employment expected to be generated in Agriculture during Five Year Plan:

	Scheme	Employment Potential
1.	Additional areas under Cultivation to be brought Under oilseeds and pulses	0.35 Million man years
2.	NWDPRA	0.50 Million man years
3.	Horticulture	1.20 Million man years
4.	On Farm Management	1.25 Million man years
5.	Agri Clinics and Seed Production	0.15 Million man years
6.	Tractors	0.10 Million man years
	Total	3.55 Million man years

Annexure – A(b)

Greening the Country for Food, Livelihood and Environmental Security

For Ecological security following areas have to be greened on priority basis:

1)	Degraded forest areas	31 million hectares
2)	Wastelands	50 million hectares
	Total	81 million hectares

2. The Task Force on greening the country (Planning Commission) has recommended the following programme during 5 years period :

(i) 10 m. ha of degraded forestland can easily be regenerated/afforested under Joint Forest Management with the involvement of people on share and care basis. Two million ha. can be greened annually on watershed development basis *involving 2 million people*. A "food for work" scheme maintaining 50:50 ratio of food and cash will be ideal. Cash expenditure of Rs.4500 crores will be required on yearly basis. The area being hilly, integrated watershed development will conserve soil, water and bio-diversity. Cultivation of bamboo, medicinal plants, Jatropha and other multipurpose species will meet food, fodder, fuel, fibre, water and energy needs of the forest dwellers (mostly tribal and majority of them living below poverty line). Availability of water and crude drugs will provide preventive and curative health care. Production of fodder and industrial raw-material will further generate employment in secondary and tertiary sectors. Jatropha oil will substitute for kerosene oil and diesel. Bamboo and timber production will provide cash income to each family and help in construction of their houses. Thus during implementation of the project each beneficiary will get cash wage and food and from the second year onwards forest produce. Surplus forest products are easily marketable yielding cash income to the beneficiaries. JFM will alleviate poverty and eliminate hunger and starvation deaths.

(ii) About 20 million ha. of rainfed agricultural area is available for agroforestry. At present, such areas are monocropped and crop failures are common. Lands are mostly owned by SC, ST and other backward classes. Each family owns about 2 ha. of land. Agroforestry is proposed on field bunds by providing technology, planting material under "food for work" scheme. Thus 10 million families can be covered in 5 years period. Two million families can be provided employment and food annually on a sustainable basis. Agroforesty is expected to conserve rainwater, augment biomass production, increase productivity and improve drainage. Appropriate technology, extension, financial support and removal of various constraints can alleviate poverty of 10 million families. Annual investment required will be of the order of Rs.6000 crore which includes 40% of food component. At present the country is importing forest products worth Rs.8500 crore annually. Prior to 1986 India was net exporter of forest products. Import of forest produce from 1987 onwards has reduced employment opportunities and increased poverty, hunger and unrest in backward areas. Without greening activities floods and drought, land degradation, advancing of deserts and environmental pollution cannot be halted. Thus JFM & Agroforestry can easily employ 4 million people under "food for work" scheme for greening the degraded areas.

(iii) *Development of Medicinal Plants for Employment Generation* – India, identified as one of the 8 important global centres for plant diversity is immensely rich in medicinal and aromatic plants growing in diverse ecosystems. Enormous opportunity exists worldwide not only for Indian System of Medicine (ISM) but also for the growth of herbal sector. The herbal sector opens fresh opportunities for the production of a whole range of therapeutics as also for food supplements, cosmetics, toiletries, nutraceuticals and veterinary medicine. The Task Force on medicinal plants (Planning Commission) has made following recommendations:

- Identification and establishment of MPDA/Vanaspati Van over an area of 1 million ha. in forest areas for intensive management of medicinal plants. Under "food for work" scheme 10 lakhs people will get productive employment and food.

- Nearly 1 lakh people will get employment in 10,000 pharmacies, health tourism and manufacture of various products.

- Globalisation of ISM can easily earn Rs.10,000 crore on yearly basis.

On the recommendation of the Task Force, the Medicinal Plant Board has come in existence. GMP (Good Manufacturing Practices) has been introduced to ensure quality, safety and efficacy of drugs. Health tourists have started visiting Kerala and Varanasi, Students from abroad have started coming to our Ayurvedic institutions. Concerted effort in identified sectors can easily generate 1.1 million jobs on a yearly basis.

(iv) *Bamboo Development* – Bamboo is an important feature in many parts of India. It has more than 1500 uses. Recent technological developments have given birth to new generation products, which are in great demand inside as well as outside the country. The Task Force on greening India had made following recommendations for this developing sector:

- All existing sawmills and plywood industries may reconstruct themselves to substitute timber by bamboo as their raw material. Use of timber is not permitted by Supreme Court order for environmental reasons. Nearly 3 million jobs are lost due to this. This change over with bamboo will require heavy investments. Private firms owning these industries need loans from the banks.

- Bamboo technology mission should provide technology to the industries for producing quality bamboo products for export.

- CAPART can motivate the growers and NGOs to cultivate useful bamboo species.
- For retarding climatic change global consensus is to change over from timber to bamboo use. For boosting the export, establishment of "Bamboo Board" will be desirable.

All these activities can generate additional employment to 2 million people. According to a study of INBAR, India has potential to boost the bamboo trade to the extent of Rs.30,000 crore annually. The global market will absorb it by the end of this decade.

Therefore, the total potential of additional employment generation from different programmes comes to 7.1 million employment by the end of the Tenth Plan. This is shown in Table A6, alongwith the assessment of Special Group.

Table – A6

Employment Generation in Forestry, Medicinal Plants and Bamboo Development during Tenth Five Year Plan: Projections by the relevant Task Forces and the Special Group*

	Scheme	Employment Potential
1.	Forestry and agro forestry	4 million (1.5 million)
2.	Medicinal Plants	1.1 Million (0.5 million)
3.	Bamboo Development	2 Million (1.5 million)
	Total	7.1 Million (3.5 million)

* (i) Task Force on Greening India;
(ii) Task Force on Medicinal Plants.

NB : Brackets denote the Special Group's estimates

Annexure – A(c)

Few more innovative areas – Energy Plantations for Bio-mass Power Generation

1. Cultivation of fast growing trees such as casuarina equistifolia and bush crops such as prosopis juliflora can serve as biomass fuel for establishing a national network of decentralized rural power plants. These power plants, ranging in size from 10-25 MW, can generate thousands of megawatts of power from renewable, forest based fuel sources in a cost effective manner. This would reduce India's dependence on imported fuel oils, stimulate private investment in the power sector, and generate massive income and employment opportunities for the rural poor.

2. In order to meet pent up demand, India needs to create an additional 100,000 MW of power generation capacity during the Tenth Plan period. Establishment of 10 million hectares of energy plantation will be sufficient to generate 25,000 MW of power generation and provide year-round employment for 7.5 million people.

3. *Casuarina* is a fast growing tree that can be cultivated on marginal wasteland and harvested on a rotating basis from the third to fourth year onwards. Casuarina is already commercially cultivated over wide tracks in the southern States, primarily as a rain-fed crop for fuel and construction. It can also be used as pulp for papermaking. It is an excellent species for environmental control of erosion, stabilization of soils and reclamation of poor soils. It requires 10,000 tonnes of casuarina to generate one megawatt for a year. By harvesting the crop on a rotating basis, a standing plantation of 250 hectares is sufficient to generate one megawatt of power. A 2500-hectare casuarina energy plantation can support a 10-12 MW power plant. Assuming a net farm selling price of Rs.700 per tonne, one hectare of casuarina can generate year round net income of Rs.28000. Allocating one hectare per person, each 10 MW power plant can provide employment for 2500 persons.

4. *Prosopis* is a thorny plant that grows wild on extensive areas of wasteland and serves as a fence, but is not being harvested or utilised for commercial purposes. It grows rapidly, producing

about 10 tonnes of biomass on dry-weight basis per hectare per annum. The biomass is an excellent raw material for power generation. 1000 hectares of rainfed prosopis can provide sufficient fuel to generate one MW of electric power. One hectare of prosopis under rainfed conditions can produce on an average 10 tonnes of fuel per hectare per year, from the 3rd year onwards. By harvesting the crop on a rotating basis, a standing plantation of 1000 hectares is sufficient to generate one megawatt of power. A 10,000-hectare prosopis energy plantation can support a 10 MW power plant. Assuming a net farm-selling price of Rs.700 per tonne, one hectare of prosopis can generate year-round net income of Rs.7,000. Each hectare requires 100 man-days per annum of labour input. Allocating two hectares per person, a 10 MW power plant can provide employment for 5000 persons, each earning Rs.14,000 per annum.

5. The challenge is how to implement the projects in a manner that will generate maximum income and employment for the rural poor. It can be done by assigning suitable land for each project in different parts of the state, leasing 50% of the required land to corporates willing to invest in the approved agro-enterprises. The balance 50% may be given to rural families for cultivation as a registered crop and supply of produce to the power plants. Cooperative power plants can also be established in regions such as Maharashtra where agricultural cooperatives have proven effective. Nationalised Banks may be directed to extend loans to the farmers.

Bio-fuel from Sugarcane – Ethanol Plantations

6. India is currently producing surplus sugar and is holding stocks equivalent to 8 months domestic requirement. Export of the sugar is not viable because low productivity and high cost of production make Indian sugar uncompetitive on the international market. Excess production of sugarcane and molasses may be utilised as raw material for the production of ethanol that can be mixed with petroleum products as a fuel for motor vehicles.

7. Ethanol can be blended with motor fuels up to 5-10% without any modification of vehicles with fuel injection system and can be used in higher blends up to 95% in modified vehicles. Ethanol blends generate significantly less pollution than alternative

petroleum-based fuels.

8. India presently consumes approximately 40 million tonnes of petrol per annum. Assuming a 10% blend of ethanol with petrol and diesel, the total requirement of ethanol would be 4.6 million tonnes per annum. With engine modification, much higher ethanol blends can be utilised. The cost of production of ethanol fuel from sugarcane will be approximately Rs.18 litre, of which 2/3rd will go as income to farmers. Total current production of ethanol in India (primarily from molasses) is 1.3 billion litres, of which 50% is used for industrial purposes and 50% for potable purposes.

9. India currently produces approximately 300 million tonnes of sugarcane annually, of which 60% is crushed for sugar production and 40% for jaggary and other products. The 180 million tonnes of cane is converted into 18 million tonnes of sugar and 8 million tonnes of molasses annually. Current domestic sugar consumption is only 15 million tonnes. Since the cost of production in India is above the international level, surplus sugar accumulates. India's current stock of surplus sugar is 10 million tonnes, equivalent to 8 months consumption. Assuming that 25 million tonnes of sugarcane is diverted from sugar production for production of ethanol fuel, an additional 1.6 billion litres of ethanol can be produced. By increasing the yield of sugarcane and increasing total area under sugarcane, additional ethanol can be produced.

10. 25 million tonnes of sugarcane (8% of total cane) may be diverted for ethanol production, resulting in production of 1.6 billion litres of ethanol fuel. Additional areas can be identified for growing sugarcane exclusively for ethanol production. By this way, additional cane production of 75 million tonnes would be available which can produce an additional 4.8 billion litres of ethanol. In addition, availability of sugarcane can be increased by a concerted effort to improve the productivity and efficiency of existing sugarcane cultivation. By this way, additional cane production of 75 million tonnes would be available which can produce an additional 4.8 billion litres of ethanol. Total ethanol production from these programmes would be 11.2 billion litres per annum. Existing distilleries can produce this ethanol because they are under utilised.

11. The programme would produce 11.2 million tonnes of ethanol fuel per annum, valued at Rs.17,000 crores, as a substitute for imported oil. The most significant benefit of the programme is that it can help meet the nation's energy requirements in a manner that generates additional rural income of Rs.10,000 to 12,000 crores, rather than by expenditure of foreign exchange to generate prosperity in petroleum producing countries. Improving the productivity of sugarcane can bring down the price of sugar to internationally competitive levels so that surplus production can be exported. The higher cane yield and additional area cultivated will generate 2.5 million additional employment opportunities. The programme can produce 30 billion units of electricity from bagasse valued at Rs.9000 crores. The employment to be generated from these programmes as well as estimates of Special Group for these programmes are given in Summary Table A7.

Table – A7

Summary Table – Energy Plantations & Employment Creation

Project	Area (Ha.)	Income Generation (Rs.crores)	Job Creation	Gestation
Energy Plantation				
Prosopis	5 million	6500	7.5	3 years
Casuarina	5 million	13500	million	5 years
	wasteland			
Ethanal Plantation	800,000	12000	2.5 million	1 year
	irrigated	5000		
		6000		
Total	10 million wasteland and 800,000 irrigated	Rs.430000	10 million jobs*	

* Special Groups has assumed 1.22 million manyears for first project and 0.79 million man years for second project for the 10th five year Plan.

12. The Special Group is of the view that this much employment generation will not be possible in the Tenth Plan. **Therefore, a conservative estimate has been taken that 2.01 million** employment opportunities would be created under this in the Tenth Plan.

Annexure – A(d)

Rural Development Programmes –

Sampoorna Gramin Rojgaar Yojana (SGRY), Swaranjayanti Gram, Swarozgar Yojana (SGSY) and Pradhan Mantri Gram Sadak Yojana (PMGSY)

I. Sampoorana Gram Rozgar Yojana (SGRY)

The Ministry of Rural Development have been operating two Schemes of Wage Employment, namely, the Employment Assurance Scheme (EAS) and the Jawahar Gram Samridhi Yojana (JGSY). While the EAS was primarily meant for creation of additional employment opportunities during the period of acute shortage of wage employment through manual work for the rural poor living below the poverty line, the JGSY was aimed at creation of need-based rural infrastructure at the village level. These programmes have contributed to a great extent in reducing rural poverty and improving the quality of rural life. These two programmes have been merged into a single wage employment programme namely, the Sampoorna Gramin Rozgar Yojana (SGRY) which was launched in September, 2001 with an annual outlay of Rs. 10,000 crores. This will enable an annual increase in allocation for employment schemes by Rs. 6000 crores. The major objective of this Scheme is to provide food security, additional wage employment and village infrastructure simultaneously. Under the Scheme 50 lakhs tonnes of foodgrains amounting to Rs. 5000 crores (at economic cost) is to be provided every year to the State Governments and UTs. The remaining funds are to be utilized to meet the cash component of wages and material cost. Under the Scheme, 100 crores mandays of employment are envisaged to be generated every year.

Past experience has shown that 50 crores mandays of employment per year have been generated under the EAS and JGSY. Although, it is targeted to generate 100 crores mandays per year under the new scheme of SGRY, in actual fact, at least 90 crores mandays per annum will be generated (depending upon the actual allocation of funds). Therefore, in any case, it can be safely estimated that 40 crores mandays per annum will be the additionality in employment under the restructured SGRY.

II. Swaranjayanti Gram Swarozgar Yojana (SGSY)

The Ministry of Rural Development implements the Swaranjayanti Gram Swarozgar Yojana (SGSY) which is a restructured Self-Employment Programme of the erstwhile IRDP and allied Schemes. The SGSY came into operation from 1st April, 1999 and it has been conceived as a holistic Programme covering all aspects of Self-Employment like organisation of the rural poor into Self-Help Groups (SHGs) and their capacity building, training, planning of activity clusters, infrastructure development, financial assistance through bank credit and subsidy and marketing support. It is expected that individuals and Group Swarozgaris will, over a period of time, establish micro-enterprises based on key activities identified taking into account the resource availability and demand potentiality in the area concerned. Under the Scheme, while subsidy is only an enabling component great reliance is placed on the credit component for successful operation of the micro-enterprises started under the Scheme. The various Evaluation Studies of the erstwhile IRDP and allied Schemes have shown that these Schemes have provided productive employment opportunities for the rural poor on a sustainable basis, although certain shortcomings were also noticed in the actual implementation at the field level. It has been possible to establish 7.42 lakhs Self Help Groups under the restructured Self-Help Groups under the restructured Self-Employment Programme of SGSY.

It is targeted to set up 14 lakhs Self-Help Groups (at least 1 SHG in every habitation of the country) by 2004. As the SGSY is a process oriented Programme, it may take some time from the stage of formation of Self-Help Groups to the final stage of setting up of micro-enterprises. Past experience of the operation of the Scheme has shown that on an average, it was possible to provide employment to 8.5 lakh persons per annum, on a sustainable basis (including group and individual swarozgaris). On this basis, it is estimated that it would be possible to provide self employment on a sustainable basis, to about 43 to 45 lakhs persons during the next five years i.e., .8 to .85 m per years. In addition, there will be indirect employment, also consequent to the setting up of micro enterprises by these persons. This estimate is based on the assumption that the current level of investment of Rs. 800 crores per annum will be maintained during the next five years under the programme.

III. Pradhan Mantri Gram Sadak Yojana (PMGSY)

The allocation for rural roads was about Rs.500 crore in the year 1999-2000. This has now been raised to Rs.2500 crore under the programme Pradhan Mantri Gram Sadak Yojana (PMGSY). The Special Group has taken a conservative estimate that 0.77 million person-years of additional employment opportunities would be created under this in the Tenth Plan, taking the norm of employment generation from the construction sector.

The Special Group on a conservative basis assessed that employment opportunities to be created under these 3 programmes would mean a net addition of 2.86 million person-years during the Tenth Plan:

Table – A8

Employment Opportunities: Three Special Programmes.

Programme	Increase in employment opportunity during 10th Plan (million persons years)
SGRY	1.29
SGSY	0.80
PMGSY	0.77
Total	2.86

Annexure – A(e)

Employment Generation in Small Scale Industries (SSI) Sector

1. Employment generation has always been one of the main objectives of the policies aimed at economic development and growth of the nation. A rise in economic growth has always led to increased employment opportunities and similarly enhanced employment generation has always contributed significantly towards economic growth. However, identifying and creating employment opportunities has always been a challenging task in our country, the reasons for which are plenty and well known. More disturbing in this context is the realization that there has not been commensurate growth in employment vis-à-vis economic growth as demonstrated by the GDP indicators over the past decade.

2. The Small Scale Sector currently provides employment to over 18.5 million persons. SSI Units are set up in the Private Sector. Employment in the SSI sector is mainly generated in two forms:

- Autonomous – wherein every new SSI unit set up provides employment to entrepreneurs, skilled, semi-skilled and unskilled workers; and
- Induced – through specialized employment generation programmes like the Prime Minister's Rozgar Yojana (PMRY), etc.

3. The average rate of growth of production in SSI sector is estimated at 8 per cent and average employment is about 4 per cent per annum respectively. This gives an employment elasticity of 0.5 for this sector. The target of employment generation in the SSI sector by the terminal year of the 9th Five Year Plan was 185 lakh persons in 2001-02, giving an additionality of 25 lakh persons from the base year i.e., 1996-97. The estimates of additional employment generated in the SSI sector during the 9th Plan are that of about 33 lakh persons. The SSI sector provides whole-time and sustainable and durable employment. According to 2nd All India Census of Registered SSI units (1987-88), the average employment per SSI unit is 6.3 persons. As a result of

modernization and technology upgradation of SSI sector and emergence of capital-intensive products, the average employment per unit during Ninth Five Year Plan has been estimated at 5.5 persons per unit.

4. The role of Government is to facilitate and promote entrepreneurship, technology, marketing, credit etc. so that SSI Units can compete. The policy environment enabling this sector to grow includes:

(i) SSI sector comes under the Priority Sector Lending programme of Banks

(ii) Fiscal support to SSI units in the form of Excise Exemption, some direct tax benefit by the Central Government, Sales tax/loan deferment by the State Governments

(iii) Protection through product reservation (currently 799 items out of about 8000 items manufactured in the SSI sector are reserved).

(iv) Price Preference and Purchase Preference in purchases by Government Departments.

(v) Support for technology upgradation through Small Industries Service Institutes (SISIs), Product Cum Process Development Centres (PPDCs), Regional Testing Centres (RTCs), Tool Rooms and Financial incentives for acquiring ISO 9000 certification.

(vi) Entrepreneurship development programmes conducted by various National level institutes and support to state level industries.

(vii) Encouraging Ancillaries, Vendor development, sub-contracting exchanges etc.

(viii) Development of infrastructures.

5. The targeted rate of growth for SSI Sector has been kept at 12% for the Tenth Plan on the ground that economy is expected to grow at 8% (GDP) in the Tenth Plan. With liberalization of the economy and its assimilation into the globalised world order, latest and state of the art technology needs to be adopted by new units

coming up in the Small Scale Sector, while the existing units need to carry out technological upgradation from time to time to enhance their competitive strengths. This also entails commensurate improvement in the quality of employment/labour. Emphasis would have to be given to quality of labour along with the quantity of labour to bear the onslaught of globalisation and survive in the changing economic scenario with increasing competitiveness. The Small Scale Sector is poised to be the engine of employment generation/growth in the next 5 years is clear from the projections made by the Sub-Group I of the Working Group on Small Scale Industries for the 10th Five Year Plan. The growth in employment is dependent on the growth in the number of units, growth rate of the SSI sector and nature of growth i.e. the type of industries i.e. capital intensive or labour intensive. Taking all these factors into account, the Sub-Group projected that in the terminal year of the Tenth Plan i.e. 2006-07 there will be 43.78 lakh units of small scale industries with employment of 237.17 lakhs.

The net addition of employment in the Tenth Plan will be 39 lakh persons from growth buoyancy. The average growth rate for employment for the Tenth Plan will be 4.2% per annum.

6. Taking into account the increased capital intensity in the SSI sector, the current employment per unit is estimated at 5.5 persons. Taking the 2001-02 figure of number of SSI units as the base and applying a growth rate of 4.6% per annum over it we get the number of SSI units coming into existence each year. This annual number of new units is multiplied by 5.0 i.e. the average estimated current employment per unit. A relatively lower per unit employment has been visualized for the Tenth Five Year Plan because of the increased emphasis on technology upgradation and modernization of the SSI Sector, which is considered essential in order to enhance the competitiveness necessitated by the ongoing process of liberalization globalization and adherence to the WTO agreements. There are also indications that in times to come SSI sector will be moving to product lines having higher capital intensity. There is likely to be impetus for setting up more and more self employment ventures because of introduction of Voluntary Retirement Scheme in the Public Sector Undertakings. Similarly, there are also indications that the major part of the

service sector will grow as small enterprises. All these factors will help to generate additional employment of 44.10 lakh persons.

7. There are at present nearly 33 lakh SSI units all over the country, of which about 1 lakh are in the organized (factory sector). The unorganized sector comprises of SSI units engaged in manufacturing apart from those in the handloom, handicrafts, coir and KVIs sectors. The organized sector includes powerlooms other than the manufacturing SSIs. There is also a large sub-sector within the SSI sector known as Tiny Industries, which consist of micro units, which are comparable to rural, and cottage industries.

8. The Special Group has estimated that 4.2 million additional jobs can be created by specific programme in the small industries including KVIC. KVIC submitted a plan of creating additional two million jobs from different special programmes including REGP and those recently announced; Based on the good performance during the last three years in generating new employment opportunities under REGP (Rural Employment Generation Programme) and generating 3.05 lakh new jobs in 1999-2000 and 3.50 lakhs in 2000-01 as also the sanctions already made by CCEA for 20 lakh new jobs through REGP in Tenth Plan, the assessment made by Special Group for the next five years is that KVIC will generate at least 4 lakh jobs a year on a cumulative basis, i.e. 2 million jobs over the Tenth Plan. Added to this is from special cluster development programme and other measures in SSI resulting from the recommendations of the Planning Commission's Gupta Committee and from PMRY another 2.2 million additional jobs are likely to be created. These are added to the normal growth in employment from growth buoyancy of nearly 2.2 million when the growth will be increased from 8 per cent to 12 per cent per annum.

A detailed note on KVIC, its objectives and strategies are given in Chapter V of this Report.

Table – A9

The final break up of potential areas of job creation is as follows:

(Million persons years)

I	Program Based	a)	KVIC in REGP	2.00	4.20
		b)	PMRY in SSI	1.65	
		c)	SSI : Cluster Development	0.55	
		(i)	**Small Manufacturing**		
II	Growth induced	a)	SSI	3.86	7.42
		b)	Coir	0.10	
		c)	Handloom	0.40	
		d)	Power loom	0.10	
		e)	Handicraft	0.93	
		f)	Sericulture	0.50	
		g)	Wool (unorganised sector)	0.10	
		(ii)	**Large Manufacturing**	1.43	
	Total Manufacturing		*(including SME's & Special Employment Programmes in Rural Areas)*		11.62

Annexure – A(f)

Community Services

A. Employment in Education Sector

Employment in Education Sector may be seen from the following table obtained from Ministry of Human Resource Development.

Table – A10

Assessment of present trends in Employment in Elementary Education and Literacy

Schemes	Estimate of employment Opportunities		Nature of Activities & Establishments
	2002	2007	
Teachers	16,92,159	32,23,757	Primary and upper primary teachers employed under OBB, DPEP, SSA, Lok Jumbish, Shiksha Karmi, AS/EGS, ECCE, Mahila Samakhya, continuing education, SRC & JSS
DIET, BRC, CRC, engineering Staff, SPO, DPO	56,469	1,51,890	Resource persons and project staff employed under DPEP and SSA
Mid-day-meal	4,00,000	4,60,000	Cook and Helper employed for mid day meal scheme
Total	21,48,628	38,35,647	

Note:

- OBB – OPERATION BLACK BOARD
- DPEP – District Primary Education Programme
- SSA – Surva Siksha Abhiyan
- AS/EGS – Alternative Schooling/Education Guarantee Scheme
- ECCE – Early Childhood Care and Education
- SRC – State Resource Centre
- JSS – Jan Shikshan Sansthan
- DIET – District Institute of Education and Training
- BRC – Block Resource Centre
- CRC – Cluster Resource Centre
- SPO – State Project Office
- DPO – District Project Office

B. Employment in Health and Child Development

Employment in health and child development may be seen from the following table given by the Social Welfare Division. These estimates are based on the Ninth Plan achievements of the sector and the projections for Tenth Plan are as follows:

Table – A11

Employment in Women and Child Development Sector

	Programmes	Additional Employment
1.	Integrated Child Development Projects (ICDS)/ Angan Wadi Workers (AWWs)/ Angan Wadi Helpers (AWHs)	3.00 lakh
2.	Support for Training and Employment Programme (STEP)	1.25 lakh
3.	Employment and Income Generation, Training-cum-Production Centres for Women (NORAD)	1.39 lakh
4.	Socio Economic Programmes (SEP)	1.70 lakh
5.	Condensed Courses of Education and Vocational Training for Adult Women for Employment Generation	1.00 lakh
6.	National Handicapped Finance and Dev. Corporation*	1.00 lakh
	Total	9.34 lakh

* Income generating activities for 9755 persons in Ninth Plan (assumed to be around 10,000 in the Tenth Plan)

The Special Group has assumed that additional 1.7 million employment will be generated in Elementary Education and 0.8 million from Health and Child Development and other Self-Employment Programmes.

Annexure – B

General Comments on Task Force Report on Employment Opportunities and other relevant Sources

(a) The Task Force Report:

One of the terms of reference of this Group (Annexe C), is the consideration of the relevant findings of the earlier Task Force Report constituted on 21.1.1999 and submitted on 1.7.2001 in preparing the present Report. The earlier Task Force Report like the present one also depended primarily on the NSSO 55th Round Survey data for estimating employment and unemployment in the economy. It used UPSS method of NSSO for estimating the movements of employment and unemployment in India. The Special Group's assessment of this method is given in Chapter 2. Because of using this method, it has derived an estimate of unemployment, which excludes large number of persons unemployed over a period of six months or less of the year and sometimes even marginally employed for a few hours in their working days. Thus, the Estimates of unemployment on this definition underestimated the Plan's task in generating new employment. Indeed, this has precisely happened when the estimates of Task Force gave as low an unemployment rate in 1999-2000 as 2.2 per cent of the labour force. This estimate of unemployment therefore does not reflect fully the economic and social pressure in the job market from a large number of persons who are employed and unemployed. This definition of employment, including a large proportion of unemployment/ underemployment, therefore, cannot match with the concept behind the Prime Minister's target of creating ten million gainful jobs a year and 50 million over the Tenth Plan period. Hence the Special Group switched over to the concept of current daily status, the estimates of which are also given in the NSSO Survey. To quote NSSO, "the CDS measure of unemployment is widely agreed to be the one that most fully captures open unemployment in the country". This raises the unemployment immediately to above 7 per cent in 1999-2000. The Task Force report also admitted that CDS method gives better measurement of unemployment.

Secondly, the Task Force depended largely on the potentials

of job creation on the past employment elasticities with a few minor ad-hoc corrections in some sectors and without giving any specific explanations. The implications of the change in policies in future and the impact of special employment and rural development programmes have not been explicitly dealt with. The Task Force assessed that in the agriculture future job creation potentials are near zero. But the Special Group views that because agriculture has not been given priority in 90s reforms process, there has been no growth in agricultural employment between 1993-94 and 1999-2000. The Special Group thinks that agriculture has still a very high potential for contributing to additional employment, if proper policies are undertaken regarding restructuring and deregulation along with Tapping new areas in agriculture and allied activities.

The Task Force further assumed that the GDP growth is the key generator of employment but even by assuming as high as eight per cent growth rate, it came out with an unemployment rate near doubling at the end of Tenth Plan. These findings clearly demonstrate that the growth *per se* will not be able to tackle the unemployment problem unless the patterns of growth and the major policies are changed. The Task Force recommended as an alternative scenario a further increase in the growth rate to 9 per cent per annum but still it has not been able to reduce the unemployment rate from the present. The Special Group however considers that it is not feasible to sustain such high growth rate at this point of time, given India's present savings and investment constraints and many other constraints, arising from unsatisfactory infrastructures, absence of good governance and inept implementation machinery. The Task Force further asserted that the target of creation of ten million jobs per year is not required and a lesser number of jobs will fulfill the plan needs. To quote "Projected growth rate for the labour force growth (1.8 per cent assumed) imply that the expected scale of addition to the labour force and therefore the need for new employment opportunities will be significantly less than the assumed in our Terms of Reference". This view, does not take the large base period pool of unemployment of around 26 million estimated on CDS basis. The Task Force used a projection model to estimate employment and unemployment and left a heavy unemployment as residual. The Special Group has however treated employment generation as a target variable and has worked out appropriate policies and programmes to achieve this goal.

On the basis of their findings, both the Task Force and the Special Group emphasise the need for improving the job quality i.e., generating gainful employment. However, the Task Force does not think of unemployment as a problem and centered its policy focus basically on improving the quality of jobs. The Special Group thought that the quality of employment and the lack of employment opportunities in the market should be treated simultaneously considering that with large unemployment in the market, it is very difficult to improve the terms of employment. This is especially in the unorganised labour market where labourers have no protection from exploitation.

The Task Force gave top priority to accelerating the growth of the organised sector because it provides much better quality jobs and concentrates most of its policies to help the growth of the organised sector. It, however, overlooked the fact that the private sector segment of the organised sector at the moment contributes hardly 2.7 per cent of the total employment in the economy. As a result even if this sector grows above 20 per cent per annum over the Tenth Plan period, its marginal (additional) contribution will be to the extent of 0.5 to 1.0 per cent of the total volume of employment generated. The public sector segment of the organised sector, because of its almost zero employment elasticity, is ruled out from making any significant contribution to employment in the near future. The Task Force further recommended that the organised sector, by a faster growth will ease out the less competitive unorganised sector in future. The Special Group has concluded that to solve the employment problem over the Tenth Plan period, along with the organised sector, we have no alternative but to take measures to accelerate the growth of productivity and income of those working in the unorganised sector which provides at present 92 per cent of employment; This could be achieved by improving skills, providing more timely and easy credit, better technology and infrastructure and using better marketing know-hows. All these policies have been spelt out in the present Special Group Report. In terms of priority areas for generation of additional employment, the Task Force gave highest priority to the services sector, projecting that 70 per cent of the employment of the economy will still be provided by the services sector. But the Special Group concluded from its projections that agriculture will still be the highest single sector for providing employment, followed by small and medium industries and the different services sectors. The public sector over the Tenth Plan has a major role in providing infrastructure, especially in social sector but should not be regarded as a major source of job creation except in some segments of social and financial services.

According to the Special Group, the contribution to employment from the services sector, on incremental term will lie around 50 per cent of the total employment and not as high as 70 per cent projected by the Task Force. In selecting the policy packages, the Special Group has been benefited by the analysis made on different policy options by the Task Force. But the Task Force has deliberated mainly on those policy issues, which pertain to growth only and not specifically to employment generation like the policies to increase the employment intensities of output by proper choice of technology over the medium term period. The Task Force also has not considered in its estimates the effect of the likely downsizing of the Government and retrenchment of the labour force both in public undertakings and the private sector in the near and medium term period. The Special Group has made some approximate estimates, which show that the magnitude may be more than four million persons.

Finally, the Special Group in general benefited from many recommendations of the Task Force report barring but in certain areas, where the Special Group expressed its reservations primarily because of the nature of their immediate effect on employment. Those policies are as follows:

1. The Task Force Report recommended the lowering of import tariffs to the levels prevailing in East Asia over a three-year period. The Special Group, however, thinks that although the reduction of tariff, by reducing some input costs encourage an increase in export helping additional employment generation, in specific cases, it can also adversely affect employment among certain domestic industries at least in near future, by possible larger competition from imports. No specific study has been available to give the net

effect of tariff reduction on the economy as a whole. Indeed a detailed study must be made on this aspect. Therefore, the Special Group has decided not to take any view until more information is available.

2. The Task Force recommended that the Agro Companies should be allowed to buy, develop, cultivate and sell the degraded wastelands after taking this land out of the purview of tenancy laws.

However, the Special Group views that such a scheme should be treated only in the form of a time-bound lease in which the interests of local landless labour, marginal farmers etc., should also be considered and as opposed to "once for all" transfers to different bodies including the agro companies.

3. The Task Force recommends in favour of the freedom of conversion of rural land into urban usage and laws to facilitate private development townships and estates. In the opinion of the Special Group, it should be done only in selected wastelands and not as a general rule.

4. The Task Force recommended dereservation of SSI within four years, and increase in the FDI investments.

The Special Group is of the view that the dereservation should be done on case-by-case basis as a gradual process without giving a time limit for total phasing as recommended by the Committee on Development of Small Enterprises constituted by the Planning Commission. Any increase in the ceiling of FDI Investment at the moment is not needed.

5. The Task Force recommended a fast switch to modern retail trade and removal of ban on FDI in this sector.

The Special Group is of the opinion that on the ground of employment and its benefits from dispersion across regions, the retailing should be allowed to continue both in the modern and traditional sectors and all help should be given to the traditional sector to improve their productivity and quality of services. Over a long-term period, the merging of the two may come. The special group does not recommend FDI in retail sector for the Tenth Plan.

6. Regarding special employment programmes

The Task Force's view is that they are not effective in giving employment and entail wastage and, therefore, pending review, these programmes should be frozen at the current price level. The Special Group feels that there is scope for tightening and rationalizing the special employment programmes by proper mergers and partial weeding, but the scale of operation should not be reduced, because it has a very effective role in generating employment especially during slack season and in areas where market is not functioning properly.

7. Hiring and Firing

The Task Force recommended that there should be flexibility in the hiring and firing of labour, where no permission from government will be needed. It is only then that there will be incentive to use labour-intensive production. The Special Group thinks that its relaxation may create more firing than hiring in the near future, given that the market is carrying excess labour and government is following its downsizing policy. In the long run this relaxation may result in more hiring but no study until now is available as to the net effect. Besides even if amended, by relaxing provision for hiring and firing, it should be along with the social security coverage, when full care should be taken to protect the retrenched labour. The ensuing National Labour Commission Report in this context should be examined. The Group therefore decided not to form any view, without more information from the Labour Commission Report.

8. Labour Laws

The Task Force recommended suitable amendment of the Contract Labour Act. This issue is lying with the Group of Ministers for their decision. The Special Group in principle agrees with the Task Force's recommendations but thinks that it should be preceded by appropriate social security and other measures for protection of the interests of labour. Proper regulatory authorities are to be created to watch the recruiting agencies, for protecting the employees' interests. It may be pointed out that most of the labour laws that the Task force has recommended for change, pertain only to the organised sector covering hardly 8 per cent or less of the labour force. The Task Force has not discussed much about the labour laws, rules and regulations applicable to the unorganised sector. The Special Group has discussed its problems in detail.

(b) Population Census of India

The population census provides decadal growth of the main workers and also of the marginal workers. Main workers are defined as those who have work for the major part of the reference period (i.e., 6 months or more). The marginal workers are those who had not worked for the major part of the reference period. The estimates of workforce as percentage to population are available on all-India basis, also state-wise and in the union territories. In this Census Report, however, the concepts of employment and unemployment are different from the ones given in the NSSO Report. Therefore, a strict comparison with Special Groups estimates of workforce should not be attempted; only their broad trends can be compared.

Table 14 gives the decadal growth rate of the work force over the 1990s. Here again we notice the growth of workforce comprising the main workers (we have taken the main workers separating the marginal workers since it is closer to the concept of the workforce measured on the CDS basis) has decelerated significantly from the 1980s of around 2.34 per cent to 0.81 per cent in the 1990s. These estimates are not strictly comparable with NSSO estimates because of their differences in the concept and measurement use for the workforce. But both the NSSO and the Census clearly demonstrate that there has been a significant deceleration in the growth of workforce (from the eighties to the nineties). As to the rate of growth of the marginal workers in the Census grew much faster compared to the main workers; This is corroborated also by the fast growth of casual workers in the NSSO Survey. But here again one should be careful in trying any strict comparisons between the two sets of estimates.

The regional trends in employment during 1991-2001 are rather disturbing from the labour perspective (Table 14). States, which are still very far, intime, from demographic transition have recorded slow growth or even a decline in number of main workers; Orissa (-0.81%), Uttar Pradesh (0.11%), Madhya Pradesh

(0.47%) and Bihar (0.72%) as compared to all India average of 0.81%). Implicit in this are sharp escalations in inter-state migration. If we rely on economic growth processes alone, to balance labour supply and demand, at regional level the job quality will tend to reach rather highly exploitative levels in some pockets of the country. Social ramifications of these are easy to imagine. At the same time freedom to migrate is essential because otherwise, regional inequalities in unemployment and income will accentuate still further. The Special Group therefore, suggests in chapter V that the planning process needs to lock closely at the migrant workers. Emphasis on more and better work opportunities in agriculture and allied areas in particular in the States having high labour supply growth is therefore considered as of crucial importance to sustain job quality of the average worker of the country.

(c) Employment Exchange

The third source is the data given by employment exchanges. There are nearly 958 employment exchanges spread all over India which record registration for jobs in the live register on a time series basis; but there are major limitations in using the information from this source, because of the following reasons.

(i) All the job seekers registered with the employment exchange are not necessarily unemployed.

(ii) All job seekers or unemployed do not register themselves with the employment exchange, given the fact that in most of the states the employment exchanges are concentrated in the urban areas.

(iii) In some exceptional cases, there is a chance of duplication in the register.

(iv) The job seekers who find employment through agencies other than employment exchanges do not always report to the employment exchanges for deletion of their names.

(v) Employers also do not intimate the employment exchanges when selections are done from the employment exchanges' list.

(vi) There are cases when a default to renew the cards results in deletion of their names.

Here also, we notice, on an annual basis, the number in the live register of the employment exchange is increasing over time and it has reached a level of 41.3 million persons in the year 2000. Keeping in mind the limitations of this source, it can only be loosely compared with the unemployment figures derived by the CDS method, based on NSSO data. The latter gives an unemployment level of 27 million person years. Both figures are very large. Therefore, they warrant special attention in preparing the Tenth Plan's programmes, policies and fund allocations.

(d) Economic Census

The fourth source is the Economic Census of 1998 brought out by the India's Central Statistical Organisation. This census provides among several data, the data on the growth of the workforce. Here of course the farm sector (i.e., the crop production and plantation) is excluded. To quote "The census included all enterprises engaged in economic activity, both agricultural and non agricultural, whether employing hired work or not except in crop production and plantation". The definition of workers in the Economic Census, however, is not comparable with the NSSO definition. Therefore the data can be used only to have a broad comparison in trends on employment and unemployment with the NSSO data.

Table – B1

Growth of Workers – Economic Census

	1980	1990	1998
Rural	24226528	32175787 (2.88)	38132534 (2.15)*
Urban	28952165	38210417 (2.81)	42498707 (1.34)
Combined	53178693	70386204 (2.84)	80631241 (1.71)

( ) denote growth rate (%)

* Establishments recorded in Economic Census exclude farms, and therefore bulk of the rural workers. Hence, Economic Census 1998 reflects a slower decline in rural workforce than the NSSO Employment Survey (1999-2000) and Demographic Census (2001).

This result broadly corroborates the findings of NSSO and population Census when the growth rate exhibited significant deceleration in the 90's compared to 80's. However as already explained no direct comparability with our estimates based on NSSO will be possible.

(e) McKinsey Report

The fifth source is the McKinsey Report, the growth imperative and employment generation in India brought out by McKinsey Global Institute working in collaboration with McKinsey India office on the economic performance of India. This report, like the Special Group, used CDS basis of estimation of employment and unemployment and relevant parameters from NSSO 55th round. It then provides an estimate of employment for the year 2010, based on a growth rate of 10 per cent per annum supported by an exhaustive reform package; but it also ends with an unemployment rate even after a 10 year period of almost at the same level, as in the base. This exercise like ours has used the measurement of unemployment on CDS basis. This report therefore clearly fails to give answer to India's problem of unemployment and improvement in job quality of an average Indian labour supply household.

Table – B2

The Employment and Unemployment Scenario (1993-94 – 2006-07) : Special Group & Task Force Exercise

	Special Group Report (Tenth Plan)					Task Force Report UPSS		
	1993-94	1999-2000	2001-02*	2006-07**		1993-94	1999-2000	2006-07@
1. Labour Force (person years)	335.97	363.33 (1.31)	378.21	413.50 (1.80)	1. Labour Force (million persons)	381.94	406.05 (1.03)	462.12 (1.80)
2. Work Force (person years)	315.84	336.75 (1.07)	343.36 (2.70)	392.35	2. Work Force (million persons)	374.45	397.00 (0.98)	442.40 (1.50)
3. No. of unemployeds (person years)	20.13	26.58 (4.74)	34.85 (- 9.51)	21.15	3. No. of unemployeds (million persons)	7.49	9.05 (3.20)	19.72 (11.34)
4. Percentage unemployed	5.99	7.32	9.21	5.11	4. Percentage unemployed	1.96	2.23	4.27

* estimated on the basis of CSO's Quick and Advance estimates of GDP and sector composition with minor adjustments.

** Projections with changed Industrial Structure

( ) denote rate of growth

(m) denote million

UPSS: Usual Principal and Subsidiary Status.

@ 8% GDP Growth Scenario

Annexure – C

No. P- 12049/01-LEM/ERS
Government of India
Planning Commission
(LEM Division)
Yojana Bhawan, Sansad Marg,
New Delhi – 1 : dated 5.9.2001

ORDER

Subject: *Constitution of "Special Group on Targeting 10 Million Employment Opportunities per year over the Tenth Plan Period".*

It has been decided that a Special Group in the Steering Committee on Labour and Employment for the Tenth Five-Year Plan should prepare the strategy and programme for employment generation. This will be done by a "Special Group and Targeting 10 Million Employment Opportunities per year over the Tenth Plan Period".

2. The composition of the "Special Group on Targeting 10 Million Employment Opportunities per year over the Tenth Plan Period" will be as follows.

1.	Dr. S.P. Gupta, Member (LEM) & Chairman, Tenth Plan Steering Committee on Labour and Employment	Chairman
2.	Chairman (KVIC)	Member
3.	Sh. R.P. Sinha, Pr. Adviser (LEM)	Member
4.	Secretary (Labour)	Member
5.	Secretary (Rural Development)	Member
6.	Secretary (Urban Employment & Poverty Alleviation)	Member
7.	Secretary (Small Scale Industry)	Member
8.	Secretary (Agro and Rural Industries)	Member
9.	Secretary (Social Justice and Empowerment)	Member
10.	Director General, NSSO	Member
11.	Adviser (LEM)	Member-Secretary

Co-opted subsequently through Order dated 14.12.2001

1.	Secretary, Department of Agriculture & Cooperation	Member
2.	Secretary, Department of Food Processing Industries	Member
3	Secretary, Department of Animal Husbandry & Dairying	Member
4	Secretary, Department of Elementary Education and Literacy	Member
5	Secretary, Department of Family Welfare	Member
6.	Secretary, ISM&H, Ministry of Health and Family Welfare	Member
7.	Secretary, Ministry of Health and Family Welfare	Member
8.	Secretary, Road Transport, and Highways	Member
9.	Secretary, Ministry of Tourism	Member
10.	Secretary, Ministry of Textiles	Member
11.	Secretary, Development Commissioner (Handlooms)	Member
12.	DC(SSI), Department of Small Scale Industries	Member
13.	Dr. H. Ramachandran, Director, IAMR	Member
14.	Dr. Gary Jacobs, The Mother's Society, Pondicherry	Member
15.	Prof. Amitabh Kundu, JNU	Member

3. The terms of reference of this Group are :

3.1 To suggest strategies and programmes in the Tenth Plan for creating gainful employment opportunities for 10 million people a year.

3.2 To consider all relevant studies and recommendations including the Report submitted on July 2, 2001 by the Task Force on Employment Opportunities.

3.3 To look into sectoral issues and policies having a bearing on employment generation, and to recommend sectoral programmes for creation of employment opportunities.

3.4 To consider the Reports, proceedings and other available documents prepared for the labour intensive sectors by the Planning Commission Workings Groups and Steering Committees constituted for the Tenth Plan.

3.5 To consider any other matter related with or incidental to above terms of reference.

4. The Chairman of the Group may co-opt any other person as Member of the Group.

5. The Chairman may invite specialists to particular meetings of the Special Group.

6. The Group will submit its report by November 30, 2001. The LEM Division in the Planning Commission will provide the Secretariat for the Group.

7. The expenses towards TA/DA of the official members will be met by respective Government Departments/Institutions to which they belong. The TA/DA of non-official Members and invitees to meetings will be paid by Planning Commission as admissible to Grade I officers of the Government of India.

8. Smt. Padmaja Mehta, Director (LEM), Room No. 561, Yojana Bhavan, Sansad Marg, (Tel. 3325978) will act as Nodal Officer and any further communication in this regard may be made with Nodal Officer.

Sd/-

(K. K. Chhabra)

Under Secretary to the Government of India

Table – 1

Present Sectoral Employment Scenario (1999 - 2000)

Sectors	Employment Elasticity	Employment Elasticity	Total: Current Daily Status (CDS)			Organised: Public Sector	Organised: Private Sector	Organised: Total	% of organised sector to total sectoral employment	% of public sector to total Emp.	% of public sector to total Org.	% of private sector to total Org.	Absolute employment % composition	Sectoral GDP Growth %	Sectoral GDP Growth %
	1983 to 1993 -1994	1993-94-2000	1983	1993-94	1999-2000	1999	1999	1999						1983 to 1993-94	1993-94 to 2000
0	1	2	3	4	5	6	7	8	9	10	11	12	13	14	15
1. Agriculture	0.70	0.01	151.35	190.72	190.94	0.52	0.87	1.39	0.73	0.27	37.16	62.84	56.70	2.9	3.1
2. Mining & quarrying	0.59	-0.41	1.74	2.54	2.26	0.93	0.09	1.01	44.69	41.15	91.41	8.59	0.67	6.2	4.7
3. Manufacturing	0.38	0.33	27.69	35.00	40.79	1.57	5.18	6.75	16.55	3.95	23.25	76.75	12.11	6.0	7.8
4. Electricity, gas & water supply	0.63	-0.52	0.83	1.43	1.15	0.96	0.04	1.00	96.96	83.48	95.91	4.09	0.34	8.4	6.8
5. Construction	0.86	0.82	7.17	11.02	14.95	1.11	0.07	1.18	7.90	7.42	93.97	6.03	4.44	4.9	6.3
6. Trade, hotels and restaurents	0.68	0.62	18.17	26.88	37.54	0.16	0.32	0.49	1.31	0.43	33.54	66.46	11.15	5.6	9.2
7. Transport, storage & communication	0.55	0.63	6.99	9.88	13.65	3.08	0.07	3.15	23.08	22.56	97.81	2.19	4.05	6.1	8.7
8. Financing, insurance, real estate and business services	0.45	0.64	2.10	3.37	4.62	1.30	0.36	1.65	35.71	29.14	78.34	21.66	1.38	10.1	8.4
9. Community, social and personal services	0.68	-0.25	23.52	34.98	30.84	9.79	1.70	11.49	37.26	31.74	85.21	14.79	9.16	5.7	8.4
All	**0.52**	**0.16**	**239.57**	**315.84**	**336.75**	**19.42**	**8.70**	**28.11**	**8.34**	**5.77**	**69.06**	**30.94**	**100.0**	**5.2**	**6.7**

Source : National A/ c ; CSO, NSSO : 55th round, Economic Survey

Table – 1(a)

Sectoral NDP Scenario : Organised & Unorganised Sectors

GDP in Rs. Crores

Sectors	NDP at factor cost		NDP Organised Sector		%age Sectoral GDP (Organised)		%age GDP Organised to total	% age employment (Private organised to total)	%age employment organised sector to total	employment elasticity organised sector	employment elasticity Total economy
	1993-94	1999-2000	1993-94	1999-2000	1993-94	1999-2000	1999-2000	1999-2000	1999-2000	1993-94 to 1999-2000	1993-94 to 1999-2000
	—— (Rs. Crore at 1993-94 prices) ——										
Agriculture	229829	274858	8046	8808	3.5	3.2	0.9	0.26	0.41	-0.61	0.01
Mining & quarrying	14950	20648	13861	19156	92.7	92.8	1.9	0.03	0.30	-0.25	-0.41
Manufacturing	103739	148121	65774	90168	63.4	60.9	8.8	1.54	2.0	0.165	0.33
Electricity, gas and water supply	8801	14609	8169	13766	92.8	94.9	1.4	0.01	0.30	0.056	-0.52
Construction	38749	55696	18929	24107	48.9	43.3	2.4	0.02	0.35	-0.136	0.82
Trade, hotels and restaurent	96627	164064	10865	32751	11.2	20.0	3.2	0.10	0.15	0.069	0.62
Transport, storage and communication	37721	66110	21000	30801	55.7	46.6	3.0	0.02	0.94	0.024	0.63
Financing, insurance, real estates and business services	80541	131527	39706	78739	49.3	59.9	7.7	0.11	0.49	0.358	0.64
Community, social and personal services	87035	143712	70499	120033	81.0	83.5	11.8	0.50	3.4	0.081	-0.25
Total	**697992**	**1019345**	**256849**	**418920**	**36.8**	**41.1***	**41.1**	**2.58**	**8.34**	**0.066**	**0.165**

* Organised private sector 15% of GDP

Table – 1 (b)

Past and Present Macro Scenario on Employment and Unemployment (CDS Basis) (Person years)

ALL INDIA

	(Million)			Growth per annum (%)	
	1983	1993-94	1999-2000	1983 to 1993-94	1993-94 to 1999-2000
Population	718.2	894.01	1003.97	2.0	1.95
Labour Force	261.33	335.97	363.33	2.43	1.31
Workforce	239.57	315.84	336.75	2.7	1.07
Unemployment rate (%)	(8.3)	(5.99)	(7.32)		
No. of unemployed	21.76	20.13	26.58	-0.08	4.74
RURAL					
Population	546.61	658.83	727.5	1.79	1.67
Labour Force	204.18	255.38	270.39	2.15	0.96
Workforce	187.92	241.04	250.89	2.40	0.67
Unemployment Rate (%)	(7.96)	(5.61)	(7.21)		
No. of unemployed	16.26	14.34	19.5	-1.19	5.26
URBAN					
Population	171.59	234.98	276.47	3.04	2.74
Labour Force	57.15	80.60	92.95	3.33	2.40
Workforce	51.64	74.80	85.84	3.59	2.32
Unemployment Rate (%)	(9.64)	(7.19)	(7.65)		
No. of unemployed	5.51	5.80	7.11	0.49	3.45

Schedule Caste Population

	1993-94	1999-2000	1993-94 to 1999-2000 Growth per annum (%)
Population	142.93	179.87	3.91
Labour Force	54.84	66.57	3.28
Workforce	50.26	60.17	3.04
Unemployment rate (%)	(8.34)	(9.60)	
No. of unemployed	4.58	6.40	5.75
Schedule Tribe Population			
Population	65.56	81.72	3.74
Labour Force	29.56	34.80	2.75
Workforce	28.29	32.96	2.58
Unemployment rate (%)	(4.32)	(5.30)	
No. of unemployed	1.28	1.84	6.31
Schedule Caste & Schedule Tribes			
Unemployment rate (%)	(6.94)	(7.77)	(5.90)

Source : NSSO & Population Census
All estimates are on CDS (Current Daily Status basis)
( ) denote percentage

Table – 2

Manufacturing Sector - Labour Intensity in the Organised Segment relative to the Unorganised

	Employment				GDP (gross) (at 1993-94 prices)				
Manufacturing	1993-94	1999-2000	Growth per annum	Manufacturing	1993-94	1999-2000	Growth per annum	Employment elasticity	Labour intensity 1999-2000 Organised/unorganised
	(Million)		(%)		(Rs. Crores)		(1994-2000)	(%)	
Organised	6.40 (18.29)	6.74 (16.52)	0.87	**Registered**	81873 (65.2)	124993 (63.5)	7.31	0.119	0.1136 i.e. for equal output when unorganised sector generates employment of 100 persons, organised sector 11.4 persons
Unorganised	28.60 (81.7)	34.05 (83.48)	2.95	**Unregistered**	43620 (34.8)	71770 (36.5)	8.66	0.341	
TOTAL	35.00 (100.0)	40.79 (100.0)	2.58		125493 (100.0)	196763 (100.0)	(7.8)	0.331	

NB : Organised and unorganised sectors roughly equated with registered and unregistered sectors.

Table – 2 (a)

Employment elasticities in organised and unorganised sectors (1993-94 to 1999-2000)

Employment in million
GDP (Net) in crores at
1993-94 prices

	Employment (CDS)		Growth per annum	Net Domestic Product at factor cost		Growth per annum	Employment Elasticity	Relative Employment elasticities unorganised/ unorganised
	1993-94	1999-2000	(%)	1993-94	1999-2000	(%)		
Organised	27.18 (8.6)	28.11 (8.34)	0.56	256849 (36.8)	418920 41.10	8.50	0.066	3.23
Unorganised	288.66 (91.4)	308.64 (91.66)	1.12	491143 (63.2)	697992 58.9	5.27	0.213	
Total	315.84 (100)	336.75 (100)	1.07	697992 (100)	1019345 (100)	6.52	0.165	

NB : Brackets give the percentage composition

Table – 3

Employment Scenario from 8% growth per annum and extrapolated industrial structure

Based on Actual Elasticity (1994-2000) -CDS & 1.8% p. a. Growth in L. F.

	Unit	1999-2000$	2001$$	2002$$	2007	2012	Employment Growth over 10th plan per annum
Labour Force (1.8% p. a. Growth)	million	363.33	371.52	378.21	413.50	451.53	1.8%
Employment ** #	million	336.75	340.82	343.36	373.03	403.52	1.7%
(Unemployment rate)	(%)	7.32	8.26	9.21	9.79	10.63	
No. of Unemployed	million	26.58	30.70	34.85	40.47	48.01	3.0%

** Based on 8% Growth in GDP during 2002-07

\# Current Daily status basis

$ 1999-2000 figures related to NSS 55th (July, 1999 - June, 2000) rd.

$$ Based on 5.2% GDP Growth during 2000-01 and 2001-02

Note : Actual elasticities (1994-2000) are given in Table - 8

Table – 3 (a)

*Employment Opportunities sectorwise over the Tenth Plan**

Employment in million

Sectors	GDP Gr. 2000-01 % QE	GDP Gr. 2000-01 % SG	GDP Gr. 2001-02 % AE	GDP Gr. 2001-02 % SG	High Growth (8.0%) SG	Projected Elasticity* 2000-02 & 2002-07	CDS Emp. (1993-94) (1.1.1994)	CDS Emp. (1999-00) (1.1.2000)	Projected Employment# Empl. 2000-01 (1.4.2001)	Empl. 2001-02 (1.4.2002)	Empl. 2002-07 (1.4.2007)	Rate of Growth in Employment (%) 1993-94 to 1999-2000	1999-2000 to 2000-01	2001 to 2002	2002 to 2007
1. Agriculture	-0.2	0.2	5.7	3.4	4.2	0.01	190.72	190.94	190.95	191.01	191.42	0.02	0.00	0.03	0.04
2. Minings and quarrying	3.3	3.7	1.4	1.1	4.7	-0.41	2.54	2.26	2.22	2.21	2.01	-1.91	-1.52	-0.46	-1.93
3. Manufacturing	6.7	5.6	3.3	2.6	10.0	0.33	35.00	40.79	41.73	42.09	49.51	2.58	1.85	0.85	3.30
4. Electricity, gas and water supply	6.2	4.7	5.2	3.7	8.3	-0.52	1.43	1.15	1.11	1.09	0.88	-3.55	-2.44	-1.92	-4.32
5. Construction	6.8	5.5	2.9	2.8	8.3	0.82	11.02	14.95	15.80	16.16	22.46	5.21	4.51	2.30	6.81
6. Trade, hotels and restaurent	3.8	6.9	6.3	5.8	8.0	0.62	26.88	37.54	39.56	40.99	52.22	5.72	4.28	3.62	4.96
7. Transport, storage & communication	8.2	6.9		5.8	10.3	0.63	9.88	13.65	14.39	14.92	20.43	5.53	4.35	3.67	6.49
8. Financing, insurance, real estate and business services	2.9	9.1	7.5	11.1	10.0	0.64	3.37	4.62	4.96	5.32	7.25	5.40	5.82	7.11	6.40
9. Community, social & personal services	6.0	7.8	6.0	7.0	7.6	-0.25	34.98	30.84	30.09	29.57	26.86	-2.08	-1.95	-1.74	-1.90
All Sectors	4.0	5.2	5.4	5.2	8.0	0.21	315.84	336.75	340.82	343.36	373.03	1.07	0.97	0.75	1.67

\# ROG in employment has been projected by taking into account observed Sectoral elasticities based on CDS Employment during 1994-2000 and sectoral growth in GDP at 5.2% for 2000-01 and 2001-02 & 8% during 2002-07

* Observed Elasticity during 1994-2000 based on CDS

QE = Quick estimates

AE = Advance estimates

S. G = Special Group Estimates

Note : 1. Projected employment is based on sectoral employment elasticities and sectoral growth in GDP

2. Projections may not be adjusted for Repair Services because 3- digit data on workers distribution by industries on CDS basis is not available.

Table – 4

*Employment Scenario on * 8% growth per annum and changed industrial structure on the basis of proposed poilcy and programmes in the 10th Plan*

	Unit	1999-2000	2001-2002	2006-2007	2011-2012	Growth over 10th Plan percentage per annum
Labour Force	million	363.33	378.21	413.50	453.52	1.8
Employment	million	336.75	343.36	392.35	451.53	2.7
Unemployment rate	(%)	7.32	9.21	5.11	0.44	
No. of unemployeds	million	26.58	34.85	21.15	1.99	-9.5

Special group estimates,

* on CDS basis

Table – 4 (a)

The implicit movement in the labour productivity (i.e., out put per labour)

Per cent per annum

	1983 to 1993-94	1993-94 to 1999-2000	Projected 2001-2002	Projected 2006-2007
(A) Based on 1994-2000 elasticities				
GDP (growth)	5.2	6.7	5.2	8.0
Work force	2.7	1.07	0.98	1.67
Employment elasticities	0.538	0.160	0.188	0.209
Labour productivity	2.3	5.6	4.2	6.2
(B) Based on 1994-2000 elasticities with changes in policies and programmes				
Work force	2.7	1.07	0.98	2.7
Employment elasticities	0.538	0.160	0.188	0.338*
Labour productivity	2.3	5.6	4.2	5.2

* implicit employment elasticity including employment on special programmes

Table – 5

Estimates of Generation of Sectoral Employment opportunities over the Tenth Plan

Sectors	Sectoral GDP Growth (%) 10th Plan	Base employment (CDS) (million) 2001-2002	Increased employment opportunities over 10th Plan: on estimating employment elasticities	Program and Policy Based **	Total Incre-mental	(million) Total Employ-ment 2007
Agriculture & Allied (Incl. Rural activity)*	4.2	191.01 (55.63)	0.41	9.06	9.47	200.48 (51.09)
Mining & Quarrying	4.7	2.21 (0.64)	-0.20		-0.20	2.01 (0.51)
Manufacturing & SSI (PMRY & REGP) Pradhan Mantri Rozgar Yojana and Rural Employment Generation Programme	10.0	42.09 (12.26)	7.42	4.2	11.62	53.71 (13.70)
Gas, Electricity & Water	8.3	1.09 (0.32)	-0.21		-0.21	0.88 (0.22)
Constructions	8.3	16.16 (4.71)	6.30		6.30	22.46 (5.72)
Trade, Hotel & Restaurant	8.0	40.99 (11.94)	11.23		11.23	52.22 (13.28)
Transport, Storage & Communications	10.3	14.92 (4.35)	5.51		5.51	20.43 (5.21)
Financial Institutions, Real Estate & Business Services	10.0	5.32 (1.55)	1.93		1.93	7.25 (1.84)
Community Services, Social & Personal Services	7.6	29.57 (8.61)	-2.71	3.2	0.49	30:06 (7.64)
Sampoorna Gramin Rozgar Yojana (SGRY)				1.29	2.09	2.09
Swaranjayanti Gram Swarojgar Yojana (SGSY)				0.8		
Pradhan Mantri Gram Sadak Yojana (PMGSY)				0.77	0.77	0.77
Aggregate	8.0	343.36	29.67	19.32	48.99	392.35

Brackets denote percentage composition to total.

** Detailed breakup is given in annexure A and summarised in Table 7 estimates based on person years basis.

Table – 6A

Low Growth Scenario (6.5% Growth over 10th Plan Period). Projection of Employment Opportunities

CDS basis

Items	Unit	1999-2000	2001-2002	2006-2007
Labour Force (1.8%) per annum	Million	363.33	378.21	413.50
Employment	Million	336.75	343.36	367.44
No. of unemployed	Million	26.58	34.85	45.56
Unemployment rate	percentage	7.32	9.21	11.0

Table – 6B

Low Growth Scenario with recommended programmes & policy changes

CDS basis

Items	Unit	1999-2000	2001-2002	2006-2007
Labour Force	Million	363.33	378.21	413.50
Employment	Million	336.75	343.36	375.0
No. of unemployed	Million	26.58	34.85	38.5
Unemployment rate	percentage	7.32	9.21	9.30

CDS : Current Daily Status

Table – 7

"Programme-generated" incremental employment, over 10th plan

(million person years)

(a) Agriculture & Allied		
1. Diversion to oilseeds and pulses:	0.35	
2. National Watershed Development Project for Rainfed Areas (NWDPRA)	0.50	
3. Horticulture	1.20	
4. On Farm Management	1.25	
5. Agriculture Clinics and Seed production	0.15	
6. Training and employment of tractor drivers	0.10	
	————>	3.55
(b) Greening the country through Agro Forestry		
1. Joint Forest Management (JFM)	1.50	
2. Development of medicinal plants	0.50	
3. Bamboo Development	1.50	
	————>	3.50
(c) Energy Plantation for Biomass power Generation		
1. Energy Plantation Prosopis and Casuarina	1.22	
2. Ethanol (Biofuel from sugarcane plantation)	0.79	
	————>	2.01
(d) Rural Sectors and SMEs		
Prime Minister's Rojgar Yojana (PMRY-SSI)	1.65	
Cluster Development	0.55	
Rural Employment Generation Programme (REGP-KVIC)	2.00	
Sampoorna Gramin Rojgar Yojana (SGRY)	1.29	
Pradhan Mantri Gram Sadak Yojana (PMGSY)	0.77	
Swarnajayanti Gram Swarojgar Yojana (SGSY)	0.80	
	————>	7.06
(e) Education and Literacy		
1. Education	1.53	
2. Mid day meals	0.06	
3. DIET, BRC, CRC, Engineering Staff SPO, DPO	0.09	
	————>	1.70
Employment through ICT Development		0.70
Health, Family and Child Welfare		0.80
GRAND TOTAL		19.32

NB : Details are in Annexure (A)

Table – 8

Employment elasticities 1993-94 - 1999-2000 & implicit over the Tenth Plan by changes in sectoral composition

CDS Basis

Sectors	Growth of Employment 1994-2000	GDP Growth (%) 1994-2000	Elasticities 1994-2000* (%)	Elasticities assumed in the 10th Plan: With policy changes including special employment programmes	Elasticities assumed in the 10th Plan: Without policy changes
1. Agriculture & Allied (incl. Rural activities)	0.02	3.1	0.006 ****	0.231	0.006
2. Mining & quarrying	-1.91	4.7	-0.41	-0.41	-0.41
3. Manufacturing	2.58	7.8	0.33	0.500	0.33
4. Electricity, gas and water supply	-3.55	6.8	-0.52	-0.52	-0.52
5. Construction	5.21	6.3	0.82	0.82	0.82
6. Trade, hotels & restaurents	5.72	9.2	0.62	0.62	0.62
7. Transport, storage and communication	5.53	8.7	0.63	0.63	0.63
8. Financing, insurance, real estate and business services	5.40	8.4	0.64	0.64	0.64
9. Community, social & personal services	-2.08	8.4	-0.25	0.043	-0.25
Total	1.07	6.7	0.16	0.338***	0.21**

* Based on actual observed elasticties (1994-2000)
** Based on Growth and without Policy changes
*** Based on Growth and Policy changes over the 10th Plan
**** Approx to 0.01

Table – 9

Employment Scenario Statewise

CDS basis

States Major Ones	Employment ('000) 1999-2000	Employment Growth 1993-94 to 1999-2000 (% pa)	Unemployment Rate		Employment elasticity 1993-94 to 1999-2000	GDP Growth (% per annum) 1993-94 to 1999-2000
			1999-2000 (%)	1993-94 (%)		
Andhra Pradesh	30614	0.35	8.03	6.69	0.067	5.2
Assam	7647	1.99	8.03	8.03	0.737	2.7
Bihar	30355	1.59	7.32	6.34	0.353	4.5
Gujarat	18545	2.31	4.55	5.70	0.316	7.3
Haryana	5982	2.43	4.77	6.51	0.420	5.8
Himachal Pradesh	2371	0.37	2.96	1.80	0.052	7.1
Karnataka	20333	1.43	4.57	4.94	0.188	7.6
Kerala	8902	0.07	20.97	15.51	0.013	5.5
Madhya Pradesh	28725	1.28	4.45	3.56	0.272	4.7
Maharashtra	34979	1.25	7.16	5.09	0.216	5.8
Orissa	11928	1.05	7.34	7.30	0.262	4.0
Punjab	8013	1.96	4.03	3.10	0.426	4.6
Rajasthan	19930	0.73	3.13	1.31	0.104	7.0
Tamil Nadu	23143	0.37	11.78	11.41	0.052	7.1
Uttar Pradesh	49387	1.02	4.08	3.45	0.185	5.5
West Bengal	22656	0.41	14.99	10.06	0.056	7.3
All India	336736	1.07	7.32	5.99	0.160	6.7

Table – 10

Comparison of employment & labour force growth estimated on UPSS & CDS basis. 1993-94 - 1999-2000

	% Change per annum in employment growth 1999-2000/1993-94		Employment in million			
			1993-94	1993-94	1999-2000	1999-2000
Sector	UPSS#	CDS*	UPSS#	CDS*	UPSS#	CDS*
Agriculture	-0.34	-0.12	242.46	190.72	237.56	190.94
Mining & quarrying	-2.85	-2.55	2.70	2.54	2.27	2.26
Manufacturing	2.05	2.66	42.50	35.00	48.01	40.79
Electricity, gas & water supply	-0.88	-3.43	1.35	1.43	1.28	1.15
Construction	7.09	5.22	11.68	11.02	17.62	14.95
Trade, hotels and restaurents	5.04	5.85	27.78	26.88	37.32	37.54
Transport storage and communication	6.04	5.61	10.33	9.88	14.69	13.65
Financing, insurance, real estate and business services	6.20	5.62	3.52	3.37	5.05	4.62
Community, social and personnel services	0.55	-2.0	32.13	34.98	33.20	30.84
All India Work Force	0.98	1.07	374.45	315.84	397.00	336.75
All India Labour force	1.07	1.31	381.46	335.97	406.85	363.33
Unemployment Rate (%)			1.88	5.99	2.2	7.32

Based on Old Population Census and Technical Group.

* Based on 2001 Population Census

Table – 11

Unemployment Rates : Alternative Measures

(Percentage of Labour Force)

	Usual Principal Status (UPS)	Usual Principal and Subsidiary Status (UPSS)	Current Weekly Status (CWS)	Current Daily Status (CDS)
RURAL				
1977-78	3.26	1.54	3.74	7.70
1983	1.91	1.13	3.88	7.94
1987-88	3.07	1.98	4.19	5.25
1993-94	1.80	1.20	3.00	5.63
1999-00	1.96	1.43	3.91	7.21
URBAN				
1977-78	8.77	7.01	7.86	10.34
1983	6.04	5.02	6.81	9.52
1987-88	6.56	5.32	7.12	9.36
1993-94	5.21	4.52	5.83	7.43
1999-00	5.23	4.63	5.89	7.65
ALL INDIA				
1977-78	4.23	2.47	4.48	8.18
1983	2.77	1.90	4.51	8.28
1987-88	3.77	2.62	4.80	6.09
1993-94	2.56	1.89	3.63	6.03
1999-00	2.81	2.20	4.41	7.32

Note : These estimates of Employment are based on NSS data combined with census data. The NSS gives Labour Force Participation Rate (LFPR) and Work Force Participation Rate (WFPR) for four categories : rural male (RM), rural female (RF), urban male (UM) and urban female (UF) separately. We obtain estimates of the total labour force and total work force in each year by applying LFPR and WFPR to the total population of each category (RM. RF. UM & UF) obtained from the interpolation for inter-census years. However, for the year 2001 the four component (RM. RF. UM & UF) are not available in the key results of Census released in April 2001. Hence, estimates of populations for these four categories made by the Technical Group (which was chaired by Registrar General) in 1996 have been used to combine the component-wise LFPR's and WFPR's to the level of Rural, Urban and All India.

Table – 12

Unemployment Rates by Household Monthly Per Capita Expenditure Class (1999-2000)

Monthly Per Capita Expenditure Class (Rs.)		Unemployment Rate (CDS) per cent of labour force	
Rural	Urban	Rural	Urban
0 - 225	0 - 300	11.31	9.61
225 - 255	300 - 350	9.62	9.67
255 - 300	350 - 425	8.12	8.20
300 - 340	425 - 500	7.46	9.20
340 - 380	500 - 575	6.56	9.20
380 - 420	575 - 665	6.18	8.63
420 - 570	665 - 775	6.48	8.19
470 - 525	775 - 915	6.14	7.18
525 - 615	915 - 1120	5.60	6.65
615 - 775	1120 - 1500	6.06	5.68
775 - 950	1500 - 1925	5.57	4.67
950 & above	1925 & above	5.25	4.10
All	All	7.21	7.65

Source : NSSO Survey 55th Round (1999-00)

Table – 13

Rate of Growth of Employment in Organised and Unorganised sectors.

Activities	Employment Weight (Total) 1999-2000	Organised Sector Growth* (% per annum) 1994-2000	Unorganised** Sector Growth (% per annum) 1994-2000
Agriculture	56.7	-1.00	0.03
Mining and quarrying	0.67	-1.30	-2.40
Manufacturing	12.11	0.87	2.95
Electricity, gas and water supply	0.34	0.51	-17.00
Construction	4.44	-0.69	5.85
Trade, hotels and restaurents	11.15	1.43	5.79
Transport, storage and communication	4.05	0.21	7.59
Financing, insurance, real estate and business services	1.38	1.27	8.30
Community, social and personal services	9.16	0.8	-3.56
All Sectors	100.0	0.56	1.12

* DGE&T

** Derived from NSSO

Table – 14

SECTION A

Workforce increase between 1981-1991 & 1991- 2001 based on Census

(million)

		1981	1991	% growth 1981-91	2001	% growth (1991-2001)
1.	Population (million)	683.33	846.30	2.16	1025.25	1.94
2.	Participation rates (%) (Main workers)	33.50	34.10	0.18	30.50	-1.11
3.	Work Force (million) (Main workers)	228.92	288.59	2.34	312.70	0.81
4.	Marginal Worker (%) participation rates	3.20	3.40	0.61	8.70	9.85
5.	No. of marginal worker (million)	21.87	28.77	2.78	89.20	11.98

SECTION B

Growth in Workforce for major states 1991-2001 (Census) (Main Workers)

States	Workforce Growth	States	Workforce Growth
Andhra Pradesh	0.19	Madhya Pradesh	0.47
Assam	0.13	Maharashtra	1.41
Bihar	0.72	Orissa	-0.81
Gujarat	1.46	Punjab	2.53
Haryana	2.83	Rajasthan	2.28
Himachal Pradesh	1.0	Tamil Nadu	0.38
Karnataka	1.13	Uttar Pradesh	0.11
Kerala	-0.08	West Bengal	1.16
		All India	0.81

Table – 15

Unemployment Rate for the Persons of Age 15 years and above with Different Educational Attainments (1999-2000)

(on usual (adj) basis

All- India per '000

Different approaches	General Educational Level						
	not literate	literate & upto primary	middle	secondary	higher secondary	graduate & above	secondary & abvoe
(1)	(2)	(3)	(4)	(5)	(6)	(7)	(8)
Rural males							
usual (adj.)	3	9	23	43	61	82	56
	(2)	(4)	(22)	(50)	(73)	(98)	(65)
Rural Females							
usual (adj.)	1	6	32	98	143	298	146
	(2)	(5)	(30)	(113)	(199)	(274)	(160)
Urban Males							
usual (adj.)	13	28	52	51	77	63	62
	(9)	(23)	(54)	(56)	(75)	(56)	(60)
Urban Females							
usual (adj.)	5	19	79	120	167	147	143
	(3)	(29)	(109)	(157)	(192)	(189)	(182)

Note : Figures in parentheses give the corresponding rates for NSS 50th Round.- 1993-94

Table – 16

Unemployment Rate among the Youth (15-29 years)
(1999-2000)

CDS Basis

Age groups (year)	Unemployment rate (per cent of labour force) Male	Female
	Rural India	
15-19	13.1 (9.0)	12.8 (8.3)
20-24	11.7 (10.3)	12.1 (8.2)
25-29	9.2 (7.7)	7.7 (6.5)
15-29	11.1 (9.0)	10.6 (7.6)
	Urban India	
15-19	19.0 (16.2)	18.0 (18.6)
20-24	17.1 (17.0)	25.9 (28.5)
25-29	10.3 (9.3)	13.1 (15.5)
15-29	14.7 (13.7)	19.1 (21.2)

Note : The figures in parentheses give the corresponding rates for NSS 50th round (1993-94)

Table – 17

Current daily status unemployment rates for each State and U.T. (1999-2000)

	Unemployment Rate (per cent of labour force)					
	Rural			Urban		
	Male	Female	Persons	Male	Female	Persons
1	2	3	4	5	6	7
Andhra Pradesh	8.1	8.1	8.1	7.2	8.9	7.6
Assam	6.4	12.5	7.4	9.9	21.9	11.9
Bihar	7.2	6.2	7.0	8.7	13.5	9.3
Gujarat	5.1	4.2	4.8	4.0	5.4	4.2
Haryana	5.3	1.8	4.7	4.5	4.9	4.5
Himachal Pradesh	3.4	9.0	2.4	7.0	11.9	7.8
Karnataka	4.4	4.0	4.3	5.3	5.9	5.4
Kerala	20.0	26.1	21.7	15.5	28.2	19.1
Madhya Pradesh	4.0	3.5	3.8	7.2	5.7	7.0
Maharashtra	6.3	6.9	6.5	7.7	10.0	8.1
Orissa	7.6	5.6	7.1	9.8	8.2	9.5
Punjab	4.2	1.7	3.7	4.8	5.3	4.9
Rajasthan	3.3	1.9	2.8	4.7	3.5	4.5
Tamil Nadu	14.3	12.3	13.5	9.0	8.6	8.9
Uttar Pradesh	4.0	2.1	3.6	6.3	5.0	6.2
West Bengal	15.2	25.1	17.0	10.0	13.9	10.6
All India	**7.2**	**7.0**	**7.1**	**7.3**	**9.4**	**7.7**

Table – 18

Current daily status unemployment rate among the youth (15-29) for each State and U.T.

Rural

State/U.T	Unemployment Rate (per cent of labour force)		
	Male	Female	Persons
Andhra Pradesh	10.8	8.7	9.9
Assam	12.3	24.9	14.6
Bihar	11.5	8.8	11.0
Gujarat	6.8	6.4	6.7
Haryana	9.0	2.4	8.1
Himachal Pradesh	8.1	2.8	6.1
Karnataka	6.0	5.6	5.8
Kerala	32.3	45.8	36.3
Madhya Pradesh	5.4	4.0	4.9
Maharashtra	11.3	8.9	10.4
Orissa	12.6	8.4	11.3
Punjab	8.0	3.6	7.0
Rajasthan	5.0	3.3	4.4
Tamil Nadu	19.7	15.3	18.1
Uttar Pradesh	6.8	2.0	6.1
West Bengal	23.0	39.1	26.6
All India	11.1	10.6	11.0

Table – 19

Current daily status unemployment rate among the youth (15-29 years) for each State and U.T.

Urban

State/U.T	Unemployment Rate (per cent of labour force)		
	Male	Female	Persons
Andhra Pradesh	14.3	16.7	14.8
Assam	22.4	42.7	26.6
Bihar	24.0	28.0	24.4
Gujarat	8.0	11.4	8.5
Haryana	8.0	9.9	8.3
Himachal Pradesh	16.8	37.5	20.5
Karnataka	10.4	10.3	10.5
Kerala	26.6	50.4	34.3
Madhya Pradesh	14.9	12.3	14.6
Maharashtra	15.6	21.1	16.5
Orissa	26.8	20.1	25.5
Punjab	8.9	13.9	9.5
Rajasthan	8.4	10.4	8.8
Tamil Nadu	15.5	15.6	15.6
Uttar Pradesh	12.4	12.7	12.5
West Bengal	23.4	27.2	24.0
All India	14.7	19.1	15.4

Table – 20

Growth of Workers - Economic Census

		1980	1990	1998
Rural*				
	Workers (million)	24.2	32.2	38.1
	Growth rate (%)		2.88	2.15
Urban				
	Workers (million)	29.0	38.2	42.5
	Growth rate (%)		2.81	1.34
Combined				
	Workers (million)	53.2	70.4	80.6
	Growth rate (%)		2.84	1.71

* The Rural Sector in Economic Census excludes farm sector and plantation

Table – 21

Sectoral Employment growth on CDS basis

Sector	Employment (in million)				Annual Growth (%)			
	1983	1987-88	1993-94	1999-2000	1983 to 1987-88	1987-88 to 1993-94	1983 to 1993-94	1993-94 to 1999-2000
Agriculture	151.35	163.82	190.72	190.94	1.77	2.57	2.23	0.02
Mining & quarrying	1.74	2.40	2.54	2.26	7.35	1.00	3.68	-1.91
Manufacturing	27.69	32.53	35.00	40.79	3.64	1.23	2.26	2.58
Electricity, gas and water supply	0.83	0.94	1.43	1.15	2.87	7.19	5.31	-3.55
Construction	7.17	11.98	11.02	14.95	12.08	-1.38	4.18	5.21
Trade, hotels and restaurant	18.17	22.53	26.88	37.54	4.89	2.99	3.80	5.72
Transport, storage and communication	6.99	8.05	9.88	13.65	3.21	3.46	3.35	5.53
Financial, insurance, real estate and business services	2.10	2.59	3.37	4.62	4.72	4.50	4.60	5.40
Community, social and personal services	23.52	27.55	34.98	30.84	3.57	4.06	3.85	-2.08
All Sector	**239.57**	**272.39**	**315.84**	**336.75**	**2.89**	**2.50**	**2.67**	**1.07**

Table – 22

Sectoral Employment Elasticities on CDS Basis

Sectors	Employment Elasticity		
	1983 to 1987-88	1983 to 1993-94	1993-94 to 1999-2000
Agriculture	0.87	0.70	0.01
Minings and quarrying	1.25	0.59	-0.41
Manufacturing	0.59	0.38	0.33
Electricity, gas and water supply	0.30	0.63	-0.52
Construction	2.81	0.86	0.82
Trade, hotels and restaurant	0.87	0.68	0.62
Transport, storage and communication	0.47	0.55	0.63
Financing, insurance, real estate and business services	0.49	0.45	0.64
Community, social and personal services	0.52	0.68	-0.25
ALL	**0.68**	**0.52**	**0.16**

Note : Elasticity may change after adjustment of workers of Repair services

Source : NSSO; Different Rounds of Employment & Unemployment Survey

Table – 23

Gross Domestic Product: at 1993- 94 Prices (Rs. Crores)

Sectors	1977-78	1983-84	1987-88	1993-94	1999-2000*	Annual Growth Rates (%) in GDP 1977-78 to 1983-84	1983-84 to 1987-88	1987-88 to 1993-94	1983-84 to 1993-94	1993-94 to 1999-2000*
Agriculture ** (3 years average)	**154538**	**178087**	**193149**	**243292**	**289877**	**2.4**	**2.1**	**3.9**	**3.2**	**3.0**
Agriculture	158132	182498	182899	241967	290334	2.4	0.1	4.8	2.9	3.1
Minings & quarrying	7278	11010	13836	20092	26446	7.1	5.9	6.4	6.2	4.7
Manufacturing	50885	70306	89374	125493	196763	5.5	6.2	5.8	6.0	7.8
Electricity, gas and water supply	5668	8470	12200	18984	28225	6.9	9.6	7.6	8.4	6.8
Construction	23274	25216	29843	40593	58728	1.3	4.3	5.3	4.9	6.3
Trade, hotels and restaurant	44165	57706	71878	99369	168355	4.6	5.6	5.5	5.6	9.2
Transport, storage & communication	20719	28307	36864	51131	84477	5.3	6.8	5.6	6.1	8.7
Financial Institutions, real estates and business services	23739	34391	49598	90084	146546	6.4	9.6	10.5	10.1	8.4
Community, social and personal services	40122	53838	70286	93632	152117	5.0	6.9	4.9	5.7	8.4
All Sectors GDP at factor cost	373982	471742	556778	781345	1151991	3.9	4.2	5.8	5.2	6.7

* Quick estimates

** Three years moving average

Source : National Accounts Statistics Back Series, 1950- 51 to 1992- 93, & PRESS NOTE OF CSO, JUNE 2001

Table – 24

Net Domestic Product by Organised/ Unorganised Sectors

(Rs. Crores)

INDUSTRY	1993-94						1999-2000					
	at current prices			at 1993-94 prices			at current prices			at 1993-94 prices		
	orga-nised	unorga-nised	total	orga-nised	unorga-nised	total	orga-nised	unorga-nised	total	orga nised	unorga nised	total
1. Agriculture, forestry and fishing	**8046**	**221783**	**229829**	**8046**	**221783**	**229829**	**13999**	**422844**	**436843**	**8808**	**266050**	**274858**
1.1 agriculture	6263	204656	210919	6263	204656	210919	13071	387536	400607	8262	244957	253219
1.2 forestry & logging	1779	9387	11166	1779	9387	11166	910	17417	18327	606	11599	12205
1.3 fishing	4	7740	7744	4	7740	7744	18	17891	17909	9	9425	9434
2. Mining and quarrying	**13861**	**1089**	**14950**	**13861**	**1089**	**14950**	**28944**	**2255**	**31199**	**19156**	**1492**	**20648**
3. Manufacturing	**65774**	**37965**	**103739**	**65774**	**37965**	**103739**	**127387**	**82419**	**209806**	**90168**	**57953**	**148121**
4. Electricity, gas & water supply	**8169**	**632**	**8801**	**8169**	**632**	**8801**	**21350**	**1307**	**22657**	**13766**	**843**	**14609**
5. Construction	**18929**	**19820**	**38749**	**18929**	**19820**	**38749**	**43941**	**57580**	**101521**	**24107**	**31589**	**55696**
6. Trade, hotels and restaurant	**10865**	**85762**	**96627**	**10865**	**85762**	**96627**	**47110**	**188888**	**235998**	**32751**	131313	**164064**
6.1 Trade	9374	81950	91324	9374	81950	91324	40761	180030	220791	28378	125337	153715
6.2 Hotels & Restaurants	1491	3812	5303	1491	3812	5303	6349	8858	15207	4321	6028	10349
7. Transport, storage & communication	**21000**	**16721**	**37721**	**21000**	**16721**	**37721**	**45437**	**52088**	**97525**	**30801**	**35309**	**66110**
7.1 Railways	6792	0	6792	6792	0	6792	11094	0	11094	9284	0	9284
7.2 Transport by other means	7118	15770	22888	7118	15770	22888	15473	49993	65466	8680	28047	36727
7.3 Storage	240	344	584	240	344	584	581	587	1168	319	322	641
7.4 Communication	6850	607	7457	6850	607	7457	18289	1508	19797	17976	1482	19458
8. Financing, Insurance, real estate and business services	**39706**	**40835**	**80541**	**39706**	**40835**	**80541**	**119377**	**80032**	**199409**	**78739**	**52788**	**131527**
8.1 Banking & insurance	37376	2734	40110	37376	2734	40110	103560	10609	114169	69110	7080	76190
8.2 Real estate, ownership of dwelling business & legal services	2330	38101	40431	2330	38101	40431	15817	69423	85240	10268	45069	55337
9. Community, social & personal services	**70499**	**16536**	**87035**	**70499**	**16536**	**87035**	**198997**	**39257**	**238254**	**120033**	**23679**	**143712**
9.1 Public administration & defence	38760	0	38760	38760	0	38760	105594	0	105594	63653	0	63653
9.2 Other services	31739	16536	48275	31739	16536	48275	93403	39257	132660	56368	23691	80059
10. Net domestic product at factor cost	**256849**	**441143**	**697992**	**256849**	**441143**	**697992**	**646542**	**926670**	**1573212**	**418920**	**600425**	**1019345**

Note : Components of organised and unorganised by industry at 1993- 94 prices will not add up to total in view of the defalator used at individual / total level.

Source : CSO

Table – 25

Gross & Net Enrolment Rates between 1993-94 to 1999-2000

	1993-94			1999-2000		
	Boys	Girls	Total	Boys	Girls	Total
1	2	3	4	5	6	7
ALL INDIA						
TOTAL ENROLMENTS	101290751	9242014	110532765	106401936	77460260	183862196
[Classes I to XII]						
Including Pre-Degree Intermediate						
DROP OUT RATE	36.07	39.05	37.32	38.67	42.28	40.25
NET ENROLMENT	39511494	2827611	67820386	39314547	28576740	67883492
[IN CLASSES I - V]						
ENROLMENTS	24213399	15701183	39914582	25082351	16982847	42065198
[IN CLASSES VI-VIII] MIDDLE						
DROP OUT RATE	49.95	56.78	52.80	51.96	58.00	54.53
NET ENROLMENT	12118806	6786051	18839682	12049561	7132796	19127045
[IN CLASSES VI-VIII]						
ENROLMENTS	10179372	5603869	15783241	11292663	7288837	18581500
[IN CLASSES I-X]						
SECONDARY						
DROP OUT RATE	68.41	74.54	70.90	66.58	70.60	68.28
NET ENROLMENT	3215664	1426745	4592923	3774008	2142918	5894052
[IN CLASSES I - X]						
ENROLMENT (GROSS)						
ALL INDIA						
a) HIGHER SECONDARY (10+2 NEW PATTERN) XI - XII Classes	3415130	1704444	5119574	4387053	2857866	7244919
b) INTERMEDIATE /JUNIOR COLLEGE Pre - Degree / Pre - University	1678541	766288	2444829	1566580	821458	2388038
TOTAL	5093671	2470732	7564403	5953633	3679324	9632957

NOTE : GOVT SCHOOLS, GOVT. RECOGNIZED SCHOOLS, LOCAL BODIES

SOURCE : SELECTED EDUCATIONAL STATISTICS - 1993-94 and 1999-2000 DEPT. OF EDUCATION, M/O HRD.

Table – 26

*Proportion of Vocationally Trained among the youth in Labour Force -International Comparison**

Country	Age Group	Vocationally trained (percent of those in labour force)
India (1999-2000)	20-24	5.35**
Developing Countries		
Botswana	20-24	22.42
Colombia (1998)	20-29	28.06
Mauritius (1995)	20-24	36.08
Mexico (1998)	20-24	27.58
Developed Countries		
Australia (1998)	20-24	64.11
Canada (1998)	20-24	78.11
France (1997)	20-24	68.57
Germany (1998)	20-24	75.33
Israel (1998)	18-24	81.23
Italy (1997)	20-24	43.88
Japan (1997)	15-24	80.39
Korea Republic (1998)	20-24	95.86
New Zealand (1997)	20-24	63.03
Russian Federation (1998)	20-24	86.89
Singapore (1998)	20-24	66.24
United Kingdom (1998)	20-24	68.46

Note: * Only those who have received formal vocational training are shown as trained. Skills in India are acquired through informal methods, including training in the family.

** Estimates are based on (NSSO Report No. 458 and Results of 55th round.

Table – 27

All India. 1961-1999-2000

(in '000s)

	1961	1993-94	1999-2000
NCO 1968 Divisions			
Professional & Technical and Related Workers	3236	13707 (4.6)	14574 (1.02)
Administrative, Executive & Managerial Workers	1812	7132 (4.33)	12218 (9.39)
Service Workers	5558	12752 (2.6)	16336 (4.22)
Production and Related Workers Trspt Eqpt. Operator and Labourers	29286	65934 (2.54)	78141 (2.87)

( ) brackets gives Rate of Growth over the previous year.

Table – 28

Number of Selected Workers in Identified 2-digit Occupation-groups & their growth All India. 1961-1999-2000

(in '000s)

	1961	1993-94	1999-2000
NCO 1968 Occupational Groups			
Nursing & other Medical & Health Technicians	323	767 (2.71)	1142 (6.86)
Teachers	1582	6340 (4.4)	7456 (2.74)
Transport & Communication Workers & Supervisors	669	1433 (2.38)	1729 (3.18)
Launders, Hair Dressers, Beauticians etc.	1828	3229 (1.77)	4184 (4.41)
Food & Beverage Processors	1837	2528 (1.0)	3187 (3.94)
Machines & Workers, Tool makers & Operators	3871	11813 (3.59)	13179 (1.84)
Brick layers & other Constructions workers	-	6617	10,453 (7.92)
Transport Equipment Operator	1207	6249 (5.22)	9133 (6.53)

Source: Prof. K. Sundaram. Paper submitted in Golden Jubilee Seminar of NSSO, May 2001

( ) brackets gives rate of growth over the previous year

Table – 29

Unemployment Rates (%) amongst Educated Youth 1983 to 1999-2000*

Year	Secondary education and above			All types of Technical Education		
	Rural	Urban	Combined	Rural	Urban	Combined
1983	20.4 (2.5)	30 (10.7)	20.7 (4.2)	25	23.9	24.4
1987-88	15.9 (3.8)	16.6 (12.1)	16.2 (5.4)	24	20.7	22.1
1993-94	17 (2.9)	20.8 (10.8)	18.5 (4.6)	29	25.9	27.3
1999-2000	12.5 (3.7) (11.0)**	18.3 (11.2) (15.4)**	14.8 (5.4)	22.8	24.5	23.7

* On Usual Status Basis

Note: i) Technical Education comprises of Additional Diplomas or certificates in Agriculture, Engineering/Technology, medicines, crafts and other subjects

ii) Youth means age group 15-29

iii) Figures in the parentheses show the unemployment rate among youth as a whole

iv) Figures in the parentheses with ** show the unemployment rate among youths as a whole on CDS basis.

Table – 30

Distribution of Workers (Usual Status) by Category of Employment

(Per cent)

Year	Category of Employment		
	Self Employment	Regular Salaried	Casual
1. Rural Areas			
1977-78	62.6	7.7	29.7
1983	61.0	7.5	31.5
1987-88	59.4	7.7	32.9
1993-94	58.0	6.4	35.6
1999-00	56.0	6.7	37.3
2. Urban Areas			
1977-78	42.4	41.8	15.8
1983	41.8	40.0	18.2
1987-88	42.8	40.3	16.9
1993-94	42.3	39.4	18.3
1999-00	42.1	40.1	17.8
3. Rural and Urban Combined			
1977-78	58.9	13.9	27.2
1983	57.4	13.9	28.7
1987-88	56.0	14.4	29.6
1993-94	54.8	13.2	32.0
1999-00	52.9	13.9	33.2

Figures for the share of self employed, regular salaried employed and casual workers for the year 1972-73 are 61.4 per cent, 15.4 per cent and 23.2 per cent respectively for the Rural and Urban combined.

Source: NSSO Surveys

Table – 31

Jobseekers on the live Register of the Employment Exchange

Year	No. in the live register (in million)
1983	22
1988	30
1994	37
2000	41

Source : DGE&T

Table – 29

Unemployment Rates (%) amongst Educated Youth*
1983 to 1999-2000

Year	Secondary education and above			All types of Technical Education		
	Rural	Urban	Combined	Rural	Urban	Combined
1983	20.4 (2.5)	30 (10.7)	20.7 (4.2)	25	23.9	24.4
1987-88	15.9 (3.8)	16.6 (12.1)	16.2 (5.4)	24	20.7	22.1
1993-94	17 (2.9)	20.8 (10.8)	18.5 (4.6)	29	25.9	27.3
1999-2000	12.5 (3.7) (11.0)**	18.3 (11.2) (15.4)**	14.8 (5.4)	22.8	24.5	23.7

* On Usual Status Basis

Note: i) Technical Education comprises of Additional Diplomas or certificates in Agriculture, Engineering/Technology, medicines, crafts and other subjects

ii) Youth means age group 15-29

iii) Figures in the parentheses show the unemployment rate among youth as a whole

iv) Figures in the parentheses with ** show the unemployment rate among youths as a whole on CDS basis.

Table – 30

Distribution of Workers (Usual Status) by Category of Employment

(Per cent)

Year	Category of Employment		
	Self Employment	Regular Salaried	Casual
1. Rural Areas			
1977-78	62.6	7.7	29.7
1983	61.0	7.5	31.5
1987-88	59.4	7.7	32.9
1993-94	58.0	6.4	35.6
1999-00	56.0	6.7	37.3
2. Urban Areas			
1977-78	42.4	41.8	15.8
1983	41.8	40.0	18.2
1987-88	42.8	40.3	16.9
1993-94	42.3	39.4	18.3
1999-00	42.1	40.1	17.8
3. Rural and Urban Combined			
1977-78	58.9	13.9	27.2
1983	57.4	13.9	28.7
1987-88	56.0	14.4	29.6
1993-94	54.8	13.2	32.0
1999-00	52.9	13.9	33.2

Figures for the share of self employed, regular salaried employed and casual workers for the year 1972-73 are 61.4 per cent, 15.4 per cent and 23.2 per cent respectively for the Rural and Urban combined.

Source: NSSO Surveys

Table – 31

Jobseekers on the live Register of the Employment Exchange

Year	No. in the live register (in million)
1983	22
1988	30
1994	37
2000	41

Source : DGE&T